Sexual Orientation at Work

Sexual Orientation at Work: Contemporary Issues and Perspectives brings together contemporary international research on sexual orientation and draws out its implications for lesbian, gay, bisexual, trans and heterosexual employees and managers. It provides new empirical and theoretical insights into sexual orientation employment discrimination and equality work in countries such as South Africa, Turkey, Australia, Austria, Canada, the US and the UK.

This book is novel in its focus on how sexual orientation intersects with other aspects of difference such as age, class, ethnicity and disability. It adopts new theoretical perspectives (e.g., queer theory) to analyze the rise of new 'gay-friendly' organizations and examines important methodological issues in collecting socioeconomic data about sexual minorities.

Providing an accessible account of key issues and perspectives on sexual orientation in the workplace, *Sexual Orientation at Work* caters to a wide range of readers across business, feminist and LGBT/queer studies fields.

Fiona Colgan is a senior lecturer (teaching and research) in the faculty of business and law at London Metropolitan University (UK). She has published on a range of topics in equality, diversity and employment relations. Her research on LGBT workplace issues can be found in *Equality, Diversity and Inclusion*, *Gender, Work and Organization* and the *HRM Journal*.

Nick Rumens is professor of organization behaviour at Middlesex University London (UK). His research interests are LGBT sexualities in organization, workplace friendships and queer theory. He has recently published journal articles on these topics in *Human Relations and Organization*, and a book, *Queer Company: Friendship in the Work Lives of Gay Men* (Ashgate, 2011).

Routledge Studies in Management, Organizations and Society

This series presents innovative work grounded in new realities, addressing issues crucial to an understanding of the contemporary world. This is the world of organised societies, where boundaries between formal and informal, public and private, local and global organizations have been displaced or have vanished, along with other nineteenth-century dichotomies and oppositions. Management, apart from becoming a specialized profession for a growing number of people, is an everyday activity for most members of modern societies.

Similarly, at the level of enquiry, culture and technology, and literature and economics, can no longer be conceived as isolated intellectual fields; conventional canons and established mainstreams are contested. **Management, Organizations and Society** addresses these contemporary dynamics of transformation in a manner that transcends disciplinary boundaries, with books that will appeal to researchers, student and practitioners alike.

For a full list of titles in this series, please visit www.routledge.com

Sexual Orientation at Work

Contemporary Issues and Perspectives

**Edited by Fiona Colgan
and Nick Rumens**

NEW YORK AND LONDON

First published 2015
by Routledge
711 Third Avenue, New York, NY 10017

and by Routledge
2 Park Square, Milton Park, Abingdon, Oxon OX14 4RN

Routledge is an imprint of the Taylor & Francis Group, an informa business

Library of Congress Cataloging-in-Publication Data

Sexual orientation at work : contemporary issues and perspectives / edited by
Fiona Colgan and Nick Rumens.
  pages cm. — (Routledge studies in management, organizations and
society ; 31)
 1. Sexual minorities—Employment.   2. Diversity in the workplace.
3. Sexual orientation.   4. Personnel management.   I. Colgan, Fiona.
II. Rumens, Nick.
  HF5549.5.S47.S49   2015
  331.5'3—dc23
  2014006631

ISBN: 978-0-415-53649-3 (hbk)
ISBN: 978-0-203-11145-1 (ebk)

Typeset in Sabon
by Apex CoVantage, LLC

Printed and bound in the United States of America by Publishers Graphics,
LLC on sustainably sourced paper.

Fiona: For Maureen Colgan, who has always made the world a better place to be.
Nick: For Danny, with love, for his unfaltering love and affection.

Contents

Tables and Figure

Tables

Figure

Acknowledgments

We would both like to thank Pauline and Peter, Fiona's and Nick's respective partners, for providing us with unending fortitude, love and encouragement throughout the process of developing this book.

This book benefitted also from generous support and patience of the editorial and commissioning team at Routledge. It has been a pleasure to work with Routledge, and we extend our appreciation to Terry Clague, Laura Stearns, Dave Varley, Lauren Verity, Manjula Raman and Stacy Noto, all of whom have supported this project from the beginning.

Equally, this book profited from the insight, energy and commitment of our contributors. We would like to thank our contributors for providing us with engaging and pertinent chapters that breathe fresh air into contemporary issues and perspectives on sexual orientation in the workplace. Also as editors we would like to acknowledge and thank the many individual research participants for sharing their life experiences and providing us all with rich insights into their lives and organisations as well as possible avenues for progress in the future.

1 Understanding Sexual Orientation at Work

Fiona Colgan and Nick Rumens

INTRODUCTION

What does sexual orientation have to do with organisation, with the workplace? The same question has been raised in regard to gender in edited collections similar to this one (Ely, Foldy and Scully, 2003; Jeanes, Knights and Yancey Martin, 2011). In both instances, these questions underscore a widespread and flawed assumption that the workplace is a neutral zone into which such things as sexual orientation and gender are imported. We do not agree. One point of departure for this edited collection is the idea that sexual orientation and the workplace can be considered as mutually influencing, not only in the sense that places of work shape how sexual orientations are understood and experienced but also in the sense that the workplace is sexualised through how sexual orientations are constructed and attributed meaning at work. In this vein, sexuality may be understood to have an orientation that can be turned (in)appropriately towards the people to whom one is attracted sexually and emotionally (Bohan, 1996).

Indeed, the (in)appropriateness of orienting sexuality in one direction or another is structured and regulated by a dominant mode of understanding sexual orientation as dichotomous (heterosexual and nonheterosexual, where the latter stands in for lesbian, gay, bisexual and trans [LGBT] sexualities). This in turn pivots on a widely accepted model of sex as either male or female. As the chapters in this edited collection concede in various ways, these are false dichotomies which cause problems for LGBT people at work, with many subscribing to a view that the categories used to define sexuality as culturally contingent and subject to change over time, of which Foucault's three volumes of the *History of Sexuality* (1979, 1985, 1986) is often cited to support this understanding of sexuality. The salience of sexual orientation as a focal point of analysis, and indeed as a term used to title this edited collection, is that within 'institutions, structures of understanding, and practical orientations that make heterosexuality not only coherent—that is, organised as a sexuality—but also privileged' (Berlant and Warner, 1998: 548), we tend to understand sexual orientation in regard to nonheterosexual sexualities. Ahmed (2006: 69) reflects on this point in a similar way: 'The emergence of the idea of "sexual orientation" does not position the figures of the homosexual and heterosexual in a relation of equivalence. Rather, it is the homosexual who is constituted as having an "orientation": the heterosexual would be presumed to be neutral'. In this way, the homosexual is positioned as deviant from the supposedly neutral heterosexual. For the purposes of this book, Ahmed's framing of sexual orientation is vital because it trains attention on how LGBT sexualities are constructed as '(ab)normal' in the workplace, a focal point which has frequently been beyond the purview of social scientists including organisation studies scholars. In another respect, the association of sexual orientation with LGBT sexualities is limiting in that heterosexuality itself is taken for granted as being 'natural', leaving unanswered questions about how it might be understood and experienced otherwise.

When this knowledge is coupled to an assumption that the workplace is asexual, employers are confronted by the prospect of having to manage sexual orientations in particular, and sexualities more generally. Typically in ways that maximise their potential for improving organisational productivity while minimising the risk of interfering with getting the job done. This belief has fuelled countless managerial incursions into organising, controlling and suppressing sexual orientation at work through dress codes, equality and diversity initiatives, sexual harassment policies and so on (Hearn and Parkin, 1995; Skidmore, 2004; Colgan et al., 2009; Brower, 2013). We can see this at work in other ways, too, particularly how heterosexuality is regarded as axiomatic to the extent that the heterosexuality of organisational life becomes invisible. Conversely, other sexual orientations categorised as LGBT are rendered visible, observed in how they have been variously constructed as 'abnormal', as 'Other', and, thus, susceptible to forms of persecution and discrimination in many places of work around the world (ILGA, 2013). However, in other work contexts, some LGBT sexualities are prized as valuable organisational resources in policy making, enhancing professionalism in human services, penetrating niche markets and creating 'diverse' workforces (Humphrey, 1999; Deverell, 2001; Colgan et al., 2009; Rumens, 2011). Clearly sexual orientation in the workplace matters and as such warrants serious scholarly attention as to how it is understood and experienced by organisations and those individuals who occupy and traverse different sexual identity categories.

In light of the above, another point of departure for this edited collection is the argument that LGBT sexualities have not always been paid the attention they deserve by organisation scholars. It is not true to say that research has been 'silent' on sexuality generally. Early research focused in two main areas: sexual harassment and sexual minorities (Pringle, 2008). A number of these early works have explored sexuality, work and organisation, using a gender and feminist lens including for example, Hearn, Sheppard, Tancred-Sheriff and Burrell's edited collection *The Sexuality of Organization* (1989) and Brewis and Linstead's *Sex, Work and Sex Work*

(2000). Although this research has shown that sexuality pervades every aspect of organisation, this is still not conventionally acknowledged. Of all the equality strands, sexual orientation remains one of the most 'sensitive', and indeed 'invisible', areas of diversity; it is much less researched in management and organisation studies than other 'visible' forms such as gender or race and ethnicity (Bowen and Blackmon, 2003; Colgan and McKearney, 2011). Assumptions of heterosexuality as natural and privileged obscure the fact that LGBT people are an important constituency of countless organisations who must negotiate the norms, values and practices of knowledge coded in heteronormativity (Pringle, 2008). If we fail to confront the heteronormative bias that pervades many workplaces and the 'theoretical heterosexism' (Dunne, 2000: 134) still evident in many studies of organisations, work and family life, we risk becoming blind to the causes and effects of inequalities grounded in organisational heteronormativities and how they impact on LGBT lives. Under these circumstances, individuals and organisations alike are neither engaged nor challenged by the issues raised by LGBT people in the workplace, which we argue ought to be an integral part of understanding the reproduction of myriad inequalities within different workplaces around the globe. The implications of this argument should have particular resonances for those individuals targeted by and charged within organisations to bring certain marginalised groups of people forward from the fringes, including those who identify as LGBT (Bell et al., 2011; Klarsfeld et al., 2014). As many of our contributors argue, part of this enterprise must involve addressing and challenging organisational heteronormativities if we are to understand more fully the needs, interests and voices of LGBT people who are employed in these institutions. As such, this volume offers new research to explain and examine why sexual orientation has been and continues to be a pressing issue at work. As such, it is important and helpful for the reader if we situate this edited collection within the sexuality of organisation literature that has grown over the last three decades or so.

WAVES OF RESEARCH ON LGBT SEXUALITIES IN THE WORKPLACE

Organisational scholarship on LGBT sexualities may be understood as occurring in waves. We employ a wave metaphor here which resonates with but is not a direct copy of how feminism has been conceptualised in terms of emerging and competing politics and theories. In the feminist literature 'first', 'second' and 'third' waves have been used as labels to denote differences in feminist theories, vocabularies, generations and political strategies, sometimes inadvertently obscuring the similarities between each wave (Laughlin et al. 2010). The organisational literature on LGBT sexualities is not as well developed as feminist scholarship, with some scholars criticising the former as theoretically and methodologically limited

(Creed, 2005; Ragins and Cornwell, 2001; Croteau, 1996). We agree to some extent, but we point to the progressive signs apparent in the scholarship that has been published over the last decade or so, some of which has been informed by the advancements made by feminist and race studies (for example, Butler, 1990, 2004; Crenshaw, 1991; Acker, 2000; Yuval-Davis, 2006), social constructionism, poststructuralism and queer theory (Ward and Winstanley, 2003; Williams, Giuffre and Dellinger, 2009; Taylor, Hines and Casey, 2011; Rumens, 2012). It is no coincidence that it is these conceptual resources which have allowed unprecedented inroads into analysing sexuality and gender more broadly, uprooting essentialist accounts that treat gender and sexuality as fixed, intrinsic properties of individuals. However, much of the research has, thus far, been limited to a relatively small section of the population in specific parts of the world. As Ozturk (2011) suggests, in addition to developing the research agenda in North America, Europe, Australia and New Zealand, there is a need to expand research relating to heteronormativity and LGBT rights and concerns in other parts of the world where limited conceptual or empirical work has been done (Colgan and McKearney, 2011). These caveats notwithstanding, the wave metaphor is useful because it helps us to carve out and make sense of the shifting contours of LGBT organisational research that have arisen and continue to rise today, to which this edited collection is a vibrant contribution, indicative of a field of inquiry that is fluid and expanding in both ambition and scope.

The First Wave

The first wave dates to the late 1970s and played a leading role in directing attention to the significance of sexual orientation as an organisational issue. Early research mainly focused on the presence, nature and effects of discrimination towards lesbians and gay men in the workplace. For example, UK surveys published in the 1980s (Beer, Jeffrey and Munyard, 1983; GLC, 1985; Taylor, 1986) showed that employment discrimination on the grounds of sexual orientation was widespread, legal, expected by lesbian and gay employees and seldom questioned by employers. These studies were important for the concern they displayed about how lesbian and gay workers who suspected that their sexual identity, presumed or known by employers and colleagues, influenced decisions not to recruit and promote them or, in the worst cases, to dismiss them from the workplace. The same research exposed the dire consequences of 'coming out' to some employers and colleagues, documented in accounts of bullying, harassment, persecution and violence inflicted on many of those individuals who struggled to participate openly in organisational life.

In this regard, early studies shone a revealing light on homophobia in the workplace, *homophobia* being a term often used to describe a dread of gay people—as well as an irrational fear of homosexuality—and the behaviours emanating from this fear or 'phobia' of homosexuals (Herek, 2004). As organisational research on LGBT sexualities grew and developed, homophobia has regularly been in the spotlight of researchers keen to problematise it not just as individual attitudes and behaviours but also as sexual prejudice that is rooted in social institutions. It is important to note that a number of scholars have employed the term *heterosexism* alongside or instead of *homophobia*, with the former describing an 'ideological systems that denies, denigrates, and stigmatizes any nonheterosexual form of behaviour, identity, relationship, or community (Herek, 1990: 317). The relationship between *homophobia* and *heterosexism* is complex insomuch as these two terms are sometimes regarded as being mutually exclusive, and/or they are used interchangeably and universally to refer to a prejudice against gays and lesbians. For our purposes, we subscribe to the view put forward by O'Brien (2008), who submits that homophobia and heterosexism are mutually constitutive, not least because individuals who hold anti-gay/anti-lesbian attitudes feel justified in expressing them, particularly within contexts where these attitudes and behaviours are culturally sanctioned. Such prejudice reinforces ideologies and practices of 'intolerance and hostility and reinscribe homosexuality as something that should be despised and feared and should remain hidden' (2008: 498).

In one sense the concerns addressed in early organisational research reflected the types of issues being raised in the midst of wider social, cultural and political shifts that were underway in North America, Europe, Australasia and elsewhere (Adam, Duyvendak and Krouwel, 1999). The 1960s was witness to a great deal of social and political unrest which manifested itself in, among other things, antiwar demonstrations, student protests, the rise of second wave feminism and the advent of black and ethnic minority civil rights movements. In 1969 the infamous Stonewall riots took place in the Greenwich Village neighbourhood in New York City, which served as a flash point for the birth of the gay liberation movement. As Richardson and Monro (2012) note, the sexual politics of the late 1960s and early 1970s was radical and militant. Political groups sought to bring to light the discrimination faced by LGBT people in all areas of life, regarding it as a serious social problem (Adam, 1987; Cruikshank, 1992). The tenor of political activism was highly critical of the meanings traditionally attributed to the sexual orientation of 'homosexuality' as a psychiatric and medical disorder, disease, perversion and sin, and thus a threat to the moral and social fabric of everyday life. At the same time, the gay liberation movement began to fracture as sexual politics between lesbians and gay men exposed political differences between these groups, most notably around gay men's presumed ability to access gender privilege (Jeffreys, 1993). Tensions elsewhere within the women's movement (e.g., ignoring the perspectives of lesbian identified women) also fuelled some lesbians to organise separately. Additionally, bisexuals and trans people experienced exclusion from gay and lesbian movements, propelling bi and trans politics along different but sometimes intersecting lines of flight (Richardson and Monro, 2012). Despite these political differences and tensions, organisational research on LGBT sexualities in this period may be understood as being part of a wider move to expose and critique the nature and extent of objectionable treatment of LGBT sexualities in all areas of life, often with the aim of seeking to transform rather than folding LGBT sexualities into the heteronormative fabric of society (Lorde, 1980; Weeks, 2008).

Nonetheless, to what extent the radicalism of wider LGBT political activism percolated into organisational research of the time is debatable. Research in this period reinforced the bold demands made by lesbian and gay rights movements for legislation that would ban employment discrimination against lesbians and gay men on the grounds of sexual orientation (Levine, 1979; Levine and Leonard, 1984). Often these studies adopted the self-chosen terms *lesbian* and *gay*, thus marking an important shift from the term *homosexual*, increasingly criticised as a construction of 'pseudo-scientific theory of sexuality', which, as Watney (1994: 17) argues, 'more properly belongs to the age of the steam engine than to the late twentieth century'. But early organisational research was limited in its ambition. Some of the first review articles on employment discrimination focused on gay men (Levine, 1979) and lesbians (Levine and Leonard, 1984), ignoring the employment experiences of bisexual and trans employees. And whereas early calls for legislation introducing citizenship rights (Weeks, 1998) and outlawing job discrimination were important steps (and still are needed today in many countries), it is arguable whether legal reforms can produce the transformative effects on societies that continue to privilege heterosexuality as a 'natural' and 're/productive' sexual orientation (Richardson, 2000; Skidmore, 2004). In other words, legal reforms and policy initiatives are not enough to dislodge the normative foundations of heterosexuality that maintain the heteronormative and patriarchal contours of societies. However, over the course of the 1980s, organisational research on LGBT sexualities gathered momentum, raising new issues that encouraged theoretical diversity and nurtured a more expansive set of aims and questions regarding the experiences of LGBT people in the workplace.

The Second Wave

A second wave of organisational research surged forward during the 1990s, focusing on a wider range of employment issues affecting LGBT people. Discrimination in the workplace remained a key subject for analysis, with research examining the discriminatory practices directed at LGBT workers employed within a wider range of organisational settings such as those within private sector corporations (Woods and Lucas, 1993; Shallenberger, 1994), the police services and the armed forces (Burke, 1993; Hall, 1995), local government (Humphrey, 1999) and education (Tierney, 1997; Taylor and Raeburn, 1995; Knopp, 1999; Skelton, 2000). Research also considered the 'double jeopardy' faced by lesbians given gendered patterns of occupation segregation in the workplace (Khayat, 1992; Driscoll, Kelley and Fassinger, 1996). Dunne's research on lesbians (1997, 2000) was particularly important in challenging the 'blind spot' in accounts of gender inequality as a consequence of the heterosexual bias in research on work and family life. A prominent and recurrent focal point of analysis within this corpus of research is how LGBT people construct, disclose and manage sexual identities at work. Whereas coming out was embraced and promoted as a political strategy among lesbian and gay movements to counter heterosexism within society (Richardson and Monro, 2012), the everyday realities of disclosing as LGBT revealed how difficult such a strategy might be to enact and sustain.

Woods and Lucas's (1993) US study of gay male professionals is well cited in that respect. They identified three main strategies for managing a gay male identity in the workplace that continue to inform research in this area: (1) counterfeiting; (2) avoidance; (3) and integration. Counterfeiting refers to efforts made by gay men to 'pass' as heterosexual in the workplace, thereby giving out the 'wrong' message about their gay identity, which remains concealed. Strategies of avoidance include attempts to disclose as little personal information as possible, deflecting attention away from the issue of sexuality. In contrast, strategies of integration refer to 'coming out' as gay in the workplace. This usually involves saying or doing something explicit to disclose as gay to colleagues. Some men made indirect remarks to colleagues about their sexuality whereas others tried to normalise their sexual identity, by conforming to prevailing expectations and cultural norms around sexuality and gender. In each strategy individuals manage what information about their sexual identity is disclosed, to whom, how and when. The angle of analysis then is typically slanted towards evaluating the costs of these strategies in terms of the unrealised benefits of disclosing. Crucially, opting to come out of the corporate closet to publicly express a minority sexual identity carries the risk of amplifying the individual's susceptibility to discrimination, as Humphrey's (1999) UK study of LGB public sector workers also illustrates vividly. As such, identity disclosure and management dilemmas and strategies have underscored an array of factors (e.g., personal, environmental and organisational) that influence LGBT employees' disclosure decision-making processes. For example, studies during the 1990s started to throw light on the significance of nonheterosexist and homophobic organisational cultures, senior management support and nondiscriminatory work policies (Shallenberger, 1994; Ellis and Riggle, 1995; Day and Shoenrade, 1997) in helping LGBT employees to participate in organisational life in ways that produce desirable personal and organisational outcomes (e.g., personal integrity, identity development, higher levels of job satisfaction, reduced turnover, improved productivity).

Another conspicuous focal point in second wave LGBT organisational research is the impact of homophobia and heterosexism on LGBT careers in terms of concerns, trajectories, coping strategies and adjustments (Croteau and Hedstrom, 1993; Chojnacki and Gelberg, 1994; Chung and Harman, 1994; Chung, 1995; Boatwright et al., 1996). The bulk of this research has been conducted from a psychology perspective that suggests life and work are so interconnected as to be inseparable at the level of analysis, especially as homophobia and heterosexism shape how LGBT people construct relationships and identities, and pursue and adjust careers. One important contribution made by this literature was to treat sexual orientation as an influencing factor in career decision making and development, thus countering the heterosexist bias that had previously coloured this scholarship. In a likewise fashion, researchers started to investigate the impact of sexual orientation on the economic position of LGBT people within the labour market, proceeding on the basis that economic differences exist between people with differing sexual orientations producing (un)expected (dis)advantages (Badgett, 1995; Gluckman and Reed, 1997).

Taken together, the second wave of organisational LGBT research echoed earlier studies, showing many employers to be ill-disposed towards the employment and presence of LGBT people in the workforce, particularly where their sexuality is either known or presumed. It is little wonder then that much of the second wave LGBT organisational literature makes for grim reading: the world of work is often constructed as being replete with hazards and risks for LGBT employees who are 'out' and/or closeted. However, the same raft of studies go beyond simply exposing employment discrimination on the grounds of sexual orientation and documenting the identity disclosure dilemmas and management strategies faced and developed by LGTB people at work. They extend scholarly knowledge about LGBT agency and the ways in which work environments may be made more accepting and supportive settings for LGBT people to come out as workers and clients. The types of measures for improvement in that respect vary, from advocating legal reform, to the introduction of organisational policies and practices that are inclusive of LGBT employees, to management and staff training on sexual orientation alongside other equality strands and establishing LGBT support networks (McNaught, 1993; Rasi et al. 1995; Winfield and Spielman, 1995). It is no coincidence that during this period studies focused on how LGBT might organise politically in the workplace in order to effect such changes. This has included campaigns as both workers and service users to improve provision within the public services (Cooper, 1994; Epstein, 1994; Rayside, 1998). LGBT people have always been active in their trade unions, however after the 1980s the workplace became an important 'site of activism', in order to challenge the 'blatantly discriminatory' policies and practices LGBT people encountered at work (Hunt, 1999: 2). In the absence of antidiscrimination legislation, one of the five major reasons LGBT workers gave for being able to be 'out' at work in the UK was their union's commitment to LGBT issues (LRD, 1992). Trade unions, particularly public sector and unions with predominantly female memberships, were initially the most progressive in their response during these early years (Hunt, 1999). Research sought to chart and share the progress LGBT activism made in unions through education and organising; equality bargaining on LGBT issues; and the campaigns for and strategic use of LGBT and equality self-organised structures (Franzway, 1997; Colgan, 1999; Humphrey, 1999; Hunt, 1999; Krupat and McCreery, 2001).

Theoretically, much of the research cited above has been more attuned to wider developments in theorising sexuality in the social sciences and humanities. The study of sexual orientation is increasingly seen as forming part of a broader perspective on sexuality that focuses on sexual identities, desires, relations, fantasies and ethics. Closer to home, during the mid to late 1980s, a number of landmark publications on organisation and sexuality paved the way for thinking about organisation and sexuality as mutually constitutive and about the sexuali*ties* of organisation (Burrell, 1984, 1987; Hearn et al., 1989). In addition, feminist studies of organisation, also increasingly focused on both gender and sexuality when analysing barriers and resistance to equal opportunity and diversity policies and practices within organisations (Walby, 1990; Cockburn, 1991; Itzin and Newman1995; Halford and Leonard, 2001). Drawing from this literature and the social sciences scholarship on sexuality more generally, organisational research on LGBT sexualities during the second wave is loosely bound together by a common thread: the idea that sexuality is constructed, multiple and fluid, although the specific theorising of sexuality as such within this literature differs markedly. This emergent sense of theoretical diversity begins to unfold in a third wave of scholarship.

The Third Wave

A third wave of LGBT organisational research has developed over the last decade or so, evident in much of the concern it shows for understanding how organisations have addressed sexual and gender diversity in the workplace. This wave of literature has been conditioned, in part, by the changes, both positive and negative, taking place in work contexts around the globe. South Africa paved the way to LGBT rights and recognition in the public sphere by being the first country in the world to include lesbian and gay equality in its constitution in 1996 (Jara, Webster and Hunt, 1999). In 2000, the European Union introduced the 2000 Framework Equality Directive, which required European member states to introduce legislation to tackle discrimination on grounds of sexual orientation. As other countries have taken similar steps, the issue of global LGBT equality is now a topic for discussion at international summits with figures such as US Secretary of State Hillary Clinton talking of the necessity of linking 'gay rights' with human rights (US Department of State, 2011) as one indicator of corporate social responsibility (Colgan, 2011). These changes combined with evidence of seemingly more relaxed social attitudes towards LGBT people in a growing number of countries (Weeks, 2007) means that for some employees in specific work contexts, organisations have become more tolerant places to work openly as LGBT. Evaluating the impact of such changes on LGBT people in the workplace has been a significant topic of investigation within this third wave of research.

For example, talk within academic circles and the popular business press of a 'new' organisational form—the 'gay-friendly' organisation—has caught the attention of organisational researchers, not least because the term seems to be underpinned by an implicit assumption of an ethics of tolerance and liberalism within the work environment. Correia and Kleiner assert that 'gay friendly' employers are those organisations that foster an atmosphere considered hospitable to gay, lesbian and bisexual employees (2001: 95). Continuing, Correia and Kleiner suggest that the offerings of a gay-friendly organisation ought to include an employment policy covering sexual orientation and gender identity that is 'consistently enforced', domestic partnership benefits for same-sex couples, LGB support groups, diversity training on sexual orientation and gender, respectful advertising to LGB stakeholders and charitable support for LGB communities. This allows us to recognise and begin to understand the conditions of possibility for 'gay-friendly' organisations to emerge.

For example, Colgan et al. (2007) examine sixteen UK 'good practice' organisations and suggest that, whereas the legal protection provided by the (Sexual Orientation) Regulations (2003) is not a panacea for LGBT workplace discrimination, it has exerted a positive influence as another driver for equality action. Previously, social justice and business case arguments for addressing sexual orientation at work served as the stimulus for employers to develop formal gay-friendly signals such as policies that address sexual orientation and include LGBT networks and support groups. Typically, organisations in the public sector have been in the vanguard here, with some heralded as beacons of 'good practice' (Colgan et al., 2007). At the same time, Colgan and McKearney (2012) argue that the initial impetus for developing a more inclusive work environment for LGBT employees can crystallise out of the activism of LGBT employees and their allies. In line with Raeburn's US based research (2004), they cite LGBT company network groups as contemporary examples of LGBT activism that appear to offer new employee voice mechanisms in the UK. The same studies caution against facile understandings of what *gay-friendly* means, arousing the suspicions of those who feel that the term veils over how and why particular sexualities are validated at the expense of others (Woodruffe-Burton and Bairstow, 2013; Rumens and Broomfield, 2014). Indeed, the unacknowledged meanings attached to gay-friendly organisations are potentially revealing of what the term avoids asking: do organisational sexualities continue to be categorised around a heterosexual/homosexual binary, and who benefits from the heteronormative logic that reproduces these divisions? Such concerns have yet to structure much of the emergent literature on gay-friendly organisations, although there are some notable exceptions (Giuffre, Dellinger and Williams, 2008; Rumens and Kerfoot, 2009; Williams, Giuffre and Dellinger, 2009; Williams and Giuffre, 2011).

At the same time, third wave scholarship has continued to critically consider issues raised by earlier waves of research, such as workplace discrimination (Skidmore, 2004; Ward and Winstanley, 2006; Croteau, Anderson and VanderWal, 2008; Losert, 2008; Ryniker, 2008; Willis, 2012), identity disclosure and management issues (Button, 2004; Ragins, 2004, 2008; Ward and Winstanley, 2005; Ragins, Singh and Cornwell, 2007; Rumens and Kerfoot, 2009) and forms of LGBT organising and activism (Colgan and Ledwith, 2002; Creed, 2003; Cooper, 2006; Hunt and Rayside, 2007), although the directions and theoretical lenses used by scholars to come at and study these issues are considerably more varied. For example, important research examines how LGBT employees are not passive victims of organisational heteronormativity; they can operate as 'tempered radicals': individuals who experience the competing demands of being both effective, contributing organisational insiders as well as outsiders 'because they represent ideals or agendas that are somehow at odds with the dominant culture' in their organisations (Meyerson, 2001: 5). In this body of work, which aligns itself within neoinstitutionalist/social movements frameworks (Myerson and Scully, 2005; Creed, 2003; Creed, 2005), it is argued that part of this process involves challenging norms that denigrate alternative sexualities and acting as workplace advocates for improvements in equality and diversity initiatives and agendas (Creed and Scully, 2000). In this sense, LGBT employees figure as potential institutional change agents who demonstrate loyalty to their employing organisation but display commitment to developing a more inclusive organisational culture for LGBT employees (Creed, DeJordy and Lok, 2010).

Workplace heterosexism and homophobia continue to be areas of significant scholarly concern. Over the last decade researchers have bemoaned the enduring prevalence of employment discrimination on the grounds of sexual orientation, as noted in Ryniker's (2008) study of workplace discrimination against lesbians in the US, Öztürk's (2011) analysis of LGBT employees' work experiences in Turkey, and Bowring and Brewis's (2009) study of LGBT people employed in Canada, regarded by the authors as a supposedly 'queer friendly' nation. Of considerable note also is that the study of workplace discrimination in this third wave becomes more refined, with terms such as *biphobia*, *bi-negativity* and *transphobia* being used to analyse the particular forms of gender and sexual discrimination experienced by particular groups within the LGBT acronym. It is during this period that studies emerge on the specific employment experiences of bisexuals (Green, Payne and Green, 2011) and trans identified employees (Hines, 2010), two groups of people either previously overlooked or unceremoniously lumped together with gay men and lesbians under variations of the LGBT acronym in the organisational literature.

For example, Green, Payne and Green (2011) conducted an international survey of the experience of bisexual people in the workplace, which indicated that being 'out' as bi at work is linked to a higher quality of work life, especially when employers are committed to developing policies and organisational practice that targets both sexual orientation and gender identity issues. At the same time, being out is a risky enterprise due to the pervasiveness of bi-negativity. Notably, many study respondents reported that gay and heterosexual colleagues misunderstood bisexuality, found they were not accepted as 'legitimate' members of LGBT employee resource groups and felt they were perceived by colleagues as 'untrustworthy', 'unreliable and/or indecisive'. Many survey participants felt this had a damaging effect on their career advancement prospects. A comparable picture is painted by Chamberlain's (2009) research conducted through the UK LGB charity Stonewall. Somewhat similarly, recent studies on the work experiences of trans people also reveal a disturbing picture of employment discrimination, persecution and violence at and outside work (Connell, 2010; Richardson and Monro, 2012; Jones, 2013).

Theoretically, third wave research exhibits a pronounced interest in examining the diversity across and within the LGBT acronym, with some researchers extending the acronym to include intersex and queer or questioning people (LGBTIQ). Nonetheless, we cannot ignore the enduring tensions between all of the groups that comprise the LGBT acronym (see Richardson and Monro, 2012), and organisational research on LGBT people has not always been sensitive to or acknowledged these differences. Trans issues, for instance, have often been framed only in gendered terms excluding them from the LGBT acronym in some contexts, but trans sexualities are complex and diverse in ways that may rupture the distinct sexual orientation categories on which LGBT identities are based (Thanem, 2011). Debates about the diversity within and across the groups that form the LGBT moniker are gathering momentum, partly as third wave research has reacted to wider and relatively recent developments in the study of sexuality in the social sciences and humanities. A growing interest in intersectional analysis is one outcome of this momentum. It draws on earlier feminist and sociological research which sought to escape simplistic dichotomies and address issues of identity, inequality and difference through 'intersectionality' (Crenshaw, 1991; Yuval-Davis, 2006). In recent years researchers seeking to explore sexuality and the complex ways it intertwines with other identities including class, race, ethnicity, age and disability have explored the possibilities and limitations of intersectional analysis in considering the ways in which sexuality is 'lived' alongside these other social divisions and subjectivities (Monro, 2010; Casey et al., 2010; Taylor, Hines and Casey, 2011; Wright, 2013).

The influence of postmodernism and poststructuralism has so far perhaps had the greatest effect, prising open opportunities for researchers to pierce the darkness that had previously surrounded sexuality in much of the traditional organisational literature (Burrell, 1984, 1987; Hearn et al., 1989) and transcending essentialist conceptions of sexuality that reinforce the heterosexual/homosexual binary that sustains heteronormativity. Strains of postmodern and poststructuralist thinking have permeated third wave research (Ward and Winstanley, 2003; Bowring and Brewis, 2009; Öztürk, 2011; Rumens, 2012), supplementing existing accounts that draw on social psychology (Ragins, 2008) and sociology (Richardson and Monro, 2012). They have also paved the way for the introduction of new theoretical lenses. For instance, queer theory has a postmodern and poststructuralist heritage and for that reason has been enormously popular within the social sciences and humanities since the 1990s as a denaturalising critique and destabilising politics of heteronormativity (Warner, 1993; Edelman, 2004; Ahmed, 2006; Taylor and Addison, 2013). Despite its inroads there, it has only recently started to creep into some organisational research on how particular workplaces condition possibilities for LGBT people to conform and resist organisational heteronormativity (Williams, Giuffre and Dellinger, 2009; Öztürk, 2011; Rumens, 2012, 2013; Rumens and Broomfield, 2014) and critique approaches to diversity management (Bendl, Fleischmann and Hofmann, 2009). More than most this work has revealed, in varying degrees, the normalisation of certain LGBT sexualities in the workplace, a process by which some LGBT people are seeking to normalise by 'fitting into' (see Seidman, 2002) rather than transforming existing work cultures and societies that remain heteronormative.

Indeed, third wave LGBT organisational research is set against a broader sexuality of organisation literature that has become increasingly concerned with the study of sexuali*ties*. In theory, heterosexuality is eligible for scrutiny but, as much of the extant sexuality of organisation literature demonstrates, it frequently evades scholarly interrogation, with the exception of what Hearn and Parkin (1987: 43) indicated has been the research on sexual harassment, or more specifically the 'heterosexual' harassment of women by men. One promising and relatively new area of research concerns the role, motivations and activities of heterosexuals, termed *straight allies* within the North American literature, who actively work in support of LGBT and workplace equality (Brooks and Edwards, 2009; Russell, 2011). Otherwise the presumed naturalness and apparent ubiquity of heterosexuality in organisational life makes it difficult to study. It is for this very reason at least that we urgently require analyses of heterosexuality in organisational settings, in order to understand how it might subvert its own privileged status as 'natural', revealing important tensions in the dynamic between heterosexuality and heteronormativity.

Where Next?

As the discussion so far reveals, a great deal of change has occurred within organisational landscapes for LGBT employees across the globe, with some being dubbed as 'progressive'. But it is crucial to acknowledge that such progressive changes are uneven, not uniformly understood and felt by all LGBT employees, and, in some situations (e.g., those marked by a politics of economic austerity and conservatism), hard won equality gains may be jeopardised and even reversed. As much as some individuals might be tempted to cleave to a sentiment of 'things can only get better', sometimes carried in a widespread and uncritical belief that there will be less sexual prejudice as each generation passes, we cannot rely on a naïve and linear concept of progress to understand what the future might hold for LGBT people at work. For example, the recent reversal of fortunes for LGBT people in Russia, most noticeably implemented in legislation banning propaganda of 'nontraditional sexual relations' among minors, which effectively prohibits. among other things, gay Pride events and speaking in defence of LGBT people, acts as a tart corrective to romantic notions of progress (Colgan and McKearney, 2014). What exactly has changed and where and by how much are important questions that still require scholarly investigation if we are to avoid crass generalisations about how things have or might become progressively and universally better for LGBT people at work across the world. For instance, we might hope that future research will be less reliant on a 'Western' (Anglo-North American) tradition (Kulpa and Mizielinska, 2011) and informed by postcolonialist critiques of a universal 'global' LGBT rights–based approach and its perceived alignment with neoliberal capitalism (Kollman and Waites, 2009; Lind, 2010). Indeed, many of the chapters in this book provide ideas for advancing scholarship along different trajectories as well as giving us reasons to be concerned about how LGBT people go about their working lives. Here, then, it is useful to introduce the chapters, underlining their contribution to the field. It is important to point out that there is no strict categorisation or thematic ordering of chapters. We have abandoned traditional academic protocols in that respect, opting instead to organise the book in a way that furthers the reader's understanding. As such, the chapters at the beginning consider the ways in which LGBT people are navigating changes in their work contexts following the introduction of increased rights and recognition in their organisations; the chapters which follow focus on diversity of perception and experience within the LGBT acronym before leaving Australasia, Europe and North America to explore LGBT experiences in the differing contexts provided by South Africa and Turkey. Simpson's chapter broadens the literature by exploring gendered and heteronormative work contexts for both LGBT and heterosexual subjects. The last four chapters provide useful reflections on the opportunities, challenges and contradictions in developing and implementing policy and practice on sexual orientation, equality and diversity at work taking account of contemporary issues and perspectives.

In 'Navigating Service and Sexuality in the Canadian, UK and US Militaries', Michèle Bowring and Joanna Brewis examine how LGB people navigate their sexuality in the military: an occupation, which until relatively recently, LGB people were formally banned from joining and from which, if identified, they could be expelled. Their research provides valuable insights on the evolution of an organisation where policies and culture foreground issues of gender and sexuality within a hypergendered context. Their chapter concludes that although the repeal of the bans on LGB service has brought progress and has been beneficial for LGB people, this has not been sufficient to mitigate the ongoing effects of heterosexism and discrimination on those still serving in and retired from the military.

Following on, Catherine Connell in 'Reconsidering the Workplace Closet: The Experiences of Lesbian and Gay Teachers' turns her attention to the very different working environment provided within schools. She argues that despite the recent rise of gay-friendly workplaces, the classroom remains a hostile work environment for many lesbian and gay teachers, even in US states with laws prohibiting sexual orientation discrimination. This chapter examines how teachers negotiate their sexual and professional identities in the classroom and reveals that standards of professionalism which are constructed as neutral are in fact still deeply imbued with heterosexual privilege. She concludes that challenges to the status quo are too often left to the individual teacher rather than taken up at the organisational level. Visibly lesbian and gay teachers may thus face a no-win situation: either emphasise their commonality with heterosexual teachers and reproduce normative standards, or risk being punished for transgressing gender and sexuality norms.

Todd Brower then moves on to investigate whether institutions such as the courts, which he argues have cultural and legal mandates to be societal institutions dedicated to equal justice, can deliver fairness and equal treatment for LGBT people at work. His chapter 'Courts as Workplaces for Sexual Orientation Minorities' reviews four empirical studies on LGBT court employees' experiences in the US and UK to consider this question. His research drawing on Kahan (2000) suggests that visibility of LGBT sexual orientation can influence employees' perceptions and treatment at work but that legal and workplace protections, although important, may not necessarily create equal treatment or social change for LGBT employees.

Next, John Broomfield's chapter adopts a social constructionist view of 'Gay Men in the UK Police Services'. It is encouraging to see that the landscape of policing has been transformed such that many 'out' gay men can exude confidence in their roles as police officers and are able to point to equality policy as an important factor in the construction of open gay identities at work. However, although he suggests many of his participants no longer need to construct 'double lives', most still need to manage the performance of a gay identity within the masculine working environment the chapter describes. Broomfield suggests that to be accepted as a gay police officer requires the tailoring of the gendered performance of homosexuality in order to conform to heteronormative gender norms (thus paralleling Connell's findings with teachers). The chapter finds that the acceptance of gay men in the police service has thus come at a price—the valorisation of 'the normal gay' and the marginalisation and Othering of effeminate (gay) men.

Elizabeth McDermott's chapter moves from a consideration of LGBT experiences within a specific occupation or sector to a regional study in the North West of England. It explores how lesbian identity and social class may influence attitudes to paid work and the impact this may have on well-being. The chapter draws on Bourdieu's (1984) conceptualization of social class and is one of the chapters in the book stressing the importance of an intersectional perspective to studies of LGB people, work and wellbeing. McDermott's study challenges both the heteronormative research frameworks of enquiry into women's employment and the insufficient attention paid to social class in the experiences of LGB people and employment. The chapter ' "I Felt like the Dad in the House": Lesbians' Wellbeing, Class and the Meanings of Paid Work' concludes that although all of the lesbian participants expected to be economically self-sufficient, the middle-class lesbians were more likely to be in employment which enhanced their wellbeing.

In 'Organisational Life within a UK "Good Practice Employer": The Experiences of Black and Minority Ethnic and Disabled LGBT Employees', Fiona Colgan also adopts an intersectional approach in order to consider the crossover of dimensions of diversity and make visible heterogeneous LGBT employee perceptions and experiences of organisational life. Her research across sixteen good practice employers found that despite progress on equality across all 'protected characteristics' covered by the Equality Act (2010), black and minority ethnic (BME) and disabled LGBT participants perceived that sexual orientation, gender identity and gender reassignment were not accorded the same status as the other equality strands. In addition, their organisations were not perceived to be particularly sensitive to issues of 'dual discrimination', nor were they aware of the benefits to employees and the organisation of taking a more intersectional and thus more inclusive approach to equality/diversity policy and practice. Colgan's chapter is welcome in addressing a research gap in the LGBT literature by providing insights on the ways in which LGBT people who self-identify as having a disability and/or as BME experience and negotiate their working lives.

Another welcome addition to the literature is provided by Paul Willis's chapter, 'Working across Differences in Sexuality and Age: Australian Stories of Young LGBQ Workers' Experiences in Paid Employment'. The study provides evidence that, despite formal protections from age- and sexuality-based discrimination under Australian law, many young LGBQ Australians are vulnerable to poor treatment given their overrepresentation in casual, low skill and nonunionised work. Willis uses a relational approach to theorise sexuality and power in his examination of how LGBQ young workers experience heteronormative, 'precarious' work environments. The chapter also explores how social differences in age and sexuality shape the interactions of young LGBQ workers with other employees and members of management. Notwithstanding the hardships identified and discussed within the research, it is heartening to learn that the young people faced with discursive and material violence adopted a range of strategies to challenge their situation. Thus as Willis concludes, young LGBQ employees can bring fresh perspectives and make valuable contributions in developing inclusive work policies and practices.

Mikki van Zyl's chapter encourages us to consider LGBTI experiences in a South African context. As she points out, nearly twenty years ago, South Africa became the first country in the world constitutionally to guarantee freedom from discrimination against people on the basis of sexual orientation. Thus in 'Working the Margins: Belonging and the Workplace for LGBTI in Post-Apartheid South Africa', van Zyl asks how South African LGBTI people have been negotiating their lives during this dramatically changing time. Using a lens of 'belonging' (Yuval-Davis, 2011) to examine unevenness in entitlements to rights, inclusion and recognition, her chapter illuminates the dialectic between the formal rights enshrined in citizenship and everyday homoprejudice. As a result, her research participants managed their identities strategically in order to feel secure as appropriate to their situation. Despite the resurgence of a discourse about homosexuality being 'unAfrican' fuelled in part by religious fundamentalists following 'imported' colonial faiths, van Zyl concludes that the judicial framework of rights has provided a strong foundation for LGBTI employees to 'be themselves' in the new South Africa.

The next chapter, 'From Cradle to Grave: The Lifecycle of Compulsory Heterosexuality in Turkey' by Mustafa Bilgehan Öztürk and Mustafa Özbilgin, is also welcome in helping us to move the LGBT literature on organisation and work beyond the conventional coverage of Australasia, Europe and North America. Turkey straddles the borders of Europe and Asia geographically and symbolically and, although a secular state since its foundation by Mustafa Kemal Atatürk in 1923, is currently governed by the Justice and Development Party, a socially conservative democratic party with close ties to political Islam (Öztürk, 2011). This is one of the chapters in the book which draws on queer theory to question and destabilize the politics of gender and heteronormativity. Öztürk and Özbilgin do this in order to problematize the lifecycle of compulsory heterosexuality within institutional settings as experienced by gay men. There is no national regulation or governmental body that affords legal protection against discrimination on grounds of sexual orientation in Turkey. Thus Öztürk and Özbilgin argue that it provides an interesting setting in which to study compulsory heterosexuality and the agency and resilience of LGBT people. However, they conclude that despite the EU accession process and a number of promising changes such as the annual Pride march in Istanbul and the increasing availability of LGBT networks and social venues, the lifecycle of compulsory heterosexuality is unlikely to be susceptible to change in Turkey in the near future.

Next, 'Sexual Spaces and Gendered Dynamics: The Experiences of Male Cabin Crew' by Ruth Simpson signals the growing and broadening interest in exploring sexuality and gender beyond sexual minorities in the workplace. This chapter examines the gendered and sexualised meanings which may be attached to space and place and highlights how space and sexuality intersect through a spatially aware heteronormative gaze. Simpson highlights the instability and socially constructed nature of space so taking us beyond space as mere context or 'container' of experience. She does so through a study of male airline cabin crew, exploring the performative nature of space during the onboard service encounter within an aircraft by considering how male crew mobilise and utilise the spaces of their working lives. Having shown how the cabin of an aircraft is sexualized and sexualizing, gendered and gendering, Simpson's research illustrates how male crew become associated with femininity and with a denigrated (homo)sexuality irrespective of their actual sexual orientation.

Although, LGBT people have gained rights and recognition in the public sphere as illustrated in most of the chapters above, it is clear there is still a need to identify effective strategies to ensure the full equality of sexual minorities at work. Nick Rumens's chapter. 'Is Your Workplace "Gay Friendly"? Current Issues and Controversies', uses a queer theory perspective to interrogate the term *gay-friendly* and question whether the construction of workplaces as gay-friendly actually represents a progressive step forward for LGBT employees. He argues that *gay-friendly* is a polysemous term with multiple uses and meanings, which doesn't acknowledge the complexity of lived diversities in LGBT lives; is not easily subject to 'measurement; and too often means dovetailing with the bottom line. Although Rumens concedes that research shows that some gay-friendly workplaces may be more accepting and welcoming to LGBT people, he argues this comes at a price, where heteronormative power relations may require the heteronormalisation of LGBT identities to take place. Thus he cautions against reading workplaces framed as gay-friendly as a 'natural' and logical step forward in the development and materialisation of LGBT equalities at work, envisioning instead 'queer organisations' which may permit employees to (re)contruct and live different identity categories, realities and possibilities at work.

In 'Moving from 'Invisibility' into National Statistics? Lesbians and the Socioeconomic Sphere', Roswitha Hofmann, Karin Schönpflug and Christine Klapeer also concern themselves with the contradictory implications of 'categorisation' and 'measurement' of LGB identities when collecting quantitative research data on LGB people. The official recognition of sexual orientation as an equality strand in many European countries has highlighted the need to consider sexuality as an analytic category in need of audit (alongside gender, ethnicity, disability and so forth) in order to be able to quantify the effects of discrimination in the socioeconomic sphere. Hofmann, Schönpflug and Klapeer's chapter outlines the current methodological challenges of empirical research and statistical data collection procedures using examples from two research projects on the socioeconomic status of lesbian women. Using a queer-feminist and governmentalist perspective in their analysis, they conclude that data generation procedures need to be sensitive to the heteronormative and homophobic contexts within which many LGB people still live. Also, current data collection efforts illustrate the tensions between being able to quantify discrimination and the dangers of 'normalisation' as the LGB population group is 'counted' using 'normative' frameworks and 'official' categories which render the fluidity and complexity of sexual and gender identifications invisible.

Suzanne Franzway's chapter focuses on 'Sexual Politics and Queer Activism in the Australian Trade Union Movement', organisations which she argues have historically been dominated by masculine heterosexuality. In recent years, as in other countries, Australian unions have come to recognise the need to recognise and represent an increasingly diverse workforce and trade union membership, including LGBTI workers. Franzway uses a feminist analysis to discuss the sexual politics and self-organising which has been integral to the progress being made by Australian unions on equality issues. Recognising that 'queer' can be playful but also difficult and confrontational as it represents a challenge to the heteronormative dominance of unions and cultures, Franzway's chapter draws on recent examples of queer activism in the Australian trade union movement to examine the sexual politics involved in bringing LGBTI issues onto the industrial, social and political agenda. She concludes that queer activism in the Australian union movement, although dependant on the intermittent and uneven efforts of relatively small groups of activists and their allies, continues to have a critical role to play in ensuring the workplace rights of LGBTI workers.

The final chapter, 'Going Global: International Labour and Sexual Orientation Discrimination', is welcome in its consideration of sexual orientation workplace issues in a global context. It illustrates how far unions have come in addressing issues related to sexual orientation. Gerry Hunt's chapter, while recognising the advances that have been secured for LGBT workers in some parts of the world (often with the assistance and support of organized labour), also points to blatant discrimination and illegality, often with severe punishments, which is the reality for LGBT people in parts of Africa, Asia, the Caribbean, the Middle East and Russia. His chapter shows that many of the countries with the weakest record on LGBT rights also have national labour movements which are underdeveloped and weak and/or co-opted by governments so have been able to offer little by way of support to LGBT workers. In this context, Hunt considers the potential importance of international labour organisations acknowledging and tackling sexual orientation discrimination through policy directives, education, support and campaigning activities at the international level. It also points to the protection which may be provided through International Federation Agreements signed between multinational corporations and one or more global union. Hunt's research shows that one-third of these agreements includes nondiscrimination provisions for LGBT workers and asks whether these agreements provide a significant and potentially transformative workforce gain for LGBT workers in locations where no other legislative protections currently exist.

In conclusion, we hope readers of all kinds will find this edited collection engaging and apposite, although we readily acknowledge the limitations and imperfections of this collection as different readers will come at this text with different expectations—we cannot account for all possibilities here. Limitations and imperfections notwithstanding, this edited collection bears testimony to the prospects within organisation studies for conducting research on LGBT sexualities. Business and management schools, for instance, may afford scholars opportunities to research LGBT employment issues, especially if they are framed as 'mainstream' business issues that affect organisational outcomes such as productivity and job satisfaction. Equally, however, such academic settings may be challenging for carrying out research on LGBT sexualities, not least because such organisations are themselves marked by heteronormativity (Creed, 2005; Fotaki, 2011; Giddings and Pringle, 2011), which has presented barriers to undertaking research on LGBT sexualities (Taylor and Raeburn, 1995; Klawitter, 1998). We cannot be complacent about the conditions of possibility within academic institutions for producing new knowledge on organisational sexualities, which in itself constitutes an important avenue of ongoing research that deserves more scholarly attention. This book bears testimony to the current possibilities for pursuing organisational research on sexualities, which we hope will foment thinking, research and activism in the areas covered by our contributors, nurturing the growth of future waves of organisational research on the sexualities of the workplace.

REFERENCES

Acker, J. (2000) 'Revisiting Class: Thinking from Gender, Race and Organizations', *Social Politics*, 7 (2): 192–214.

Adam, B. (1987) *The Rise of a Gay and Lesbian Movement*, Boston: Twayne Publishers.

Adam, B., Duyvendak, J. and Krouwel, A. (1999) *The Global Emergence of Gay and Lesbian Politics*, Philadelphia: Temple University Press.

Ahmed, S. (2006) *Queer Phenomenology: Orientations, Objects, Others*, Durham, NC: Duke University Press.

Badgett, M.V.L. (1995) 'The Wage Effects of Sexual Orientation Discrimination', *Industrial and Labor Relations Review*, 48 (4): 726–739.

Beer, C. R., Jeffrey, R. and Munyard, T. (1983) *Gay Workers: Trade Unions and the Law*, London: NCCL.

Bell, M., Ozbilgin, M., Beauregard, T. and Surgevil, O. (2011) 'Voice, Silence and Diversity in 21st Century Organizations: Strategies for Inclusion of Gay, Lesbian, Bisexual and Transgender Employees', *Human Resource Management*, 50 (1): 131–146.

Bendl, R., Fleischmann, A. and Hofmann, R. (2009) 'Queer Theory and Diversity Management: Reading Codes of Conduct from a Queer Perspective', *Journal of Management and Organization*, 15 (5): 625–638.

Berlant, L. and Warner, M. (1998) 'Sex in Public', *Critical Inquiry*, 24 (2): 547–566.

Boatwright, K. J., Gilbert, M. S., Forrest, L. and Ketzenberger, K. L. (1996) 'Impact of Identity Development upon Career Trajectory: Listening to the Voices of Lesbian Women', *Journal of Vocational Behavior*, 48 (2): 210–228.

Bohan, J. S. (1996) *Psychology and Sexual Orientation: Coming to Terms*, New York: Routledge.

Bourdieu, P. (1984) *Distinction*, London: Routledge and Kegan Paul.

Bowen, F. and Blackmon, K. (2003) 'Spirals of Silence: The Dynamic Effects of Diversity on Organizational Voice', *Journal of Management Studies*, 15 (5): 625–638.

Brewis, J. and Linstead, S. (2000) *Sex, Work and Sex Work*, London: Routledge.

Brooks, A. K. and Edwards, K. (2009) 'Allies in the Workplace: Including LGBT in HRD', *Advances in Developing Human Resources*, 11 (1): 136–149.

Brower, T. (2013) 'What's in the Closet: Dress and Appearance Codes and Lessons from Sexual Orientation', *Equality, Diversity and Inclusion*, 32 (5): 491–502.

Burke, M. (1993) *Coming Out of the Blue: British Police Officers Talk about Their Lives in 'The Job' as Lesbians, Gays and Bisexuals*, London: Cassell.

Burrell, G. (1984) 'Sex and Organizational Analysis', *Organization Studies*, 5 (2): 97–118.

Burrell, G. (1987) 'No Accounting for Sexuality', *Accounting, Organizations and Society*, 12 (1): 89–101.

Butler, J. (1990) *Gender Trouble: Feminism and the Subversion of Identity*, London: Routledge.

Butler, J. (2004) *Undoing Gender*, London: Routledge.

Button, S. (2004) 'Identity Management Strategies Used by Gay and Lesbian Employees: A Quantitative Investigation', *Group & Organization Management*, 29 (4): 470–494.

Casey, M., Hines, S., Richardson, D. and Taylor, Y. (2010) 'Introduction', *Sociology*, 44 (5): 803–810.

Chamberlain, B. (2009) *Bisexual People in the Workplace: Practical Advice for Employers*, London: Stonewall.

Chojnacki, J. T. and Gelberg, S. (1994) 'Toward a Conceptualization of Career Counseling with Gay/Lesbian/Bisexual Persons', *Journal of Career Development*, 21 (1): 3–10.

Chung, Y. B. (1995) 'Career Decision Making of Lesbian, Gay, and Bisexual Individuals', *The Career Development Quarterly*, 44: 178–190.

Chung, Y. B. and Harmon, L. W. (1994) 'The Career Interests and Aspirations of Gay Men: How Sex-Role Orientation Is Related', *Journal of Vocational Behavior*, 45 (2): 223–239.

Cockburn, C. (1991) *In the Way of Women: Men's Resistance to Sex Equality in Organizations*, Basingstoke: Macmillan.

Colgan, F. (1999) 'Recognising the Lesbian and Gay Constituency in UK Trade Unions: Moving Forward in UNISON', *Industrial Relations Journal*, 30 (5): 444–463.

Colgan, F. (2011) 'Equality, Diversity and Corporate Social Responsibility: Sexual Orientation in the UK Private Sector', *Equality, Diversity and Inclusion*, 30 (8): 719–734.

Colgan, F., Creegan, C., McKearney, A. and Wright, T. (2007) 'Equality and Diversity Policies and Practices at Work: Lesbian, Gay, and Bisexual Workers', *Equal Opportunities International*, 26 (6): 590–609.

Colgan, F. and McKearney, A. (2011) 'Spirals of Silence', *Equality, Diversity and Inclusion*, 30 (8): 624–632.

Colgan, F. and McKearney, A. (2012) 'Visibility and Voice in Organisations: Lesbian, Gay, Bisexual and Transgendered Employee Networks', *Equality, Diversity and Inclusion*, 31 (4): 359–378.

Colgan, F., McKearney, A., Bokovikova, E., Kosheleva, S. and Zavyalova, E. (2014) 'Employment Equality and Diversity Management in a Russian Context', in Klarsfeld, A. Booysen, L. Ng, E. Roper, I. and Tatli, A. (eds), *International Handbook in Diversity Management at Work*, Cheltenham: Edward Elgar.

Colgan, F., Wright, T., Creegan, C. and McKearney, A. (2009) 'Equality and Diversity in the Public Services: Moving Forward on Lesbian, Gay and Bisexual Equality?', *Human Resource Management Journal*, 19 (3): 280–301.

Connell, C. (2010) 'Doing, Undoing, or Redoing Gender? Learning from the Workplace Experiences of Transpeople', *Gender & Society*, 24 (1): 31–55.

Cooper, D. (1994) *Sexing the City: Lesbian and Gay Politics Within the Activist State*, London: Rivers Oram Press.

Cooper, D. (2006) 'Active Citizenship and the Governmentality of Local Lesbian and Gay Politics', *Political Geography*, 25 (8): 921–943.

Correia, N. and Kleiner, B.H. (2001) 'New Developments Concerning Sexual Orientation Discrimination and Harassment', *International Journal of Sociology and Social Policy*, 21 (8/9/10): 92–100.

Creed, W.E.D. (2003) 'Voice Lessons: Tempered Radicalism and the Use of Voice and Silence', *Journal of Management Studies*, 40 (6): 1503–1536.

Creed, W.E.D. (2005) 'Seven Conversations about the Same Thing – Homophobia and Heterosexism in the Workplace', in Konrad, A. M., Prasad, P. and Pringle, J.K. (eds), *Handbook of Workplace Diversity*, London: Sage.

Creed, W. D., DeJordy, R. and Lok, J. (2010) 'Being the Change: Resolving Institutional Contradiction through Identity Work', *Academy of Management Journal*, 53 (6): 1336–1364.

Creed, W. D. and Scully, M. A. (2000) 'Songs of Ourselves: Employees' Deployment of Social Identity', *Journal of Management Inquiry*, 9 (4): 391–412.

Crenshaw, K. (1991) 'Mapping the Margins: Intersectionality, Identity Politics and Violence against Women of Colour', *Stanford Law Review*, 43 (6): 1241–1299.

Croteau, J.M. (1996) 'Research on the Work Experiences of Lesbian, Gay, and Bisexual People: An Integrative Review of Methodology and Findings', *Journal of Vocational Behavior*, 48 (2): 195–209.

Croteau, J. M., Anderson, M. Z. and VanderWal, B. (2008) 'Models of Workplace Sexual Identity Disclosure and Management', *Group & Organization Management*, 33 (5): 532–565.

Croteau, J. M. and Hedstrom, S. (1993) 'Integrating Commonality and Difference: The Key to Career Counseling With Lesbian Women and Gay Men', *The Career Development Quarterly*, 41 (3): 201–209.

Cruikshank, M. (1992) *The Gay and Lesbian Liberation Movement*, London: Routledge.

Day, N.E. and Schoenrade, P. (1997) 'Staying in the Closet versus Coming Out: Relationships between Communication about Sexual Orientation and Work Attitudes', *Personnel Psychology*, 50 (1): 147–163.

Deverell, K. (2001) *Sex, Work and Professionalism: Working in HIV/AIDS*, London: Routledge.

Driscoll, J., Kelley, F. and Fassinger, R. (1996) 'Lesbian Identity and Disclosure in the Workplace: Relation to Occupational Stress and Satisfaction', *Journal of Vocational Behaviour*, 48: 229–242.

Dunne, G. (1997) *Lesbian Lifestyles: Women's Work and the Politics of Sexuality*, Basingstoke: Macmillan Press.

Dunne, G. (2000) 'Lesbians as Authentic Workers? Institutional Heterosexuality and the Reproduction of Gender Inequalities', *Sexualities*, 3 (2): 133–148.

Edelman, L. (2004) *No Future: Queer Theory and the Death Drive*, Durham, NC: Duke University Press.

Ellis, A. L., and Riggle, E.D.B. (1995) 'The Relation of Job Satisfaction and Degree of Openness about One's Sexual Orientation for Lesbians and Gay Men', *Journal of Homosexuality*, 30 (2): 75–85.

Ely, R. J., Foldy, E. G and Scully, M. A. (2003) (eds) *Reader in Gender, Work and Organization*, Oxford: Blackwell.

Epstein, D. (ed.) (1994) *Challenging Lesbian and Gay Inequalities in Education*, Buckingham: Open University Press.

Fotaki, M. (2011) 'The Sublime Object of Desire (for Knowledge): Sexuality at Work in Business and Management Schools in England', *British Journal of Management*, 22 (1): 42–53.

Foucault, M. (1979) *The History of Sexuality Volume 1: An Introduction*, London: Allen Lane.

Foucault, M. (1985) *The Use of Pleasure: The History of Sexuality Volume II*, Pantheon: New York.

Foucault, M. (1986) *The Care of the Self: The History of Sexuality Volume III*, Pantheon: New York.

Franzway, S. (1997) 'Sexual Politics in Unions', in Pocock, B. (ed.), *Strife: Sex and Politics in Labour Unions*, St Leonards, NSW: Allen and Unwin.

GLC (1985) *Danger! . . . Heterosexism at Work*, London: GLC.

Gluckman, A. and Reed, B. (1997) (eds) *Homo Economics: Capitalism, Community, and Lesbian and Gay Life*, London: Routledge.

Giddings, L. and Pringle, J. (2011) 'Heteronormativity at Work: Stories from Two Lesbian Academics', *Women's Studies Journal*, 25 (2): 91–100.

Giuffre, P., Dellinger, K. and Williams, C. L. (2008) 'No Retribution for Being Gay?: Inequality in Gay-Friendly Workplaces', *Sociological Spectrum*, 28 (3): 254–277.

Green, H. B., Payne, N. R. and Green, J. (2011) 'Working Bi: Preliminary Findings from a Survey on Workplace Experiences of Bisexual People', *Journal of Bisexuality*, 11 (2–3): 300–316.

Halford, S. and Leonard, P. (2001) *Gender, Power and Organisations*, Basingstoke: Palgrave.

Hall, E. (1995) *We Can't Even March Straight: Homosexuality in the British Armed Forces*, London: Random House.

Hall, M. (1989) 'Private Experiences in the Public Domain: Lesbians in Organizations', in Hearn J., Sheppard, D., Tancred-Sheriff, P. and Burrell, G. (eds), *The Sexuality of Organization*, London: Sage.

Hearn, J. and Parkin, W. (1987) *Sex at Work: The Power and Paradox of Organisation*, Brighton: Wheatsheaf.

Hearn, J. and Parkin, W. (1995) *Sex at Work: The Power and Paradox of Organisation Sexuality*, New York: Macmillan St Martin's Press.

Hearn J., Sheppard, D., Tancred-Sheriff, P. and Burrell, G. (1989) (eds), *The Sexuality of Organization*, London: Sage.

Herek, G. M. (1990) 'The Context of Anti-Gay Violence: Notes on Cultural and Psychological Heterosexism', *Journal of Interpersonal Violence*, 5: 316–333

Herek G. M. (2004) 'Beyond "Homophobia": Thinking about Sexual Prejudice and Stigma in the Twenty-First Century', *Sexuality Research and Social Policy*, 1 (2): 6–24.

Hines, S. (2010) 'Queerly Situated? Exploring Negotiations of Trans Queer Subjectivities at Work and Within Community Spaces in the UK', *Gender, Place & Culture: A Journal of Feminist Geography* 17 (5): 597–613.

Humphrey, J. (1999) 'Organizing Sexualities, Organized Inequalities: Lesbians and Gay Men in Public Service Occupations', *Gender, Work & Organization*, 6 (3): 134–151.

Humphrey, J. (2000) 'Self-Organization and Trade-Union Democracy', *The Sociological Review*, 48 (2): 262–282.

Hunt, G. (1999) *Labouring for Rights: Unions and Sexual Diversity Across Nations*, Philadelphia: Temple University Press.

Hunt, G. and Rayside, D. (2007) *Equity, Diversity, and Canadian Labour*, Toronto: University of Toronto Press.

International Lesbian, Gay, Bisexual, Trans and Intersex Association (2014) *Global Interactive Map: LGBT Rights*, available at http://www.ilga.org (accessed 19 January 2014).

Itzin, C. and Newman, J. (1995) *Gender, Culture and Organizational Change*, London: Routledge.

Jara, M., Webster, N. and Hunt, G. (1999) 'At a Turning Point: Organized Labor, Sexual Diversity and the New South Africa', in Hunt, G. (ed.), *Labouring for Rights: Unions and Sexual Diversity Across Nations*, Philadelphia: Temple University Press.

Jeanes, E., Knights, D. and Yancey Martin, P. (2011) (eds) *Handbook of Gender, Work and Organization*, Oxford: Wiley.

Jeffreys, S. (1993) *The Lesbian Heresy: A Feminist Perspective on the Lesbian Sexual Revolution*, Melbourne: Spinifex Press.

Jones, J. (2013) 'Trans Dressing in the Workplace', *Equality, Diversity & Inclusion*, 32 (5): 503–514.

Kahan, D. (2000) 'Gentle NUDGES vs. Hard Shoves: Solving the Sticky Norm Problem', *University of Chicago Law Review*, 67: 607–645.

Khayatt, M. D. (1992) *Lesbian Teachers: An Invisible Presence*, New York: State University of New York Press.

Klarsfeld, E. Booysen, L., Ng, E., Roper, I. and Tatli, A. (eds) (2014) International Handbook on *Diversity Management at Work*, Cheltenham: Edward Elgar.

Klawitter, M. M. (1998) 'Why Aren't More Economists Doing Research on Sexual Orientation?', *Feminist Economics*, 4 (2): 55–59.

Kollman, K. and Waites, M. (2009) 'The Global Politics of Lesbian, Gay, Bisexual and Transgender Human Rights: An Introduction', *Contemporary Politics*, 15 (1): 1–17.

Knopp, L. (1999) 'Out in Academia: The Queer Politics of One Geographer's Sexualisation', *Journal of Geography in Higher Education*, 23 (1): 116–123.

Krupat, K. and McCreery, P. (2001) *Out at Work: Building a Gay-Labor Alliance*, Minneapolis: University of Minnesota Press.

Kulpa, R. and Mizielinska, J. (2011) *De-Centring Western Sexualities*, Farnham: Ashgate.

Labour Research Department (1992) *Out at Work: Lesbian and Gay Workers Rights*, London: LRD.

Laughlin, K., Gallagher, J., Cobble, D. S., Boris, E., Nadasen, P., Gilmore, S. and Zarnow, L. (2010) ' Is It Time to Jump Ship? Historians Rethink the Waves Metaphor', *Feminist Formations*, 22 (1): 76–135.

Levine, M.P. (1979) 'Employment Discrimination against Gay Men', *International Review of Modern Sociology*, 9: 151–163.

Levine, M. P. and Leonard, R. (1984) 'Discrimination against Lesbians in the Work Force', *Signs*, 9 (4): 700–710.

Lind, A. (2010) 'Introduction: Development, Global Governance and Sexual Subjectivities', in Lind, A. (ed.), *Development, Sexual Rights and Global Governance*, London: Routledge.

Lorde, A. (1980) 'I Am Your Sister: Black Women Organizing across Sexualities', in Blasius, M. and Phelan, S. (eds), *We are Everywhere*, London: Routledge.

Losert, A. (2008) 'Coping with Workplace Heteronormativity Among Lesbian Employees: A German Study', *Journal of Lesbian Studies*, 12 (1): 47–58.

McNaught, B. (1993) *Gay Issues in the Workplace*, New York: St. Martin's Press.

Monro, S. (2010) 'Sexuality, Space and Intersectionality: The Case of Lesbian, Gay and Bisexual Equality Initiatives in UK Local Government', *Sociology*, 44 (5): 803–810.

Meyerson, D. E. (2001) *Tempered Radicals: How People Use Difference to Inspire Change at Work*, Boston: Harvard Business School Press.

Meyerson, D. E. and Scully, M. A. (1995) 'Crossroads Tempered Radicalism and the Politics of Ambivalence and Change', *Organization Science*, 6 (5): 585–600.

O'Brien, J. (2008) 'Complicating Homophobia', *Sexualities*, 11 (4): 496–512.

Öztürk, M. B. (2011) 'Sexual Orientation Discrimination: Exploring the Experiences of Lesbian, Gay and Bisexual Employees in Turkey', *Human Relations*, 64 (8): 1099–1118.

Pringle, J. (2008) 'Gender in Management: Theorising Gender as Heterogender', *British Journal of Management*, 19 (1): 110–119.

Raeburn, N. (2004) *Changing Corporate America from Inside Out: Lesbian and Gay Workplace Rights*, Minneapolis: University of Minnesota Press.

Ragins, B. R. (2004) 'Sexual Orientation in the Workplace: The Unique Work and Career Experiences of Gay, Lesbian and Bisexual Workers', *Research in Personnel and Human Resources Management*, 23 (35–120).

Ragins, B. R. (2008) 'Disclosure Disconnects: Antecedents and Consequences of Disclosing Invisible Stigmas across Life Domains', *Academy of Management Review*, 33 (1): 194–215.

Ragins, B. R. and Cornwell, J. M. (2001) 'Pink Triangles: Antecedents and Consequences of Perceived Workplace Discrimination against Gay and Lesbian Employees', *Journal of Applied Psychology*, 86 (6): 1244–1261.

Ragins, B. R., Singh, R. and Cornwell, J. M. (2007) 'Making the Invisible Visible: Fear and Disclosure of Sexual Orientation at Work', *Journal of Applied Psychology*, 92 (4): 1103.

Rasi, R., Min, D., Rodriguez-Nogues, L. and Ed, D. (1995) *Out in the Workplace: The Pleasures and Perils of Coming Out*, Los Angeles: Alyson Publications.

Rayside, D. (1998) *On the Fringe: Gays and Lesbians in Politics*, Ithaca: Cornell University Press.

Richardson, D. (2000) 'Constructing Sexual Citizenship: Theorizing Sexual Rights', *Critical Social Policy*, 20 (1): 105–135.

Richardson, D. and Monro, S. (2012) *Sexuality, Equality and Diversity*, Basingstoke: Palgrave Macmillan.

Rumens, N. (2011) *Queer Company: The Role and Meaning of Friendship in Gay Men's Work Lives*. Farnham, Ashgate.

Rumens, N. (2012) 'Queering Cross-Sex Friendships: An Analysis of Gay and Bisexual Men's Workplace Friendships with Heterosexual Women', *Human Relations*, 65 (8): 955–978.

Rumens, N. (2013) 'Queering Men and Masculinities in Construction: Towards a Research Agenda', *Construction Management and Economics*, 31 (8): 802–815.

Rumens, N. and Broomfield, J. (forthcoming) 'Gay Men in the Performing Arts: Performing Sexualities within 'Gay-Friendly' Work Contexts', *Organization*, 21 (3): 362–379.

Rumens, N. and Kerfoot, D. (2009) 'Gay Men at Work: (Re)constructing the Self as Professional', *Human Relations*, 62 (5): 763–786.

Russell, G. (2011) 'Motives of Heterosexual Allies in Collective Action for Equality', *Journal of Social Issues*, 67 (2): 376–393.

Ryniker, M. R. (2008) 'Lesbians still Face Job Discrimination', *Journal of Lesbian Studies*, 12 (1): 7–15.

Seidman, S. (2002) *Beyond the Closet: The Transformation of Gay and Lesbian Life*, London: Routledge.

Shallenberger, D. (1994) 'Professional and Openly Gay: A Narrative Study of the Experience', *Journal of Management Inquiry*, 3 (2): 119–142.

Skelton, A. (2000) 'Camping It Up to Make Them Laugh? Gay Men Teaching in Higher Education', *Teaching Higher Education*, 5 (2): 181–193.

Skidmore, P. (2004) 'A Legal Perspective on Sexuality and Organization: A Lesbian and Gay Case Study', *Gender, Work & Organization*, 11 (3): 229–253.

Taylor, D. (1986) (ed.) *All in a Day's Work. A Report on Anti-Lesbian Discrimination in Employment and Unemployment in London*, London: Sweet and Maxwell.

Taylor, Y. and Addison, M. (2013) (eds) *Queer Presences and Absences*, Basingstoke: Palgrave Macmillan.

Taylor, V. and Raeburn, N. (1995) 'Identity Politics as High-Risk Activism: Career Consequences for Lesbian, Gay and Bisexual Sociologists', *Social Problems*, 42 (2): 252–273.

Taylor, Y., Hines, S. and Casey, M. (2011) *Theorizing Intersectionality and Sexuality,* Palgrave Macmillan: Basingstoke.

Thanem, T. (2011) 'Embodying Transgender in Studies of Gender, Work, and Organization', in Jeanes, E., Knights, D. and Martin, P. Y. (eds), *Handbook of Gender, Work, and Organization*, Oxford: Wiley.

Tierney, W. G. (1997) *Academic Outlaws: Queer Theory and Cultural Studies in the Academy*, Thousand Oaks, CA: Sage.

Trau, R. and Hartel, C. (2004) 'One Career, Two Identities: An Assessment of Gay Men's Career Trajectory', *Career Development International*, 9 (7): 627–637.

United States Department of State (2011) *The Department of State's Accomplishments Promoting the Human Rights of Lesbian, Gay, Bisexual and Transgender People*, 6 December, available at www.state.gov/r/pa/prs/ps/2011/12/178341. htm (accessed 19 January 2014).

Walby, S. (1990) *Theorizing Patriarchy*, Oxford: Blackwell.

Ward, J. and Winstanley, D. (2003). 'The Absent Present: Negative Space within Discourse and the Construction of Minority Sexual Identity in the Workplace', *Human Relations*, 56 (10): 1255–1280.

Ward, J. and Winstanley, D. (2005) 'Coming Out at Work: Performativity and the Recognition and Renegotiation of Identity', *The Sociological Review*, 53 (3): 447–475.

Ward, J. and Winstanley, D. (2006) 'Watching the Watch: The UK Fire Service and Its Impact on Sexual Minorities in the Workplace', *Gender, Work & Organization*, 13 (2): 193–219.

Warner, M. (1993) *Fear of a Queer Planet: Queer Politics and Social Theory*, Minneapolis: University of Minnesota.

Watney, S. (1994) *Practices of Freedom: Selected Writings on HIV/AIDS*, Durham: Duke University Press.

Weeks, J. (1998) 'The Sexual Citizen', *Theory, Culture and Society*, 15 (35): 1–19.

Weeks, J. (2007) *The World We Have Won*, London: Routledge.

Weeks, J. (2008) 'Regulation, Resistance, Recognition', *Sexualities*, 11 (6): 787–792.

Williams, C. and Giuffre, P. (2011) 'From Organizational Sexuality to Queer Organizations: Research on Homosexuality and the Workplace', *Sociology Compass*, 5 (7): 551–563.

Williams, C., Giuffre, P. A. and Dellinger, K. (2009) 'The Gay-Friendly Closet', *Sexuality Research & Social Policy*, 6 (1): 29–45.

Willis, P. (2012) 'Witnesses on the Periphery: Young Lesbian, Gay, Bisexual and Queer Employees Witnessing Homophobic Exchanges in Australian Workplaces', *Human Relations*, 65 (12): 1589–1610.

Winfield, L. and Spielman, S. (1995) *Straight Talk about Gays in the Workplace*, New York: AMACOM.

Woods, J.D. and Lucas, J.H. (1993) *The Corporate Closet: The Professional Lives of Gay Men in America*, New York: The Free Press.

Woodruffe-Burton, H. and Bairstow, S. (2013) 'Countering Heteronormativity: Exploring the Negotiation of Butch Lesbian Identity in the Organisational Setting', *Gender in Management: An International Journal*, 28 (6): 359–274.

Wright, T. (2013) 'Uncovering Sexuality and Gender: An Intersectional Examination of Women's Experience in UK Construction', *Construction Management and Economics*, 13 (8): 832–844.

Yuval-Davis, N. (2006) 'Intersectionality and Feminist Politics', *European Journal of Women's Studies*, 13 (3): 193–209.

Yuval-Davis, N. (2011) *The Politics of Belonging: Intersectional Contestations*, London: Sage.

2 Navigating Service and Sexuality in the Canadian, UK and US Militaries

Michèle A. Bowring and Joanna Brewis

INTRODUCTION

This chapter represents an empirical contribution to the literature on what is still—despite the significant body of scholarship exploring the experiences of lesbian, gay and bisexual (LGB) workers—an occupational sector about which we know comparatively little. It reports findings from qualitative interviews with three current and eight former members of the Canadian, UK and US militaries, all of whom identify as nonheterosexual. At the time of writing, research based on in-depth primary data, which indexes the actual experiences of LGB service members, is relatively scarce. This is unsurprising given that until fairly recently there was only one acceptable presentation of sexuality in the militaries of all three countries discussed here: heterosexuality. In 1992 this changed in Canada and in 2000 in the UK; it was not until December 2010, however, that the US followed its counterparts in the relaxation of the heterosexual standard. The military therefore represents a critical case in terms of understanding how individuals navigate nonheterosexual identities at work because it was only some two decades ago when LGB men and women were either debarred from serving in these three militaries altogether or had to engage in an elaborate concealment of their sexual orientation in order to do so.

We start with a brief overview of military policy regarding LGB soldiers in Canada, the UK and the US, followed by a critical excavation of the rationale for the various bans on these soldiers' service.

NATIONAL CONTEXT AND CHANGING MILITARY POLICY

Since 1992, Canada's official policy has been that there is no discrimination on the basis of sexual orientation in the Canadian Forces (CF). Until 1988 it was entirely prohibited for lesbians and gay men to serve, and members were required to inform superior officers if they suspected a fellow soldier was gay or lesbian. After this requirement was dropped, although openly gay and lesbian recruits were still turned away, existing members who were discovered to be gay or lesbian were no longer dismissed. They did, nonetheless, face an end to promotions, security clearances, transfers and reenlistment (Belkin and McNichol, 2001). In 1992, the Department of National Defense repealed the exclusion in response to the Canadian Charter of Rights and Freedoms (1982) and a Supreme Court challenge brought by former service member Michelle Douglas, who had been dishonourably discharged on the basis of her sexuality (Poulin, Gouliquer and Moore, 2009: 498). As a result, the CF adopted an equality stance in all its dealings with service members. No special treatment of any kind was to be accorded to members because of sexual orientation, with regard to issues such as billeting and deployment, on-base accommodation, sanitation facilities and eligibility for partner benefits. Sexual harassment regulations were also amended to include the possibility that both men and women could perpetrate and be the victim of such behaviours. At the same time, enhanced training was introduced in order to dispel myths such as those suggesting lesbians and gay men will make indiscriminate and unwanted advances towards anyone of the same sex. Instead it was stipulated that 'sexual harassment can be exhibited by anyone, regardless of their sexual orientation' (Sexual Harassment and Racism Prevention, cited in Belkin and McNichol, 2000: 13).

It is interesting to note that, just as with the combat exclusion for women (which was overturned in 2001), the ban on gay and lesbian members of the Canadian military was lifted as a result of external, judicial pressure rather than an internal change of mindset. Indeed there were many opponents of the repeal within the CF and dire predictions of mass resignations, an increase in sexual harassment by gay soldiers, more gay bashing and the refusal of vast numbers of members to work for or with gay and lesbian soldiers. But Belkin and McNichol found, some years after the fact, that 'while the removal of the ban may not be universally liked among heterosexual soldiers, it does appear to be universally accepted' (2000: 37). Equally, they found gay and lesbian service members were less stressed and more easily able to accomplish their jobs without fear of discovery. Of course Canada is, in general, a LGB-friendly country that was an early adopter of policies requiring equal treatment on the basis of sexuality (Hunt and Eaton, 2007; Poulin, Gouliquer and Moore, 2009: 498), and certainly in comparison to the UK and the US. Nevertheless, these findings have been echoed in studies of the Israeli, German, Swedish and Australian militaries after these countries repealed extant bans.[1]

The British military lifted its ban on gay and lesbian personnel in 2000. Previously, rather as in Canada prior to 1992, it was felt that 'homosexual behaviour can cause offence, polarise relationships, induce ill-discipline, and, as a consequence, damage morale and unit effectiveness' (Ministry of Defence, 1996: 7). Gay and lesbian recruits were turned away and gay and lesbian members were dishonourably discharged if discovered. Skidmore (1998: 46) comments that the first attempt at organised resistance to the ban was the formation of Rank Outsiders in 1991, a pressure group closely affiliated with LGB charity Stonewall. Rank Outsiders and Stonewall gave evidence at a House of Commons Select Committee on the military in 1992 on this basis (Stonewall, n.d.). A subsequent series of court challenges stemmed from the dishonourable discharge of four servicemen and women on the grounds of sexual orientation. Although their actions for judicial review were rejected by the Divisional Court in June 1995 and the Court of Appeal in November of the same year, and leave to appeal to the House of Lords was likewise rejected in March 1996, Skidmore suggests that this case 'helped considerably in exposing the prejudice of the armed forces' (1998: 47). Indeed the consequent groundswell culminated in a European Court of Human Rights ruling in September 1999 that the ban violated gay and lesbian members' right to privacy (Walker, 2001; Stonewall, n.d.). In response, the Ministry of Defence introduced a new set of regulations that lifted the ban on gay men and lesbians serving in the military in the January of the following year.

In their early study of the effects of British military integration, Belkin and Evans (2000) found no adverse effects. Although we have been unable to locate any more recent studies, certain facts suggest that the repeal of the ban has been relatively unproblematic, at least at a macro level. For example, the Royal Navy, initially the most resistant of the services, went on a drive in 2006 to increase its diversity by recruiting more gay and lesbian personnel. During Gay Pride celebrations in London in 2008, members of all three branches of the British military marched in full uniform, with the military's approval, for the first time. The lack of discussion of this integration in the popular media also points to the relative absence of controversy, given the usually high profile of the issue in the past, and Stonewall (n.d.) report that 'the armed forces [themselves] have stated that the new policy has caused no problems'. All three branches of the services are, moreover, now Stonewall Diversity Champions and as such have publicly committed 'to promote good working conditions for all existing and potential employees and to ensure equal treatment for those who are lesbian, gay and bisexual' (ibid.). The Stonewall Diversity Champions scheme offers participants access to the Workplace Equality Index so that they can assess their work in the area against best practice, as well as an 'allocated client account manager with knowledge of best practice in your sector or region', regular seminars which are free to attend for any employee of a Champion and access to Stonewall Consult for 'in-depth pieces of work such as staff surveys or leadership development on a consultancy basis' (ibid.).

The US is a different context again. Until 1993 there was an outright ban on gays and lesbians in the US military, and periodic purges resulted in thousands of people being dishonourably discharged every year. As part of his presidential campaign, Bill Clinton pledged to repeal the ban if elected.

In 1992, once in office, he began to pursue this course of action but met with stiff opposition from the Joint Chiefs of Staff, Congress and sectors of public opinion (Martinez, Hebl and Law, 2012: 462). In a compromise move, Clinton instituted 'Don't Ask, Don't Tell' (DADT), enshrined in the National Defense Authorization Act (1994). Under DADT, gay and lesbian members were allowed to serve 'if they were not open and if they did not engage in homosexual conduct' (Frank, 2004: 7). The policy therefore prohibited openly homosexual behaviour, effectively continuing to ban gay men and lesbians from service unless they denied or repressed their sexual orientation. Members who admitted to being gay, or who were discovered engaging in homosexual conduct or dating same-sex partners, were dishonourably discharged. Despite the fact that DADT included 'Don't Pursue' and later 'Don't Harass', ostensibly offering additional protection for gay and lesbian service members, there were in excess of 13,000 dishonourable discharges during the policy's lifetime; there is also evidence that homophobic harassment did not significantly reduce either (Moradi, 2006, 2009; Estrada and Laurence, 2009; Martinez, Hebl and Law, 2012; Rich, Schutten and Rogers, 2012).

Although from its introduction there were continuous attempts to challenge DADT, as we have seen, it was not until December 2010 that the ban was actually lifted. Barack Obama pledged to repeal DADT during his first presidential campaign in 2008. However, in the ensuing twenty-four months, critical personnel such as Arabic–English translators continued to be dishonourably discharged because of their sexual orientation, and this at a time when the US military was stretched increasingly thin in Iraq and Afghanistan (Moradi, 2009: 514). Despite recommendations for repeal that came—ironically—from former high-profile supporters of the ban such as Colin Powell and a clear statement from the Chair of the Joint Chiefs of Staff in February 2010 that DADT should be abolished, there was still considerable resistance.

In fact, even after the ban was repealed, actual implementation was held off for several months (until 20 September 2011) so that appropriate transition plans could be worked out, in case the repeal caused furore in the ranks. This was despite a Department of Defense survey of 115,052 respondents released in late 2010 suggesting that '70% of service members felt ending the policy would not negatively affect unit readiness' (Rich, Schutten and Rogers, 2012: 270). In the end, DADT ended not with a bang but with a whimper—just as with Canada and the UK, no adverse consequences have been reported to date. Indeed, twelve months after its implementation, 'the first scholarly effort to assess the accuracy of . . . predictions about the impact of DADT repeal on military readiness' (Belkin et al., 2012: 3) was released. The authors conclude that 'DADT repeal has had no negative impact on overall military readiness or its component parts: unit cohesion, recruitment, retention, assaults, harassment or morale' (ibid.: 33).

BUT WHY BAN LGB SERVICE MEMBERS AT ALL?

One reason for all of the bans cited here has been the argument that homosexual service members somehow undermine unit cohesion, identified as central to military effectiveness. And yet numerous scholarly studies—including the most recent, by Belkin et al. (2012)—have tested this assumption and found no support for it. Kier (1998), for example, cites meta-analyses of military cohesion studies as uncovering nothing more than a small positive correlation—*and no proven causality*—between cohesion and performance. She adds that the high turnover of members of small units in the military, because personnel are moved around as needed and because of casualties in time of combat, is antithetical to the supposed importance of cohesion anyway.

Relatedly, Moradi (2009) and Trivette (2010) both establish the reverse relationship, with their data suggesting that, where lesbian and gay soldiers were out to colleagues, this *improved* unit cohesion, even under bans such as DADT. Moreover, as Scheper *et al.* (2008: 426) point out, the relevant research has only ever established 'occasional and isolated problems of adjustment' after bans have been revoked. Neither have these studies identified 'any overall decrease in cohesion, readiness, morale, or recruiting as a result of . . . policy transitions' (ibid.).

As we have established above, such studies include the militaries of Canada, Israel, Australia, the UK, Germany, Sweden and, most recently, the US. Equally, in Moradi's (2009) data there was an *inverse* relationship between concealment of orientation and respondents' assessment of unit cohesion, due to the stress involved in hiding a nonnormative sexuality. Trivette concurs, suggesting that for many of the twenty-four US veterans, both men and women, whom he interviewed 'the effect of maintaining the identity privacy required by DADT puts a barrier between them and those with whom they serve . . . damaging the very cohesion DADT is intended to protect' (2010: 219).

Privacy has been another central reason for excluding lesbians and gay men from these militaries, although most commentators contend that there is, likewise, little evidence that privacy is important in recruiting and retaining soldiers. Belkin and Embser-Herbert (2002) add that lesbians and gays *already* serve in the military where bans exist and thus share close quarters with heterosexual members. Indeed the LGB US veterans in Frank's (2004) study suggested that more and more nonheterosexual members were being open about their orientation with their close primary unit members and/or immediate superiors with no apparent adverse consequences; again—as with Moradi and Trivette's findings—DADT notwithstanding.

Estes (2005) also interviewed gay US veterans and collected narratives spanning some sixty years of military history, during all of which time gay and lesbian service members were either banned outright or expected to hide their sexuality from recruiters, superiors and peers. These oral histories told of continued fear of discovery leading to lies about the respondents and their partners and an inability to let other unit members get close for fear of disclosing too much information. Implications for their effectiveness as serving personnel included reduced capacity to bond with peers, to develop trust within their units, to discuss personal matters and to achieve maximum productivity in their working lives as fighters and support personnel. As a result, a proportion of Estes's soldiers who served in Iraq during the current campaign had already left the military or decided not to reenlist.

Importantly, because Estes' work chronicles both official and unofficial US military policy towards gays and lesbians since World War II, it suggests that experiences of nonheterosexual members also vary according to two criteria: the attitudes of their superior officers and whether it was peacetime or not. Certainly during periods such as World War II, Vietnam, the first Gulf War and the current conflicts in Iraq and Afghanistan attitudes towards lesbian and gay service personnel seem to relax somewhat as a matter of exigency. Discussions in the online groups contacted in our initial search for participants, as well as numerous published accounts of personnel known to be gay being sent to the front line (Scheper et al., 2008: 431–432), and the fact that DADT dishonourable discharges fell from 1,273 in 2001 to 612 in 2006, with the wars in Iraq and Afghanistan both starting in this five-year period (Moradi and Miller, 2009: 399), all back this up. Indeed Trivette (2010: 216) actually quotes the National Defense Authorisation Act's statement that 'known homosexuals . . . will not be removed if it is deemed to not be in the military's best interest'. We return to this specific issue later but for now provide a summary of the methodology underpinning the collection of our qualitative research data.

METHODOLOGY

A mix of purposive, snowball and self-selection sampling was used to recruit the respondents in this research. Various approaches were deployed, including posts to relevant online discussion groups, requests to networks of colleagues and former students and asking respondents to identify others who might be willing to participate. In the end, eleven respondents took part. These were two serving members (Charlotte, who identifies as lesbian, and Joy, who identifies as bisexual) and two veterans of the Canadian military (Sally, who identifies as a lesbian, and Carla, who identifies as bisexual); one serving member of the UK military (Henry, who identifies as gay) and two veterans of the UK military (Andrea and Susan, who both identify as lesbian); and four veterans of the US military (Caleb, who identifies as gay, and Miranda, Tanya and Jane who all identify as lesbian).[2] They were, with two exceptions, also all women. As such, we draw out gender differences in the data when they seem to be germane, but it is true to say that in many other respects our findings mirror mixed gender studies in the extant literature on LGB military service. In addition, Michèle's gender may have impacted differently on the willingness of LGB men and women to join the study, although of course this is something we can only speculate about.

The respondents took part in semi-structured interviews, either face to face or over the telephone, between 2005 and 2007. Careful ethical safeguards were put in place, including the written securing of informed consent, offering the interview guide ahead of time, mechanisms to protect respondents' identities and to ensure confidentiality (for example, password protection of any electronic records and locking away hard copy information relating to the interviews), as well as allowing respondents to withdraw from the project at any point. Recruiting participants from the US military proved especially challenging because DADT was still in force at the time. Other researchers have recruited veterans to address just this dilemma (Frank, 2004; Estes, 2005; Moradi, 2009; Trivette, 2010). However, even if they no longer serve, habit, fear of reprisal from the Veteran's Administration, including loss of pension and benefits, and fear of censure by the military more generally has stopped many members from participating in this and other studies of LGB experience in the US armed forces as governed by DADT. In the present study a number of potential US respondents—both serving members and veterans—asked a lot of questions about anonymity and then decided not to participate, stating that they were too concerned about repercussions if the military found out about their sexual orientation. These men and women also expressed their concerns about the Internet being vulnerable to government surveillance.

In the next section we analyse the interview data against the backdrop of the extant scholarship on how LGB members experience their military service.

THOSE WE LOVE: LGB SEXUALITY AND THE EXPERIENCE OF MILITARY SERVICE

The first issue that came up was of course the fear of discovery that these LGB participants had lived with, given they had all served during periods when there was a ban on gay and lesbian soldiers. As Tanya, who served in the US military for twenty years—latterly as an officer—and only discovered after two years in that she was a lesbian, explains, 'Once I figured out I was a lesbian I was scared and paranoid for the next eighteen years'. Similarly, Andrea and Susan told of bed checks and surprise inspections in the British military in order to discover women in sexual situations with other women. Andrea explained that in all-female barracks it was difficult to pursue a relationship unless one of the parties was billeted in a single room. Even then, surprise inspections made it very difficult to spend intimate time together. She did comment, however, that the surprise inspections and bed checks were quite often unsuccessful in discovering illicit relationships because there would usually be a tip-off ahead of time. Susan also told a story about an occasion when a tip-off didn't come early enough and two women were almost caught. One of them quickly jumped under the bed and grabbed on to the bedsprings, lifting herself up off the floor as she tried to wait out the inspection. Unfortunately, she was not able to hang on long enough—she fell to the floor with a thump, was discovered and eventually cashiered out of the army. Andrea recounted a similar anecdote about another woman who jumped out of a window in order to escape an inspection and broke her leg.

The Canadian Forces had their own share of what Sally called 'witch hunts' in the years preceding the 1992 repeal. She explained that the military could bug and tape record conversations in off-base apartments if they wanted to, in order to ensure that lesbians and gay men were caught and dishonourably discharged. When Sally, who was out as a lesbian before she joined the CF, was asked why she had joined up when she knew her sexual orientation was problematic in this context, she responded:

> I knew I was gay, knew if I got caught I get booted out with a dishonourable discharge and that would follow me around . . . but it was easy to blend in—what was scary was the witch hunts.

Poulin, Gouliquer and Moore (2009: 500) suggest that these witch hunts, during the early 1980s in particular, were 'especially virulent' in their targeting of lesbian service members and could be triggered by something as innocuous as joining the softball team. They also document the significant health problems their lesbian respondents suffered as a result of being dishonourably discharged, as well as being socially ostracised and in some cases experiencing relationship difficulties when their partner was still serving (2009: 505–506). Sally's fears, then, were clearly not unfounded.

Nonetheless, other LGB soldiers explained that, whereas they knew that their sexual orientation could be grounds for dishonourable discharge, they had joined up out of a desire to serve their country, because the lifestyle appealed to them or because they felt that this was a place where they could make an important contribution. To them, their sexual orientation was irrelevant to their potential performance in the military. These respondents expected that they would be able to keep this aspect of their identity separate from their day-to-day working lives and thus be successful in achieving their objectives. In the end, though, much like the participants in Frank's (2004) and Estes' (2005) studies, having to hide their sexual orientation often led to anger, resentment and eventual exit from the military. Jane, who actually reenlisted in the middle of transitioning out of the US military when the first Gulf War started, explained:

> DADT really bothered me, living a double life got to be really old. It was depressing . . . Every day that I put on a uniform I was publicly

stating 'This is my job and I'm putting my life on the line for you and your rights. I'm on the front line of defence for the Constitution of the United States. I have sworn to defend it from enemies, foreign and domestic'. Yet I'm a gay soldier—*my domestic enemies are here in the US . . .* Overseas, it was 'we don't care who you are, what you do in your spare time, as long as you can do your job'. I wasn't good enough to be in the peacetime army but I was good enough to bleed for them— potentially get killed. (emphasis added)

We have already seen that wartime created a different set of priorities for US military brass when the ban was in operation and Jane's powerful narrative brings this to life in terms of its effects on her own service. Her comments also echo the 1993 Congressional Research Service finding that, during wars, suspected gay and lesbian service personnel have been 'allowed or ordered to serve at the risk of their own lives with the probability of forced discharge when hostilities end if their sexuality becomes an issue' (cited in Scheper et al., 2008: 431). Similarly, Skidmore (1998: 45) summarizes British activist and commentator Peter Tatchell's argument concerning 'the state's hypocrisy in accepting gay and lesbian personnel willingly in times of armed conflict—such as the Gulf War, Vietnam—but discharging them as soon as possible thereafter'.

Jane eventually decided to leave the military, in part because of the way that hiding her sexual orientation made her feel: 'Keeping quiet, after a while it killed my naturally boisterous personality. I didn't like who I was becoming because I couldn't be me'. Jane is not unusual in her decision, as Gates (cited in Trivette, 2010: 219) points out. He suggests that DADT forced between 3,000 and 4,000 personnel to voluntarily quit the US military every year. Similarly, Trivette's respondent Harry said that when he retired and was able to live 'a life of integrity', it was as if he had changed from 'a small, 1950's portable black and white' television to a 'wide screen, high definition TV' (2010: 224). Jane also resented what was, to her, the two-faced way in which many soldiers behaved towards her: 'I got tired of hearing "good job" to my face and "dyke" behind my back'. Likewise, Caleb, who also served in the US forces, never told anyone he worked with that he identified as gay for fear of the consequences. He generally accomplished this by dividing up his life: 'I compartmentalised . . . It was a matter of prioritising: job/position/discharge ranking versus my personal life. And later I chose never to disclose that I was gay when I went to VA doctors'.

Caleb, Jane and also Sally often refrained from getting too close to peers in order to hide their sexuality. They avoided official social functions so they didn't have to bring false 'dates' or show up alone and have to explain why. Jane actually volunteered to take duty shifts in order to avoid this dilemma at official functions but feels that her nonappearance exacerbated an already difficult situation. As also recorded by Frank (2004) and others

(Estes, 2005; Moradi, 2009; Trivette, 2010), this had the effect of isolating these respondents in their daily working lives. Sally remarked:

> You can only reveal so much of yourself to your friends. Never party too hard 'cause you never know what'll happen. But because you're not as emotionally bonded with the people it's easier to do the more difficult things. It was easier for me, not having the strong emotional attachments to people.

Sally differs from other veterans' experiences documented elsewhere (see Kaplan and Ben-Ari, 2000) in the positive inflection that she gives to her isolation. Other respondents grew very disenchanted with the concealment strategies they felt compelled to use:

> I was fed up with having to hide my sexuality. It was wrong—it was part of me. I began to resent that. (Andrea)

> I left because I didn't want to give away the next twenty years of my social life. My roommate and I would have been life partners if we'd been in civilian life. (Caleb)

Notably, in fact, very few of the participants in this project were still serving after the various bans were repealed—most had already left either because they were tired of hiding their sexual orientation or they had been dishonourably discharged. Nonetheless, not one LGB veteran expressed regret at serving in the military, although they had to leave in the end.

A smaller number of other soldiers such as Jane and Miranda, like the male and female respondents in Estes' (2005), Moradi's (2009) and Trivette's (2010) research, had been out to peers and to their immediate superiors as well. Their superior officers generally did not care as long as they did a good job and would refrain from instituting dishonourable discharge proceedings. Typically, most peers did not care either, at least in the sense that they would not 'out' gay or lesbian colleagues to the military authorities. However, that did not mean that these coworkers felt comfortable with LGB personnel in their midst and that they did not make disparaging remarks when they thought such colleagues were out of earshot (Johnson and Burke, 2006).

Significantly then Charlotte was the only LGB participant who was in the military before the repeal of the ban and continues to serve today. She explained that, when she originally joined, 'I lied to get in and it pissed me off'. After the repeal of the ban, she became very open about her sexual orientation: 'I decided I was going to be a poster child. I was senior enough for there to be no repercussions—in this way I could make it easier for others coming behind me'. When asked why she would take on such a task, she replied, 'Because I'm that much of a feminist'. Charlotte is now open about her sexual orientation to her peers and to her superiors. As well, it often comes up when dealing with junior personnel. When Michèle commented that it was very brave of her to be out in such an unapologetic and complete way in her working life, she replied, 'Brave? Not really. It would only be if there was a real risk they would attack me'.

But Charlotte suggested that one of the things that allowed her to be out to this degree was her chosen occupation, music. She was very clear that there were many places in the military where it would be much more difficult to be out and added that it would be far more difficult for a gay man than for a lesbian: 'If you're an infantier, if you're on a ship, especially if you're a man, it's like pinning a target on your head—slashed tyres, painted car, broken windows. I would be afraid of it if I were a man'. It is worth underlining that Charlotte was speaking nearly two decades after the full repeal of the ban on homosexual personnel serving in the CF and that she also suggests life for gay men in the service is much harder per se than for lesbians. The profound masculinism of military culture, as discussed most recently by Hale (2012) and Godfrey, Lilley and Brewis (2012), undoubtedly plays a key role here. So, for instance, a lesbian service member may well be understood, if she is out to colleagues, as more masculine (and thus more 'soldierly') than her gay male counterpart. However, Charlotte went on to say that a change in CF policy has not been enough to make a comprehensive difference:

> There's a policy here that we don't discriminate, but attitudes haven't changed. Now they're recognising the need to address belief and that's more difficult since they get hung up on freedom of religion. In any case, I don't have to wait long to hear a homophobic joke or comment.

CONCLUSION

We suggest that this project is a valuable addition to the extant scholarship on LGB experiences of military service for several reasons. First, it offers an interesting cross-national perspective, especially on service in the hostile conditions of the bans described earlier. This in and of itself is unique as far as we have been able to ascertain. Second, it underlines and augments findings from previous studies, especially around the constant fear of being outed; the potentially disastrous consequences of such discovery; and the fact that hiding one's sexuality as a result *negatively affects* unit cohesion, performance, individual well-being and job satisfaction. Then there is the micro-level at which being out to selected superiors and coworkers does not inevitably lead to significant problems for the LGB soldier, but even for those whose sexuality is an open secret (like Jane) or a matter of full disclosure (like Charlotte), what results could in fact only be a hypocritical and surface tolerance from others. More than this, Jane's narrative adds to the considerable evidence that, under policies like DADT, LGB soldiers might not have been 'good enough to be in the peacetime army' but they were often 'good enough to bleed . . . potentially get killed'.

These findings taken together lead us to concur with Poulin, Gouliquer and Moore (2009: 511–512) in their call for the Canadian Forces to publicly apologise for the 'persecution, discrimination, and humiliating discharges perpetrated against soldiers for reasons of homosexuality'; to allow serving members and veterans access to all records of such investigations and to request that they be expunged; to permanently memorialise the 'adversity and the sacrifice LGBT people made in the face of discrimination' as well as creating a 'special military medal that ex- or currently-serving members can request to commemorate the ordeal'; to commemorate the ordeal'; and to introduce a thorough going educational programme within the CF aimed at eliminating any discrimination against LGBT members going forward.

Our own research suggests to us that the same recommendations both can and should apply to the militaries of the US and the UK, although it is a very welcome step forward that the UK has already begun to financially compensate LGB soldiers for career and health-related losses (ibid.); also welcome is the aforementioned participation by these forces in the Stonewall Diversity Champions programme.

As we have also argued, the military is a very useful context within which to examine the ways in which LGB people manage their identity because its policies and culture foreground issues of gender and sexuality within a hypergendered context. It is often policy-makers at levels far removed from the barracks who decide laws and policies that affect LGB personnel. For example, although the US military ban on lesbian and gay personnel was repealed in September 2011, the spouses of lesbian and gay members are still not allowed to receive the same benefits as the husbands and wives of heterosexual members, even when they are legally married, because of the Federal Defense of Marriage Act (DOMA). Indeed, lesbian and gay spouses are not even recognized as their partners' 'family' by the US government, as exemplified in the case of Staff Sergeant Tracy Dice Johnson whose wife, Staff Sergeant Donna Johnson, was killed in action in Afghanistan (Jowers, 2013). Unlike heterosexual spouses, Tracy Dice Johnson is not entitled to a monthly survivor's pension, nor is she entitled to Army widows' health care and education benefits—all of this because DOMA prevents her from being treated equally. What effect, we could ask, does this continuing double standard have on LGB members' well-being and decisions to come out?

Thus it is important to follow the evolution of organisations such as the military as they change in this regard. It is also crucial to highlight the ways in which changing policies is not enough by researching the ways in which LGB employees manage their sexual identity in such contexts, whether or not they choose to be out, and the effect that the attitudes of coworkers has on that process.

NOTES

1. See Scheper et al. (2008, n. 38) and Frank (2010) for a useful summary of this research.
2. The empirical research was carried out by Michèle as part of her doctoral project on the connections between sex, gender, sexuality and leadership in the military and in nursing (Bowring, 2009). The twenty-two military respondents represented all three Canadian service branches (Army, Navy and Air Force); the Army and the Navy in the UK; and the Army, Navy and Air Force in the US.

REFERENCES

Belkin, A. and Embser-Herbert, M. (2002) 'A Modest Proposal: Privacy as a Flawed Rationale for the Exclusion of Gays and Lesbians from the US Military', *International Security*, 27 (2): 178–197.

Belkin, A., Ender, M., Frank, N., Furia, S., Lucas, G. R., Packard, G., Schultz, T. S., Samuels, S. M. and Segal, D. R. (2012) *One Year Out: An Assessment of DADT's Repeal on Military Readiness*, Palm Center, September 20. Available at www.palmcenter.org/publications/dadt/one_year_out.

Belkin, A. and Evans, R. L. (2000) *Effects of Including Gay and Lesbian Soldiers in the British Armed Forces: Appraising the Evidence*, Palm Center White Paper, November 1. Available at www.palmcenter.org/publications/dadt/british_soldier_motivation.

Belkin, A. and McNichol, J. (2000) *Effects of the 1992 Lifting of Restrictions on Gay and Lesbian Service in the Canadian Forces: Appraising the Evidence*, Palm Center White Paper, April 1. Available at www.palmcenter.org/publications/dadt/effects_of_the_1992_lifting_of_restrictions_on_gay_and_lesbian_service_in_the_canadian_forces_appraising_the_e.

Belkin, A. and McNichol, J. (2001) 'Homosexual Personnel Policy in the Canadian Forces', *International Journal*, Winter: 73–88.

Bowring, M. (2009) 'Leading at the Border: Gender, Sex and Sexuality in Hypergendered Organizations', unpublished PhD thesis, University of Leicester, UK.

Estes, S. (2005) 'Ask and Tell: Gay Veterans, Identity and Oral History On a Civil Rights Frontier', *Oral History Review*, 32 (2): 21–47.

Estrada, A. X. and Laurence, J. H. (2009) 'Examining the Impact of Training on the Homosexual Conduct Policy for Military Personnel', *Military Psychology*, 21 (1): 62–80.

Frank, N. (2004) *Gays and Lesbians at War: Military Service in Iraq and Afghanistan Under "Don't Ask, Don't Tell"*, Palm Center White Paper, September 1. Available at www.palmcenter.org/publications/dadt/gays_and_lesbians_at_war_military_service_in_iraq_and_afghanistan_under_don_t_ask_don_t_tell.

Frank, N. (2010) *What Does the Empirical Research Say About the Impact of Openly Gay Service on the Military? A Research Memo*, Palm Center, March 3. Available at www.palmcenter.org/publications/dadt/what_does_empirical_research_say_about_impact_openly_gay_service_military.

Godfrey, R., Lilley, S. and Brewis, J. (2012) 'Biceps, Bitches and Borgs: Reading *Jarhead*'s Representation of the Construction of the (Masculine) Military Body', *Organization Studies*, 33 (4): 541–562.

Hale, H. (2012) 'The Role of Practice in the Development of Military Masculinities', *Gender, Work and Organization*, 19 (6): 699–722.

Hunt, G. and Eaton, J. (2007) 'We Are Family: Labour Responds to Gay, Lesbian, Bisexual, and Transgender Workers', in G. Hunt. and D. Rayside (eds), *Equity, Diversity, and Canadian Labour,* Toronto: University of Toronto Press, pp. 130–155.

Johnson, W. B. and Buhrke, R. A. (2006) 'Service Delivery in a "Don't Ask, Don't Tell" World: Ethical Care of Gay, Lesbian, and Bisexual Military Personnel', *Professional Psychology: Research and Practice,* 37 (1): 91–98.

Jowers, K. (2013) 'Soldier, Lesbian, War Widow Frustrated by the System', *Army Times,* 7 January. Available at www.armytimes.com/news/2013/01/PRIME-military-same-sex-marriage-widow-010713/.

Kaplan, D. and Ben-Ari, E. (2000) 'Brothers and Others in Arms: Managing Gay Identity in Combat Units of the Israeli Army', *Journal of Contemporary Ethnography,* 29 (4): 396–432.

Kier, E. (1998) 'Homosexuals in the US Military: Open Integration and Combat Effectiveness', *International Security,* 23 (1): 5–39.

Martinez, L. R., Hebl, M. R. and Law, C. L. (2012) 'How Sexuality Information Impacts Attitudes and Behaviors toward Gay Service Members', *Military Psychology,* 24 (5): 461–471.

Ministry of Defence (1996) *Report of the Homosexuality Policy Assessment Team,* February. Available at http://www.mod.uk/NR/rdonlyres/C801AAED-2EFE-4D33-A845-EFD103438BF2/0/HPAT_report_Feb_1996.pdf.

Moradi, B. (2006) 'Perceived Sexual-Orientation-Based Harassment in Military and Civilian Contexts', *Military Psychology,* 18 (1): 39–60.

Moradi, B. (2009) 'Sexual Orientation Disclosure, Concealment, Harassment, and Military Cohesion: Perceptions of LGBT Military Veterans', *Military Psychology,* 21 (4): 513–533.

Moradi, B. and Miller, L. (2009) 'Attitudes of Iraq and Afghanistan War Veterans toward Gay and Lesbian Service Members', *Armed Forces & Society,* 36 (3): 397–419.

Poulin, C., Gouliquer, L. and Moore, J. (2009) 'Discharged for Homosexuality from the Canadian Military: Health Implications for Lesbians', *Feminism & Psychology,* 19 (4): 496–516.

Rich, C., Schutten, J. K. and Rogers, R. A. (2012) ' "Don't Drop the Soap": Organizing Sexualities in the Repeal of the US Military's "Don't Ask, Don't Tell" Policy', *Communication Monographs,* 79 (3): 269–291.

Scheper, J., Frank, N., Belkin, A. and Gates, G. J. (2008) ' "The Importance of Objective Analysis" on Gays in the Military: A Response to Elaine Donnelly's *Constructing the Co-Ed Military',* *Duke Journal of Gender Law and Policy,* 15 (2): 419–448.

Skidmore, P. (1998) 'Sexuality and the UK Armed Forces: Judicial Review of the Ban On Homosexuality', in T. Carver and V. Mottier (eds), *Politics of Sexuality: Identity, Gender, Citizenship,* London: Routledge, pp. 45–56.

Stonewall (n.d.). Available at www.stonewall.org.uk.

Trivette, S. (2010) 'Secret Handshakes and Decoder Rings: The Queer Space of Don't Ask, Don't Tell', *Sexuality Research and Social Policy,* 7 (3): 214–228.

Walker, K. (2001) 'Moving Gaily Forward? Lesbian, Gay and Transgender Human Rights in Europe', *Melbourne Journal of International Law,* 2 (1). Available at www.austlii.edu.au/au/journals/MelbJIL/2001/4.html.

3 Reconsidering the Workplace Closet
The Experiences of Lesbian and Gay Teachers

Catherine Connell

INTRODUCTION

Despite the rise in gay-friendly workplaces (Williams, Giuffre, and Dellinger, 2009), the public school classroom remains a hostile work environment for lesbian and gay teachers, even in locales with laws prohibiting discrimination against them (Colgan and Wright, 2011; Connell, 2012; Friend, 1993; Harbeck, 1997; Irwin, 2002; Jackson, 2007; Kissen, 1996; Walters and Hayes, 1998). This chapter examines how lesbian and gay teachers negotiate their sexual and professional identities in these competing contexts. Their experiences offer unique insights into the heterosexual norms embedded in schools.

Lesbian and gay teachers must contend with professional norms that categorize coming out as inherently unprofessional and are thereby often denied the taken-for-granted benefits that their heterosexual counterparts enjoy, including talking about romantic partners, displaying family photos in the classroom, bringing partners to school functions, and seeing themselves reflected in the curriculum. Visibly lesbian and gay teachers face a no-win situation: either emphasize their commonality with heterosexual teachers and reproduce repressive norms in the process, or risk being punished for transgressing gender and sexuality norms. This chapter details how this double bind operates in the lives of lesbian and gay teachers and concludes with a discussion of how it might be undermined.

BECOMING A PROFESSIONAL

Despite the common presumption of its irrelevance to most workplaces, sexuality is in fact significant to the organization in all kinds of work and occupations (Hearn and Parkin, 1987). This is most obvious in the patterns of exclusion, discrimination, and harassment that lesbian and gay employees have experienced in the workplace, which demonstrate that one's sexual identity does indeed have a bearing on career success and occupational location. Less obvious yet equally important is the way that bureaucratic and organizational forms are themselves embedded in gender and sexuality norms. For example, feminist scholars have identified how the job expectations of high pay, high prestige employment are incompatible with child-care and domestic responsibilities, the bulk of which often fall to women, thereby making such employment difficult for women and especially for mothers (Acker, 1990; Blair-Loy, 2003; Hochschild, 1997; Williams, 1996). The organization of work, then, is predicated on the sexual division of labour in the household (Hartmann, 1976).

Another way that work and occupations are infused with sexuality is through norms of professionalism. Every job has its own occupationally specific standards of what it means to be professional, but generally speaking, professionalism is associated with rationality, technical expertise, and subdued emotional character, all of which are also tied to notions of masculinity (Connell, 1987). Feminist analyses of the workplace have pointed out the ways that this association of professionalism and masculinity has disadvantaged women (Acker, 1990; Bruni and Gherardi, 2001; Whitehead, 2002), but less has been said about how it relates to sexuality. Woods and Lucas (1993) explored this connection in their study of gay male professionals and found that coming out was consistently defined as an 'unprofessional' act. They argue that coming out threatens professional identity-making because professionalism is not only inherently gendered but also sexualized. That is to say that the professional ideal is not only masculine, as feminist scholars have argued, but also heterosexual. Gay men who want to achieve professional status must conform to this ideal, which in Woods and Lucas's study (1993) meant remaining closeted and distancing themselves from what were perceived to be feminine behaviours or attributes.

More recent work shows that whereas the professional closet is becoming a thing of the past, the process of negotiating an identity as a gay professional continues to be difficult for many (Rumens and Kerfoot, 2009). A significant proportion of US employers now offer nondiscrimination protections for lesbian and gay workers (Human Rights Campaign, 2013; Raeburn, 2004), many going so far as to identify themselves as 'gay-friendly' (Williams, Giuffre, and Dellinger, 2009). In such workplaces, the stakes of coming out are significantly lowered; increasingly, lesbian and gay employees report that coming out on the job is routine and unremarkable (Rumens and Kerfoot, 2009; Seidman, 2002; Williams, Giuffre, and Dellinger 2009).

This movement away from the closet, though, has not lessened the gender normative expectations of gay employees that Woods and Lucas (1993) describe. In fact, some argue that the professional demands of gender normativity for such employees have intensified since the decline of the closet. For example, Rumens and Kerfoot (2009) find that whereas gay professionals in the UK are able to come out on the job, they feel increasingly constrained to a strictly masculine, normative presentation of self. Williams, Guiffre, and Dellinger (2009) suggest that the 'old' version of the closet, which forbade publicly declaring a homosexual identity, has been replaced with the 'gay-friendly closet', which allows for the disclosure of homosexuality but demands that lesbians and gays appear 'normal', or just like their heterosexual counterparts. This demand creates what Duggan (2002) calls 'the new homonormativity': to the extent that mainstreaming lesbian, gay, and bisexual identities has been successful, it has brought with it intensified demands to accept the gendered, raced, and classed status quo. In the work realm, this has meant increased acceptance for openly lesbian and gay employees but only for those who are willing and able to conform to the narrow standards of professionalism.

The teaching profession is a unique case for a couple of key reasons. First, unlike the workplaces studied by Rumens and Kerfoot (2009) and Williams, Giuffre, and Dellinger (2009), which were defined as gay-friendly, schools as workplaces are markedly less gay-friendly in climate. Previous research suggests that lesbian and gay teachers experience significant harassment and discrimination on the job (Friend, 1993; Harbeck, 1997; Irwin, 2002; Jennings, 1994; Jackson, 2007; Kissen, 1996; Walters and Hayes, 1998). Teachers are routinely fired for being gay or lesbian (Biegel, 2010; Davis, 1972; Irwin, 2002). In 1978, The Briggs Initiative nearly made it illegal for gays and lesbians to teach in US public schools, and more recently gay and lesbian teachers have been used as scapegoats in efforts to block federal nondiscrimination legislation (McCreery, 1999). It stands to reason, then, that the closet remains a central feature of teaching employment, in which case a study of teachers adds an important caveat to the body of literature suggesting that US workplaces are 'beyond the closet' (Seidman, 2002).

Second, professionalism in teaching has a moral dimension that makes it distinct from the professional norms of most occupations. Teachers are expected to develop a moral character in children as part of their professional duties, and their own morality is closely scrutinized in kind. To the extent that homosexuality is defined as beyond the bounds of morality, then, it is in tension with the norms of teaching professionalism. Whereas the normalization of lesbian and gay sexualities might suggest that homosexuality is no longer considered immoral, nearly half of surveyed Americans continue to believe that homosexuality is 'morally wrong' (Pew, 2012), and these beliefs are only intensified when it comes to exposing young children to homosexuality. Whereas recent survey data show that attitudes may be shifting toward acceptance, a sizable proportion of the US population continues to disapprove of gays and lesbians teaching at the elementary and high school level (Jones, 2009). This suggests that the moral dimension of teaching makes the accomplishment of a professional identity more fraught for lesbian and gay teachers than for other lesbian and gay professionals.

METHODOLOGY

The data for this chapter are derived from a comparative study of the experiences of lesbian and gay public school teachers in California, a US state with a high level of sexuality nondiscrimination protections, and Texas, a state with low levels of such protections. The study includes in-depth interviews with 45 lesbian and gay teachers and administrators (24 in California and 21 in Texas) and multiple field observations with 8 teachers and administrators (5 in California, 3 in Texas) between June and December 2008. In the same time period, I also interviewed 6 'straight allies' (heterosexual teachers, administrators, and advocates who self-identify as gay rights supporters)—2 in California and 4 in Texas—for a total of 51 interviews. Interviewees were recruited via snowball sampling and a subsample of interviewees were selected for observation, which included sitting in on classes and attending relevant events, including Gay Straight Alliance (GSA) meetings, meetings of a lesbian and gay teacher advocacy group, and a pride parade march with a group of teachers and students. The majority of the interviews in California were conducted in the greater Los Angeles area,

Table 3.1　Demographic Composition of Sample

	CA sample	TX sample
Age		
Under 40	11	12
Over 40	15	13
Race		
White	17	19
Latino	6	3
Black	0	3
Asian	2	0
Biracial	1	0
Gender		
Man	14	11
Woman	12	14
Sexual Identity		
Gay	14	11
Lesbian	9	10
Bisexual	1	0
Straight	2	4
Teaching Level		
Elementary school	4	8
Middle school	3	7
High school	13	5
Administration	6	1
Not a teacher	0	4

whereas the majority of the Texas interviews were conducted in the Central Texas 'triangle' of Houston, Dallas, and Austin.

The sample includes roughly the same number of men and women. It is diverse with respect to age, years of teaching experience, and type of education work (elementary teaching, middle school teaching, high school teaching, and administration). However, the sample is fairly racially homogenous, comprised of mostly white participants, despite attempts to include more teachers of colour. Furthermore, the sample is limited to mostly lesbian-, gay-, and straight-identified individuals; only one respondent identified as bisexual. Because it is difficult to make comparable claims about the bisexual experience with only one bisexually identified participant, the focus of this chapter is the experiences of the lesbian and gay participants. This study did not include transgender-identified teachers, in part because of the uniquely complex dynamics of the transgender work experience (Connell, 2010).

COMING OUT IN THE CLASSROOM IS 'UNPROFESSIONAL'

Within the context of teaching, coming out continues to be seen as contrary to standards of professionalism. In interviews, this tension was especially evident in discussions of coming out to students. Lesbian and gay teachers in this study said that overt displays of sexuality, which included by their definition, coming out, are 'unprofessional' and 'inappropriate' in the classroom. Teachers, they said, should present themselves as asexual in the classroom. On the surface, this asexual expectation applies to all teachers, gay or straight. However, the reality is that some expressions of sexuality are implicitly legitimized in the teaching context. This distinction privileges heterosexuality and further marginalizes lesbian and gay teachers.

When I asked Hugh, a gay Latino middle school Texas teacher, if he comes out as gay to his students, he responded:

> I don't approach that with my kids. I don't bring up anything personal with my kids ... just because ... children are impressionable and I don't want to have to explain myself to a child. So I never come out to my students. I just don't think it's appropriate to bring up.

This type of response was common among teachers in both states, who felt that coming out was too 'personal' and irrelevant to their teaching responsibilities. For example, Cheryl, a Latina lesbian special education teacher in California, asserted:

> No, [I'm not out at school] because I think, first and foremost, I see myself as a teacher. I don't mix my sexual orientation with my career. You know, it's my career first. I've never even thought about it.

Cheryl's statement implies that sexual identity and career are mutually exclusive—and mutually opposed—components of identity and self.

Lesbian and gay teachers sometimes argue that sexuality has no place in the classroom context, but when the subject turned to heterosexuality in the classroom, they readily identified how their straight colleagues reference their sexual identity in their daily interactions with students. When asked how straight teachers' sexuality impacts on their students, Rufus, a white gay middle school California teacher, explained:

> [Heterosexuality] is a range of experience, a way of being. [Straight teachers] talk about their husbands, wives, their straight lives in way that has an impact on their students and their ideas.

Mary, a retired white lesbian health teacher, also in California, held the position that gay and lesbian teachers have a responsibility to be out and justified this standpoint by referencing the ways straight teachers make their sexualities known at school:

> The assumption is that you are heterosexual until proven otherwise. For the most part, people assume heterosexuality. And so that's why teachers who are heterosexual don't feel the need to 'come out'; it's just assumed. [Heterosexual teachers] talk about their husbands and wives and their children and have photos of their families in the classroom. I think, likewise, we need to participate in that in the same way.

Although married straight teachers displayed their sexuality through references to, pictures of, and classroom visits from their spouses, these same displays were considered 'unprofessional' if performed by lesbian and gay teachers. This illustrates an interesting paradox in the interviews. Namely, most lesbian and gay teachers say that sexuality itself in the classroom is unprofessional, yet they recognize displays of married, monogamous heterosexuality as acceptably professional classroom behaviour. Defining coming out as professionally questionable while acknowledging the compatibility between (married) heterosexuality and professionalism shows how heterosexuality is legitimized through the professional expectations of the teaching occupation. When lesbian and gay teachers say sexuality in the classroom is 'unprofessional', what they perhaps really mean is that *homosexuality* in the classroom is unprofessional. This dissonance—between what is acceptable for lesbian and gay versus straight teachers—reveals the way that the norms of teaching professionalism privilege heterosexuality.

DEVELOPING A PROFESSIONAL IDENTITY AS A LESBIAN OR GAY TEACHER

Despite this formidable obstacle, lesbian and gay teachers do usually manage to develop a sense of professional competence, using two key strategies.

First, they reframe the moral dimensions of teaching to include role modelling and protecting vulnerable lesbian, gay, and bisexual and questioning students. Second, to the extent they can make their sexuality visible on campus, there is a tendency toward homonormative (Duggan, 2002) interpretations of the acceptable avenues for such visibility.

Moral Authority

When asked to explain the value they placed on being visible as a lesbian and gay teacher, such teachers often emphasized the way teacher visibility might positively impact on students. Susan, a white lesbian administrator on a California textbook adoption board, believed in the importance of visibility for affirming marginalized students in the classroom curriculum, which included lesbian and gay visibility. She explained:

> Sexual orientation and gender identity are invisible [in schools]. And we know how important it is for children to see themselves in their curriculum. You know, we actually sit down and count, when doing textbook adoption, and count—how many pictures in here are of Latino students, African American students, Asian American or white students? You know, when we have the picture of the drug dealer, the drug buyer, and the drug user—what colour are these people? You know, and the reason we think about this is like—also, in our literature classes—who reflects our history, our stories. We want out students to see themselves in the curriculum. And we should have that same consideration for our [sexual] minority students. So that's why it's important to be out.

Susan considers the importance of visibility from a pedagogical perspective, in the context of the research and standards of practice that suggest the importance of seeing one's marginalized race, class, gender, and sexual position reflected in curriculum. Amy, a white lesbian California high school teacher, agreed that lesbian and gay teacher visibility was key to supporting lesbian, gay, bisexual, and transgender students:

> I think it's up to the individual teacher, but I think the more that we're visible, the better it will be for everybody. And I think that, you know, we help our students, too, by being visible. Because, you know, if they don't see adults feeling comfortable with their own sexuality, what's it saying to them? How does it affect them? If you're coy about it or secretive or whatever.

In positioning the visibility of lesbian and gay teachers as a way of protecting students who might themselves be or become lesbian, gay, or bisexual, Susan and Amy are able to carve out a kind of moral expertise for lesbian and gay teachers. In the process, they co-opt the rhetoric of morality and child welfare that has historically been used to block lesbians and gays from teaching to make an argument for their inclusion.

Anthony, a gay Latino administrator in California, believed that lesbian and gay visibility is important not just for teachers but also for administrators. He suggested that administrative visibility promotes a culture of safety in schools. He explained:

> [The board members of our lesbian and gay teacher support organisation] always felt that if there were out administrators, out principals, out assistant principals, superintendents, directors that were out, then teachers would then feel safe to come out and then those teachers that are out can serve as direct role models for their students, as well as the school site administrators. So that was our plan, our strategy to make the students feel safe in the school, to make a safer environment.

Anthony's argument underscores the role modelling argument and adds another rationale for visibility: the creation of a safe school environment through the visibility of high profile figures in the school district. This 'trickle down' rationale echoes the arguments of mainstream gay rights politics, which often demand that public figures such as politicians, artists, and actors come out on the basis that their visibility fosters a safer climate for others. By emphasizing safety, Anthony also picks up on the near-ubiquitous discourse about school safety and bullying in contemporary education to legitimize lesbian and gay teachers and administrators as uniquely qualified to support students through role modelling.

Homonormative Presentations of Self

In addition to claiming moral authority through role modelling, lesbian and gay teachers manage the dissonance between being lesbian/gay and being a teaching professional by highlighting their similarities to their heterosexual counterparts. In interviews, research participants articulated the contours of the acceptable—and unacceptable—visibly lesbian or gay teacher. In doing so, they contrasted certain kinds of lesbian/gay performances in a way that constructed differences between what they imagined to be a 'good' lesbian/gay teacher and a 'bad' lesbian/gay teacher. The differences between the 'good' and 'bad' lesbians/gays hinged on ideas about normality, productivity, gender expression, and sexual activity.

Mary, a retired white lesbian teacher, had fought for decades for lesbian and gay inclusion within one California school district. Her arguments in favour of normalizing lesbian and gay identities in schools directly articulated the expectations of 'virtual normality' (Sullivan, 1996). She argued, 'I think we just have to put a face on ourselves that we are normal and productive citizens like everyone else so people can begin to know that we exist, and who we are and that we're teachers and neighbors and family members, aunts and uncles, and you know, whatever career we're in'. This emphasis on normality and productivity epitomized the expectations of the 'good' lesbian/gay teacher that were echoed across interviews in both states. Similar to claims about the unique moral authority of lesbian and gay teachers, Mary's statement that lesbian and gay teachers are 'normal and productive citizens like everyone else' is a compelling argument for inclusion and support of lesbian and gay teachers. Troublingly, though, it also reinforces a narrow code of conduct for lesbians and gays in the classroom; what about those who will not—or cannot—put on that face of normalcy?

Charles, a white gay retired teacher in California, reiterated the emphasis on normality and productivity established in Mary's comments, saying: 'The thing is that we need to keep working, to get people to see that we are *regular people*' (emphasis added). David, a Latino gay Texas teacher, further emphasized the importance between the growing visibility of lesbian and gay teachers and the projection of an image of normality in the following exchange:

> *INTERVIEWER:* What do you think we could do to improve the way schools are organized or the culture around schools to make it a more gay-friendly climate?
>
> *DAVID:* I think really what we need—and this is hard to say because I think it would jeopardize a lot of people—is we need more media coverage. And positive coverage. Because a lot of time, the public, all they see, and there's nothing wrong with this, but all they see is our friends out there marching in gay pride and they've got a wedding dress on and a beard, and it's like, they need to know that we're people, too. And we're fighting for the same goals they are—educating our children and making our lives better. A lot of times I think when straight people look at us, they look at us as deviants. And that bothers me, because I feel, I personally feel that I would have more in common with a straight man that likes to do the things that I do than with a gay man that likes to do the complete opposite.

David hesitated when describing the 'good' lesbian/gay image because of the jeopardizing impact it might have on more marginalized lesbian, gay, bisexual, and transgender people. Yet David ultimately underscored that the visibility of 'acceptable' lesbian/gay identities is the key to achieving 'gay-friendly' schools. Acceptability is defined here as conforming to conventional norms of gendered dress, raising children, and possessing the same interests, hobbies, and aesthetics of straight men—an agenda very much in line with the ideal of homonormativity.

Part of what David and other teachers were struggling with is the constraining power of stereotyping. David, in part, might be reacting to the stereotypes of lesbians and gays as gender transgressors, finding them limiting and frustrating as someone who does not fit that stereotype. Teachers referenced these stereotypes frequently when talking about their experiences; for example, white lesbian Texas teacher Elizabeth lamented: 'One of the biggest things is public perception about what being gay is. Because those stereotypes . . . you have those even with high schoolers and those carry on into your adult life . . . For instance, every lesbian has short hair or a mullet and plays softball, things like that'. Teachers like David and Elizabeth feel understandably frustrated by these very narrow definitions of what a lesbian/gay person should look like. Ideally, representations of lesbians and gays would include a whole range of being and not rely on stereotypes. One problem, though, with the way that David and others are reacting to these stereotypes is how they depict gender nonnormative queers as somehow contributing to stereotyping and therefore damaging to the agenda of advancing gay rights. The person with a beard in a wedding dress becomes a distracting spectacle, rather than a person who also has legitimate needs under the umbrella of 'gay rights'.

What is especially disconcerting about this emphasis on normality is the corresponding disdain that emerged with respect to those who do not toe the line. When asked what advice he would offer newly minted gay and lesbian teachers, Charles admonished: 'Well, it's up to the gay or lesbian teacher to act like a person, and not have bizarre or flamboyant character'. He went on to explain that flamboyance would be an inappropriate distraction in the classroom: 'It distracts from what they are trying to present and they are supposed to be presenting the subject matter, primarily, and that [would be distracting]. So nothing that distracts from the overall tone and presentation is appropriate'. Charles references both the neutral ideal of teaching professionalism—nothing 'distracting' from the expected tone and presentation of teaching—as well as the homonormative ideal of avoiding 'bizarre' or 'flamboyant' presentations of self. Further, Charles's directive—'it's up to the gay or lesbian teacher to act like a person'—is in line with neoliberal discourses that locate change at the individual level rather than critique the institution that demand such narrow and normative presentations.

Research participants counterposed an ideal lesbian/gay identity—be normal, productive, just like everyone else—against a 'bad' lesbian/gay archetype. Some teachers contrasted their own status as a 'good' lesbian/gay with the 'bad' lesbians/gays their students otherwise encounter. Larry, a white gay high school teacher in California, defined his presence as an openly gay teacher in direct contrast to the gay men and trans women he presumes his students encounter in their communities. He explained this in the following exchange:

INTERVIEWER:	Do you think it's important for teachers to be out in their classrooms?
LARRY:	I think so.
INTERVIEWER:	Why is that?
LARRY:	It's just, um, especially in our neighbourhood, a neighbourhood that's 90 percent Hispanic, the only gay people they see are what the kids call the 'half trannies'. The really effeminate Hispanic gay men, they keep the bottom and get boobs in Mexico City, really cheap boobs. And they're hookers and prostitutes or something . . . [In their communities], there's no such thing as gay. Not like, 'I'm going to live with a guy, spend the rest of my life with a guy, and you know, we're going to share a life'. No.

In this interview excerpt, Larry referenced a 'bad' gay man—effeminate, possibly trans-identified men of colour who participate in sex work—which he juxtaposes against himself to shore up his identity as a potential gay role model. Larry must participate in this process of distancing himself from 'those' gays in order to reconcile his conflicting professional and sexual identities. In this process, he draws upon assumptions about US gay identities as more evolved than those in the Global South, positing his white, upper middle-class presentation of gay identity as superior. Larry's use of the 'bad' gay archetype carves out a place for himself as a gay professional, but it also reinforces negative stereotypes of queer men of colour. It posits whiteness as a more enlightened and progressive racial identity with respect to lesbian and gay identity and rights.

Interestingly, in interviews, depictions of the 'bad' lesbian/gay referred mostly to gay men, rather than lesbians. I speculate that this may be connected to the history of visibility—and vilification—of gay men, particularly in the context of working with young children (Sears, 1998). The gendered dynamics of the teaching profession are perhaps also contributing to this trend in the interviews.

Women and men working in feminized occupations are often stereotyped. Women doing this work are often assumed to be maternal and inherently caring, which fits with gendered stereotypes, whereas men who cross over into these occupations are stereotyped as effeminate and assumed to be gay (Williams, 1995). This larger sociological context of occupations predominately occupied by women perhaps makes gay men in teaching more readily visible, whereas lesbians are overlooked. Other research suggests women may actively try to remain less visible as a way to avoid compounding gender discrimination with sexual identity discrimination (Colgan, Creegan, and McKearney 2008; Colgan and Wright 2011). The gendered implications of this are double-edged; in one respect, it contributes to the invisibility of lesbians, whereas in another, it stigmatizes gay men, effeminate gay men in particular, in the teaching context.

Although the 'bad' gay teacher was often the imagined target, some interviewees did reference a corresponding stereotype of the 'bad' lesbian teacher. For example, Christi, a white lesbian Texas middle school teacher, contrasted her own presentation as conventionally gendered with the archetypical butch lesbian. She said:

> It sounds callous but I've said for years that the girls want to be me and the boys want to 'do' me. And that is why I get along so well with my students. I just operate on knowing that 13-year-old boys and 13-year-old girls just want attention. And between the two of them, they all want attention. I think if I were butch, it would be very difficult.

Christi recognized the added burden carried by gender transgressing teachers, who must 'battle' to develop legitimacy in the school context. Christi herself drew on her presentation as a conventionally feminine woman to negotiate her relationship with her students, who she assumes are heterosexual themselves. She acknowledges this advantage, saying later: 'Yeah, that heterosexual privilege? Hell yeah, I'm gonna use it'. Her belief that her success as a teacher hinged on her gender presentation as well as her perception that a more gender nonconforming presentation of self would be difficult to navigate in the school context, underscores the limited choices that gay and lesbian teachers perceive—either conform to acceptable presentations of a visible lesbian/gay self and find acceptance or stand out and face possible persecution. Whereas Christi was able to negotiate her professional and sexual identity through her own fairly conventional gender presentation, not all teachers have access to this strategy. Further, her strategy relies on the compromise that is at the troubling heart of homonormativity—that is, giving up a critique of systems of privilege in order to secure a place for oneself in the institutions that continue to exclude others.

CONCLUSION

Much like the gay men in previous research (Woods and Lucas, 1993), lesbian and gay teachers in the contemporary public school context continue to experience coming out as antithetical to standards of professionalism. They attribute this tension to the ostensibly sexually neutral presentation of self that teachers are expected to abide by. Yet they also readily identify how certain behaviours, such as displaying photos of or talking about partners, are interpreted as unprofessionally sexual for gay and lesbian teachers but not for heterosexual teachers. What this reveals is that standards of professionalism, which are constructed as being sexually neutral, are in fact deeply imbued with heterosexual privilege. This heterosexualized 'ideal worker norm' (Williams, 2000) disadvantages lesbians and gays, who must either try to conform or risk failure, which can entail discrimination and harassment.

In this context, how is it that lesbian and gay teachers develop a sense of professionalism? As I have shown above, they do so in two key ways. First, they take the rhetoric of morality that teaching professionalism is so deeply steeped in and turn it on its ear by claiming a unique moral authority as protectors of lesbian, gay, bisexual, and transgender children, the bullying of whom has become the recent subject of much educational reform and concern. They also emphasize the ways that lesbian and gay teachers can (and should) be just like their straight counterparts. By projecting an image of 'virtual normality' (Sullivan, 1996), they are able to recoup some authority and legitimacy and distance themselves from the more damning stereotypes of homosexuality that might otherwise impede their professional success. In the process, though, they further marginalize those who are not able or willing to draw on this presentation of self. Specifically, gender nonnormative teachers and teachers disadvantaged by race, class, and other marginalized statuses are left behind in the individualized pursuit of equality through normality.

Further, these strategies put the burden of change on the individual, rather than agitating for change at the institutional level. What this analysis of gay and lesbian teachers' experiences has shown is that heterosexual privilege is built into the very foundation of what it means to be professional in this occupational context. For the purposes of brevity, this chapter does not include a discussion of the experience of straight allies, but my forthcoming book, *School's Out: Gay and Lesbian Teachers in the Classroom*, demonstrates that their performances of teaching professionalism are not burdened by the same kinds of considerations as gay and lesbian teachers. In fact, they feel freer to advocate for gay rights in their classrooms because there are less vulnerable to accusations about pushing a personal agenda. Accordingly, efforts to redress the discrimination and harassment that lesbian and gay teachers face should happen at the structural level and not remain the responsibility of individual teachers, who may or may not have the privilege of speaking out.

Whereas creating policy that would unseat heterosexual privilege and homonormativity is a daunting task, one small first step might be taken in the framing of nondiscrimination law and policy. At present, there are no federal nondiscrimination protections of lesbian, gay, bisexual, and transgender employees, meaning that the teachers I interviewed in Texas can be legally discriminated against. The teachers in California do benefit from statewide protections, but federal nondiscrimination could go far to benefit both groups of teachers, as it would provide not just concrete protection but also would symbolically reinforce the protections that do exist at the state and local level.

Additionally, teachers' unions have historically been significant in protecting teachers from discrimination. Teachers unions are especially influential in California; local and nationally affiliated teachers' unions such as the American Federation of Teachers (AFT), the National Education Association (NEA), and United Teachers Los Angeles (UTLA) have been very vocal in their support of lesbian, gay, bisexual, and transgender teachers and their rights in schools (GLBTQ, 2009). In contrast, teacher unions under Texas's 'right to work' employment conditions have very little political power. There, unions cannot represent teachers in labour disputes, including disputes about sexual harassment and discrimination on the basis of sexual identities. In addition to strengthening federal nondiscrimination protections, broadening the protective powers of unions in states like Texas would be beneficial to lesbian and gay teachers. Overall, union strength in US has seen a massive decline since the 1950s (Wallerstein and Western, 2000), suggesting that improving and strengthening unions not be only an issue for 'right to work' states but rather a national concern.

Various iterations of the Employment Nondiscrimination Act (ENDA) has been introduced—and blocked—in US Congress since the 1990s. After a contentious history over the scope of protections it should provide, the pending version of the bill includes not just sexual identity nondiscrimination but also gender expression, which is intended to protect transgender employees in addition to lesbian, gay, and bisexual employees. This broader constituency of employees who would be protected by ENDA would be an important step toward deconstructing heterosexual privilege in the teaching profession for two reasons. First, by including transgender employees, this bill would protect not just more teachers, but some of the most marginalized— whatever advancement we have seen with respect to accepting lesbians and gays (and to a lesser extent, bisexuals) has not come with corresponding levels of acceptance for transpeople (Norton and Herek, 2012), meaning they are especially vulnerable to discrimination and harassment. Second, the symbolic potential of including 'gender expression' in the bill's wording could be used to contest the homonormative expectations of teaching professionalism. Successful legal challenges to discrimination on the basis of 'gender expression' that interpret it to include unequal treatment because of gender nonconformity could bring the issue of homonormativity to the fore. By including a critique of the normativity that the teaching profession demands, such legal challenges would be more effective in uncovering and dismantling heterosexual privilege and homonormativity than claims based in sexual identity discrimination alone. Consequently, any movement to improve the working conditions of lesbian and gay (as well as bisexual and transgender) teachers would be well served by the successful passage of a broad and inclusive federal nondiscrimination policy. From there, more occupationally specific policies and practices can begin to bolster the transformation of the profession, which has for too long limited who can and cannot teach.

REFERENCES

Acker, J. (1990) 'Hierarchies, Jobs, Bodies: A Theory of Gendered Organizations'. *Gender & Society,* 4, 2, 21–27.

Biegel, S. (2010) *The Right to be Out: Sexual Orientation and Gender Expression in America's Public Schools.* Minneapolis: University of Minnesota Press.

Blair-Loy, M. (2005) *Competing Devotions: Career and Family Among Women Executives*. Cambridge, MA: Harvard University Press.

Bruni, A. and Gherardi, S. (2001) 'Omega's Story: The Heterogeneous Engineering of a Gendered Professional Self', in Dent, M. and Whitehead, S. (eds), *Managing Professional Identities: Knowledge, Performativity and the 'New' Professional*, pp. 174–98. London: Routledge.

Colgan, F., Creegan, C., McKearney, A., and Wright, T. (2008) 'Lesbian Workers: Personal Strategies amid Changing Organisational Responses to "Sexual Minorities" in UK Workplaces'. *Journal of Lesbian Studies*, 12,1, 31–45.

Colgan, F. and Wright, T. (2011) 'Lesbian, Gay and Bisexual Equality in a Modernising Public Sector: Opportunities and Threats'. *Gender, Work and Organization*, 18,5, 548–70.

Connell, C. (2010) 'Doing, Undoing, or Redoing Gender?: Learning from the Workplace Experiences of Transpeople'. *Gender & Society*, 24,1, 31–55.

Connell, C. (2012) 'Dangerous Disclosures'. *Sexuality Research & Social Policy*, 9,2, 168–77.

Connell, C. (2013) *School's Out: Gay and Lesbian Teachers in the Classroom*. Berkeley: University of California Press.

Connell, R. W. (1987) *Gender and Power*. Stanford, CA: Stanford University Press.

Davis, J. C. (1972) 'Teacher Dismissals on Ground of Immorality'. *Clearing House*, 46,7, 418–23.

Duggan, L. (2002) 'The New Homonormativity: The Sexual Politics of Neoliberalism', in Castronovo, R. and Nelson, D. D. (eds), *Materializing Democracy*, pp. 175–94. Durham, NC: Duke University Press.

Friend, R. A. (1993) 'Choices, Not Closets: Heterosexism and Homophobia in Schools', in Weis, L. and Fine, M. (eds), *Beyond Silenced Voices: Class, Race, and Gender in United States Schools*, pp. 209–31. New York: State University of New York Press.

GLBTQ Encyclopedia (2009) 'Teachers'. Available online at www.glbtq.com/social-sciences/teachers,6.html. Accessed February 2013.

Harbeck, K. M. (1997) *Gay and Lesbian Educators: Personal Freedoms, Public Constraints*. Malden, MA: Amethyst Press and Productions.

Hartmann, H. (1976) 'Capitalism, Patriarchy, and Job Segregation by Sex'. *Signs*, 1,3, 137–69.

Hearn, J. and Parkin, W. (1987) *"Sex" at "Work": The Power and Paradox of Organisation Sexuality*. New York: St. Martin's Press.

Hochschild, A. (1997) *The Time Bind: When Work Becomes Home and Home Becomes Work*. New York: Metropolitan Books.

Human Rights Campaign (2013) *Corporate Equality Index 2013: Rating American Workplaces on Lesbian, Gay, Bisexual, and Transgender Equality*. Washington, DC: Human Rights Campaign.

Irwin, J. (2002) 'Discrimination against Gay Men, Lesbians, and Transgender People Working in Education'. *Journal of Gay & Lesbian Social Services*, 14,2, 65–77.

Jackson, J. M. (2007) *Unmasking Identities: An Exploration of the Lives of Gay and Lesbian Teachers*. Lanham, MD: Lexington Books.

Jennings, K. (1994) *One Teacher in 10: Gay and Lesbian Educators Tell Their Stories*. Boston: Alyson Publications.

Jones, J. (2009) 'Majority of Americans Continue to Oppose Gay Marriage'. Available online at www.gallup.com/poll/118378/Majority-Americans-Continue-Oppose-Gay-Marriage.aspx. Accessed February 2013.

Kissen, R. M. (1996) *The Last Closet: The Real Lives of Lesbian and Gay Teachers*. Portsmouth, NH: Heinemann Publishing.

Lewis, G. B. and Taylor, H. E. (2001) 'Public Opinion toward Gay and Lesbian Teachers: Insights for All Public Employees'. *Review of Public Personnel Administration*, 21, 133–51.

McCreery, P. (1999) 'Beyond Gay: "Deviant" Sex and the Politics of the ENDA Workplace'. *Social Text,* 17, 39–58.

Norton, A. T. and Harek, G. M. (2012) 'Heterosexuals' Attitudes toward Transgender People: Findings from a National Probability Sample of U.S. Adults'. *Sex Roles.* Available online at www.springerlink.com/content/w615567201950w12/. Accessed August 2012.

Pew Research Center (2012) 'Homosexuality and Morality'. Available online at http://pewresearch.org/databank/dailynumber/?NumberID=880. Accessed August 2012.

Raeburn, N. C. (2004) *Changing Corporate America From Inside Out: Lesbian and Gay Workplace Rights.* Minneapolis: University of Minnesota Press.

Rumens, N. and Kerfoot, D. (2009) 'Gay Men at Work: (Re)constructing the Self as Professional'. *Human Relations,* 62, 763–86.

Seidman, S. (2002) *Beyond the Closet? The Transformation of Gay and Lesbian Life.* New York: Routledge.

Sullivan, A. (1996) *Virtually Normal.* New York: Vintage.

Wallerstein, M. and Western, B. (2000) 'Unions in Decline? What Has Changed and Why'. *Annual Review of Political Science,* 3, 355–77.

Walters, A. S. and Hayes, D. M. (1998) 'Homophobia Within Schools: Challenging the Culturally Sanctioned Dismissal of Gay Students and Colleagues'. *Journal of Homosexuality,* 35,2, 1–23.

Whitehead, S. M. (2002) *Men and Masculinities.* Cambridge: Polity Press.

Williams, C. L. (1995) *Still a Man's World.* Berkeley: University of California Press.

Williams, C. L., Giuffre, P., and Dellinger, K. (2009) 'The Gay-Friendly Closet'. *Sexuality Research & Social Policy,* 6,1, 29–45.

Williams, J. C. (1996) 'Restructuring Work and Family Entitlements around Family Values'. *Harvard Journal of Law & Public Policy,* 19, 753.

Williams, J. C. (2000) *Unbending Gender.* New York: Oxford University Press.

Woods, J. D. and Lucas, J. H. (1993) *The Corporate Closet: The Professional Lives of Gay Men in America.* Mankato, MN: The Free Press.

4 Courts as Workplaces for Sexual Orientation Minorities

Todd Brower

INTRODUCTION

Courts have cultural and legal mandates to be societal institutions dedicated to equal justice, including fairness for LGBT people. These mandates conform to their traditional institutional role: to resolve disputes (Rottman, 2005). However, courts also employ sexual minorities and serve as their workplaces. That function of judicial bodies has been less often studied. This chapter draws on four empirical studies that examined court employees' employment experiences a decade ago (Brower, 2003 UK Report; Brower, 2005 UK Report; California Judicial Council, [CAJC] 2001; New Jersey Supreme Court [NJSC], 2001) to explore common patterns in LGBT persons' work experiences. Because only these four data sets exist, this chapter necessarily focuses on UK and US courts.

The interaction of law, workplace mandates, norms, and discrimination is complex. Confronted with societal discrimination, researchers such as Becker (1971) argued that nondiscrimination laws are unnecessary whereas others suggested that market forces alone cannot end discrimination (Darity and Mason, 1998). According to the latter view, collective action and social and workplace norms are important influences supporting discrimination, especially because people often view LGBT persons as outsiders—contravening traditional gender roles and societal customs (Colgan and McKearney, 2012). Other discrimination theories suggest that LGBT persons' visibility triggers mistreatment (Fleming, 2007; Woods, 1993). Qualitative research on LGBT lawyers surveyed about sexual orientation discrimination supports this perspective: 'I don't think the firm would care if a lawyer *was* gay, but would care if he/she was *openly* gay at the office, social events, etc.' (Los Angeles County Bar Association Report [LACBA], 1994, pp. 28–29). The National Association for Law Placement (2013) reported the percentage of openly LG lawyers in the US increased from 1.88 percent in 2011 to 2.07 percent in 2012, but those numbers are still low. Thus, despite the increasing acceptance of LGBT people in modern life (Green, 2010; Pew Research Center, 2012), sexual minorities may still prefer to remain hidden in legal workplaces (McNish, 2006). Theoretical models of workplace discrimination falter when presented with empirical jobsite data. Each judiciary reporting data (CA, NJ, UK) had unambiguous protections against sexual orientation discrimination during the survey periods. Consistent with those policies, we might expect fair treatment of LGBT court employees (Colgan, et al., 2007; Skidmore, 2004). However, Balakrishnan and Bauer (2006) found that explicit legal rules and employment policies did not necessarily improve LGBT employees' job environments. Rather, degrees of sexual orientation visibility (Badgett, 1996; Brower, 2007) and supervisorial commitment to fairness may be greater influences on work life (Huffman, Watrous-Rodriguez, and King, 2008).

Finally, LGBT employees' treatment in workplaces explicitly focused on fairness may elucidate how sexual minorities navigate other, more traditional jobs without legal protections or strong societal equality expectations. Court workplaces also illustrate the 'sticky norms' problem: individuals' reluctance to fully implement legal regulations designed to change an embedded social norm (Kahan, 2000). Accordingly, this chapter explores how sexual orientation visibility influences court employees' perceptions and personal experiences and interacts with fairness norms and legal mandates.

THE FOUR COURT EMPLOYEE STUDIES

The four court employee studies on sexual minorities' treatment illustrate how law and legal institutions combine with sexual identity visibility to profoundly influence LGBT persons' employment. During the survey periods, each court had workplace policies prohibiting sexual orientation discrimination (Brower, 2003 UK Report; Brower, 2005 UK Report; CAJC, 2001; NJSC, 2001), but external legal protections were mixed. California and New Jersey had state laws against sexual orientation discrimination in employment, although the US federal government still does not (Lindemann, Grossman, and Weirich, 2012). In the UK, the Employment Equality (Sexual Orientation) Regulations 2003 went into effect in the period between the two surveys. Thus, 2000 to 2005 provides a particularly rich period to study the interaction among workplace norms and legal regulations because the various protection schemes were in flux. Concomitantly, LGBT employees and their heterosexual colleagues were adjusting their expectations and behaviours to those changes, a significant factor when law seeks to modify social norms successfully (Kahan, 2000).

All four surveys emphasized court employees' direct experiences, observations, and perceptions of the court system. California asked people to report their experiences and observations in 2000, the year preceding the survey, and during their employment with the courts generally; the New Jersey instrument used the reporting period of 1995 to 2000; and the two UK Reports were deployed in 2003 and 2005.[1] The study populations varied, as did response rates. The California Judicial Council sent questionnaires to 5,500 of the approximately 17,000 California court employees around the state, including court clerks, reporters, administrators, and attorneys; approximately 28 percent responded (n=1,525) (CAJC, 2001). Sixty-four respondents identified as LGB; California did not ask about transgender persons (Brewer and Gray, 1999a). Of LGB court employees, over one-third were totally out at work; over one-third were selectively out there; over one-quarter were not out. California court employee respondents were full-time, permanent court employees (98%) and were predominantly white, heterosexual, married women (93%).

In the UK, researchers surveyed the Rainbow Network, the LGBT court employee group. The 2003 survey had a 67.4 percent response rate. Of 97 respondents, 70 respondents identified as LGBT 'Full Members of the Network', 25 as heterosexual 'Friends of the Network', and 2 as other. A majority of 2003 UK survey respondents were white, had at least an A-level degree, and often lived with a same-sex partner. They worked primarily at court administrative headquarters, and in the South Eastern Circuit, although other respondents were employed throughout England and Wales. Of respondents replying to the question about sexual orientation visibility at work, nearly half were totally out, almost one-fifth were selectively out, and less than 10 percent were not out (Brower, 2003 UK Report). The survey was repeated in spring 2005 for the then-current Rainbow Network membership (Brower, 2005 UK Report).

In New Jersey, approximately 21,000 questionnaires were distributed and 2,594 were returned for a response rate of 12 percent. Nearly 70 percent of respondents who identified their relationship to the New Jersey courts were court employees, with lawyers and judges comprising nearly one-quarter. Seven percent who identified their sexual orientation were LGB; the New Jersey survey also did not ask about transgender issues or identity. No information was given about education, income, geographic distribution, marital status, race or ethnicity, or other demographic information (NJSC, 2001).

VISIBILITY AND INVISIBILITY IN THE COURTS

Whereas sexual orientation is complex and may be measured by identity or behaviour, identity is often the salient characteristic in the workplace (Badgett, 1996). Because most LGBT people are not visibly identifiable (Blumenfeld and Raymond, 1993), Eskridge (1997) showed LGBT people often expressly communicated that identity to break the assumption of heterosexuality engendered by silence. Silence allows some gay people to hide their identity and avoid the negative consequences of visibility (Eskridge, 1997). Nevertheless, forced invisibility is a form of inequality, not a solution to anti-gay discrimination (Schacter, 1997). A New Jersey respondent disclosed:

> As a gay employee there is not much that I can say about this delicate subject because I cannot even be myself at my place of employment.

I have to lead two different lives. Sometimes my co-workers ask me if I have a girlfriend, if I am married, how many children I have, and I have to answer with a lie. All this makes me feel very unhappy. In addition, sometimes the people that I work with make fun of gay people in front of me, and I have to laugh about it and pretend that it does not bother me.

(NJSC, 2001: 48–49)

Additionally, silencing identity reinforces LGBT marginalisation because gay people must deny an essential difference between them and others (CAJC, 2001) or not share in everyday workplace social interactions to mask certain aspects of their lives (Ho, 2006; LACBA, 1994). These restrictions can estrange LGBT employees from colleagues, triggering more discomfort for all parties.

Thus, open self-identity is more significant for LGBT people than for heterosexuals (Eskridge, 1997) and carries greater consequences. During the historical time period discussed here, the LACBA (1994) found that nearly one-half of all respondents, regardless of sexual orientation, believed that merely revealing the sex of one's partner would harm an LG attorney's career. As one UK court employee commented, '[I was] not invited to senior office meetings as partners were invited and they did not want me to attend with my same-sex partner' (Brower, 2003 UK Report, p. 37). Heterosexuals may not feel any pressure to voice their sexual orientation explicitly but may simply display pictures of a spouse at work, use an opposite sex pronoun when describing joint activities, or allow people to presume heterosexuality (Biewen, 1997). However, publicly acknowledging one's LGBT identity constitutes deliberate, continuing choices, calibrated to setting, comfort level, consequences (Ragins and Cornwell, 2001), disclosure tradeoffs (Woods, 1993), and often shared first with trusted individuals or other gay people (Friskopp, 1996; Ragins, Cornwell, and Miller, 2003). Visibility is important to assimilation at work, to integration into courts and other societal institutions, and to self-worth generally. As the empirical studies on LGBT persons' court experiences demonstrate, visibility affects treatment in multiple ways. It forms an additional dimension when studying LGBT persons' experiences not typically relevant in visibly diverse populations like race or gender (Badgett, 1996).

LGBT PERSONS' EXPERIENCES AND
TREATMENT IN THE COURTS

Consistent with explicit workplace sexual orientation protections in all three jurisdictions during the survey periods, over 76 percent of UK respondents and 94 percent of California employees believed that written court policies were fair to LGBT people. Most court employee respondents believed that LGBT people were treated the same as other employees (Brower, 2003

UK Report; CAJC, 2001). Nevertheless, the predominant pattern for LGBT employees was a perceived deterioration in treatment and fairness perceptions when asked about specific observations, experiences, and quotidian workplace policy applications (Brower, 2005 UK Report; CAJC, 2001; NJSC, 2001). This chapter explores that discrepancy.

Contemporaneous workplace behaviour studies show similar patterns. Formal equality and legal protections do not necessarily create actual equal treatment or positive experiences (Badgett, 1996; Ragins and Cornwell, 2001). Collegial and peer group pressures may undermine formal mandates (Balakrishnan and Bauer 2006; Ragins, Singh, and Cornwell 2007). Other studies, however, reflect that legal context may change LGB workplace experiences (Colgan, et al., 2007). Further, Skidmore (2004) suggested that despite law's shortcomings as a regulatory apparatus, it shaped organisational policy and practice, and the eventual modification of cultural norms. Kahan's (2000) work suggests one resolution of these potentially conflicting results between affirmative workplace and legal protections against sexual orientation discrimination and persistent negative job experiences by LGBT court employees. He posits that the relationship between law and social norm change is counterintuitive. In order for law effectively to change societal norms and behaviour, legal restrictions cannot get too far ahead of the majority's beliefs. A 'no tolerance policy for violations' or 180-degree norm change is likely to be counterproductive. If law censures behaviour substantially more severely than does a typical decision maker or societal actor, then the actor's personal aversion to the overly harsh condemnation will overcome her desire to follow the law; she will resist enforcing the legal requirements. Conversely, if the legal rule censures behaviour only slightly more than does the social norm, the decision maker will follow the law despite personal disinclination.

These dynamics are self-reinforcing. Reluctance to enforce laws will strengthen others' resistance; willingness to enforce will also reinforce others' conformity to the law. Finally, those who are victims of the illegal behaviour and/or who are sympathetic to the law will resent underenforcement of strict legal protections and view that reluctance as condoning illegal activity. Consequently, positions harden on both sides of the divide and induce more negative behaviours and hostility as polarisation develops (Kahan, 2000). Thus, a gentle legal nudge is more effective than a hard shove to modify engrained social norms. Kahan's theory (2000) finds support in court employee data on workplace experiences. Despite explicit rules mandating sexual orientation fairness in the courts during the studied time period, other workplace dynamics may have undermined legal equality requirements and may have inhibited the effectiveness of statutory or regulatory workplace protections. For example, a workplace norm discouraged sexual minorities' visibility. NJSC (2001) found that most people believed homosexuality was a private matter inappropriate in the workplace. One

New Jersey respondent commented that most LGBT people would prefer to hide their sexuality. This belief may be backwards; heterosexual coworkers' preferences may require secrecy.

> The thing that concerns me most about my [workplace] is a general attitude that being gay is simply not an issue and shouldn't even be addressed in the work context. This attitude pervades to the extent that I personally feel pressure not to raise 'gay' issues, even when it otherwise seems appropriate to do so
>
> (Hennepin County Bar Association [HCBA], 1995, pp. 31–32)

Judicial workplace studies found that coworkers counselled/expected LGBT employees to hide their sexuality or criticised disclosure (Brewer and Grey, 1999a; Brower, 2003 UK Report; NJSC, 2001). Sixteen percent of LG New Jersey respondents and 2 percent of all court employees regardless of sexual orientation heard a coworker, supervisor, or judge criticise an employee or applicant for openly identifying as LG. Twenty-one percent of LG employees and 1 percent of all employees reported that someone in their office was advised or asked to conceal their sexual orientation (NJSC, 2001). Over 26 percent of UK court employees thought that LGBT employees should keep their sexual orientation hidden at work. Indeed, some sexual minorities may have wished to be open, but others in the courts forced them to stifle their nonmajority identity (Brower, 2003 UK Report).

These pressures are consistent with other workplace studies. Moore (1993) found that 37 percent of Americans stated that they did not want LG people to disclose their sexuality. Some might object to 'private behaviour'/sexuality appearing in the public workplace; others may resent confronting their otherwise latent antipathy towards sexual minorities (Badgett, 2001). Other contemporaneous empirical studies confirm these findings but conclude that legal requirements are important but not determinative in sexual minorities' workplace experiences and visible LGBT identity (Ragins and Cornwell, 2001). Ragins, Singh, and Cornwell (2007) found also that fears associated with disclosure predicted job attitudes, psychological strain, work environment, and career outcomes. Law and workplace norms are filtered through sexual minority employees' experiences and affect LGBT identity disclosure. Court responses buttress those conclusions, even in institutions requiring formal equality:

> The judge asked all prospective jurors to state marital status and what their spouse's occupation was. I have a long-term domestic partner, so I felt that answering the question honestly required me to reveal my sexual orientation and to state my partner's occupation even though legally my marital status is single Stating 'single' would have felt like lying.
>
> (Brewer and Gray, 1999a, p. 33)

Remaining silent caused lesbians and gay men to feel they deceived others in court and elsewhere, although some opted for that choice.

Ragins and Cornwell (2001) also speculated that disclosure might lead to increased reports of discrimination in more hostile environments. As in other workplaces (Croteau, 1996; HCBA, 1995; LACBA, 1994), open LGBT court employees often experienced more discrimination and negative treatment. Over 32 percent of all 2003 UK respondents thought that people used sexual orientation to devalue some LGBT employees' credibility. Moreover, nearly 28 percent believed that openly LGBT employees lacked the same promotion opportunities as heterosexuals, whereas over 16 percent said hiring was harder if people suspected you were LGBT. Finally, over 5 percent believed that LGBT employees received less favourable work assignments than heterosexuals (Brower, 2003 UK Report). The 2005 UK data were similar, as were California employees' responses to the same questions (Brewer and Gray, 1999a ; Brower, 2005 UK Report).

Openness

Unlike LGBT court users who may have limited exposure to the courts, LGBT employees have repeated contact with judicial institutions because they work there. Thus, no employees described their court experience as a sexual orientation–neutral event—a frequent comment of California LG court users in the companion study to the court employee report (Brower, 2003a). For example, a California judicial worker stated, 'I could never understand why all of a sudden I was treated with disrespect by management. Then a co-worker told me that she thought management hated gays and that they were told by a different co-worker that I was gay' (Brewer and Gray, 1999a, p. 59). A New Jersey lesbian court employee heard that her sexuality caused her not to be promoted (NJSC, 2001, p. 47). British examples were similar and show the disjunction among openness, formal work policies, and actual treatment. One British court employee reported: 'In short, 15 years ago I was offered the post of Principal Private Secretary of the Lord Chancellor; [I] came out; and the offer was withdrawn'. Another said: 'My working relationship with a young, female line Manager broke down when she discovered I was gay . . . Having previously worked together harmoniously before she discovered I was gay, she started to pick fault with me once she was aware' (Brower, 2003 UK Report, p. 47).

As court data illustrate, a visible LGBT work identity coloured employees' experiences. Jolls (2006) found that the salience of minority identity increased bias. The more distinct a group appeared from the majority, the more likely the majority disproportionately ascribed out-group/minorities' failures to group characteristics and to individual fault. In contrast, in-group/majority persons' failures were attributed to situations beyond the individuals' control and not to their membership in a particular social group. Similarly, people remembered and judged more harshly the undesirable behaviour of out-group members than of in-group members (Krieger, 1995). The historical distinctiveness of open LGBT identity helps translate these findings to workplace experiences. Ordinarily, heterosexuals are not separately characterised by sexual orientation or behaviour. Accordingly, we rarely perceive heterosexuality because we measure difference against that baseline (Brower, 2007). For example, sexual orientation protections apply to LGBT and heterosexual persons, but heterosexuals seem not to need antidiscrimination laws; they do not normally appear different enough to provoke negative reactions. Indeed, the few reported situations of sexual orientation discrimination against heterosexuals occur when they are minorities in gay environments (Apilado, 2011; *The Providence Journal*, 2006).

People view open LGBT employees differently from open heterosexual court workers. All court reports found significant disparities in work experiences of LGBT versus heterosexual employees. Unsurprisingly, few heterosexual court employees suffered negative treatment based on sexual orientation. California LG employees were over five times more likely to experience negative actions or discrimination or hear comments based on sexual orientation than were heterosexuals (Brewer and Gray, 1999a). The 2005 UK study reported similar findings (Brower, 2005 UK Report). Consistent with the polarisation that Kahan (2000) predicted for law-based hard shoves against persistent social norms, gay and heterosexual court employees witnessed different behaviours by coworkers and had different fairness perceptions. Thirty percent of all New Jersey respondents regardless of sexual orientation, but 78 percent of LG respondents heard a coworker, supervisor, or judge make derogatory statements or inappropriate jokes about homosexuals. Moreover, 14 percent of all judicial employees but 49 percent of LG workers heard those remarks or jokes about a colleague because that person was or was perceived to be LG (NJSC, 2001). A California court employee reported: 'There were quite a few gay men who worked at our court and were openly harassed because of it' (Brewer and Gray, 1999a, pp. 48–49).

Heterosexual and LGBT court employees' opinions also diverged on the courts' success in resolving disputes. UK and California court employees rated the courts less fair to LGBT people than to the general population, with sexual minorities rating the courts significantly lower than their heterosexual colleagues (Brower, 2003 UK Report; Brower, 2005 UK Report; CAJC, 2001). The degradation in fairness perceptions and equal treatment because of minority status is consistent with other court studies on minority identities, like race or ethnicity (Rottman and Hansen, 2001). Congruent with dissimilar workplace experiences and perceptions, homosexuals and heterosexuals also differently assessed the risks/benefits of disclosing sexual orientation in the judicial workplace. A greater percentage of heterosexual than homosexual UK court employees believed LGBT persons were able to be open about their sexual orientation at work (Brower, 2003 UK Report).

UK court employee demographics underscore this contrast. Remember heterosexuals surveyed all affiliated with the LGBT employee network due to their interest in and sensitivity to sexual orientation issues. If even those persons undervalued workplace disclosure risks compared to their LGBT colleagues, stronger disparities should occur in the more randomly drawn New Jersey court employee sample, where heterosexual respondents had no particular affinity for LGBT issues. Indeed, on virtually every question in which data were disaggregated by respondents' sexuality, New Jersey LGBT employees reported worse experiences or observations than did their heterosexual counterparts (NJSC, 2001).

Despite the strong connexion between sexual orientation openness and adverse treatment and heterosexual colleagues' significant preference for invisible LGBT sexuality, data on court worker visibility are not uniformly negative. As in other workplaces, sexual orientation openness correlated with some positive fairness perceptions. Griffith and Hebl (2002) linked openness with lower job anxiety. Day and Schoenrade (2000) found that open LGBT employees were more committed to their workplaces and had higher job satisfaction and lower conflict between work and home. Open LG workers were more satisfied with that degree of visibility than were more closeted employees (Croteau, 1996). The UK reports reflect similar findings. In 2005, a larger percentage of open British LGBT court employees than their closeted coworkers reported that the court's policies were fair to LGBT people (Brower, 2005 UK Report). British respondents in 2003 who were more open at work believed that it was unnecessary to hide one's sexual orientation. They also more likely disagreed that (1) an open LGBT person would have a harder time being hired; (2) people made jokes about LGBT persons behind their backs; and (3) prejudice was widespread at work (Brower, 2003 UK Report). Nevertheless, a more pessimistic data interpretation is possible. Colleagues may simply hide prejudices when openly gay people are present. Over 40 percent of California court employees acknowledged that people joked or commented about gay people behind their backs (Brewer and Gray, 1999a); in the 2005 UK study, nearly 47 percent made that same point (Brower, 2005 UK Report). In addition, employees who were not identified as LGBT heard more negative comments about sexual minorities and perceived more widespread workplace prejudice than did their more open colleagues.

Visibility sometimes pushed bias underground: 'I hope they will begin to think about what they are saying, as I confront their behaviour every time. I am worried though, that they will just stop saying things in front of me, which means I can no longer try to change their behaviour and/or attitudes' (Brower, 2003 UK Report, p. 39). These comments reflect that LGBT people felt obligated to improve their workplaces and colleagues (Harding, 2006). However, this need may lead to frustration and/or powerlessness in the face of covert workplace norms and behaviours, or it may lead to increased disenchantment and polarisation (Kahan, 2000). Because sexual orientation is not always observable, it also affected heterosexual colleagues' workplace identity, dynamics, and experiences. Minority sexuality may provoke an associative stigma: heterosexuals or assumed heterosexuals might be reluctant to associate with gay people because they fear misidentification as LGBT. One closeted UK gay court employee experienced this associative stigma:

> I joined the [LGBT] Network on the pretext of being a 'friend' whereas I am a full member but not 'out'. I received widespread negative comments and ridicule from junior staff through to senior managers. I felt very uncomfortable and I was able to see people's reaction as if is assumed I was totally straight and why was I joining supporting this bunch of 'weirdos'.
>
> (Brower, 2003 UK Report, pp. 59–60)

Courts and discrimination researchers should recognise that bias and prejudice may not be eliminated but may merely lie dormant until the openly gay person leaves the room. NJSC (2001, p. 49) noted: 'Several gay or lesbian respondents said that because co-workers and others do not know that they are gay, they feel free to make gay jokes in their presence'. Consequently, LGBT people may suffer negative treatment although colleagues attempt to hide their prejudices (Brower, 2007). Compounded by the associative stigma affecting heterosexual or assumed heterosexual employees, ingrained workplace norms may be resistant to change (Kahan, 2000).

Hiding or Passing

Despite explicit workplace protections for LGBT identity, every court jurisdiction had at least one respondent who reported passing as heterosexual rather than face mistreatment as LGBT (Brewer and Gray, 1999b; Brower, 2003 UK Report; Brower, 2005 UK Report; NJSC, 2001). An English judicial appointee reported a similar choice (Moran, 2006).

One New Jersey court employee noted:

> I am not open about my lifestyle at my job for fear of retaliation and/ or job loss. I have appeared in many of the different county courthouses as a part of my State job. I have heard and seen, countless times, gay/ lesbian jokes, comments, disparaging looks, mocking behavior, etc. I have seen many instances of discrimination towards gays and lesbians in the New Jersey courts … How surprised all the judges and lawyers I deal with on a continuing basis would be if I was allowed to be open and honest about my life.
>
> (NJSC, 2001, p. 49)

Even more than their visible LGBT colleagues, these closeted employees express frustration and fear about visible sexual identity and their inability to report unequal treatment or to have legal protections address these issues. Unsurprisingly, contemporaneous, noncourt workplace studies also found that LGBT employees were less likely to disclose their sexuality when they experienced or witnessed discrimination (Croteau, 1996; Ragins and Cornwell, 2001). Further, even successful passing as heterosexual may produce job-related, economic effects, may create higher absenteeism or job turnover (Ragins and Cornwell, 2001), and may reduce productivity or increase stress (Escoffier, 1975; HCBA, 1995). The conscious effort involved in passing also means avoiding potentially awkward workplace social interactions where sexual orientation may be exposed (Badgett, 1996). Two gay attorneys remarked:

> I knew that I would lose work if any of the [bosses] found out that I was gay ... I was conscious of having to remain somewhat distant to most people. I did not get close to people because in their natural course of conversation most people talk about their spouses and families ... I only spoke about work-related matters, never joined any group of co-workers for a drink, and never went to any firm events except those that were absolutely obligatory, and then I left as soon as possible.
>
> (HCBA, 1995, p. 37)

> [At social events] gay and lesbian attorneys are most likely to feel and be perceived as 'different'—usually attending events without a date/spouse, making it more difficult to enjoy the event and participate fully. As a result, they are often perceived by other attorneys as antisocial or mysterious ... not fitting in.
>
> (LACBA, 1994, p. 33)

Estrangement from work colleagues and diminished participation in workplace life is significant. Ragins and Cornwell (2001) found that equal social interactions with heterosexual colleagues had the strongest inverse relationship to perceived discrimination. Similarly, not participating equally in workplace culture may mean that LGBT court employees fail to develop allies or mentors important for advancement (Kantor, 1977; Ragins and Cornwell, 2001). In corporations, the lack of mentoring and placing women and LGBT workers in jobs without contacts and experience led to fewer promotions and the glass ceiling (Federal Glass Ceiling Commission, 1995; Frank, 2004). Interestingly, gender glass ceiling studies illustrate the persistence of customary gender roles and anti-gay workplace norms within organisations (Stonewall, 2008), with lesbians especially affected. Shuler (2003) found that women who broke gender glass ceilings were always depicted with traditional gender-conforming indicia to avoid a lesbian stigma. Accordingly, visibility can sometimes present difficult choices for LGBT people as they negotiate workplace identity.

Hidden LGBT workers also felt an associative stigma. Some did not report anti-gay incidents because they feared being outed as LGBT (NJSC, 2001). Over 7 percent of California court employees who did not report incidents of negative work behaviours that they had experienced said it was because of this fear (Brewer and Gray, 1999a); over 9 percent of UK court employees behaved similarly (Brower, 2003 UK Report). One New Jersey judicial system employee noted he either kept quiet or participated in anti-gay comments to deflect suspicion that the employee was LGBT (NJSC, 2001). Thus, the desire to hide their sexuality adversely affected LGBT court workers' environment.

CONCLUSION

LGBT visibility carried consequences for court experiences; once uncovered, LGBT identity remained salient and affected workers' treatment. Indeed, as with Kahan (2000), visibility and complaints about underenforcement of workplace protections may harden resistance to those regulations where social norms appreciably conflict with legal protections. The ways in which visible LGBT employees negotiate professional, sexual and sexual orientation identities, and workplace relationships may reflect paths to which their less open LGBT coworkers may not have access (Rumens, 2012).

Socio-legal scholars have shown that law and societal norms are not abstract, formal doctrines divorced from individuals' lived experiences (Harding, 2006; Skidmore, 2004). The court employee surveys reflected how LGBT workers expressed their relationship to their employer, their workplaces, and legal institutions and structures. Accordingly, theories about how LGBT people construct identities within legal regimes must consider how visibility affects those identity narratives, and theoretical models should reflect the range of visibility choices. As a necessary first step, data collection and analysis should reflect visibility so that information is available to assess findings along that metric.

Finally, this chapter illustrates that even institutions explicitly focused on fairness like courts can still harbour adverse treatment and negative reactions to LGBT visibility. Traditional gender norms can also undermine the integration and experiences of visible LGBT workers, despite legal and workplace protections (Rumens and Broomfield, 2012). Further, those protections do not necessarily create equal treatment or social change. During the relevant years (2000–2005), even organisations highly rated on Stonewall's (UK) various metrics still reflected an 'implementation gap' between those policies and the treatment of LGBT persons (Bond, Hollywood, and Colgan, 2009; Colgan and McKearney, 2011). Accordingly, we should cautiously assign significance to the consistent appearance of courts, law firms, and other organisations on lists of top workplaces for LGBT people (Stonewall, 2012). Nevertheless, visibility may have positive effects on law, legal institutions, and LGBT workers' experiences (Colgan, et al., 2007; Skidmore, 2004). As sexual minorities come out at work, LGBT identity becomes normalised and less salient. The less people perceive others as different, the more they incorporate diversity into their in-group, and the more they perceive people as individuals. Normalisation should also encourage social customs to adapt to the presence of LGBT workers as colleagues and friends. Consequently, it may provide the more effective, gentle nudges to transform those norms.

NOTE

1. This chapter's author was the designer and drafter of the two UK studies and was a primary author of the California report. He was uninvolved in the New Jersey study.

REFERENCES

Apilado v. North American Gay Amateur Athletic Alliance, Case No. C10-0682-JCC (Dist. Ct Wash, 10 Nov. 2011).

Badgett, M.V.L. (1996). 'Employment and Sexual Orientation: Disclosure and Discrimination in the Workplace'. In Ellis, A. L., and Riggle, E.D.B., (eds), *Sexual Identity on the Job: Issues and Services*, Philadelphia: Haworth Press.

Badgett, M.V.L. (2001). *Money, Myths and Change: The Economic Lives of Lesbians and Gay Men*, Chicago: University of Chicago Press.

Balakrishnan, A., and Bauer, E. (2006, July 28). 'Gay Men Earn Less and are More Likely to be Jobless, Survey Shows', *The Guardian* (UK), at F25.

Becker, G.S. (1971). *The Economics of Discrimination*, Chicago: University of Chicago Press.

Biewen, J., and Siegel, R. (1997, Oct. 21). 'Gay Teacher Files First Amendment Lawsuit in Utah', *All Things Considered* (NPR).

Blumenfeld, W.J., and Raymond, D. (1993). *Looking at Gay and Lesbian Life* 86. Boston: Beacon Press.

Bond, S., Hollywood, E., and Colgan, F. (2009). *Integration within the Workplace*, Manchester: Equality and Human Rights Commission.

Brewer, D. J., and Gray, M. J. (1999a). *Report on Sexual Orientation Fairness in California Courts*.

Brewer, D. J., and Gray, M. J. (1999b). *Survey Data, Preliminary Report Draft 3/31/99*. Reported in 9 Apr. 1999 materials of the Subcommittee on Sexual Orientation Fairness.

Brower, T. (2003). *Report on the Survey of the Lord Chancellor's Department, Rainbow Network: Sexual Orientation Fairness in the Courts of England and Wales*, Lord Chancellor's Department (UK).

Brower, T. (2005). *Report On The 2005 Survey Of The Department For Constitutional Affairs, Rainbow Network: Sexual Orientation Fairness in the Courts of England and Wales*, Department for Constitutional Affairs (UK).

Brower, T. (2007). 'Multistable Figures: Sexual Orientation Visibility and Its Effects on the Experiences of Sexual Minorities in the Courts', *Pace Law Review* 27(2): 101–198.

California Judicial Council—Access and Fairness Committee (2001). *Sexual Orientation Fairness in the California Courts*. San Francisco.

Colgan, F., Creegan, C., McKearney, A., and Wright, T. (2007). 'Equality and Diversity Policies and Practices at Work: Lesbian, Gay and Bisexual Workers', *Equal Opportunities International* 26(3): 590–609.

Colgan, F., and McKearney, A. (2011). 'Creating Inclusive Organisations: What Do Lesbians, Gays and Bisexuals in the Private Sector Think Makes a Difference?'. In Wright, T., and Conley, H. (eds), *Gower Handbook of Discrimination at Work*, Farnham: Gower Publishing.

Colgan, F., and McKearney, A. (2012). 'Visibility and Voice in Organisations: Lesbian, Gay, Bisexual and Transgendered Employee Networks', *Equality, Diversity and Inclusion* 31(4): 359–378.

Croteau, J.M. (1996). 'Research on the Work Experiences of Lesbian, Gay and Bisexual People: An Integrative Review of Methodology and Findings', *Journal of Vocational Behavior* (48)195: 201–203.

Darity, W., Jr., and Mason, P. L. (1998). 'Evidence on Discrimination in Employment: Codes of Color, Codes of Gender,' *Journal of Economic Perspectives* 12(2): 63–90.

Day, N.E., and Schoenrade, P. (2000). 'The Relationship among Reported Disclosure of Sexual Orientation, Anti-Discrimination Policies, Top Management Support and Work Attitudes of Gay and Lesbian Employees', *Personnel Review* 29(3), 346–363.

Escoffier, J. (1975, Jan.). 'Stigmas, Work Environment, and Economic Discrimination Against Homosexuals', *Homosexual Counseling Journal* (2), 8–17

Eskridge, W., Jr., (1997). 'A Jurisprudence of "Coming Out": Religion, Homosexuality, and Collisions of Liberty and Equality in American Public Law', *Yale Law Journal* (106), 2411–2443.

Federal Glass Ceiling Commission (1995). *Report*. Washington, DC.

Fleming, P. (2007). 'Sexuality, Power and Resistance in the Workplace', *Organization Studies* 28(2), 239–256.

Frank, J. (2004). *Gay Glass Ceilings*, Discussion Papers Series 2004–20. Royal Holloway, University of London.

Friskopp, A. and Silverstein, S. (1996). *Straight Jobs, Gay Lives: Gay and Lesbian Professionals, the Harvard Business School, and the American Workplace*. New York: Simon & Shuster.

Green, J. (2010). 'Social Attitudes Survey Finds Greater Acceptance of Homosexuality', *Pink News*. Retrieved from www.pinknews.co.uk/2010/01/26/social-attitudes-survey-finds-far-greater-acceptance-of-homosexuality/.

Griffith, K.H. and Hebl, M.R. (2002). 'The Disclosure Dilemma for Gay Men and Lesbians: 'Coming Out' at Work', *Journal of Applied Psychology* 87(6), 1191–1199.

Harding, R. (2006). 'Dogs Are "Registered", People Shouldn't Be: Legal Consciousness and Lesbian and Gay Rights', *Social & Legal Studies* (15), 511–533.

Hennepin County Bar Association Lesbian and Gay Issues Subcommittee (1995). *Legal Employers' Barriers to Advancement and to Economic Equality Based on Sexual Orientation*. Minneapolis.

Ho, J. (2006, Aug. 8). 'Attracting Gay MBAs', *Businessweek Online*. Retrieved from http://archive.is/YqgTs.

Huffman, A. H., Watrous-Rodriguez, K. M. and King, E. B. (2008). 'Supporting a Diverse Workforce: What Type of Support is Most Meaningful for Lesbian and Gay Employees'? *Human Resource Management* 47(2), 237–253.

Jolls, C. (2007). 'Antidiscrimination Law's Effects on Implicit Bias'. In Gulati, M. and Yelnosky, M. (eds), *Behavioral Analyses of Workplace Discrimination*. Alphen aan den Rijn, NL: Kluwer Law International.

Kahan, D.M. (2000). 'Gentle Nudges vs. Hard shoves: Solving the Sticky Norm Problem', *University of Chicago Law Review* 67, 607–645.

Kantor, R. M. (1977). *Men and Women of the Corporation.* New York: Basic Books.

Krieger, L. H. (1995). 'The Content of Our Categories: A Cognitive Bias Approach to Discrimination and Equal Employment Opportunity', *Stanford Law Review* 47, 1161.

Lindemann, B, Grossman, P. and Weirich, C. G. (2012). *Employment Discrimination Law* (5th ed.). Arlington: BNA Books.

Los Angeles County Bar Association Committee on Sexual Orientation Bias (1994) *Report.*

McNish, J. (2006, June 14). 'Can Lawyers Be Too Gay'? *Globe and Mail (Toronto).* Retrieved from www.globeinvestor.com/servlet/story/RTGAM.20060614.wxlaw column14/GIStor.

Moore, D. W. (1993). 'Public Polarized on Gay Issue', *Gallup Poll Monthly* 331, 31–34.

Moran, L. J. (2006). 'Judicial Diversity and the Challenge of Sexuality: Some Preliminary Findings', *Sydney Law Review* (28), 565–598.

NALP (2013). LGBT Representation up in 2012, *NALP Bulletin.* January. Retrieved from www.nalp.org/lgbt_representation_up_in_2012

New Jersey Supreme Court (2001). *Final Report of the Task Force On Sexual Orientation Issues.* Trenton, NJ.

Pew Research Center for People and the Press (2012). *Growing Public Support for Same-Sex Marriage.* Retrieved from www.people-press.org/2012/02/07/ growing-public-support-for-same-sex-marriage/.

Ragins B. R. and Cornwell, J. M. (2001). 'Pink Triangles: Antecedents and Consequences of Perceived Workplace Discrimination Against Gay and Lesbian Employees', *Journal of Applied Psychology* 86(6), 1244–1261.

Ragins, B. R., Cornwell, J. M. and Miller, J. S. (2003). 'Heterosexism in the Workplace: Do Race and Gender Matter?' *Group & Organization Management* 28(1), 45–74.

Ragins, B. R, Singh, R. and Cornwell, J. M. (2007). 'Making the Invisible Visible: Fear and Disclosure of Sexual Orientation at Work', *Journal of Applied Psychology* 92(4), 1103–1118.

Rottman, D. B. (2005). *National Center for State Courts, Trust and Confidence in the California Courts: A Survey of the Public and Attorneys, Part I: Findings and Recommendations 26.* Administrative Office of the Courts on behalf of the California Judicial Council. San Francisco.

Rumens, N. (2012). 'Queering Cross-Sex Friendships: An Analysis of Gay and Bi Men's Workplace Friendships with Heterosexual Women', *Human Relations* 65(8), 955–978.

Rumens, N. and Broomfield, J. (2012). 'Gay Men in the Police: Identity Disclosure and Management Issue', *Human Resource Management Journal* 22(3), 283–298.

Schacter, J. (1997). '*Romer v. Evans* and Democracy's Domain', *Vanderbilt Law Review* 50, 361–371.

Shuler, S. (2003). 'Breaking through the Glass Ceiling without Breaking a Nail: Women Executives in Fortune Magazine's "Power 50" List', *American Communication Journal* 6(2), 1–26.

Skidmore, P. (2004). 'A Legal Perspective on Sexuality and Organization: A Lesbian and Gay Case Study', *Gender, Work and Organization* 11(3), 229–253.

Stonewall (2008). *The Double-glazed Glass Ceiling: Lesbians in the Workplace.* London: Stonewall.

Stonewall, (2012). 'Top 100 Employers 2012'. Retrieved from www.stonewall.org. uk/at_work/stonewall_top_100_employers/default.asp.

Woods, J. D. (1993). *The Corporate Closet: The Professional Lives of Gay Men in America.* New York: Free Press.

5 Gay Men in the UK Police Services

John Broomfield

INTRODUCTION

The UK police service has received intense criticism from academics and other commentators in the field of equality and diversity regarding the position of women, ethnic, racial and sexual minority employees (Brown, 1998; Burke, 1994; Cashmore, 2001; Dick and Cassell, 2004; Metcalfe and Dick, 2002). Accounts of truncated career trajectories, stereotyping, bullying, harassment and loss of employment figure prominently in this research, all of which suggests that workplace discrimination on the grounds of sex, race and sexuality has plagued the UK police service. In this vein, Burke (1993) provided a glimpse into the tumultuous working lives of lesbian, gay and bisexual (LGB) police officers. His study confirmed that LGB officers were likely to experience heightened ambivalence within the service against pervasive conditions of machismo and institutionalised homophobia; embrace masculine signifiers associated with conventional images of police work; and adopt dual roles—heterosexual(ised) workplace personas and 'homosexual' off-duty identities. Nevertheless, times have changed, as highlighted by recent research (Davies and Thomas, 2008; Loftus, 2008, 2010). Police services are now under increasing pressure to understand themselves as 'sites of diversity' (Loftus, 2008). In fact, constabularies regularly feature in Stonewall's annual Equality Index, implying that the UK police service has cultivated fertile ground for the construction of minority sexual identities at work (Stonewall, 2013). Currently, however, few academic studies explore how lesbian, gay, bisexual and trans (LGBT) employees negotiate identities and selves within police work cultures that have been subject to change and reform.

Drawing on data from a wider research project, carried out in the UK between 2008 and 2009, on the negotiation of gay identity within perceived 'gay hostile' and 'gay-friendly' work sites, this chapter aims to provide a contemporary account of the effects of police culture on one sexual minority group: gay men employed as police officers. After providing a brief account of gay male sexualities in the police, I show that 'out' gay men can exude confidence in their roles as police officers and articulate equality policy as an important mediating factor in the construction of gay identity at work.

I then go on to highlight that, although study participants no longer engage in the dramaturgy associated with the 'double lives' of the 1990s, some continue to face formidable challenges associated with managing a gay identity within a highly masculine police working culture. Importantly, I conclude by showing that the acceptance of homosexuality in the police force has come at a price—that of a strict associated gender identity whereby processes of 'normalisation' have significantly restricted the expression of certain gay identities, resulting in the intense marginalisation of some effeminate workers in the UK police service.

GAY MEN IN THE UK POLICE SERVICES

The central theme common to studies on policing is that officers work within contexts dominated by 'machismo' or 'hegemonic masculinity'; police work tends to be characterised as brutal or tough work and is usually associated with images of white, working-class masculinity (Burke, 1994; Chan, 1996; Dick and Cassell, 2004; Dick and Jankowicz, 2001; Kiely and Peek, 2002; Loftus, 2008; Miller, Forest and Jurik, 2003; Ward and Winstanley, 2006). This has been historically accentuated due to the sheer number of white, working-class men within the occupation, and significantly, many policing work contexts in the UK remain overwhelmingly white, heterosexual and male. This 'demographic fact' poses important challenges for those of non-conformist gender, ethnicity or sexual identity (Loftus, 2008: 757).

Gay men have particularly struggled to integrate into police culture (Burke, 1994). For example, Loftus (2008) notes that she did not meet any officers who were 'out' throughout her ethnographic research project on diversity in the police, alluding to the absence of the openly gay police officer. A noteworthy example that considers the life of the 'homosexual police officer' is found in Burke's (1994, 1993) case study. His research makes for uncomfortable reading and confirms that gay men in the police in the early 1990s faced persecution and discrimination from colleagues. Some were forced to exit the service as a result of intense emotional dilemmas and effort invested into adopting identity strategies such as 'passing' as heterosexual. Many of Burke's (1993) participants constructed an identity at work where their sexual orientation was undisclosed. Outside of work individuals may identify as gay or lesbian, but their occupation was undisclosed (1993: 92). This strategy of leading a 'double life' or having a 'dual identity' can be incredibly stressful, not least because it is difficult for individuals to be certain if they have kept their sexuality secret from colleagues, friends and family. 'Cop canteen culture' (Fielding, 1994), as it has been dubbed, is particularly influential here as a contextual factor because it is gendered in masculinity that gives license to competition, in-/out-group distinctions, aggressive physical action and homophobic, sexualised and racist banter—often among white, heterosexual men.

In contrast to the experiences of gay men, Burke (1993, 1994) found that some lesbian officers were found to be tolerated, enjoying the added benefits of an informal 'lesbian network'. As he points out, the stigma attached to the quasi-criminal legal status of male homosexuality has been absent with respect to lesbianism, and police officer colleagues have tended to assume that gay women are more, not less, likely to live up to the 'macho' expectations of work given wider stereotypes associated with lesbian identity (this is not to say that masculine occupations pose no challenges to lesbian women; see Wright, 2008). Yet the activity of 'gay bashing' by police officers (physically abusing gay men in society 'on the job'; derision towards gay male peers) has historically served a symbolic function in the police, 'helping' to affirm the heterosexual identities of participating officers. In this regard, the experiences of men in the police service as 'deviant' are not comparable to those of their female colleagues (Burke, 1994).

At the time, it is fair to say that Burke's (1993) informative and exemplary research on the police offered much needed insight into the lives of gay and lesbian officers. Nearly two decades on, however, it is still reasonable to suggest that the occupation remains hostile towards gay employees, although the landscape of policing has changed dramatically since diversity discourses have proliferated. Since the early 2000s, the police service has been trying to undermine associations between police culture, overt discourses of machismo and a poor record of equal opportunities (Dick and Jankowicz, 2001). The Macpherson Report (1999) and the Morris Inquiry (2004) prompted the service to address issues of institutionalised racism and account for reasons why equalities have been high on the agenda (Colgan et al., 2009). These inquiries had a profound knock-on effect for positive change in all areas, including sexual orientation.

Undeniably, many police services have been at the forefront of the drive to recruit, retain and promote gay men, among others; a contradictory position to the anti-gay 'witchhunts' carried out by numerous forces in the late 1980s. Enthusiastic attempts to engage with gay men have endeavoured to 'correct the numbers', as stations now aim to reflect the diversity of the communities they serve. For example, police recruitment stalls have become commonplace at local Gay Pride events. Indeed, it is no secret that the police are actively and publically seeking change with respect to the treatment and recruitment of minority groups, and given they have been overtly criticised for their excessive use of force, racism, sexism and homophobia, constabularies are attempting to melt 'the ice in the heart of the police service' with regards to 'homosexuality' particularly (Davis and Thomas, 2008: 629).

Whereas scholarship has thrown light on how gay officers have been subject to harsh forms of discrimination and experience disclosure dilemmas associated with modes of identification based on sexual identity, a dearth of UK research examines the qualitative experiences of gay men against a backdrop of the changing conditions of police culture. This chapter goes some way in updating existing scholarship. In doing so, I show the 'increasing acceptance' of gay sexuality in the police has come at a price. Although many research participants were able to disclose as gay to colleagues without fear of hostility, they were likely to maintain and manage strict heterosexualised performances of gay identity associated with constructions of the 'normal' gay man—an identity that has increasingly been integrated into society as a respected identity. As Seidman observes:

> The normal gay is presented as fully human, as the psychological and moral equal of the heterosexual . . . [He] is expected to be gender conventional, link sex to love and a marriage-like relationship, defend family values, personify economic individualism, and display national pride.
>
> (2002: 133)

As I go on to show, valorising the image of 'the normal gay' in the police appears to have marginalised the expression of other gay identities. What we appear to be witnessing is a shift in, but not the erasure of, boundaries associated with forms of gay male sexuality that are (un)acceptable—a shift that has resulted in the stark Othering of effeminate (gay) men within the police service.

METHODOLOGY

Adopting a social constructionist position within sexuality and gender studies (Jackson, 1999; Weeks, 1985, 2007), one that rejects sexuality as a 'natural' and fixed property of the individual, sexuality and gender are regarded as historically conditioned, culturally patterned constructs that have contested meanings. Linked to this is a notion of identity as an ongoing process of negotiation and (re)construction. Whereas identities can appear stable at times, they are always in a state of becoming.

Regarding method, study data were collected as part of a wider qualitative research project, carried out in the UK between 2008 and 2009, on the negotiation of gay identities within stereotypical 'gay hostile' and 'gay-friendly' work sites. Twenty gay male police officers from a number of different constabularies across England and Wales were recruited to take part in semi-structured interviews. All participants had experience of 'street duties' but were now working throughout a range of divisions including CID, traffic, sexual offences, victim support, fire arms, neighbourhood policing and antiterrorism. One officer was retired and two worked as police officer specials. Of the participants, all were white, able-bodied, *out* gay men, and ranged in age from 23 to 50.

The sample was generated using a snowball technique, typical in studies on LGBT people who represent a 'hidden' and vulnerable population (Browne, 2005; Williams, Giuffre and Dellinger, 2009). A number of personal contacts were used to recruit initial respondents. Access was gained to the remaining participants through LGBT networks. Tapping into these networks has proved particularly effective in prior research on sexual identity at work (Humphrey, 1999; Ward and Winstanley, 2004), and this study was no exception in that regard. The only requirements for participation were that interviewees identify as 'gay' and 'male' and that they had worked at an operational level within the service. Using a qualitative data analysis computer software package (Nvivo), interview data was subsequently organised into themes and subthemes. The sections that follow have been structured around some of these key themes: the police as an example of a 'gay-friendly' occupation in the context of equal opportunities; police cultures as heteronormatively masculine; and the Othering of the camp cop. Building on this final theme, I conclude by emphasising how the acceptance of gay identity in the police leaves intact constructions of effeminate gay men as Other.

'GET OFF YOUR SOAP BOX AND MAKE US A BREW!' THE POLICE SERVICES AS GAY-FRIENDLY

Equality and diversity policy featured as an important mediating factor that has not only facilitated the changing conditions of police culture but has allowed gay officers to disclose a minority sexual identity at work. Sean (inspector, antiterrorism) was eager to highlight that statistics reiterate that a 'diversity driven agenda' has paid dividends. Now an inspector at a Midlands constabulary, he proudly reflected upon the force's achievements:

> Monitoring forms show that nearly one in ten of our police force identify as LGB, most of whom are 'living out' in the workplace.

He stressed that his own force was not an exception to the rule. A recent staff monitoring survey conducted at the same site indicated that more officers were more open about their sexuality at work than than in their lives away from work. In contrast to studies carried out in the early 1990s (Burke, 1994; Chan, 1996), Sean alludes to the positive negotiation of a gay identity within a police climate that is considered to be *more* tolerant and open than external (home) situations. Ironically, these 'double lives' led by some gay officers were the reverse of those experienced by Burke's (1994) participants. This was understood by Sean as a sign of progressive change within some police authorities, particularly so against the backdrop of stereotyped images of UK constabularies as unsafe work environments for gay employees (Burke, 1994).

The research revealed that over the years, significant attention has focused on diversity awareness training and policy changes in the police. During one interview, I was initially drawn to a participant's colourful coffee mug. Inscribed on the mug was a slogan condemning transphobia. This 'organisational prop' immediately signalled me to some of the informal measures that disseminate the 'celebration of diversity' message, emulated throughout police services in the UK and found on posters, notice boards and computer mouse mats (as also found by Loftus, 2008). Beyond this, messages from senior management about stamping out inappropriate behaviour and attitudes towards LGBT employees exceeded the level of rhetoric. Jason (PC, traffic) recalled how one Chief Constable sought to achieve radical change by removing institutional and cultural obstacles that had previously prevented minorities from progressing:

> The Chief Constable closed all canteens and bars, as a way to eliminate 'canteen culture'. It was a radical idea, but it removed 'safe white space', within which officers were able to express discriminatory views. It now became far more difficult for people to have that networking capability to make transactions that were hostile towards other people.

Here, senior officers had acknowledged 'cop canteen culture' (Fielding, 1994) as a breeding ground for sexism, racism and homophobia, and had taken corrective measures. Eradicating canteens and police bars restricted the ways in which gay men (and women) and those of BME (Black, minority, ethnic) status might feel intimated by 'safe white space'. Jason (PC, traffic) highlighted that these changes had implications for the ways in which he negotiated his own sexual identity:

> We are who we are now. There are no 'hidden veil' conversations at work. We're completely open. We come to work as our 'full selves'. Previously, I would divert attention away from conversations about my personal life. Now, I don't have to.

It appears, then, that the prevailing accent on diversity has reconfigured traditional forms of identity negotiation associated with gay sexuality within the police (Loftus, 2008; for 'traditional' examples, see Burke, 1994). Changes to recruitment initiatives and forms of training have also enabled gay officers to seek validation of a gay self at work. It was clear that certain recruitment initiatives have helped to quell initial fears of marginalisation. A number of officers noted the efforts to recruit gay men at Pride events, which encouraged them to 'live out' their sexuality as a gay man from day one. In this sense, policies put at ease aspiring gay officers and helped to articulate that gay men are welcomed and accepted. Other officers felt that police forces affirmed and celebrated diversity throughout status hierarchies, thus achieving continuity with regards to the diversity agenda. Whereas research on LGBT individuals shows that being located in the 'upper echelons' impedes the coming out process (Humphrey, 1999), I interviewed a number of openly gay inspectors. Changes to the induction programme and training have also changed the ways in which new recruits are introduced to police culture and demonstrate a heightened commitment to the harnessing and nurturing of individual uniqueness along the lines of race, religion, sexuality and gender:

> A few years ago ... what we were producing was a stamped approved police officer. By the end of their probation, all officers were trained, functioning, speaking, and doing exactly the same. The individual personality of that person was eradicated. Police training now looks to value individual traits, cultures and characters.
>
> (Sean, inspector, antiterrorism)

Sean's view of police training differs significantly from the experiences of some police recruits reported in studies that show how police training can (re)produce masculine values that support a sexist, racist and homophobic police culture (Burke, 1993; Cashmore, 2001; Prokos and Padavic, 2002).

In contrast then to stereotypes that portray the police as homophobic, the significant majority of participants, who were all 'out' gay men, appeared to exude confidence in their roles, articulating policy as an attributing factor. It would be incorrect and unwise to assume that all police officers feel ill at ease 'coming out' to colleagues, as articulated by Burke (1994), but in this study gay identity can in many instances be easily integrated at work. Clive expressed it thus:

> I genuinely believe that if someone started here today, as a brand new probationer, and said 'My name's X, and I'm gay', we'd say 'Get off your soap box and make us a brew'.
>
> (Clive, PC, neighbourhood policing)

Having said this, some participants felt that diversity programmes were mainly about complying with legislation and 'getting the numbers right'. This was captured by Ben (sergeant, event planning and road policing units), who argued that the gay staff networks 'organise a few curry nights' at the financial expense of the local force but then achieve little in terms of culture change: 'At the AGM [Annual General Meeting], it's basically: "This month, we have 298 members. Last month, we had 297 members. Next month, we hope to have 299 members"'. Indeed, a small number of participants felt they were part of an organisational process of ticking boxes, suggesting they had been recruited 'purely on the basis of sexuality', with some feeling they had to 'prove themselves' on the basis of merit in order to be taken seriously by colleagues (Miller, Forest and Jurik, 2003).

POLICE CULTURES AS HETERONORMATIVELY MASCULINE

Although the section above indicates a cultural shift has taken place in some UK police services, data below confirms that some participants were still required to engage in behaviour structured around masculinity grounded in norms of heterosexuality. In particular, effeminacy in gay men was purported to represent the antithesis of traditional masculinity and effective policing. Narratives show how public expectation of the appropriately gendered, masculine police officer continues to have ubiquitous power. As a result, gender identity and masculinity were required to remain 'omni-relevant' throughout the day-to-day lives of serving police officers (West and Zimmerman, 1987). Numerous interview excerpts illustrated this, as expressed by Clive:

> Being effeminate would make it more difficult to police the streets. Whilst attitudes have changed, there are a lot of people out there who could give you abuse. With a camp guy . . . would they be able to do the job as well? What if you've got someone you need to taser? What if you need to break up a fight? You gotta [be able] to just jump on them. [In those situations], masculinity . . . it certainly helps.

Whereas it is clear that programmes of modernisation and diversity/equality management have disturbed traditional police culture, one recurring view to emerge from the research was that contemporary policing culture is still tethered to traditional masculine values and behaviours (Loftus, 2008). Where officers are required to carry out challenging and sometimes confrontational public service work, the suitability of male officers known or presumed to be gay is questioned. Clive's account confirms that policing is principally defined in terms of 'fighting crime' or 'catching criminals', and the centrality of masculinity as an interactional resource in that respect is apparent (Martin, 1999). Indeed, the majority of police officers reflected upon how openly effeminate gay male officers might struggle to negotiate with members of the public, for police officers are expected to conform to gender norms, ultimately emphasising the pressure to be seen as traditionally masculine. This prompted participants to focus on the centrality of their own 'masculine capital' (Cole, 2008) and assert that they 'do masculinity' in a traditional sense although they identify as gay. For many, a key feature of negotiating gay identity at work involved personally aligning the sense of self with conventional images of gender.

Many participants were eager to discuss how they considered themselves to be 'ideal' workers in every way other than in sexual identity. By subscribing to representations of the otherwise 'normal' gay man (Seidman, 2002), individuals were able to reaffirm their competence as 'real (police) men'. Crucially, participants drew upon the effeminate Other, contrasting it to their own masculine identities presented as stable and in accord with heterosexual norms. In particular, dis-identifying with emasculated perceptions of gay sexuality allowed police officers to feel psychologically secure 'on the job'. The account below serves as a typical illustration:

> I've always been a masculine officer . . . Some officers these days are obviously gay around the stations and far from masculine. I do wonder

how they manage their interactions with colleagues when they have feminine characteristics, which stand out in uniform quite markedly.

(Daniel; sergeant, terrorism and allied matters)

Such comments may be considered controversial because they crudely categorise gay men in terms of gender: those who display 'feminine' characteristics and those who are conventionally masculine. Not only is gender treated as a fixed property of gay men in a polarised fashion, but making gay sexuality 'obvious' by the display of 'feminine' characteristics is considered problematic and to be avoided at work. Although the Other gay man is defined rather narrowly (he has a 'polluted' status and is stereotyped as a queen—'swishy, limp-wristed, and exhibiting an exaggerated, affected feminine style' [Seidman, 2002: 128]), constructing gender identity in opposition to those who 'lacked' masculinity enabled officers to preserve their sense of ability as 'effective' police officers. Participants sought to demonstrate physical prowess by conjuring up images of the Other which, in part, served to enhance individual self-esteem. To Daniel, 'being butch' allowed him to command respect. Yet he worried that effeminate officers would not be able to perform 'butch' forms of masculinity and therefore be unable to achieve such levels of deference. Much like those women who have been constructed in the context of police work as physically and emotionally 'unfit' to perform the full range of police duties (Dick and Cassell, 2004; Prokos and Padavic, 2002), the expression of femininity among gay officers was looked upon as being equally deficient.

As we have seen, police officers are increasingly able to live 'out' in their occupation; an important and progressive development. Arguably, given that the majority of participants conform to a notion of 'the normal gay', opportunities to enact alternative sexual identities are harder to cultivate and sustain. These limiting opportunities for the expression of gay identity effectively render the service as highly problematic for particular 'types' of gay men. The next section illustrates this empirically in more detail and discusses the challenges that face the police service in its ongoing attempts to redress inequalities along the lines of sexual orientation.

THE EFFEMINATE COPPER

If you're a butch homosexual, nobody knows. It's only if you're an effeminate homosexual. If I could take a magic potion to give me a deep voice, I would take it tomorrow.

(Isaac, PC, number plate recognition)

As the discussion above reveals, participants stressed that effeminate officers can expect to struggle, negotiating feminine qualities against masculine expectations of what constitutes effective police officers and police work. As if to confirm this, three self-identified, 'visibly gay' officers spoke of experiences whereby effeminacy had triggered instances of workplace homophobia and societal abuse on the job. The very fear of harassment drove Cameron (Special Constable), a self-confessed 'Julian Clary–like' detention officer,[1] to moderate his speech when dealing with offenders: 'In front of detainees, I have to 'play it down'. 'It' referring here to effeminate or camp performances of gay identity. Isaac, too, felt that specifically because he 'wasn't butch, didn't have a deep voice or big muscles', he became the target of underhanded, covert discrimination by coworkers. At one point, Isaac was signed off work with stress and recalled:

> I am effeminate, and I would not have come up against such homophobia if I'd been seen as a butch gay man.

Christopher reflected on policing realities on the street, noting that camp officers face name calling whilst on the beat. Christopher also found that one sergeant, before giving him a chance to introduce himself by name *or* sexuality, quipped: 'Oh, you're not one of these people who throws accusations of homophobia around are you?' This reiterates that being identifiable as a gay officer can make you the target of abuse and scorn, and by nature of their effeminacy, workers can be susceptible to distinctive workplace struggles, struggles evaded by 'butch' gay police officers.

In similar fashion, other participants recalled that effeminate officers had exited the police as a result of their 'unconventional' gender:

> A friend of mine, who is that way inclined [effeminate], had quite a hard time, to the point of getting bullied out of the job.
>
> (Bryn, Special Constable)

> I know of one camp police officer. He ended up leaving the job . . . I don't think he was particularly suited to being a police officer in the traditional sense. His station used to cover an area that was a big council estate and the mentality of the people who were there . . . I don't think they would've been the most forgiving of people. Some people just aren't suited to being police officers.
>
> (Roger, sergeant, neighbourhood policing)

As if to support Roger's assessment, Elliot (retired PC, neighbourhood policing) recalled:

> For this one guy, he was obviously gay, and they all knew; the public knew. As soon as he walked out of the door, he was hassled. He was [always too busy] arresting people who were abusing him; never mind the police work!

A handful of stories, however, demonstrated that it is inadequate to solely define the camp cop as a victim of a masculinised working context. At one point, Christopher (Special Constable, response) valorised effeminacy as an interactional resource:

> I'm a man myself remember. I mean, I'm a red-blooded male the same as them. But we can offer input in certain situations from almost a female perspective and engage with them in that way, and it works, it does work!

Indeed, although it has been found that the nature of police work produces excluding effects that help 'prop up a slender range of gendered and sexual selves, emotional intimacies, and bodily appearances' (Rumens and Kerfoot, 2009: 8), a small minority of participants felt that effeminate workers had the opportunity to 'flourish'. Accounts suggest that officers who do not fit the (perceived) hegemonic masculine ideal look to departments which value their 'feminine capital' (Cole, 2008). Dealing *sensitively* with victims of rape, both male and female, in the sexual offences unit was frequently cited as a key example. Of course, the extent to which this amounts to effeminate workers being siphoned off to particular areas or departments is open to debate. For example, interview data which highlights the migration of camp officers to 'station housed' units reinforce the dualistic view that sees 'real' police work as 'street based', whilst supervisory assignments (e.g., service-related encounters that demand emotional support for victims of rape) as subordinated, weak, devalued 'feminine labour' (Martin, 1999; see also Kerfoot and Knights, 1998).

CONCLUSION

In this chapter I have examined the work experiences of gay male police officers in the context of wider changes within the UK police service to disassociate themselves from the negative images of 'traditional' police culture. On the one hand, and in line with other studies (Belkin and McNichol, 2002; Colvin, 2009; Loftus, 2008), I show diversity/equality agendas have played an important role to that end. Indeed, some participants felt the landscape of policing had transformed due to policies ranging from recruitment initiatives to the experiences of police training. These policy initiatives have helped those police officers for whom coming out as gay at work was perceived to be a perilous act, potentially putting them at risk of discrimination and persecution (Burke, 1993, 1994). It is fair to say that it would be greatly misleading to assume that policing remains an oppressively 'gay-hostile' occupation because ideas about homosexuality as deviant within society and in police work are being challenged and appear increasingly moribund. This finding is also significant because it questions previous (and often cited) research in this area (Burke, 1993, 1994). Indeed, for some participants, elements of traditional 'canteen culture' have been disturbed, enabling them to openly affirm their sexual orientation at work. Having said this, gay police officers revealed the gains *and* setbacks experienced at ground level in regard to how the police have attempted to carry the spirit of inclusivity of diversity/equality rhetoric into practice. For example, the value of some organisational initiatives targeting sexual orientation as an equality issue is experienced by some as merely a process of ticking boxes in the pursuit of a diverse workforce.

On the other hand, the research finds that to be accepted as a gay police officer requires the tailoring or tapering of the gendered performance of homosexuality, but this does not always lead to the erasure of a gay 'sexual orientation'. In a policing context, normative masculinity continues to be sought as the most valorised form of identity, and it is essentialised and celebrated as a more appropriate way of performing police work (Beusch, 2009). In short, my research suggests that the inclusion of openly gay male police officers within the police services has come at a strict price—the demonstration of conformity to heteronormative gender norms.

This has implications for effeminate gay men in the police services. As interview data reveals, some gay police officers distance themselves from constructions of the 'effeminate', often equating their own personas to idealised forms of masculinity. Striking is the extent to which the camp cop is viewed as an organization Other at work. Camp gay men are referred to in terms of the Other, and their workplace experiences are said to differ markedly from the 'normal' gay police officer, who in contrast can be respected and accepted (Seidman, 2002). Further, effeminate police officers allude to their enduring subordination. On this note, the research findings emphasise that gay men's work experiences do not depend solely on how individuals inhabit particular sexual categories. Certain gay men in the police services are marginalised and discriminated against at work due to the gendered performance of sexuality, the implications of which have yet to be elucidated fully by academics.

One effect documented above is how this influences 'feelings of self-worth and personal integrity' (Richardson, 2007: 401). As Richardson (2007) and Seidman (2002) remind us, normalisation has disrupted associations of homosexuality with concepts of shame, risk and danger, and this idea appears to be reflected in the stories recalled by some of my participants. Those police officers who felt they ascribed to gendered constructions of the normal gay man *were* able to understand homosexuality as a 'natural, good part of themselves' and 'openly participate in mainstream social life' (Williams, Giuffre and Dellinger, 2009); however, it is clear that these workers engage in a process of normalising, most noticeable when discussions centred on perceptions of effeminacy at work. Here, gender deviance, in the form of the camp cop was framed as a symbol of derision and incompetence, as gender conventional gay police personnel attempted to secure a sense of psychological satisfaction and stability.

For some gay men 'heteronormativity is not such a bad thing after all' (Rumens, 2011), bestowing upon them privileges ordinarily conferred on to heterosexuals (e.g., dignity, respect, a sense of citizenship). However, one concern here is that is valorises a specific model of heteronormative relations that leaves little room for exploring alternative ways of being gay at work. In light of this, we need to set the above 'gains' of normalising discourses in the UK police service against the question, how far do these changes reinforce dominant constructions of gender and heteronormativity within police constabularies? Indeed, might processes of normalisation be silencing or constricting the expression of a plethora of gay identities at work more generally? Within the limitations of the study sample, I argue that the answer to the last question is largely, yes, and that we can frame the accounts of effeminate gay police officers as 'backlash stories' indicative of 'forms of sexual and gender fundamentalism' (Richardson, 2007: 403). These stories show that normalising discourses at work can 'secure difference' and leave intact the association of homosexuality with Otherness. As Richardson (2007: 403) asserts, in the wake of the deconstruction of the hetero/homo binary, 'new conceptions of Otherness and their attendant identities may be created and developed to accommodate such changes'. This new Othering includes the subject position of the camp cop. Whereas effeminate gay men have been used to being framed as the Other (Nardi, 2000), I suggest that the Otherness of camp gay men can be subject to intense interrogation in some police work contexts that marginalizes those who identify as such, not just because they are gay but because they are also effeminate.

NOTE

1. Julian Clary is an openly gay, camp British comedian.

REFERENCES

Belkin, A. and McNicol, J. (2002). 'Pink and Blue: Outcomes Associated with the Integration of Open Gay and Lesbian Personnel in the San Diego Police Department'. *Police Quarterly*, 5(1), 63–95.

Beusch. D. (2008) 'Queering Nazism or Nazi Queers? A Sociological Study of an Online Gay Nazi Fetish Group', unpublished PhD thesis, University of Warwick.

Brown, J. (1998) 'Aspects of Discriminatory Treatment of Women Police Officers Serving in Forces in England and Wales'. *British Journal of Criminology*, 38(2), 265–282.

Browne, K. (2005) 'Snowball Sampling: Using Social Networks to Research Non-Heterosexual Women'. *International Journal of Social Research Methodology*, 8(1), 47–60.

Burke, M. (1993) *Coming Out of the Blue: British Police Officers Talk About Their Lives in the Job as Lesbians, Gays and Bisexuals*. London: Capsules.

Burke, M. (1994) 'Homosexuality as Deviance: The Case of the Gay Police Officer'. *British Journal of Criminology*, 34(2), 192–203.

Cashmore, E. (2001). 'The Experiences of Ethnic Minority Police Officers in Britain: Under-Recruitment and Racial Profiling in a Performance Culture'. *Ethnic and Racial Studies*, 24(4), 642–659.

Chan, J. (1996) 'Changing Police Culture'. *British Journal of Criminology*, 36(1), 109–134.

Cole, T. (2008) 'Finding Space in the Field of Masculinity: Lived Experiences of Men's Masculinities'. *Journal of Sociology*, 44(3), 233.

Colgan, F., Creegan, C., McKearney, A. and Wright, T. (2009) 'Equality and Diversity in the Public Services: Moving Forward on Lesbian, Gay and Bisexual Equality?' *Human Resource Management Journal*, 19(3), 280–301.

Colvin, R. (2009). 'Shared Perceptions among Lesbian and Gay Police Officers: Barriers and Opportunities in the Law Enforcement Work Environment'. *Police Quarterly*, 12(1), 86–101

Davies, A. and Thomas, R. (2008) 'Dixon of Dock Green Got Shot! Policing Identity Work and Organisational Change'. *Public Administration*, 86(3), 627–642.

Dick, P. and Cassell, C. (2004) 'The Position of Police Women: A Discourse Analytic Study'. *Work Employment Society*, 18(1), 52–17.

Dick, P. and Jankowicz, D. (2001) 'A Social Constructionist Account of Police Culture and its Influence on the Representation and Progression of Female Officers. A Repertory Grid Analysis in a UK Police Force'. *Policing: An International Journal of Police Strategies & Management*, 24(2), 181–199.

Fielding, N. (1995) 'Cop Canteen Culture', in T. Newburn and E. Stanko, eds. *Just Boys Doing Business: Men, Masculinity and Crime*. London: Routledge

Humphrey, J. (1999) 'Organizing Sexualities, Organized Inequalities: Lesbians and Gay Men in Public Service Occupations'. *Gender, Work and Organization*, 6(3), 134–151.

Jackson, S. (1999) *Heterosexuality in Question*. London: Sage.

Kerfoot, D. and Knights, D. (1998) 'Managing Masculinity in Contemporary Organisational Life: A Managerial Project'. *Organisation*, 5(1), 7–26.

Kiely, J. and Peek, G. (2002) 'The Culture of the British Police: Views of Police Officers'. *The Service Industries Journal*, 22(1), 167–183.

Loftus, B. (2008) 'Dominant Culture Interrupted: Recognition, Resentment and the Politics of Change in an English Police Force'. *British Journal of Criminology*, 48(6), 778–797.

Loftus, B. (2010) 'Police Culture: Classic Themes, Altered Times'. *Policing and Society*, 20(1), 1–20.

Macpherson Report (1999) *The Stephen Lawrence Inquiry. Report of an Inquiry by Sir William Macpherson of Cluny*. London: Stationary Office.

Martin, S.E. (1999) 'Police Force or Police Service? Gender and Emotional Labor'. *ANNALS of the American Academy of Political and Social Science*, 561, 111–126.

Metcalfe, B. and Dick, G. (2002) 'Is the Force Still with Her? Gender and Commitment in the Police'. *Women In Management Review*, 17(8), 392–403.

Miller, S., Forest, K. and Jurik, N. (2003) 'Diversity in Blue: Lesbian and Gay Police Officers in a Masculine Occupation'. *Men and Masculinities*, 5(4), 355–385.

The Morris Inquiry (2004) Retrieved from www.mpa.gov.uk/downloads/issues/morris/morris-report.pdf.

Nardi, P. (2000) 'Anything for a Sis Mary: An Introduction to Gay Masculinities', in P. Nardi, ed. *Gay Masculinities*. London: Sage.

Prokos, A. and Padavic, I. (2002). '"There Oughtta Be a Law Against Bitches": Masculinity Lessons in Police Academy Training'. *Gender, Work and Organisation*, 9(4), 439–459.

Richardson, D. (2007) 'Patterned Fluidities: (Re)Imagining the Relationship between Gender and Sexuality'. *Sociology*, 41(3), 457–474.

Rumens, N. (2011) *Queer Company: The Role and Meaning of Friendship in gay Men's Work Lives*. Aldershot: Ashgate.

Rumens, N. and Kerfoot, D. (2009) 'Gay Men at Work: (Re)constructing the Self as Professional'. *Human Relations*, 62(5), 763–786.

Seidman, S. (2002) *Beyond the Closet: Transformation of Gay and Lesbian Life*. London: Routledge.

Stonewall (2013) *Stonewall Top 100 Employers 2013. The Workplace Equality Index*. Retrieved from Stonewall.org.uk.

Ward, J. and Winstanley, D. (2004) 'Sexuality and the City: Exploring the Experiences of Minority Sexual Identity through Storytelling'. *Culture and Organisation*, 10(3), 219–236.

Ward, J. and Winstanley, D. (2006) 'Watching the Watch: The UK Fire Service and its Impact on Sexual Minorities in the Workplace'. *Gender, Work and Organization*, 13(2), 193–219

Weeks, J. (1985) *Sexuality and its Discontents: Meanings, Myths and Modern Sexualities*. London: Routledge.

West, C. and Zimmerman, D. (1987) 'Doing Gender'. *Gender and Society*, 1(2), 125–151.

Williams, C. L., Giuffre, P. A. and Dellinger, C. (2009) 'The Gay-Friendly Closet'. *Sexuality Research and Social Policy*, 6(1), 29–45.

Wright, T. (2008) 'Lesbian Firefighters: Shifting the Boundaries between Masculinity and Femininity'. *Journal of Lesbian Studies*, 12(1), 103–114.

6 'I Felt Like the Dad in the House'

Lesbians' Wellbeing, Class and the Meanings of Paid Work

Elizabeth McDermott

INTRODUCTION

The legal context within which lesbian, gay and bisexual (LGB) people in the UK work has been significantly changed by legislation which safeguards employees from discrimination based on their sexual orientation (HMGovernment, 2010). This is important because research demonstrates that LGB people encounter harassment, abuse and discrimination in the workplace, and this can have a negative impact on mental health (Bradford, Ryan and Rothblum, 1994, Smith and Ingram, 2004, McDermott, 2006). Research on the effect of the employment legislation on LGB workers is uneven. There is evidence that, unsurprisingly, LGB people continue to experience discrimination and hostility in the workplace (Hunt and Dick, 2008) but that LGB workers may be more likely to use the legislation if they encounter a problem in their employment setting (Colgan et al., 2006, 2009).

Paid work has long been associated with good mental health for women (Dooley, Prause and Ham-Rowbottom, 2000, Boye, 2009) and this is also likely to be the case for LGB people. There is, however, very little research in the UK which investigates the influence of employment on LGB mental health. Despite increasing attention on the relationship between sexual identity and organizations, especially public sector employment (Humphrey, 1999, Miller, Forest and Jurik, 2003, Ward and Winstanley, 2006, Monro, 2007, Colgan et al., 2009, Richardson and Monro, 2012), the mental health effects of work on LGB people remains an under-researched area. As a result, little is known about either the cost to LGB people in terms of health and quality of employment nor the cost to organizations of not including LGB people and thus losing motivated and productive LGB workers.

Mainstream health research has suggested that women's attitudes to work may be a significant factor in the relationship between employment and psychological health (Schober and Scott, 2012). So far, however, mental health research has not questioned the heterosexual premise of these investigations. In other words, research does not consider whether sexual identity may influence the meanings of work for women. In this chapter I report on UK qualitative research which sought to examine how the meanings of paid work are mediated by sexual identity and social class and the impact this may have on lesbians' wellbeing. Most research aiming to investigate the influence of sexual identity on mental health defines mental health by the presence or absence of particular psychological problems (e.g., anxiety, depression), as well as by aspects of social dysfunction like worry and difficulty in coping (McDermott, 2006). The research reported here is concerned with the positive factors involved with mental health which act to make people feel 'well'. Drawing from a wide range of research, wellbeing is conceived as a multidimensional subjective concept which may differ according to individual or group identity and experience. Wellbeing is understood as related to the social, cultural, economic and political factors an individual is exposed to and their responses to these (Walker, 2012).

The following two sections considers, first, the evidence regarding work, mental health and lesbian identity and, second, research on lesbians' attitudes to work. Subsequently, I outline the study methodology and then present substantive findings which suggest that lesbians have a variety of attitudes to employment which arise both from their position as women with a marginalized sexual identity and their social class location. Furthermore, the differing meanings and experiences of work evident in the women's narratives indicate that this is important for understanding the influence of employment on their wellbeing.

WORK, MENTAL HEALTH AND LESBIAN[1] IDENTITY

Women's increasing participation in the labour market has prompted a range of literature exploring the relationships between women's occupational status and their mental health and wellbeing.[2] In most studies, paid work has been associated with good mental health (Singleton, 2000, Klumb and Lampert, 2004). In a study of twenty-five European countries, women's wellbeing was shown to increase with increased paid working hours (Boye, 2009). Employment related factors such as work pressure, job satisfaction and 'role overload' are shown to be powerful predictors of mental health for women (Fuhrer et al., 1999, Klumb and Lampert, 2004, Wang et al., 2008). The positive effects are usually interpreted in terms of income earned, increased confidence, self-esteem, opportunities for social contact and a greater sense of control (Warr and Parry, 1982, Klumb and Lampert, 2004).The relationship between employment and psychological health becomes more complex once a woman's social and material circumstances are considered. Social class, the presence of children and education level are influential in understanding the effect of employment on women's psychological health (Elliot and Huppert, 1991, Artazcoz et al., 2004). Studies demonstrate that low education, restricted employment opportunities (Costello, 1991), financial strain (O'Campo, Eaton and Muntaner, 2004) and work/family life imbalance (Wang et al., 2008) are associated, for example, with poor mental health among women.

Whereas this body of literature on women, employment and mental health is usually based on an understanding that work is mediated by social class and gender, heterosexuality is universally assumed and remains unproblematised (McDermott, 2006, 2003). As a result much less is known about the impact of employment on the mental health of lesbians. Nevertheless, it is reasonable to surmise that, as women workers, lesbians' employment would also be a source of economic rewards, self-esteem, identity and independence (Schneider, 1998). Lesbians, however, have the additional pressure of managing a marginalized sexual identity in the workplace. Studies consistently report that negotiating a nonheterosexual identity at work can have a negative impact on psychological health. Hostility to homosexuality in the workplace has been found to induce feelings of anxiety, fear, anger, discomfort, worry and stress (Bradford, Ryan and Rothblum, 1994, Ryan-Flood, 2004, Colgan et al., 2006, McDermott, 2006, Ragins, Singh and Cornwell, 2007). In addition, psychological distress and depression has been shown to be related to experiences of occupational heterosexism (Waldo, 1999, Smith and Ingram, 2004).

Worldwide, workplace homophobia continues to be a significant feature of lesbians' employment (McDermott, 2006, Colgan et al., 2008, Eliason et al., 2011, Willis, 2011, Wright, 2011) and may be experienced differently depending on social class position (McDermott, 2006). In a survey of 1,658 LGB people in the UK, one in five experienced bullying from their colleagues because of their sexual orientation (Hunt and Dick, 2008). Significantly, those in manual and routine employment were 50 percent more likely to experience bullying that those in professional and managerial groups (Hunt and Dick, 2008). Studies investigating the management of lesbian identity in the workplace suggest that being open about sexual identity is important to job satisfaction and performance (Ellis and Riggle, 1995, Rostosky and Riggle, 2002). Workplace policies and perceived employer support and self-acceptance have been highlighted as key to sexual identity 'openess' at work (Chrobot-Mason, Button and Diclementi, 2001, Griffith and Hebl, 2002, Rostosky and Riggle, 2002, Ragins, Singh and Cornwell, 2007). Colgan et al.'s (2007) study found that working in 'gay-friendly' environments where respondents could be 'openly' LGB was connected by the majority to greater happiness, confidence and job satisfaction. However, some studies have indicated that those in the lower levels of the occupational hierarchy were less likely to be open about their sexual identity (Ryan-Flood, 2004, Colgan et al., 2006, McDermott, 2006).

LESBIAN IDENTITY AND ATTITUDES TO PAID WORK

Mainstream research on women's work preferences and attitudes demonstrates that labour force participation is complex with a range of factors involved such as caring responsibilities and childcare arrangements, educational attainment, economic resources, job opportunities, changing gender attitudes and increasing egalitarianism all influential (Schober and Scott, 2012). This body of literature has been dominated by studies of heterosexual women with dependent children and focused upon the narrow view of attitudes to work in terms of paid work and motherhood (James, 2009). Lesbians are excluded from the frames of enquiry (for exception see Duncan et al., 2003), and heterosexuality is taken for granted.

However, large scale analysis of US population data indicate that women's sexual identity is important to understanding attitudes to employment. Studies show that lesbians are more likely to work than heterosexual women (Peplau and Fingerhut, 2004) and are more likely to be employed full time than either married or unmarried heterosexual women (Tebaldi and Elmslie, 2006). Empirical studies suggest that lesbians attitudes to work are heavily shaped by the expectation to depend on themselves for economic survival (Weston and Rofel, 1984, Dunne, 1997, McDermott, 2003, Burnett, 2010, Wright, 2011). Dunne's (1997, 1998, 2000) work argues that lesbians' economic self-reliance influences their employment, training and educational choices and suggests that lesbians are more willing to work in male-orientated employment (see also, Wright, 2011) and are better paid than heterosexual women.

A contributing factor to explaining why lesbians seem to have higher labour market participation than their heterosexual counterparts is the presence of egalitarian gender attitudes to work. Egalitarian gender attitudes among men and women are linked to greater participation in the labour market for women in European countries (Boye, 2009). Research on lesbian partnerships shows strong egalitarian ideals (Dunne, 1997, Weeks, Heaphy and Donovan, 2001) and greater flexibility in negotiating the division of labour when parenting (Dunne, 1998). Although evidence on the ways that motherhood may impact on lesbians attitudes to paid employment is scarce (Peplau and Fingerhut, 2004), one US study found that lesbians living with young children were less likely to be out of the labour force compared to heterosexual women (Leppel, 2009). The combination of lesbians' economic self-sufficiency and a more equal approach to home life and caring responsibilities may partially explain lesbians' high levels of paid employment (Peplau and Fingerhut, 2004). In addition, social class has consistently been shown to be a critical factor in understanding women's attitudes to paid employment (Crompton and Lyonette, 2007). In the UK, highly educated women are more likely to be employed after childbirth than those with lower educational qualifications (Schober and Scott, 2012). James's (2008) study of heterosexual women found class differences in attitudes to work. Those in routine or manual occupations were more likely to cite financial necessity as shaping their motivation for work compared to the women in professional and managerial positions, who prioritized enjoyable work, which may be central to their identity. Social class rarely features in studies of lesbians attitudes to work.

The aim of this chapter is to explore how lesbian identity and social class may influence attitudes to paid work and the impact this may have on well-being. So far, both health research on women's employment and research on women's work preferences have not adequately 'troubled' their heteronormative research frameworks of inquiry. In addition, research on sexuality and work has paid insufficient attention to social class in the experiences of LGB people and employment. The findings reported here are an attempt to address these exclusions and gaps.

RESEARCH METHODOLOGY

The study was based on semi-structured, single interviews with twenty-four women who self-identified with a range of 'nonnormative' sexual/gender identities (e.g., lesbian, gay, dyke, transgendered, butch). The field-work took place between 2000 and 2002. The participants all lived in the North West of England and were aged between twenty-one and fifty-six years old. The sample was generated using purposeful theoretic snowball sampling (Weston, 1991) from a diverse range of starting points, using informal lesbian networks. The resulting group of women self-defined as white (17), black or mixed race (5) and Jewish (2). Fifteen lived in cities; the other nine women lived in small towns or villages. The participants were interviewed either in the respondents' homes, their friends' houses, workplaces or cafés. The interview included questions about employment, education, housing, social relations, partner relationships, sexual identity, homophobia, parenting, social class and physical health. They were recorded and a pseudonym was ascribed to participants during transcription. Data analysis and interpretation was conducted using grounded theory techniques (Miles and Huberman, 1994) (for further methodological detail, see McDermott, 2003)

The theoretical framework for the study drew on Bourdieu's (1984) conceptualization of social class. Bourdieu rejects the idea that social class divisions are defined solely by their relationship to the means of production; he suggests that class is defined by different conditions of existence and different amounts of power or capital (Bourdieu, 1984). In 'Distinction', Bourdieu specifically outlines his formula for conceptualising social class: (Habitus × Capital) + Field = Practice (Bourdieu, 1984: 101). Capital is a metaphor for social power which positions individuals in social space and Bourdieu identifies four main categories:

a. Economic capital is wealth.
b. Cultural capital is educational qualifications, cultural goods such as books, and embodied 'taste'.

c. Social capital is generated through social relationships and based on connections and group memberships.
d. Symbolic capital is a form of distinction between groups such as physical strength or status.

If access to these capitals positions individuals differentially in social space, Bourdieu's concept of habitus is a way of describing the embodiment of this social position. Bourdieu refers to habitus as 'a socialized subjectivity' (Bourdieu and Wacquant, 1992: 126). Habitus concerns a set of lasting dispositions, created and reformulated within the individual, which reflect the social conditions to which an agent is exposed—that is, their position in social space. Habitus is a concept which Bourdieu has developed to help us explain why individuals act in certain ways at an everyday level. Habitus is a system of dispositions which is a deep lattice of *tendencies* to think, feel and behave in particular ways; it is a kind of practical sense, which Bourdieu terms the 'logic of practice' (1990), for what is to be done in any given situation.

In addition to Bourdieu's conceptualization of social class, the theoretical frame work for the study approached sexual identity as a socially contingent, fluid construction with diverse and multiple meanings. Wellbeing was not defined by the absence or presence of psychiatric morbidity but explored subjectively and positively by asking the participants to talk about what was important to being 'happy, healthy and well'.

Sample

The conceptual difficulties of utilizing Bourdieu's concept of social class and the practicalities of classifying research respondents' class position has been noted by other scholars (e.g., Reay, 1998). For this study, the participants were divided into three broad class backgrounds/trajectories: working-class (10), middle-class (7) and university educated women from a working-class background (7). Social class was attributed using occupation and education. Women were categorised as 'middle-class' if they were university educated, professionally employed and one of their parents was the same. Women who had no higher education, were nonprofessionally employed and whose parents were the same were categorised as 'working-class'. Women who were university educated and whose parents had no higher education and nonprofessional jobs were categorised as 'working-class educated' (see Table. 6.1 for the participants' occupations). The purpose of defining social class in this way was an attempt to capture how differing positions in social space (as defined by access to capitals) may influenced attitudes to paid work. There are limits in a small-scale study to using three distinct groups of class when class is more contingent.

Table 6.1   Participants' Employment

Working class (w/c) (n=10)	Working class educated (w/c ed) (n=7)	Middle class (m/c) (n=7)
Class room assistant	Student/bar staff	Solicitor
Unemployed (n=3)	Unemployed (n=2)	Unemployed
Warehouse worker	Social Services	Student
Security guard	Lecturer	University lecturer
Shop worker	Student	Business director
Cleaner	Health worker	Own business (n=2)
Lab technician		
Admin assistant		

SEXUAL IDENTITY AND WORK

The women's accounts of work correspond with other research findings (Dunne, 1997, Wright, 2011) that lesbians do not expect to rely on anyone, man or woman, to provide for their economic and material security.

> I felt like the dad in the house cos I thought I want to look after me mum so if I got a job . . . it felt boss because I was bringing me own money in, as well as giving me mum money like as rent, cos it would help her you see.
>
> (Stacey, 22, white, classroom assistant, w/c)

> There was a month recently when there was no money coming in whatsoever and, er, I got really depressed, and I really felt, erm, a failure because I couldn't provide for myself and my family.
>
> (Alison, 46, white, own business, m/c)

Stacey's and Alison's extracts clearly illustrate the role of paid employment in their lives. They expect to earn a living independently, in order to support themselves and their families. Paid employment is a means of attaining financial and material security, asserting independence and living a life without relying on men. Alison's and Stacey's references to 'providing' and being 'like the dad' show that employment is important to the survival of their families. It contests the commonsense gendered notion of employment as having lesser importance for women than men—'breadwinning' can be crucial to women also.

The meaning of work for women who identify as lesbian is shaped by their positioning outside the boundaries of heterosexuality. Heterosexual women, through their relationships with men, may access the benefits of the 'male wage', which they may rely on for a livelihood or to enhance their own waged labour. Lesbians do not have the 'option' of accessing the male wage and expect to rely on themselves to attain a standard of living. In addition, lesbians must negotiate the gendered labour market in which they are less likely to have access to the premium paid, high status jobs of men (Crompton and Lyonette, 2007).

SEXUAL IDENTITY AND CLASS

Employment was highly significant to the wellbeing of the lesbians in this study but for reasons which were distinguished by social class. The working-class women's narratives indicated that the meaning of employment was different to that of the middle-class and working-class educated women. Work functioned as a basic requirement to good psychological health by meeting their material and economic needs. The working-class women explained their approaches to work in the following ways:

> It's a means to an end, my job is; it's certainly not something that I enjoy.
>
> (Mary, 48, white, administrative assistant, w/c)

> If I need money, I'll go out and work . . . I think if you need something desperately, then you'll go and get the money, won't you?
>
> (Amanda, 36, white, unemployed, w/c)

Mary and Amanda's excerpts are typical of the working-class women's view of employment. Work was something to be endured out of financial necessity; 'a means to an end'. In the main, the working-class women did not 'enjoy' their work and, in fact, did not expect to enjoy work. If their job was a source of pleasure, they expressed surprised and felt they were lucky. Employment was important to the working-class participants' wellbeing because it provided financial security and stability. A good job was 'earning regular money' that was a decent living wage and avoiding poor working conditions.

For the working-class women in this study, employment is 'the choice of the necessary' (Bourdieu, 1984: 379). The meaning of work is a product of the economic and social conditions in which individuals find themselves. So, as lesbians they must rely on themselves to earn a wage—a lesbian practice—but class habitus also shapes their meanings of employment. The working-class women have adjusted their expectations of work to fit their objective chances. On the one hand, they do not have the right capitals to successfully trade in the labour market to secure enjoyable work, but neither do they expect to; this is where class habitus is working. Employment for the working-class women was the primary means by which they maintained a safe distance from poverty and debt. As such, work protected their wellbeing. The middle-class and the employed working-class educated respondents' accounts suggest that work is important to their wellbeing for different reasons.

> INTERVIEWER: How does running the business affect your overall wellness?
>
> PATRICIA: Oh there's a definite relationship between the two; I mean the business is, is us; it's, it's a very, very important part of our lives . . . we've got to enjoy it more . . . and we're doing what we like doing.
>
> (Patricia, 56, Jewish, own business, m/c)

> LUCY: I do love it.
> INTERVIEWER: Is it the nature of the work that you love?
> LUCY: Yeah, I think it's really good at bringing out all of the things that I think I can do—like, I really enjoy people and listening to people; I love the people side of it; I don't mind the paper side of it . . . I enjoy the sort of creativity of that side of it.
>
> (Lucy, 35, white, solicitor, m/c)

It is evident from the above extracts that the middle-class women talked differently about their jobs than the working-class women. The majority of the middle-class women claimed they enjoyed their work; they felt it was an important part of their lives and influential to keeping them well. The middle-class women live at a distance from poverty and debt; the importance of work to them is not exclusively about creating a viable and stable income. During the interviews, which were conducted before the current economic crisis, when we were discussing the influence of employment on wellbeing, factors such as job security and finances where the last to be mentioned, if at all. The middle-class women in this study, and the working-class women who were university educated and successfully employed, expected work to provide more than economic recompense. They expected it to be a source of self-esteem and self-fulfilment; work promoted their wellbeing. It is fully acknowledged that in the current climate of restricted employment opportunities, professional women's attitudes to work may be more concerned with job security and working conditions.

LESBIAN IDENTITY, CLASS AND WELLBEING

I want to compare Laura and Naomi's accounts of unemployment to draw out the complex ways in which class expectations about work combine with social class positioning and lesbian identity to influence wellbeing. Laura and Naomi are both unemployed and living on benefits with one child, but their class position mediates their orientation to paid work and the type of employment they are seeking.

Laura is from a working-class background and is currently struggling to study part-time for a degree. She lives in an area of high unemployment, and despite having accrued a certain amount of educational capital, it is not sufficient to overcome the disadvantages of a single mother in the labour market. She told me in our interview that sometimes she does suffer with mental health problems. She describes below how she feels about her life at the moment:

> Erm, well, I'd say that I'm striving towards, er, you know, making life— hopefully, you know, get some sort of work out of this and be financially better off . . . I'm on the breadline and living off borrowed money and stuff at the moment . . . I'm not always happy; I keep going; I try to keep going . . . I mean there's times I do get a bit depressed; I feel like I'm stuck in my life . . . erm, sometimes life seems a struggle.
>
> (39, white, student, w/c ed.)

Later, she explains how she has tried to find paid employment:

> I were desperate . . . you're either going to sink or swim . . . I were looking through papers and thinking, what can I do? And I know chat lines will pay on the side; that's really against what I want to do, but desperation, I did phone, but I'm going to cancel it now; that was a moment of panic; that's how—to have to listen to dirty men.

Laura does not expect to rely on anyone else to provide materially for herself or her child—a lesbian practice. But the conditions in which she lives with this expectation are influenced by her social class positioning. Laura has lived in poverty for a long time; her interview is saturated with the struggle of necessity, the endless worry, a relentless tension of surviving, of trying to provide for her child and herself. She is not passive. She is working very hard with limited resources to better her situation, but she does so not in circumstances of her choosing. Her situation is one of severely restricted employment opportunities, employment which is for survival—to provide food, pay the rent, keep the electricity connected and keep a phone operating. Living so close to necessity and poverty shapes the meaning of work for Laura. She says of possible future employment:

> I wanted something that was regular; I was thinking of probation although it's controlling I know, but it could be regular work, cos you see with me daughter and everything—and also I know myself; it would be upsetting if I kept losing jobs.

Laura's proximity to survival means she has adapted her ambition to her perceived material situation—the class habitus working. Work to Laura means putting a floor in her circumstances, to attain financial security, she does not anticipate enjoying future employment. Compare Laura's account with that of Naomi, who is from a middle-class background and has been unemployed for approximately a year since completing her PhD:

> I definitely feel very privileged that I can live the way that I'm living without working, even though I want to be working; I mean the fact that I don't have to—I mean I may have a huge overdraft and debts coming out of my ears, but with a year with a proper job that would be sorted, erm, and meanwhile I can enjoy myself . . . I have a great life; I don't have to worry about—every so often I have my money worries, and I do need to do something about that but really, erm, I live in a three-bedroomed house with my child . . . to be on your own with a child could be terrible, but it's lovely.
>
> (32, Jewish, m/c)

Naomi lives in quite different circumstances to Laura. Her unemployment is relatively recent since finishing her postgraduate qualification. Before this she was employed as a university researcher. As well as claiming state benefits, Naomi receives financial support from her parents, and she lives in a leafy suburb in a large house. She is currently looking for work and applying for professional jobs. Naomi expresses a material distance from necessity and a psychological distance and is at ease with her situation. She displays the confidence of someone who has the right capitals to be successful in the labour market. Her class habitus is one where she expects to secure work, and work means a satisfying and gratifying experience. She displays the sense of freedom of self in relation to work which her class position has afforded her:

> I gave up the teaching at Easter because I just—it doesn't matter what I teach; I don't want to be a teacher . . . if you look at my CV, I should teach, something, anything—do you know what I mean? I should be a teacher of sorts; I just don't want to be . . . it's just not for me at all.

In this extract, we can see that Naomi expects work to be something she finds enjoyable and self-fulfilling. So she can afford to reject teaching as 'it's just not for me'; she is exerting choice. Whereas she is aware that financially she needs to work, she is not unduly worried. Occupation is a source of information about herself, a source of status; it provides self-identity and self-esteem as well as income. Although Naomi is not currently working, she is confident that she will secure work. Unlike Laura, Naomi's mental health does not suffer as a consequence of her unemployment. This is because her privileged class position enables her to access financial support and protect her wellbeing from some of the difficulties of unemployment.

CONCLUSION

The significance of employment to the wellbeing of lesbians has largely been ignored both in research on health inequalities and research on work and organizations. This small-scale study sought to examine how the meanings of paid work are mediated by sexual identity and social class, and the impact this may have on wellbeing. The analysis of the interview data from women who self-identified with a range of 'nonnormative' sexual/gender identities indicates that women outside the heterosexual dyad expected to be in paid employment as a means of attaining financial and material security, asserting independence and living a life without relying on men. However, the interview data suggest that the middle-class and the (employed) working-class, educated lesbians were more likely to be in work which promoted their wellbeing and that they expected to be in this kind of employment. They anticipated that their jobs would be stimulating, provide some level of control and autonomy and offer a sense of achievement. These women expected work to be a source of self-validation, social status and social networks, as well as provide financial rewards. The key point here is that whereas they may not always be in work which fulfilled these expectations, they expected their employment to provide these factors. This contrasted with the working-class lesbians who were usually employed in work characterized as boring and routine, with little autonomy, and they were poorly paid with few prospects—and this is the kind of work they expected. If the working-class women had jobs that they enjoyed, they considered themselves unusual. At best, employment protected their mental health from the worse aspects of poverty and debt. In addition, the working-class women had a greater probability of working in poor conditions which were potentially detrimental to mental health. Their accounts had far more instances of work related ill-health such as stress, anxiety, worry and depression.

This small-scale research demonstrates that further work is necessary to increase knowledge of the ways in which employment experiences are shaped by both sexuality and social class—and are associated with mental health. There are some limitations to these findings. These data were generated before the current global fiscal crisis, restricted labour market opportunities and pressurized working conditions. However, this does not negate the findings which suggest that a greater understanding of the classed ways lesbians' employment impacts on wellbeing will enable the development of policies and practices which improve the mental health and wellbeing of LGB people in, and out, of work. Furthermore, if we are to evaluate the effectiveness of the legislation which aims to protect LGB people from discrimination at work and develop greater comprehension of LGB people's attitudes to work, we must do this from an intersectional perspective. Our frameworks of enquiry must include sexuality, gender, class and race if we are to understand LGB employee wellbeing. The ability to gain employment that enhances wellbeing should not be, as Bauman (1998: 34) states, 'the privilege of the few; a distinctive mark of the elite'. We need to be interested in the multiple analytical categories of inequality which interlock and produce unequal lives if we are to comprehend the dynamics of sexuality within contemporary organizations and the labour market.

NOTES

1. The term *lesbian* is used as short hand for all women with marginalised sexual identities.
2. Research investigating work and mental health and wellbeing uses a variety of measures and is often unclear how mental health and wellbeing are being conceptualized (see Walker, 2012 for discussion).

REFERENCES

Artazcoz, L. L., Borrell, C., Benach, J., et al. (2004) 'Women, Family Demands and Health: The Importance of Employment Status and Socio-Economic Position', *Social Science & Medicine* 59: 263–274.

Bauman, Z. (1998) *Work, Consumerism and the New Poor,* Buckingham: Open University Press.

Bourdieu, P. (1984) *Distinction,* London: Routledge and Kegan Paul.

Bourdieu, P. (1990) *The Logic of Practice,* Cambridge: Polity Press.

Bourdieu, P. and Wacquant, L.J.D. (1992) *An Invitation to Reflexive Sociology,* Cambridge: Polity Press.

Boye, K. (2009) 'Relatively Different? How Do Gender Differences in Well-Being Depend on Paid and Unpaid Work in Europe?' *Social Indicators Research* 93: 509–525.

Bradford, J., Ryan, C. and Rothblum, E. D. (1994) 'National Lesbian Health Care Survey: Implications for Mental Health Care', *Journal of Consulting and Clinical Psychology* 62: 228–242.

Burnett, L. (2010) 'Young Lesbians Explore Careers and Work Landscapes in an Australian Culture', *Journal of Lesbian Studies* 14: 36–51.

Chrobot-Mason, D., Button, S. and Diclementi, J. D. (2001) 'Sexual Identity Management Strategies: An Exploration of Antecedents and Consequences', *Sex Roles* 45: 321–336.

Colgan, F., Creegan, C., McKearney, A., et al. (2006) *Lesbian, Gay and Bisexual Workers: Equality, Diversity and Inclusion in the Workplace,* London: Working Lives Research Institute, London Metropolitan University and European Community Social Fund.

Colgan, F., Creegan, C., McKearney, A., et al. (2007) 'Equality and Diversity Policies and Practices at Work: Lesbian, Gay and Bisexual Workers', *Equal Opportunities International* 26, 590–609.

Colgan, F., Creegan, C., McKearney, A., et al. (2008) 'Lesbian Workers: Personal Stratgeies Amid Changing Organisational Response to "Sexual Minorities" in UK Workplaces', *Journal of Lesbian Studies* 12: 31–46.

Colgan, F., Wright, T., Creegan, C., et al. (2009) 'Equality and Diversity in the Public Services: Moving Forward on Lesbian, Gay and Bisexual Equality?' *Human Resources Management Journal* 19: 280–301.

Costello, E. J. (1991) 'Married with Children: Predictors of Mental and Physical Health in Middle Aged Women', *Psychiatry* 54: 292–305.

Crompton, R. and Lyonette, C. (2007) 'The New Gender Essentialism—Domestic and Family 'Choices' and Their Relation to Attitudes', *British Journal of Sociology* 54: 601–620.

Dooley, D., Prause, J. and Ham-Rowbottom, K. (2000) 'Underemployment and Depression: Longitudinal Relationships', *Journal of Health and Social Behaviour* 41, 421–436.

Duncan, S., Edwards, R., Reynolds, T., et al. (2003) 'Motherhood, Paid Work and Partnering: Values and Theories', *Work, Employment & Society* 17: 309–330.

Dunne, G. (1997) *Lesbian Lifestyles: Women's Work and the Politics of Sexuality,* London: Macmillan Press.

Dunne, G. (1998) "Pioneers Behind Our Own Front Doors': Towards Greater Balance in the Organisation of Work in Partnerships', *Work, Employment & Society* 12: 273–295.

Dunne, G. (2000) 'Lesbians as authentic workers? Institutional heterosexuality and the reproduction of gender inequalities', *Sexualities* 3: 133–148.

Eliason, M. J., DeJoseph, J., Dibble, S., et al. (2011) 'Lesbian, Gay, Bisexual, Transgender, and Queer/Questioning Nurses' Experiences in the Workplace', *Journal of Professional Nursing* 27: 237–244.

Elliot, J. and Huppert, F. (1991) 'In Sickness and in Health: Associations between Physical and Mental Well Being, Employment and Parental Status in a Nationwide Sample of Married Women', *Psychological Medicine* 21: 515–524.

Ellis, A. and Riggle, E. (1995) 'The Relation of Job Satisfaction and Degree of Openness about One's Sexual Orientation for Lesbians and Gay Men', *Journal of Homosexuality* 30: 75–85.

Fuhrer, R., Stansfeld, S. A., Chemali, J., et al. (1999) 'Gender, Social Relations and Mental Health: Prospective Findings from an Occupational Cohort (Whitehall II Study)', *Social Science and Medicine* 48: 77–87.

Griffith, K. H. and Hebl, M. R. (2002) 'The Disclosure Dilemma for Gay Men and Lesbians: "Coming Out at Work"', *Journal of Applied Psychology* 87: 1191–1199.

HMGovernment (2010) *The Equality Act 2010.* Available at www.equalities.gov.uk/equality_bill.aspx.

Humphrey, J. (1999) 'Organizing Sexualities, Organised Inequalities: Lesbians and Gay Men in Public Service Occupations', *Gender, Work and Organization* 6: 134–151.

Hunt, R. and Dick, S. (2008) *Serves You Right: Lesbian and Gay People's Expectations of Discrimination,* Stonewall, London.

James, L. (2008) 'United by Gender or Divided by Class? Women's Work Orientations and Labour Market Behaviour', *Gender, Work and Organizations* 15: 394–412.

James, L. (2009) 'Generational Differences in Women's Attitudes towards Paid Employment in a British City: The Role of Habitus', *Gender, Place and Culture* 16: 313–328.

Klumb, P. L. and Lampert, T. (2004) 'Women, Work, and Well-Being 1950–2000: A Review and Methodological Critique', *Social Science & Medicine* 58: 1007–1024.

Leppel, K. (2009) 'Labour Force Status and Sexual Orientation', *Economica* 76: 197–207.

McDermott, E. (2003) 'Hidden Injuries, Happy Lives: The Influence of Lesbian Identity and Social Class on Wellbeing'. Unpublished dissertation in *Applied Social Sciences.* Lancaster: Lancaster University.

McDermott, E. (2006) 'Surviving in Dangerous Places: Lesbian Identity Performances in the Workplace, Social Class and Psychological Health', *Feminism and Psychology* 16: 193–211.

Miles, M. and Huberman, A. M. (1994) *Qualitative Data Analysis: An Expanded Sourcebook,* London: Sage.

Miller, S., Forest, K. and Jurik, N. (2003) 'Diversity in Blue: Lesbian and Gay Police Officers in a Masculine Occupation', *Men and Masculinities* 5: 355–385.

Monro, S. (2007) 'New Institutionalism and Sexuality at Work in Local Government', *Gender, Work and Organization* 14: 1–19.

O'Campo, P., Eaton, W. W. and Muntaner, C. (2004) 'Labor Market Experience, Work Organization, Gender Inequalities and Health Status: Results from a Prospective Analysis of US Employed Women', *Social Science & Medicine* 58: 585–594.

Peplau, L. and Fingerhut, A. (2004) 'The Paradox of the Lesbian Worker', *Journal of Social Issues* 60: 719–735.

Ragins, B. R., Singh, R. and Cornwell, J. (2007) 'Making the Invisible Visible: Fear and Disclosure of Sexual Orientation at Work', *Journal of Aplied Psychology* 92: 1103–1118.

Reay, D. (1998) *Class Work,* London: UCL Press.

Richardson, D. and Monro, S. (2012) *Sexuality, Equality & Diversity,* Hampshire: Palgrave Macmillan.

Rostosky, S. and Riggle, E. (2002) '"Out" at Work: The Relationship of Actor and Partner Workplace Policy and Internalizaed Homophobia to Disclosure Status', *Journal of Couseling Psychology* 49: 411–419.

Ryan-Flood, R. (2004) 'Beyond Recognition and Redistribution: A Case Study of Lesbian and Gay Workers in a Local Labour Market in Britain', *New Working Paper Series No.12.* Gender Institute, London School of Economics.

Schneider, B. E. (1998) 'Peril and Promise: Lesbians' Workplace Participation'. In Nardi, P. M. and Schneider, B. E. (eds), *Social Perspectives in Lesbian and Gay Studies: A Reader.* London: Routledge, 377–389.

Schober, P. and Scott, J. (2012) 'Maternal Employment and Gender Role Attitudes: Dissonance among British Men and Women in the Transition to Parenthood', *Work, Employment & Society* 26: 514–530.

Singleton N. (2000) *The Prevalence of Psychiatric Morbidity Among Adults Living in Private Households,* London: HMSO.

Smith, N. G. and Ingram, K. (2004) 'Workplace Heterosexism and Adjustment among Lesbian, Gay and Bisexual Individuals: The Role of the Unsupportive Social Interactions', *Journal of Couseling Psychology* 51: 57–67.

Tebaldi, E. and Elmslie, B. (2006) 'Sexual Orientation and Labour Supply', *Applied Economics* 38: 349–562.

Waldo, C. R. (1999) 'Working in a Majority Context: A Structural Model of Heterosexism as Minority Stress in the Workplace', *Journal of Couseling Psychology* 46: 218–232.

Walker, P. (2012) 'Wellbeing: Meaning, Definition, Measurement and Application. In Walker, P. and John, M. (eds), *From Public Health to Wellbeing.* Hampshire: Palgrave Macmillan, 21–42.

Ward, J. and Winstanley, D. (2006) 'Watching the Watch: The UK Fire Service and its Impact on Sexual Minorities in the Workplace', *Gender, Work and Organization* 13: 193–219.

Wang, J. L., Lesage, A., Schmitz, N., et al. (2008) 'The Relationship between Work Stress and Mental Disorders in Men and Women: Findings from a Population-Based Study', *Journal of Epidemiology and Community Health* 62: 42–47.

Warr, P. and Parry, G. (1982) 'Paid Employment and Women's Psychological Well-Being', *Psychological Bulletin* 91: 498–516.

Weeks, J., Heaphy, B. and Donovan, C. (2001) *Same Sex Intimacies: Families of Choice and Other Life Experiments,* London: Routledge.

Weston, K. (1991) *Families We Choose: Lesbians, Gays and Kinship,* New York: Columbia University Press.

Weston, K. M. and Rofel, L. B. (1984) 'Sexuality, Class, and Conflict in a Lesbian Workplace', *Signs* 9: 623–646.

Willis P. (2011) 'Laboring in Silence: Young Lesbian, Gay, Bisexual, and Queer-Identifying Workers' Negotiations of the Workplace Closet in Australian Organizations', *Youth & Society* 43: 957–981.

Wright T. (2011) 'A "Lesbian Advantage"? Analysing the Intersections of Gender, Sexuality and Class in Male-Dominated Work', *Equality, Diversity and Inclusion: An International Journal* 30: 686–701.

7 Organisational Life Within a UK 'Good Practice Employer'

The Experiences of Black and Minority Ethnic and Disabled LGBT Employees

Fiona Colgan

INTRODUCTION

Over the last three decades, lesbian, gay, bisexual and transgendered (LGBT) activism has resulted in improved employment rights and increasing visibility for LGBT people in most developed economies (Colgan and McKearney, 2012). A more inclusive climate for LGBT people emerged in the UK post-1997, following the election of a Labour Government which introduced the Employment Equality (Sexual Orientation) Regulations (2003) and the Gender Recognition Act (2004). Research has indicated that these and subsequent UK equality legislation, whilst not a panacea, have provided an important trigger to changing social attitudes and empowering LGBT people to feel able to challenge discrimination at work and in society (Whittle, Turner and Al-Alami, 2007; Stonewall, 2012).

Unfortunately there is still a lack of official data on the UK LGBT population (Mitchell et al., 2008),[1] and thus it is fortunate that there are a growing number of studies rendering LGBT people and their experiences at work visible. These include case studies focusing on specific organisations or sectors (Burke, 1993; Colgan et al., 2006; Ward, 2008; Rumens and Broomfield, 2012). Research has also begun to focus within the acronym LGBT in order to explore the diverse organisational experiences of lesbians, gay men and bisexual and trans people[2] (Dunne, 1997; Monro, 2005; McDermott, 2006; Hines, 2010; Roberts, 2011). This is a useful development as it recognises that LGBT people are not a homogeneous group. Underlying the strategic political use of the term *LGBT* are long-standing historical tensions plus different concerns and experiences (Richardson and Monro, 2012). Recent UK studies have sought to address this diversity through the adoption of queer theory focusing on how genders and sexualities may be performed and experienced at work (Browne and Nash, 2010; Williams and Guiffre, 2011; Rumens, 2012).

Intersectionality has offered another influential approach to analysing diversity, allowing the exploration of the experiences of LGBT people, taking account of factors such as age, class, disability, religion and spirituality (Beckett, 2004; Casey et al., 2010; Taylor, Hines and Casey, 2011; Wright,

2013). It rejects treating gender, race, sexual orientation, disability and other strands as separate and essentialist categories, emphasising the need instead to focus on the ways 'dimensions of difference intersect to create new and distinct social cultural, artistic and political forms' (Dill, Murray and Weber, 2001: 4). For advocates of this approach, it has been important to move away from an additive approach (Crenshaw et al., 1994; McCall, 2005; Yuval-Davis, 2006) so as to analyse the intersection of sexual orientation and gender identity and other factors in people's lives. Such intersections can be important, both in framing identity and shaping people's experiences of hierarchical power systems and the politics of personal interactions within specific social, historical and cultural locations. Adib and Guerrier (2003: 416) suggest that intersectionality is useful in allowing the empirical examination of how the crossover with a range of dimensions of diversity is articulated in specific workplaces. Acker (2000: 202) points to the value of acknowledging the views of different organisational participants by dimensions such as gender, race and class in order to make visible the 'normal violence' of organisational life and assist in identifying discriminatory behaviour and practices within it.

Given the emerging literature on LGBT people and their diverse experiences at work, it is of concern to note that a research review by the Equality and Human Rights Commission (EHRC) (Mitchell et al., 2008) found that there were few UK studies addressing the employment experiences of disabled LGBT people and none which specifically focused on LGBT people from black and minority ethnic (BME) communities. The EHRC research review found that the intersection of disability with sexual orientation was one of the most under-researched areas in the literature. Most discussion of LGBT people with a disability was in the context of the access to health and social care (Mitchell et al., 2008), whereas studies concerned with the experiences of BME LGBT people have primarily focussed on health and cultural/family dynamics, homophobic hate crime and social exclusion (Keogh, Dodds and Henderson, 2004; Mitchell et al., 2008).

Only one major UK study provides a focus on the employment experiences of LGB BME and LGB people with disabilities (Colgan et al., 2006). Aside from this academic study, the extant UK research mostly focuses on LGB rather than LGBT experiences and is found within the practitioner domain. Molloy, Knight and Woodfield (2003: 98) found that disabled LGB respondents had chosen to only seek work with public or voluntary sector employers they perceived to be 'enlightened' or had chosen not to disclose their sexuality at work. Another theme within the literature is the isolation and 'double exclusion' that LGB people with disabilities may experience, encountering discrimination from heterosexual people on grounds of their sexual orientation and from within the LGB community on grounds of their disability (Brothers, 2000). The Safra Project (2003) identified a range of difficulties facing Muslim BME women who identified as LBT and argued the need for workplaces to be all-inclusive, not allowing LGBT issues to be compromised 'in the name of cultural sensitivity or respect for religion', whilst also not tolerating Islamaphobia (2003: 25). More recently Stonewall and the Runnymede Trust produced a report focusing on the experiences of LGB people from BME backgrounds. The research estimated that over 400,000 of the UK LGB population are BME from 'Chinese, Indian, Pakistani, Black Caribbean and a whole host of other identities' (Guasp and Kibirige, 2013: 1). A key finding was that many of the participants agreed that they had felt marginalised and isolated by the general lack of recognition of LGB BME people in the UK. The report concluded that organisations needed to recognise that people belong to more than one identity, and it cautioned against creating a perceived hierarchy between different identities (Guasp and Kibirige, 2013).

In light of the above concerns, this chapter sets out to address the research gap identified in the UK LGBT employment literature by beginning to make visible the experiences of BME and disabled LGBT people at work. In doing so it recognises the need for UK research to consider the ways in which LGBT identities intersect with other forms of identity such as disability and ethnicity (Richardson and Monro, 2012) and acknowledges that LGBT research has not always succeeded in being sufficiently inclusive of all sections of the LGBT population (Humphrey, 1998; McManus, 2003). It uses the insights gained from the exploration of intersectionality 'as a lived experience' (Taylor, Hines and Casey, 2011: 4) to enhance our understanding of organisational life (Acker, 2000). The chapter will first introduce the UK public policy context and the research study before moving on to consider the empirical findings.

CHANGING UK PUBLIC POLICY CLIMATE

The Labour Government introduced a range of legislation to promote equality and social inclusion between 1997 and 2010 (Richardson and Monro, 2012). The Employment Equality (SO) Regulations and the Gender Recognition Act (2004) were followed by the Civil Partnership Act in 2004, which recognised same-sex relationships, and the Equality Act (Sexual Orientation) Regulations in 2007, which made it unlawful to discriminate on the grounds of sexual orientation in access to goods, facilities and services. However, soon after, the UK opted to revamp its equality legislation to move towards a more integrated approach to equalities so allowing it to meet the requirements of the European Union Employment Equality Directive (2000).

As a consequence, the Equality and Human Rights Commission was established in 2007 (replacing specific equality commissions such as the Race Equality Commission and the Disability Rights Commission). The Equality Act was passed by a Labour Government in 2010. It replaced pre-existing legislation addressing specific forms of inequality and discrimination including the Sex Discrimination Act (1975), Race Relations Act (1976), Disability Discrimination Act (1995), Employment Equality (Sexual Orientation) Regulations (2003), Employment Equality (Religion or Belief) Regulations (2003), Gender Recognition Act (2004) and the Employment Equality (Age) Regulations (2006). The Equality Act identified nine 'protected characteristics', including, for example, disability, gender identity and gender reassignment, sexual orientation and race. The argument was that a move to a single equality regime could streamline equality legislation and encourage a more intersectional and consistent approach to the equality agenda (Squires, 2010). This was important because sexual orientation, gender identity and gender reassignment were perceived to receive less priority than the longer established equality strands in UK workplaces (Harding and Peel, 2007). Progress, however, has been stalled by the election of a Conservative Liberal Democrat coalition government in 2010. It has not been enthusiastic about developing a more intersectional equality agenda; for example, it has stripped back 'regulation on dual discrimination' from the Equalities Act 2010 in order to reduce costs on business (Department for Business, Innovation and Skills, 2011: 7). The inclusion of the provision on dual discrimination would have made it unlawful to discriminate against an individual on the basis of two protected characteristics (e.g., race and sexual orientation or disability and gender identity) rather than on the basis of a single protected characteristic alone (Squires, 2010).

THE RESEARCH

This chapter is based on in-depth interviews with thirty LGBT employees who self-identified as having a disability and/or as being BME. The interviews took place within a two-year study (2004–2006) focusing on LGB perceptions and experiences of diversity and inclusion at work funded by the Higher Education European Social Fund (Colgan et al., 2006). The research thus took place at a fairly optimistic time for equality issues in the UK as described in the previous section. The larger study comprised interviews with 154 LGBT employees and 60 interviews with management, trade union and LGBT group representatives within 16 'good practice' organisations.[3]

In addition to an in-depth interview, all of the respondents were asked to complete a short questionnaire prior to the interview. The purpose of this questionnaire was to obtain headline demographic and attitudinal data about the research participants and to ensure diversity was built into the study sample. Table 7.1 draws on the survey data to present a profile of the thirty LGBT respondents, all of whom, as stated, self-identified as having a disability and/or being BME. It is worth noting that two-thirds of these respondents indicated that they were 'out to everyone' about their sexual orientation at work; also note, only one of the employee participants

Table 7.1 LGBT Respondents

Pseudonym	Gender	Sexual orientation	Ethnicity	Disability	Age	Sector	Occupation	Disclosure of sexual orientation at work
Fred	M	Bisexual	Black Caribbean	N	31–40	Private	Skilled trades	Out to very few people
Robin	M	Gay	Chinese	N	41–50	Private	Manager	Out to everyone
Sav	M	Gay	Asian	N	41–50	Private	Professional	Not out at work
Harinder	M	Gay	Mixed heritage	N	21–30	Private	Professional	Out to everyone
Lee	M	Gay	Chinese	N	31–40	Private	Manager	Out to very few people
Kat	W	Lesbian	Chinese	N	31–40	Private	Professional	Out to very few people
Ellen	W	Lesbian	Mixed heritage	N	31–40	Public	Teacher	Out to everyone
Tom	M	Gay	Black Caribbean	N	21–30	Public	Admin/secretarial	Out to everyone
Justin	M	Gay	Mixed heritage	N	21–30	Public	Manual	Out to everyone
Shazia	W	Lesbian	Mixed heritage	N	31–40	Public	Professional	Out to some people
Frances	W	Lesbian	Black Caribbean	N	31–40	Public	Professional	Out to everyone
Mhinder	M	Gay	Asian	N	31–40	Public	Professional	Out to some people
Mark	M	Gay	Black Caribbean	N	31–40	Voluntary	Professional	Out to everyone
Arshad	M	Gay	Asian	N	31–40	Voluntary	Professional	Out to everyone
Kiranjit	W	Lesbian	Asian	N	31–40	Voluntary	Professional	Out to everyone

Name	Gender	Sexuality	Ethnicity		Age	Sector	Occupation	Outness
Bob	M	Gay	Mixed heritage	Y	31–40	Voluntary	managerial	Out to everyone
Jo	Trans	Bisexual	White	Y	41–50	Private	Skilled trades	Out to very few people
Sue	W	Lesbian	White	Y	41–50	Private	Associate/professional & technical	Out to everyone
Graeme	M	Gay	White	Y	31–40	Private	Professional	Out to some people
Rick	M	Gay	White	Y	31–40	Private	Manager	Out to some people
Roger	M	Gay	White	Y	41-50	Private	Professional	Out to everyone
Al	W	Lesbian	White	Y	41–50	Private	Professional	Out to everyone
Tana	W	Lesbian	White	Y	41–50	Public	Manager	Out to everyone
Tricia	W	Lesbian	White Irish	Y	31–40	Public	Professional	Out to everyone
Helen	W	Lesbian	White	Y	31–40	Public	Manager	Out to everyone
Jackie	W	Lesbian	White	Y	21–30	Public	Admin/secretarial	Out to everyone
Aidan	M	Gay	White Irish	Y	41–50	Public	Admin/secretarial	Out to some people
Pauline	W	Lesbian	White	Y	41–50	Public	Manager	Out to everyone
Andrew	M	Gay	White	Y	31–40	Public	Manager	Out to everyone
Bruce	M	Gay	White	Y	51–60	Voluntary	Professional	Out to everyone

identified as 'trans'. At the time of the research, sexual orientation and gender identity issues were still a relatively new and 'sensitive' area of research in the UK, and it is important to acknowledge that those coming forward to participate in these interviews were those who felt comfortable to participate in such a research project. The data was analysed using grounded analysis techniques and is presented below under four emergent themes.

IN SEARCH OF THE 'GOOD PRACTICE EMPLOYER'

The search for an equal opportunities (EO) employer was a predominant theme within the interviews with Jackie, for example, saying that she had always sought employment within large, public sector organisations with an EO policy.

> So being gay and disabled . . . you are covered either way . . . with a safety net if anything happens . . . . it's like if I have discrimination with regards to my sexual orientation then there is a policy in place. And likewise if I am just discriminated against because of my disability, then I am covered within the policy . . . there are representatives here within the Council that are happy to represent me on either issue if needs be.

All of the respondents agreed that their organisations had moved forward in terms of formal EO policies and practices in the last four to five years. Sav said his organisation had 'moved on considerably' in terms of race and LGBT issues, and Kat said of her employer:

> It's a neutral to good place, I guess. It's certainly making efforts to try and force people into being politically correct. Sometimes I am not sure that is always a good thing. But at least they do make the effort to let people know that they will not tolerate people who are intolerant. So this is a good thing.

However, all of the respondents thought that their organisations were more hesitant in developing policy and implementing practice with respect to sexual orientation and trans issues relative to other equality strands. Justin said:

> When I first started with [the organisation], disability . . . was already predominantly out there, and the companies knew what they had to do and . . . were there shouting, 'Rarara, we are employing disabled people'. Whereas sexual orientation is quite a new thing . . . there is a difference between the corporate view and the practice and the manager's as individuals reaction to it because remember to them it's quite a new thing, whereas disability is not.

As suggested by Harding and Peel (2007), there was a perception that sexual orientation was seen as 'second class' amongst the equality strands. Jo thought that trans issues were even lower than sexual orientation on the equality agenda, seeing them viewed as the 'ones that got left behind'. As a consequence, there was perceived to be less movement in practice on LGBT than other equality issues. This view was expressed by Al:

> Well, in a theoretical way . . . I am really chuffed [organisation] . . . is in the Stonewall league, but at the end of the day I still have to come to work and sit with the same people who've been abusive to me three years ago. You know, those people haven't changed, and I don't really think the way they think has changed very much. [The company] likes to sell itself as a champion of diversity, but I do think it's more talk than action.

Thus despite being 'good practice employers', these organisations were not always perceived as comfortable places to be. Racist, sexist and homophobic 'banter' occurred in most places, and there seemed to still be a limited awareness of disability issues. As a result, it could be isolating to be in a 'minority', as Tana describes below.

> I have worked in social services for eighteen years, and there are fewer lesbian and gay people working here to my knowledge . . . Certainly when I was working in [a previous organisation], there were far more lesbian and gay people working there . . . I could identify with other people of my like then . . . I mean, there are lots of visually impaired people working in my team, and so I guess we have common ground there. But, no, it would be nice to know more lesbians as well.

In this context, organisation and trade union equality networks were considered to be very important in countering feelings of 'isolation' by putting people in touch with each other through LGBT, BME and disability networks and broader equality events (Colgan and McKearney, 2012).

The lack of role models at the top was identified as a particular problem by respondents. Sav perceived his managers as an 'old boy's network'; Kat said of her work environment, 'It's a male environment. I am used to it, but that doesn't mean that I am comfortable with it'. Even in seemingly diverse workplaces, management hierarchies were described as overwhelmingly 'male' and 'white'. Thus it was significant that nearly all respondents said they were less comfortable disclosing their sexual orientation and/or raising equality issues with male than female managers. The problems posed by the lack of diversity at the top, particularly where routes for promotion were 'opaque', are described by Kat:

> In a world where there is just a total lack of role models . . . If I ask why am I not progressing faster than I would like to, they will say, 'Oh, you

have to network'. But the thing is, in the senior level, people don't want to network with you because you are so different, right? They can't carry on a conversation with you over thirty seconds because you don't talk about the subjects they like to talk about. And you feel so out of place . . . they want to network with people who they feel comfortable with.

TACKLING THE 'NORMAL VIOLENCE' OF ORGANISATIONAL LIFE

The respondents perceived gendered and racialised power hierarchies within their organisations and described the implications for EO in practice. Mhinder, for example, saw the power of those who were 'privileged' as unquestioned and entrenched:

I would describe the organisational cultures that I work in as very heterosexist and very white . . . most discrimination is extremely hidden and . . . if you look at the social structures [and ask] how race and say sexuality is reflected at the very higher echelons—no, all those people are typically men; there is one woman, they are all white, they are all middle-class-ish and they are the usual . . . ones that feel entitled and get most of the sort of status of power in society. So there is nobody out at the top, and there is nobody Black up at the top, and there aren't that many women.

He felt fortunate in knowing a number of BME LGBT people at work, who acted as an informal sounding board for each other, but he said if he 'got hassle' he would feel unable to challenge it:

You just have to accept this is the cost of being in such organisations . . . They say, you know, we are highly visible because of our colour, but we are highly invisible, made invisible, and we feel invisible as a result of the practices and processes that go on, and finding a voice in that dynamic is really difficult.

Al also talked of feeling oppressed by the dynamics in her organisation, which she thought undermined EO policy in practice. She had previously worked in the media and had applied for her job following diagnosis of a medical condition. She thought a more stable work situation would improve her health. The company initially seemed to offer good EO policies and had agreed to allow her to work part-time. However, she found the 'straight environment' in terms of the nature of the job itself and the assumption that 'everyone is heterosexual' was a 'culture shock'. Her attempts to discuss her life 'normally' were met by a 'wall of silence' followed by email harassment, which was stressful and exacerbated her illness. However, she found it difficult to complain about her colleagues' behaviour, instead trying to put on an 'emotional suit of armour' at work:

> You know if I say, 'I think that person is treating me badly because I am gay', and I say why . . . I literally got told, 'You are imagining it; you are being paranoid'. And because unfortunately they know about my mental health . . . I feel that they've got a bit of a lever there.

Justin, working in a predominantly white, male environment as a BME, gay man concluded:

> You do have to deal with issues with people, their issues with you, but on the other hand you have to stand up and be strong . . . I think it's quite subjective what you consider harassment because basically the line is anything that makes you upset. But from my point of view, I have been striving not to get upset about things.

His view was that if he complained, he would make things worse for himself. Sav agreed, saying that 'in spite of all these legal, supportive actions' any formal challenge would jeopardise his situation at work 'because I have to work with these people, you know, for the rest of my career'. Sue experienced being bullied in the workplace and chose to accept a move down career-wise in order to escape a hostile environment. She primarily wanted to avoid 'hassle at work' and was scared that if she had taken a Tribunal case, it might have drawn the attention of the tabloid media.

Andrew achieved a more positive outcome following a very difficult period of harassment. He had been married, with children. His problems at work started when he admitted to himself he was gay, at thirty, and tried to come out. Initially work was supportive, but then he was moved to a new department. Here he experienced homophobic bullying and harassment and ended up in 'quite a bad way':

> I was hauled up in front of one of the senior managers and basically given the riot act . . . my interpretation of the conversation was that really I should go back into the closet. I was creating too much problems within the team, causing hostility . . . being so open about my sexuality . . . as a result I ended up going off sick for six months with anxiety and depression. I was on antidepressants . . . I had suicidal tendencies . . . it soon became evident I just couldn't stay there.

On return to work, he was successful in being redeployed to the training section, and although still subject to depression, he began work as an EO trainer and became active in the disabled and LGBT sections of his union. He took the opportunity to speak up on equality issues, purposely drawing on his own experiences in order to illustrate the anxiety and depression which could be triggered by poor organisational practice.

Respondents in the public and voluntary sector seemed more likely to feel able to challenge discrimination, particularly where there were visible campaigns on equality and diversity supported by senior managers and trade unions (Colgan et al., 2006). This view was less evident in the private sector, although Harinder was clear he would not put up with discriminatory behaviour:

> The fact that I'm from an ethnic minority has never restricted my opportunities. The reason for that may be twofold. I'm a confident person; people do respect you if you are, but if you're ever slightly awkward then people latch on to it. Now, I do not give a shit if they don't like the fact I'm gay.

MANAGING VISIBILITY/INVISIBILITY
AND DISCLOSURE AT WORK

Sexual orientation has been described as different than other equality strands because of the 'invisible aspect of diversity' (Bell et al., 2011). However, the interviews indicated that issues of framing identity (Crenshaw et al., 1995) and visibility/invisibility and decisions about disclosure also applied to other aspects of diversity. Respondents emphasised the energy and skills required in managing these issues.

With respect to sexual orientation, some respondents thought they were clearly visible. For example, Sue described herself as a 'textbook butch lesbian, how people imagine one to be . . . I am almost tattooed with it'; she was constantly surprised that people did not recognise her as such. Mark also expressed frustration at the constant need to disclose his sexual orientation. He thought that he was not recognised as gay at work because of societal stereotypes of black men as 'hyper-masculine'.

> So a lot of people will look at a black male in the workplace and never assume—I get this all the time—they never ever assume that I am a homosexual. It irritates the living daylights out of me . . . I think it directly impacts the community as a whole because there are not that many people who are prepared to stand up and say, 'Actually this is who I am; deal with it'. You know, it just becomes a vicious cycle.

Other BME respondents did not wish to disclose their sexual orientation at work. For example, Kat as the only woman and BME person in her team, thought that disclosure of her sexual orientation would only further complicate her workplace interactions with colleagues.

> I think what happens with sexuality is that it's much easier to just— for it to be brushed aside because it is something that you can hide. I

cannot hide the fact that I am Chinese; I cannot hide the fact that I am a woman. But the other issue, I can just not address it.

In work contexts where colleagues and their line manager showed limited awareness and support for disability issues, some disabled LGBT respondents also chose not to come 'out' at work. For example, Aidan waited seven years, until people got to know him, before he had felt confident to disclose his sexual orientation. Jo, although out about having a disability and very active in union health and safety issues at work, did not feel able to be out about being trans and/or bisexual, concluding: 'I daren't . . . my credibility would go down the drain . . . I just have to close off. I can't afford to take risks'. As a consequence Jo felt constrained to go to work 'as a man' but said, 'I'd like to be able to go out to work as a female and do my union work as a female; that would be my ideal world, but that's never going to happen'.

Most of the disabled respondents were 'out' to their employer about their disability at work. Their priority was to ensure their employers complied with the law so enabling them to do their job. However, the degree of 'outness' with colleagues and clients could vary depending on the nature of the disability. Rick described having to expend energy on other people's reactions to his disability by 'working out what you need to do to make them . . . comfortable so that you can be comfortable'. He contrasted the energy required in managing the visibility of his disability with managing the invisibility of his sexual orientation, as he was not out to everyone at work, via two workplace scenarios:

> The disability broadcasts itself . . . it's visible . . . for example, I have just had a meeting . . . with someone I had not met before, and I noticed that she spotted my hand during this meeting . . . and I am watching to see what the reaction is. Is she taking in what I am saying or is she looking at my hand? . . . some people perceive you slightly differently if you have a disability.
>
> With me being gay, it's not something I broadcast . . . I sat in an office . . . with one wall which is a glass wall to the corridor, and I was in a meeting with my boss and a young girl walked past the windows with blond hair, and he stopped talking and stared. And I thought, I know what he is going to say, and I don't know what I am going to say back . . . And that's the point where you think, I can't turn around to you and say, Well, actually I am gay.

An additional stress was caused when people did not see the designated workplace 'labels' as applicable to them. Jo said, 'The trouble is, which category do you put me in? Do you put me in male or female?' Ellen described herself as 'anti-label on many fronts'.

> I mean, I am mixed race. I was also adopted. So for a long time I didn't know where I was from. So I mean, you know those forms where they

ask you if you are of mixed heritage? For a while I was really angry about these because I didn't know where I was from, and I actually hated having to define myself. Because as far as I was concerned we are a human race; we are not a black race or white race, and I am mixed, so what? . . . [I] happen to be female, happen to be mixed race, happen to have a lesbian relationship. But my politics are about equality for everybody, you know, in terms of humanity; that's what I am interested in.

INTERSECTIONALITY AT WORK

In moving forward, most respondents were clear that they wanted to be themselves without having to hide key aspects of their identity at work. Fred said he would like to be treated as a 'black bisexual man . . . who just happens to be an engineer'. Bruce said he wanted his sexual orientation

> to have the same status as my gender, as my ethnicity, my disability . . . I want it to be given the same status. I don't want it to be an exception that I have to bring into the conversation. And also in terms of service delivery, then when we are talking about delivering services to service users, I want it to be seen as having an equal status—that it is equally as important as gender and ethnicity.

Respondents thought that employees who felt able to be themselves were more likely to feel satisfied in their work and thus more likely to stay. In addition, they pointed to the ways in which they added value to their organisations because of the insight their 'intersections' gave them. Helen, for example, said:

> One of my roles, in leading on a strategy with the remit around sexual orientation, has been about . . . being able to promote the inclusion of sexual orientation along with other areas . . . As a disabled lesbian . . . within the disability community in terms of sexual orientation you are often seen as heterosexual or not sexual at all. And similarly within the lesbian and gay community, the experience of being a disabled woman or disabled person within that is that you experience discrimination. . . . people don't always have that understanding. . . . I am able to bring those things in.

Shazia said that she too assisted her employer in developing a more intersectional approach to service delivery at work including making sure LGBT issues did not drop off the agenda:

> On the equality impact assessment thing that we did when it got to sexuality the majority of everyone was quiet . . . they were vocal on

issues around issues around gender, race, religion and disability . . . and definitely around religion, race and culture.

Robin was an active member of his organisation's BME and LGBT network groups, frequently co-organising events with the women's network. Such intersectional networking was common amongst the respondents, and a number argued that it 'added value' via the development of an intersectional knowledge base crucial to product and service innovation in an increasingly diverse UK economy.

CONCLUSION

This chapter has focused on the experiences of LGBT people who self-defined as having a disability and/or as BME in order to provide insight into the heterogeneity of LGBT people's experiences at work. All of the respondents worked for 'good practice employers' and felt able to participate in a research project on sexual orientation at work. As Ryan-Flood (2004) has pointed out, LGBT employees not in the labour force or in difficult working environments are less likely to be out and visible at work. This reminder is extremely pertinent given that the Office of National Statistics (ONS, 2011) figures indicate that just under one in every two disabled people is in employment in the UK, and official statistics illustrate substantial differences in economic activity rates and differential access to employment by ethnicity and gender (ONS, 2006).

Nevertheless, it is argued that the chapter has been valuable in offering an exploration of 'intersectionality as a lived experience' (Taylor, Hines and Casey, 2011: 4). These LGBT respondent's viewpoints have provided new insights into organisational life (Acker, 2000). Most had sought to work for 'good practice employers'. All had perceived their employers making progress across equality strands during the research period. However, crucially, their overall perception was that sexual orientation and gender identity and gender reassignment were not accorded the same status as race, disability or other equality strands within their organisations. This reinforces findings that LGBT issues remained a 'sensitive' area notwithstanding evidence that organisations had begun to adopt a more integrated approach to equalities post-2003 (Colgan, 2011; Richardson and Monro, 2012).

Despite an EO policy and a range of interventions including diversity training for managers and the establishment of equality networks, it was striking that these 'good practice' organisations were still not very comfortable places to be. For example, most of the respondents reported feeling isolated and lacking in role models, although organisation equality and trade union equality networks provided an important point of contact and support (Colgan and McKearney, 2012). The 'normal violence' of organisational life described by Acker (2000: 202) was perceived to be exacerbated by gendered and racialised organisational hierarchies and cultures. Thus despite equality legislation and EO policies, respondents, particularly those in the private sector, reported finding it difficult to challenge discriminatory attitudes and behaviour. This was particularly the case where senior and middle management did not reflect the diversity in the workplace and in predominantly male working environments. Faced with a discriminatory environment on race, disability and/or gender, it could seem 'wise' to conceal one's LGBT identity to avoid compounding any further problems which might arise in what could be perceived as a heterosexist and/or transphobic workplace (Molloy, Knight and Woodfield, 2003; Colgan et al., 2006). Alternatively, respondents adopted individual coping strategies, and/or sought support from family and friends and/or equality and trade union networks—and, in the most impossible situations, moved to escape the abuse (Ryan-Flood, 2004).

The research illustrated the effort and skills required in managing identity, visibility/invisibility and disclosure even in 'good practice employers'. Antenna had to be continuously alert in order to manage 'labels' and workplace interactions. It took skills and energy to 'live intersectionality' and develop space to be 'oneself'. Most organisations were perceived to suffer from a form of 'LGBT-blindness' generally but particularly in the case of disabled and BME respondents (Molloy, Knight and Woodfield, 2003; Guasp and Kibirige, 2013). Although the 'good practice employers' were considered to have introduced and promoted EO policies, these were perceived to have been unevenly implemented. The challenge for organisations was thus to move beyond policy to implementation in order to develop a workplace culture which allowed LGBT BME and disabled people to be themselves (i.e., not having to hide or downplay key aspects of their identity). The respondents pointed to the benefits to the organisation of developing a more inclusive culture, not just for themselves but in terms of the 'added value' intersectional knowledge bases could provide.

It is thus a matter of regret that the UK coalition government has backpedalled on the intersectional equality agenda envisioned by the establishment of the EHRC and the Equality Act (2010). In light of this, more research on the diversity of LGBT experiences is urgently required to develop understanding and positive ways forward in the equality and diversity field. This chapter concludes that intersectionality offers one useful analytical approach to provide this by exploring the 'multifaceted ways' in which sexuality and gender intertwine with other social divisions and subjectivities in specific historical and cultural locations (Casey et al., 2010: 804).

ACKNOWLEDGMENTS

I would like to thank the research participants. I would also like to thank Pauline Baseley and Chrissy Hunter for comments on an earlier draft of this chapter.

NOTES

1. Estimates of the LGBT population vary from 5 to 7 percent (Mitchell et al., 2008). Despite considerable lobbying by LGB organisations, the Office of National Statistics (ONS) decided not to include a question on sexual orientation in the 2011 UK Census. In 2009, the Office for National Statistics introduced a sexual orientation question in its Integrated Household Survey of the UK. Although disappointed at the lack of a Census question, Stonewall welcomed the ONS collection of some data on the LGB population and suggested that the number of people feeling able to identify as LGB would increase as people became more confident and sexual orientation became a routine question in official data collection (BBC, 2010).
2. *Trans* is used in this chapter as an umbrella term to refer to the range of identities within the gender identity spectrum.
3. In order to overcome difficulties in negotiating research access in a relatively new and sensitive area of research, we identified and accessed the sixteen 'good practice employers' with the assistance of employers' organisations, trade unions and LGBT groups such as Stonewall. Twelve of the sixteen organisations which agreed to participate were members of Stonewall's Diversity Champion's Programme, which brought together organisations committed to equal opportunities and to tackling sexual orientation discrimination (Colgan et al., 2006).

REFERENCES

Acker, J. (2000) 'Revisiting Class: Thinking from Gender, Race and Organizations', *Social Politics,* 7 (2): 192–214.

Adib, A. and Guerrier, Y. (2003) 'The Interlocking of Gender with Nationality, Race, Ethnicity and Class: The Narratives of Women in Hotel Work,' *Gender, Work and Organization,* 10 (4): 413–432.

Beckett, C. (2004) 'Crossing the Border: Locating Heterosexuality as a Boundary for Lesbian and Disabled Women', *Journal of International Women's Studies,* 5 (3): 44–52.

Bell, M., Ozbilgin, M., Beauregard, T. and Surgevil, O. (2011) 'Voice, Silence and Diversity in 21st Century Organizations: Strategies for Inclusion of Gay, Lesbian, Bisexual and Transgender Employees', *Human Resource Management,* 50 (1) : 131–146.

British Broadcasting Company (2010) 'UK Gay, Lesbian and Bisexual Population Revealed', available at: http://www.bbc.co.uk/news/uk-11398629 (accessed 14 Jan. 2014).

Brothers, M. (2000) *It's Not Just about Ramps and Braille: Disability and Sexual Orientation,* London: Disability Rights Commission.

Browne, K. and Nash, C. (2010) *Queer Methods and Methodologies,* Farnham: Ashgate.

Burke, M. (1993) *Coming out of the Blue,* London: Cassell.

Casey, M., Hines, S., Richardson, D. and Taylor, Y. (2010) 'Introduction', *Sociology: Special Edition on Sexuality,* 44 (5): 803–810.

Colgan, F. (2011) 'Equality, Diversity and Corporate Social Responsibility: Sexual Orientation in the UK Private Sector', *Equality, Diversity and Inclusion,* 30 (8): 719–734.

Colgan. F., Creegan, C., McKearney, A. and Wright, T. (2006) *Lesbian, Gay and Bisexual Workers: Equality, Diversity and inclusion in the Workplace,* London: COERC, London Metropolitan University.

Colgan, F. and McKearney, A. (2012) 'Visibility and Voice in Organisations: Lesbian, Gay, Bisexual and Transgendered Employee Networks', *Equality, Diversity and Inclusion*, 31 (4); 359–378.

Colgan, F. and Wright, T (2011). 'Lesbian, Gay and Bisexual Equality in a Modernising Public Sector: Opportunities and Threats', *Gender, Work and Organisation*, 18 (5): 548–570.

Colgan, F., Wright, T., Creegan, C. and McKearney, A. (2009) 'Equality and Diversity in the Public Services: Moving Forward on Lesbian, Gay and Bisexual Equality', *Human Resource Management Journal*, 19 (3): 280–301.

Crenshaw, K., Gotanda, N., Peller, G. and Kendall, T. (eds) (1995) *Critical Race Theory: The Key Writings that Formed the Movement*, New York: New Press.

Department for Business, Innovation and Skills (2011) *The Plan for Growth*, London: HM Treasury.

Dill, B., Murray, S. and Weber, L. (2001). 'Defining the Work of the Consortium: What Do We Mean by Intersections?' *Newsletter of the Consortium of Race, Gender and Ethnicity*, Spring: 4–5.

Dunne, G. (1997) *Lesbian Lifestyles: Women's Work and the Politics of Sexuality*, Basingstoke: Macmillan.

Guasp, A. and Kibirige, H. (2013) *One Minority at a Time: Being Black and Gay*, London: Stonewall.

Harding, R. and Peel, E. (2007) 'Heterosexism at Work: Diversity Training, Discrimination Law and the Limits of Individualism', in V. Clarke and E. Peel (eds), *Out in Psychology: Lesbian, Gay, Trans and Queer Perspectives*, London: John Wiley.

Hines, S. (2010) 'Queerly Situated? Exploring Negotiations of Trans Queer Subjectivities at Work and within Community Spaces in the UK', *Gender, Place & Culture: A Journal of Feminist Geography*, 17 (5): 597–163.

Humphrey, J. (1998) 'Self-Organise and Survive: Disabled People in the British Trade Union Movement', *Disability and Society*, 13 (4): 587–602.

Keogh, P., Dodds, C. and Henderson, L. (2004) *Ethnic Minority Gay Men: Redefining Community, Restoring Identity*, London: Sigma Research.

McCall, L. (2005) 'The Complexity of Intersectionality', *Signs: Journal of Women in Culture and Society*, 30 (3): 1771–1798.

McDermott, E. (2006) 'Surviving in Dangerous Places: Lesbian Identity Performances in the Workplace, Social Class and Psychological Health', *Feminism and Psychology*, 16 (2): 193–211.

McManus, S. (2003) *Sexual Orientation Research Phase 1: A Review of Methodological Approaches*, Edinburgh: Scottish Executive.

Mitchell, M., Howarth, C., Kotecha, M. and Creegan, C. (2008) *Sexual Orientation Research Review 2008*, Manchester: Equality and Human Rights Commission Research Report 34.

Molloy, D., Knight, T. and Woodfield, K. (2003) *Diversity in Disability*, London: Department of Work and Pensions Research Report No. 188.

Monro, S. (2005) *Gender Politics: Activism, Citizenship and Sexual Diversity*, London: Pluto Press.

Office of National Statistics (2006) *Focus on Ethnicity and Religion, 2006 Edition*, available at: www.ons.gov.uk/ons/rel/ethnicity/focus-on-ethnicity-and-religion/2006-edition/index.html (accessed 16 Sept. 2013).

Office of National Statistics (2011) *People with Disabilities in the Labour Market, 2011*, available at: www.ons.gov.uk/ons/rel/lmac/people-with-disabilities-in-the-labour-market/2011/rpt-people-with-disabilities-in-the-labour-market.html#tab-Just-under-1-in-every-2-disabled-people-in-employment (accessed 16 Sept. 2013).

Richardson, D. and Monro, S. (2012) *Sexuality, Equality and Diversity*, Basingstoke: Palgrave Macmillan.

Roberts, S. (2011) 'Exploring How Gay Men Manage Their Social Identities in the Workplace: The Internal/External Dimensions of Identity', *Equality, Diversity and Inclusion,* 30 (8): 668–685.

Rumens, N. (2012) 'Queering Cross-Sex Friendships: An Analysis of Gay and Bisexual Men's Workplace Friendships with Heterosexual Women', *Human Relations,* 65 (8): 955–978.

Rumens, N. and Broomfield, J. (2012) 'Gay Men in the Police: Identity Disclosure and management Issues', *Human Resource Management Journal,* 22 (3): 283–298.

Ryan-Flood, R. (2004) 'Beyond Recognition and Redistribution: A Lesbian and Gay Case Study', *Gender Institute New Working Paper Series No. 12,* London: London School of Economics.

Safra Project (2003) *Identifying the Difficulties Experienced by Muslim LGBT Women in Accessing Social and Legal Services,* London: SAFRA Project.

Squires, J (2010) 'Intersecting Inequalities: Britain's Equality Review', *International Feminist Journal of Politics,* 11 (4): 496–512.

Stonewall (2012) *Living Together: British Attitudes to Lesbian, Gay and Bisexual People in 2012.* London: Stonewall.

Taylor, Y., Hines, S. and Casey, M. (2011) *Theorizing Intersectionality and Sexuality,* Basingstoke: Palgrave Macmillan.

Ward, J. (2008) *Sexualities, Work and Organizations,* London: Routledge.

Whittle, S., Turner, L. and Al-Alami, M. (2007) *Engendered Penalties: Transgender and Transsexual People's Experiences of Inequality and Discrimination,* London: Press for Change.

Williams, C. and Guiffre, P. (2011) 'From Organizational Sexuality to Queer Organizations: Research on Homosexuality and the Workplace', *Sociology Compass,* 5 (7): 551–563.

Wright, T. (2013) 'Uncovering Sexuality and Gender: An Intersectional Examination of Women's Experience in UK Construction', *Construction Management and Economics,* 13 (8): 832–844.

Yuval-Davis, N. (2006) 'Intersectionality and Feminist Politics', *European Journal of Women's Studies,* 13 (3): 193–209.

8 Working Across Differences in Sexuality and Age

Australian Stories of Young LGBQ Workers' Experiences in Paid Employment

Paul Willis

INTRODUCTION

This chapter focuses on the experiences of young people who are in paid employment and who identify as lesbian, gay, bisexual or queer (LGBQ). Despite a sizeable literature on LGBT sexualities and workplace discrimination, little attention has been given to the work experiences of sexually diverse young people. In this chapter I shed more light on their work-based interactions with other employees and members of management. There are two aims to this chapter. The first is to examine how young workers describe heteronormative work environments; more specifically, how young people experience and respond to discursive and material violence in the workplace. The second is to explore how differences in age and sexuality shape the interactions of young LGBQ workers with other employees and managers. To achieve these aims, I present three case studies extracted from an exploratory study into the working life of younger employees (eighteen to twenty-six years) located across a range of occupations and industries in the Australian labour market. Between 2005 and 2006, thirty-four young people shared their experiences of paid employment as either fixed term (full-time and part-time) or casual employees. Focussing on case studies provides an opportunity to undertake a more in-depth analysis of young employees' stories of work participation. Throughout this discussion, I use the abbreviation LGBQ to capture the sexual identity labels referred to by the research participants.

YOUTH PARTICIPATION IN THE CONTEMPORARY LABOUR MARKET

Youth participation in the Australian labour market is compounded by a number of structural and economic factors that can limit the work opportunities available to young people under twenty-four years of age. In Australian workplaces, young people are frequently located in 'precarious' employment and working in vulnerable positions of 'low pay, employment insecurity and working-time insecurity' (White and Wyn 2008: 174). Reporting on labour market trends, Jefferson and Preston (2012: 310) indicate that the employment of young people fifteen to twenty-four years remains predominately unstable as this generation 'continue[s] to experience relatively high levels of unemployment and underutilization' in Australian employment. Part-time work is the largest source of employment for young workers in primarily service and retail industries (Jefferson and Preston 2012). McDonald et al. (2007) argue that young Australians' vulnerability in employment is heightened by their overrepresentation in casualised and low-skilled occupations and their receipt of lower earnings in comparison to older workers (referred to as 'youth wages' for employees under twenty-one in Australian industrial law). Furthermore, young people continue to be underrepresented in industrial union membership in comparison to employees over twenty-five (Bailey et al. 2010).

Under Australian law, young employees of legal working age are entitled to the same minimum standards as other employees, including protection from age- and sexuality-based discrimination (Fair Work Act 2009, cited in Fair Work Ombudsman 2013). In parallel, each state and territory has equalities legislation in place that seeks to protect employees from unfair treatment on the basis of both age and sexuality, amongst other social characteristics. However, this legislation remains weakened by a number of exemptions—federal and state legislation grant religious employers' permission to discriminate on the grounds of sexuality (Australian Human Rights Commission 2011). Whereas some young workers are legally protected from discriminatory treatment in industries such as public service or retail, young LGBQ people pursuing vocations in religious organizations, for example, or in teaching or in welfare provision may not be shielded.

A small number of empirical studies from Australia have touched on the experiences of young workers under thirty years of age who identify as LGBQ (Carpenter 2008; Emslie 1998; Hillier et al. 2010). This research indicated some overarching themes that chime with the reported experiences of other LGBQ Australian workers (Aaron and Ragusa 2011; Asquith 1999; Irwin 1999, 2002). The third national survey of same-sex attracted youth indicated that 17 percent of respondents (fourteen to twenty-one years) who reported verbal or physical violence had been targets of abuse in their workplaces (Hillier et al. 2010). Earlier survey research likewise suggests LGBQ Australians are the subject of homophobic abuse and discrimination in their workplaces, across industry and occupation (Irwin 1999). Over half the respondents (59%) in Irwin's survey of nine hundred lesbian, gay and transgender employees reported some form of homophobic or discriminatory treatment in their current and/or previous workplace (Irwin 1999: 28). In relation to economic wellbeing, Carpenter (2008) estimates that young lesbian women (twenty-two to twenty-seven years) working in Australia are more likely to earn 30 percent less than heterosexual women in similar roles and more likely to report difficulties in obtaining paid employment.

National survey research into homophobic attitudes indicates differences in opinions between Australian generations—56 percent of respondents over sixty-five years regarded homosexuality as 'immoral' in comparison to 26 percent of young people aged eighteen to twenty-four years (Flood and Hamilton 2005). Whereas this shift between generations is encouraging, it does suggest that young LGBQ workers are more likely to encounter homophobic views in their interactions with older employees in comparison to coworkers of similar age.

Research from the UK presents a more diverse picture for younger LGBQ workers. Colgan et al.'s (2006) research indicates both positive and negative experiences for young lesbian, gay and bisexual workers employed in England. The majority of young workers (sixteen to twenty-two years) participating in focus groups recounted experiences of homophobia at work and consequentially believed they could not be 'out' in the workplace. Conversely, other qualitative findings highlight how nearly two-thirds of participants in 'good practice' case studies were 'out' to everybody at work. Participants indicated a number of positive conditions in good practice organisations which enabled them to discuss their sexual identity in work relationships—for example, through organisations promoting equality policies as part of recruitment events (Colgan et al. 2006: 43).

THEORETICAL UNDERPINNINGS

This discussion is based on a relational approach to theorising sexuality and power. Burrell and Hearn (1989) assert that power and sexuality operate as relational forces in organisational environments, as power and sexual dynamics are continually constructed and negotiated in work relationships. Other authors argue that everyday interactions between employees involve sexualised performances in which heterosexuality is frequently privileged as the dominant standpoint (Bruni 2006; McDowell 2004; Valentine 2002). The repeated signifying of heterosexual metaphors can reinforce the naturalised appearance of heterosexuality. In doing so the absence of other sexualities, including LGBQ sexualities, is accentuated (Ward and Winstanley 2003). Two useful concepts in making sense of the synergy between sexuality and power in the workplace are heteronormativity and discursive violence.

Heteronormativity, according to Berlant and Warner (1998), can be defined as the saturation of heterosexual norms and values in contemporary Western societies. Heteronormative discourses relay taken-for-granted assumptions about heterosexual relations as 'natural' and 'normal' in which heterosexual experience is equated with human experience. Queer theorist Michael Warner (2000: 3) argues that the practice of publically shaming individuals about their sexual desires can be a powerful means of reinforcing the normality of heterosexual relations, as 'shame makes some pleasures tacitly inadmissible, unthinkable' in the public arena. In seeking to interrogate heteronormative logic, Yep (2002: 170) describes the effects of discursive violence: 'The words, tone gestures, and images that are used to differentially treat, degrade, pathologise, and represent lesbian and gay experiences'. Discursive violence encapsulates the everyday expressions, gestures and comments exchanged between individual agents that continually differentiate between heterosexual and nonheterosexual identities (Yep 2002). Similarly, Mason (2002) contends that homophobic violence operates as a process of subjectification by constructing knowledge claims about the intended victim and the wider collective group to which the victim is believed to belong. To illustrate, Mason (2002) examines how homophobic discourses construct negative representations about lesbian women as disruptive subjects who upset the assumed heterosexual bond between men and women.

Within youth and educational studies, increasing attention has been given to the ways in which LGBQ youth occupy subject positions outside victim discourse and seek to challenge homophobic beliefs and actions (Blackburn 2007; Hillier and Harrison 2004; McDermott, Roen, and Scourfield, 2008). Hillier and Harrison (2004) discuss the ways in which young people 'find the fault lines' in homophobic statements and construct positive identities despite the negative messages circulated in homophobic discourse. Their theoretical position echoes Michel Foucault's (1978) discussion of power as a productive force in which individuals have the capacity to exercise power within fields of application. In the case studies below I recount the ways in which young LGBQ employees attempt to exercise power in challenging work relationships.

METHOD

The case studies presented below are based on qualitative, focussed interviews with participants face-to-face. Participation was open to young people between sixteen and twenty-six years of age, who identified as nonheterosexual (or LGB) and had a minimum of six months current or recent experience of paid employment on a casual or fixed basis. The minimum age requirement was sixteen years, in line with ethical guidelines for young people to be able to give informed consent. The maximum age was set at twenty-six years in recognition of young people who may have recently completed tertiary education and entered graduate employment. Interviews ran between two to three hours and were conducted in private locations either on campus or at prearranged locations. Interview topics included quality of work relationships, perceptions of management and sources of support. The analysis of data was guided by the constructivist grounded theory method, as outlined by Charmaz (2006). Three cases have been selected as they fulfil two criteria. First, each case depicts young people's experiences in contrasting work environments across two separate industries, retail services and education. Second, these cases provide rich examples of the challenges young LGBQ employees can experience in negotiating the power relations embedded in work relationships. These cases are not intended to detract from more positive experiences of inclusive relationships; these stories are recounted elsewhere (Willis 2009).

MOSKOE'S STORY

Moskoe is a white man, twenty-three years of age; he identifies as gay. Moskoe reflected on his work experiences in two contrasting environments. In both organisations Moskoe classified himself as the 'only gay' employee. In his current position, Moskoe had been working for two years in a student support unit in a university located in a regional city with a population less than 500,000. Moskoe's current post as a disability administrative assistant was a permanent full-time post. Whereas his team members varied in age, the majority of staff were older and female. Moskoe described himself as 'out' in his current workplace, and his sexuality was common knowledge. He had formed close friendships with female colleagues of similar age, and his male partner had been included in work functions after hours. After commencing his current job, Moskoe had attempted to drop clues about his sexuality by referring to his 'partner' in conversations. However, his attempts to signal his sexuality were foiled by the androgynous name of his partner and the presumption of heterosexuality amongst other staff. As a more effective strategy, Moskoe deployed the services of the office gossip to convey information about his sexuality to the team:

> So I just said to one of them, to the finance woman here who does all the gossiping and all that business, and made it quite clear, planted the seed with her, and then she spread it around, so I knew it would happen. I just said, 'No, no [boyfriend's name] is a guy!' and then just took-off for the weekend and knew by Monday that everyone would know, and it was a lot easier doing it that way then, you know, going round telling everyone.

In spite of this convenient channel of information, Moskoe still had to endure the presumption of heterosexuality expressed by newcomers to the team.

Moskoe described his interactions with colleagues and senior staff as generally positive, respectful and inclusive. He maintained a good relationship with his older manager who he described as a 'role model'. His only source of frustration was his former colleague's use of the term *gay* as a derogatory expression—this was a younger woman who Moskoe had befriended. Their friendship enabled Moskoe to feel comfortable to challenge her comments: 'If she said something about something "being gay" then I would pull her up; I'd say, "No, no, don't use it as derogatory term!" or "Yes, that is very homosexual"—so make fun of it'.

These experiences differed significantly from his former employment in a retail store located in a major capital city with a population exceeding two million. Balancing university study with work, Moskoe had worked in a customer service role on a casual basis for a sports store which, in his words, employed mostly 'jocks' of similar age (early twenties) and of mixed gender. Whereas Moskoe had not experienced any explicit homophobic abuse, he had found it difficult to connect with other staff with his sexuality being one significant source of social difference. Moskoe felt his coworkers did not understand his sexuality nor were they prepared to. This perception was compounded by his experiences of receiving confronting questions about his sexual attractions and relationships:

> They [sports store] had a lot of jocks there, so they didn't understand me being gay and that—there was one guy there who was talking about it, all the time, just going on about it, and I was just like, 'Oh god, come on!' . . . so he was going on about it all the time; I was thinking, God, shut up already! But he was just someone who was just so involved in being straight, in the straight world, that he just didn't get it, so he was quizzing me a lot . . . At first I was a bit upset about these jock guys that knew nothing about being gay and were just drilling me as if I was a [pause] not a freak, but just abnormal.

Moskoe had attempted to reciprocate by asking his colleagues questions about their sexual encounters: 'I'd ask them [jocks] questions about, you know, picking up, and they ask me about cruising and stuff like that, so it's a healthy exchange in the end'. He had also tried to downplay differences in sexuality and build rapport with his colleagues by emphasising points of similarity between their romantic relationships and his own same-sex relationship:

> So that's why I tried to make sure that I was as functional and normal as everybody else and just acted as, like, normally—not hide the fact that I had a boyfriend, you know, just be exactly the same as any other guys but just change the gender around, change the partner sort of thing.

Despite these challenges, the job had its advantages—Moskoe felt his work was well regarded by management, and he appreciated the flexibility of casual employment, sometimes working thirteen consecutive days. This flexibility enabled him to balance his university studies with his working life.

INGRID'S STORY

Ingrid is a white woman, twenty-three years of age, and she identifies as gay. At the time of interview, Ingrid had recently graduated as a primary school teacher and was employed in her second year of teaching at a Catholic school. The school was based in a suburban area on the fringes of a regional city with a population less than 500,000. Ingrid had not felt comfortable identifying as gay to other staff and did not intend to discuss this with students. Initially, Ingrid had experienced 'paranoia' on two levels—paranoia about the ways in which older colleagues may perceive her identity as a gay woman and paranoia about parents' knowledge and reactions to her sexuality. This feeling of paranoia was amplified by her location in a religious school; she was mindful that LGBQ sexualities did not sit comfortably alongside the doctrine of the Catholic Church.

Ingrid had not experienced discrimination or harassment, but she had witnessed a number of oppressive exchanges between staff and students about lesbian and gay sexualities. These experiences left her feeling isolated as a lesbian teacher in a primarily heterosexual work environment. On one occasion Ingrid overhead an older colleague express her opinions regarding gay children over a break in the school staffroom:

> Something came up one day, and she [older teacher] had kids of her own, and she said something about—oh, she lived with a man, and they were in a relationship, and his son was gay, and she was speaking about him one day . . . she said, 'Oh if any of my girls [daughters] ever felt like that I don't what I'd do—I'd have to kick 'em out!' And just that sort of attitude that you always worry about with your own life and then think, great! There goes another option of talking to someone and revealing a part of yourself that you'd kind of hoped to, I guess.

Witnessing a colleague discuss gay sexualities as a topic of moral disapproval temporarily reinforced Ingrid's silence about her sexual identity. However, this experience had not hindered Ingrid from eventually discussing her sexual identity and same-sex partner with other staff. Ingrid disclosed her sexuality to a small group of teachers, mainly older staff and the school principal, and was relieved to not encounter any negative responses. In general, this information was received in a positive and respectful manner.

Ingrid's greatest fear was the prospect of facing complaints from parents about a lesbian teacher working with their children. Throughout her story, Ingrid continually worried about maintaining appropriate work relationships with children and adolescents. Lesbian and gay identities and relationships were believed to be morally dangerous topics to discuss with children. While Ingrid had not encountered parental accusations, it was the possibility of facing such complaints that had a debilitating effect on her interactions with pupils:

> And so I guess I'm conscious of being alone with kids at all, and I mean all teachers really have to be as you know, but I'm always in sight; I always sit by the window; I try to have more than one person in the room at once—so just, automatically.

When faced with the recurring question, 'Are you gay?' from pupils, Ingrid elected to either ignore the question or respond in third person. These difficult discussions did not prevent Ingrid from verbally challenging the derogatory use of the term *gay* by her pupils. Ingrid shared some of the strategies she deployed to highlight to her students the absurdity of referring to people and objects as 'gay': 'You can joke with them and say, "Is that chair attracted to the other one beside it? Is that what you mean?"' Ingrid helped initiate a 'queer' arm of her local teachers' union branch in collaboration with several other lesbian and gay teachers working in schools in the same state. Ingrid had felt hesitant to campaign on behalf of other LGBQ teachers. Instead, she focussed her energies on expanding the coverage of LGBQ issues in teacher training curriculums. Other members of the union group were a similar age to Ingrid, in their early to late twenties, and were women that Ingrid had identified as a source of mutual support.

PEGGIE'S STORY

Peggie is a twenty-three-year-old white woman who identifies as both gay and lesbian. When sharing her experiences of working life, Peggie described how she had been the target of abuse and bullying by senior staff members across two separate organisations. Retail and service work was the primary industry Peggie was employed in during her seven years of casual and fixed-term employment. First, Peggie recounted her experiences of verbal abuse and harassment from an older male manager while working in a large bookstore. The bookstore was located in a capital city with a population in excess of two million. This was a new franchise store in which Peggie had quickly forged friendships with other staff of varying ages. Peggie described this workplace as a primarily positive environment: 'You got to know each other a lot during that time so it was a really good bonding session [smiles] . . . so we're all pretty much a family'. This friendly atmosphere was severely dampened by the actions of the general manager, an older heterosexual man who had ran into conflict with several coworkers. Peggie had been singled out as a target for public humiliation—for example, being denied a lunch break because she was 'too fat' and later on being the subject of harassment:

> And when he found out that I was gay, he just started to say the most rudest comments, and I just thought, You're a disgusting old

man . . . just stupid things like on our daily schedule he'd put me down as 'pussy licker' rather than write my name and, um, before we'd open up the shop he'd go, 'Could the lesbi-bite please come to . . .?' [over loudspeaker system] . . . He was really a sleaze, you know.

These negative experiences culminated in Peggie resigning from her job after several coworkers had also quit. After resigning, Peggie decided to raise her concerns by writing a letter of complaint to the head office. She received a highly affirmative response as staff from the head office recognised the harassment she had endured; this action culminated in her former manager being 'fired'.

Two years later, Peggie worked as a retail assistant for a men's clothing store. The store was based in a smaller regional city with a population less than 500,000, and the staff team comprised both younger employees of similar age to Peggie and older staff in managerial roles. Initially Peggie had built a rapport with the men employed as supervising managers who were at least ten years older, were married with children and had been working at the store for a longer period of time. Despite their initial friendliness, Peggie's interactions with the managers soon became difficult to endure as she began to experience bullying as 'one of the boys':

I think that the guys, they thought that you were one of the boys, pretty much, so you looked at chicks the way they looked at chicks, you mucked around like they'd muck around—and it went from like a fun, joking sort of thing to me coming home with bruises from my shoulders to my elbows, on my arms . . . and they thought that since you were a lesbian you could take the pain threshold of a male, which certainly isn't the case.

These incidences of 'mucking around' culminated in Peggie being assaulted by two managers during a weekend shift:

I think the final straw was when one Saturday one of my managers bear hugged me from behind and took me out to the shoe room and the other manager was there, and they taped my hands up behind my back and taped my feet up together and taped my mouth up and put me on the ground and threw shoes at me . . . I was freaking out, screaming, I was like, 'Please don't do it, cause I'm claustrophobic, and I'll freak out', you know [pause] . . . as soon as I got out of it, I grabbed my bag and walked home, and I made them pay me for the rest of the day.

Peggie's experiences of bullying did not deflect her from seeking to challenge the shift managers' actions. First, Peggie discussed her concerns with the culprits, who did not appear to understand her concerns. Second, Peggie had raised the issue with the human resources manager. Consequently, all staff were required to sign an agreement to show 'respect in the workplace'.

In Peggie's opinion, this policy had no effect because it was not enforced. Finally, Peggie discussed her concerns with the store general manager:

> He said, 'I'm really sorry that you feel that way, but if you want to look for further employment feel free to. I'll employ you until then'. And I turned around and said to him, 'I shouldn't have to look for further employment; you should be looking at your managers'.

After an extended period of ill health and limited income, Peggie decided to resign: '[I] didn't feel comfortable going to work, so I thought, Bugger it—I'm leaving!'. Shortly thereafter, Peggie obtained employment in a car retail outlet; her decision to quit had resulted in only a brief period of unemployment.

CONCLUDING DISCUSSION

Discursive and Material Violence in the Workplace

The above case studies highlight a spectrum of oppressive actions exercised in work relationships. The stories conveyed in these three cases show young people working within and against heteronormative arrangements in which heterosexuality is normalised and lesbian and gay sexualities are the subject of ridicule, abuse or cross-examination. Moskoe's and Ingrid's stories highlight the oppressive functions of discursive violence—the informal and implicit comments and questions exchanged between organisational participants, which these two young people experience as isolating and alienating as LGBQ employees. Discursive violence is an implicit means of drawing dividing lines between heterosexual and LGBQ identities and reinforcing the normative stance of heterosexuality (Yep 2002). Equally, all three case studies contain examples of how the practice of shaming, or the potential to be shamed, can operate as a powerfully subjectifying discourse for alienating LGBQ employees.

As argued by Warner (2000), the public act of shaming LGBQ individuals is an effective means of accentuating differences between nonnormative sexualities and heterosexuality. Heterosexuality is upheld as a cultural yardstick by which other sexual expressions are appraised. In Ingrid's case, the potential to be shamed at work through questions about her sexual identity and professional suitability heightened her sense of vulnerability as a lesbian employee. In school environments, LGBQ employees working with children are always mindful of the heteronormative gaze from students, staff and parents in which they could be misperceived as morally dubious employees. The potential accusation of paedophilia can work to frame LGBQ employees as 'dangerous subjects'. Likewise other lesbian and gay teachers have previously discussed how they learn to conceal their sexuality to avoid harassment from staff and students or in fear of being misinterpreted as morally dubious subjects (Ferfolja 2007, 2010; Morrow and Gill 2003). For Moskoe, being continually questioned about his sexual identity and attractions limited his capacity to speak with authority about his sexual desires and relationships. Under equalities law, it is highly unlikely these experiences would constitute discrimination, if reported at all, as current antidiscrimination measures fail to recognise more subtle forms of homophobia beyond reported acts of direct or indirect discrimination. In Ingrid's case she would have little protection from sexuality-based discrimination within a faith-based school, which is exempted under antidiscrimination law. Peggie experienced verbal abuse about her lesbian identity as an attempt to shame her and as a more explicit form of material violence.

In contrast to the other two case studies, Peggie's story contains examples of material violence in the workplace, as she was the target of verbal and physical abuse. Homophobic abuse can represent what Mason (2002) identifies as acts of 'spatial management'—attempts to reclaim organisational territories as heterosexual and masculine spaces. The expression of sexually explicit language, such as 'pussy licker', could be interpreted as an attempt to publically humiliate Peggie. Sexualised expressions such as this transmit homophobic discourses that position lesbian women's bodies as a source of bodily disorder and uncleanliness (Mason 2002). The managers who assaulted Peggie at the clothing store conveyed implicit messages about Peggie's identity as abnormal and outside heterosexual femininity. These material expressions and actions reproduce the normative status of heterosexuality, in particular male heterosexuality, in work environments.

Challenging and Responding to Homophobic Violence at Work

Encountering discursive and material violence at work mobilised these three young people to pursue a number of strategies geared towards change. Their stories bring attention to young LGBQ people's strengths and resourcefulness in combating negative work environments, albeit within restricted boundaries, and demonstrate their capacity to refute homophobic expressions in everyday relationships. To borrow Hillier and Harrison's (2004) expression, these stories represent young LGBQ workers efforts in 'finding the fault lines' in homophobic discourse. This discussion contributes to wider literature in youth studies that recognises the capacity of LGBQ youth to transcend victim identities (Hillier and Harrison 2004; Blackburn 2007; McDermott, Roen, and Scourfield 2008). Both Moskoe and Ingrid attempted to challenge the ridiculing comments voiced by others. However, there are limitations to the extent these young people can challenge these comments. In Ingrid's case, her strategy of questioning the homophobic remarks of her students could result in her sexuality becoming the subject of scrutiny. Ingrid's story highlights her proactive work in helping to kickstart a queer teachers' network and to lead initiatives in promoting a more inclusive curriculum for trainee teachers. The anxiety Ingrid experienced in her teaching role did not inhibit her from leading on this work. Other young LGBQ employees may likewise have valuable contributions to make to developing inclusive work practices and policy and should not be disregarded because of their age or limited work history.

Peggie took the plunge to vacate two abusive work environments—this is a high-risk strategy that may not be an option for other young employees. Resigning sends a clear message that an injustice has occurred against the vacating employee. Conversely, vacating abusive work environments can be understood as a convenient means of control for both the organisation and for perpetrators of abuse as the victim is removed from the organisation (Lutgen-Sandvik 2006). Taking this course of action comes at a high cost with the risk of continued unemployment and the loss of income. Whereas Peggie quickly found new employment, resigning from work may not be feasible for other young workers in industries in which employment is not as readily available or for young people who are in the early stages of pursuing career pathways. For example, it would be difficult for Ingrid as a newly qualified teacher to obtain new teaching opportunities in primary education mid-term. Leaving employment also threatens young people's economic stability.

Colgan et al.'s (2006) research suggests that some young people pursuing careers are prepared to demand positive and equal treatment as LGBQ employees. Negative experiences of homophobic abuse and harassment may complicate young people's attempts to seek equal treatment or thwart their initial attempts to pursue chosen careers. Moving between employment in the retail and service sector may be highly debilitating for young workers as they may be limited to predominantly casualised, low-skilled or unstable employment, or 'underutilization' in the labour market (Jefferson and Preston 2012). It also complicates their attempts to develop trusting relationships with other staff as some young people may need time to establish rapport with colleagues before feeling safe to discuss their sexual identities.

The Social Location of young LGBQ Workers: Accounting for Differences in Age

Differences in age and organisational status permeate the stories of these three young Australians in diverging ways. In Peggie's story, she describes herself as the subject of abuse and harassment from older male members of management. This resonates with the responses of other lesbian, gay and transgender adults employed in Australian organisations who have previously reported 'managers, supervisor or employers' as the largest group of perpetrators of abuse or harassment (Irwin 1999). Whereas this did not reflect Peggie's wider experiences of working with staff members of different ages, it does raise concerns about the potential of homophobic abuse to erode younger employee's trust in management. Likewise, it undermines young LGBQ workers' sense of inclusion in their work relationships. This is an important consideration given that Hillier et al. (2005, 37) have argued: 'Resilience in young people is dependent on connectedness and trust in other people, two things that are destroyed when young people are treated as outsiders'. Colgan et al.'s (2006) UK research previously identified line managers as a possible source of support for LGBQ employees experiencing discrimination. If younger employees do not have this recourse to support, this severely limits their options for accessing help and guidance from staff in positions of higher authority.

In contrast, Moskoe's and Ingrid's stories do not contain any discernible patterns on the basis of age. Both young people had either received or overheard heterosexist remarks from older colleagues—verbal remarks in which LGBQ workers were presumed to be straight or lesbian and gay sexualities were devalued. Conversely, both individuals reported positive relationships with colleagues of different ages, which problematise attempts to perceive differences in age as a reliable indicator of unequal treatment. At the same time, similarities in age between staff cannot be assumed to guarantee support or inclusion among employees. Moskoe's interactions with his peers in the sports store highlight how likeness in age does not necessarily bridge differences in sexual identity.

Finally, and in conclusion, it is important to emphasise that differences in both age and sexuality did not prevent all three young people from forming positive and validating work relationships in their workplaces. Whereas heteronormative assumptions may overshadow some work environments, this dominant discourse is by no means immobilising; employees of different sexualities and age continually form and maintain inclusive work relationships within its field of application.

REFERENCES

Aaron, David J. and Angela T. Ragusa. 2011. 'Policy Implications of Gay Men's Workplace Experiences: Public Service Employees in Australia's Capital, Canberra'. *Policy Studies* 32 (6): 615–630.

Asquith, Nicole. 1999. 'Sexuality at Work: A Study of Lesbians' Workplace Experiences'. *New Zealand Journal of Industrial Relations* 24 (1): 1–19.

Australian Human Rights Commission. 2011. *Addressing Sexual Orientation and Sex and/or Gender Identity Discrimination: Consultation Report.* www.hreoc. gov.au/human_rights/lgbti/lgbticonsult/report/index.html (accessed 1 November 2012).

Bailey, Janis, Robin Price, Lin Esders, and Paula McDonald. 2010. 'Daggy Shirts, Daggy Slogans? Marketing Unions to Young People'. *Journal of Industrial Relations* 52 (1): 43–60.

Berlant, Laurent and Michael Warner. 1998. 'Sex in Public'. *Critical Inquiry* 24 (2): 547–566.

Blackburn, Mollie. 2007. 'The Experiencing, Negotiation, Breaking, and Remaking of Gender Rules and Regulations by Queer Youth'. *Journal of Gay and Lesbian Issues in Education* 4 (2): 33–54.

Bruni, Attila. 2006. 'Have You Got a Boyfriend or Are You Single?': On the Importance of Being "Straight" in Organisational Research'. *Gender, Work and Organisation* 13 (3): 299–316.

Burrell, Gibson and Jeff Hearn. 1989. 'The Sexuality of Organisation'. In *The Sexuality of Organisation*, edited by Jeff Hearn, Deborah L. Sheppard, Peta Tancred-Sheriff, and Gibson Burrell, 1–28. London: Sage Publications.

Carpenter, Christopher. 2008. 'Sexual Orientation, Income, and Nonpecuniary Economic Outcomes: New Evidence from Young Lesbians in Australia'. *Review of Economics of the Household* 6 (4): 391–408.

Charmaz, Cathy C. 2006. *Constructing Grounded Theory: A Practical Guide through Qualitative Analysis*. London: Sage Publications.

Colgan, Fiona, Chris Creegan, Aidan McKearney, and Tessa Wright. 2006. *Lesbian, Gay and Bisexual Workers—Equality, Diversity and Inclusion in the Workplace*. www.workinglives.org/londonmet/library/c85513_3.pdf (accessed 1 December 2009).

Emslie, Mic. 1998. ' "Paying for an Identity": Issues Facing Young Gay People in the Workplace'. In *Against the Odds: Young People and Work*, edited by Judith Bessant and S. Cook, 159–168. Hobart: Australian Clearinghouse for Youth Studies.

Fair Work Ombdusman. 2013. *Best Practice Guide; A Guide for Young Workers*. www.fairwork.gov.au/BestPracticeGuides/04-A-guide-for-young-workers.pdf (accessed 1 November 2012).

Ferfolja, Tania. 2007. 'Teacher Negotiations of Sexual Subjectivities'. *Gender and Education* 19 (5): 569–586.

Ferfolja, Tania. 2010. Lesbian teachers, harassment and the workplace. *Teaching and Teacher Education* 26 (3): 408–414.

Flood, Michael and Clive Hamilton. 2005. *Mapping Homophobia in Australia*. www.glhv.org.au/files/aust_inst_homophobia_paper.pdf (accessed 21 July 2011).

Foucault, Michel. 1978. *The History of Sexuality, Volume 1: An Introduction*. London: Penguin Books.

Hillier, Lynne and Lyn Harrison. 2004. 'Homophobia and the Production of Shame: Young People and Same Sex Attraction'. *Culture, Health & Sexuality* 6 (1): 79–94.

Hillier, Lynne, Tiffany Jones, Marisa Monagle, Naomi Overton, Luke Gahan, Jennifer Blackman, and Anne Mitchell. 2010. *Writing Themselves In 3—The Third National Study on the Sexual Health and Wellbeing of Same Sex Attracted and Gender Questioning Young People*. http://www.glhv.org.au/files/wti3_web_sml.pdf (accessed 30 June 2011)

Hillier, Lynne, Alina Turner, and Anne Mitchell. 2005. *Writing Themselves in Again—6 Years On. The 2nd National Report on the Sexual Health & Well-Being of Same Sex Attracted Young People in Australia*. Melbourne: Australian Research Centre in Sex, Health & Society, La Trobe University.

Irwin, Jude. 1999. *The Pink Ceiling is Too Low—Workplace Experiences of Lesbians, Gay Men and Transgender People*. Sydney: Australian Centre for Lesbian and Gay Research, University of Sydney.

Irwin, Jude. 2002. 'Discrimination against Gay Men, Lesbians and Transgender People Working in Education'. *Journal of Gay & Lesbian Social Services* 14 (2): 65–77.

Jefferson, Therese and Alison Preston. 2012. 'Labour Markets and Wages in Australia in 2011'. *Journal of Industrial Relations* 54 (3): 293–311.

Lutgen-Sandvik, Pamela. 2006. 'Take This Job and . . . : Quitting and Other Forms of Resistance to Workplace Bullying'. *Communication Monographs* 73 (4): 406–433.

Mason, Gail 2002. *The Spectacle of Violence—Homophobia, Gender and Knowledge*. London: Routledge.

McDermott, Elizabeth, Katrina Roen, and Jonathan Scourfield. 2008. 'Avoiding Shame: Young LGBT People, Homophobia and Self-Destructive Behaviours'. *Culture, Health and Sexuality* 10: 815–829.

McDonald, Pauline, Janis Bailey, Damian Oliver, and Barbara Pini. 2007. 'Compounding Vulnerability? Young Workers' Employment Concerns and the Anticipated Impact of the WorkChoices Act'. *Australian Bulletin of Labour* 33 (1): 60–88.

McDowell, Linda. 2004. 'Sexuality, Desire and Embodied Performances in the Workplace'. In *Sexuality Repositioned: Diversity and the Law*, edited by Belinda Brooks-Gordon, Loraine Gelsthorpe, Martin Johnson, and Andrew Bainham, 85–107. Oxford: Hart Publishing.

Morrow, Ronald G. and Diane L. Gill. 2003. 'Perceptions of Homophobia and Heterosexism in Physical Education'. *Research Quarterly for Exercise and Sport* 74 (2): 205–214.

Valentine, Gill. 2002. 'Queer Bodies and the Production of Space'. In *Handbook of Lesbian and Gay Studies*, edited by Diane Richardson and Steven Seidman, 145–160. London: Sage Publications.

Ward, James and Diana Winstanley. 2003. 'The Absent Presence: Negative Space Within Discourse and the Construction of Minority Sexual Identity in the Workplace'. *Human Relations* 56 (10): 1255–1280.

Warner, Michael. 2000. *The Trouble with Normal—Sex, Politics, and the Ethics of Queer Life*. Cambridge: Harvard University Press.

White, Rob and Johanna Wyn. 2008. *Youth & Society—Exploring the Social Dynamics of Youth Experience*. 2nd edition. Melbourne: Oxford University Press.

Willis, Paul. 2009. 'From Exclusion to Inclusion: Young Queer Workers' Negotiations of Sexually Exclusive and Inclusive Spaces in Australian Workplaces'. *Journal of Youth Studies* 12: 629–651.

Yep, Gust A. 2002. 'From Homophobia and Heterosexism to Heteronormativity: Toward the Development of a Model of Queer Interventions in the University Classroom'. *Journal of Lesbian Studies* 6 (3/4): 163–176.

9 Working the Margins

Belonging and the Workplace for Lgbti in Post-Apartheid South Africa

Mikki van Zyl

INTRODUCTION

This chapter addresses how South African lesbians, gays, bisexuals, transgender and intersex people (lgbti)[1] negotiate the disjunctions between citizenship—which promises equality, inter alia, on the basis of sex, gender and sexual orientation—and everyday homoprejudice in the workplace. The Bill of Rights in the South African Constitution Act 108 of 1996, names a comprehensive list of identities for nondiscrimination. Understandably, post-apartheid studies on workplace equity focus predominantly on race, and whereas some address gender, they are mostly delimited to women in the workplace. This study contributes to the paucity of research on sexual orientation in the workplace in South Africa. Using a lens of 'belonging' it illuminates the dialectic between formal rights in citizenship and everyday homoprejudice. First I sketch the South African context, and then I examine lgbti citizenship through reference to the concept of active citizenship and apply Yuval-Davis's (2011) analytical framework for belonging to understand how twenty-two lgbti South Africans negotiate marginalisation at work—that is, 'work the margins'.

SOUTH AFRICAN CONTEXT

In 1996, South Africa was the first country in the world to provide constitutional protection against discrimination for sexual orientation. The foundations for these provisions were laid through lgbti mobilisation during the anti-apartheid struggle (Van Zyl 2005a). To redress historic inequalities and prevent discrimination, especially in the workplace, numerous policies and laws were enacted. The Employment Equity Act (No. 55 of 1998) (EEA) and the Promotion of Equality and Prevention of Unfair Discrimination Act (No. 4 of 2000) (PEPUDA) are keystones in labour equality. Although the laws are inclusive of the full range of marginalised groups as listed in the Bill of Rights, in practice a hierarchy of in/equalities has emerged with race discrimination the most frequent challenge in the Constitutional Court

(Mokgoro 2003). Twenty years after the end of apartheid, white economic and social privilege is still pervasive in South Africa; the country also has one of the biggest gaps between rich and poor in the world (Oswin 2007). Although a wealthy black élite and burgeoning black middle-class have emerged, most poor people are black women (Armstrong, Lekezwa and Siebrits 2008). In spite of gender equality measures on paper, South Africa consistently records the highest incidences of gender hate crimes (Mkhize et al. 2010). Therefore South Africa simultaneously boasts one of the best legislative and policy frameworks for gender equity and protection against discrimination, and an environment where women and lgbti people encounter cultures suffused with coercive heteropatriarchal norms.

Civil society movements have been essential in struggles for gender and sexual rights. The National Coalition for Lesbian and Gay Equality—now the Lesbian and Gay Equality Project—embarked on a deliberate strategy of challenging remaining discriminatory legislation through the courts (Oswin 2007). It succeeded in having numerous laws overturned, amended or enacted to ensure legal equality in all spheres of life for lgbti (Van Zyl 2005b). Yet, the majority of precedent-setting cases were contested by government, often all the way to the Constitutional Court. Whereas South Africa prided itself on its constitution, a discourse about homosexuality being 'unAfrican' had been reverberating amongst other African leaders. For the first ten years, African National Congress (ANC) leaders stood by the principles of equality in a constitutional democracy, whilst simultaneously implementing neoliberal economic policies. These laid the foundation for expressions of popular discontent with the country's levels of poverty, in turn bolstering the political ascendancy of Jacob Zuma in 2006. As president, and in defiance of the constitution, he undermines previous gains in gender equality through sexist and homophobic comments (Msibi 2011), feeding populist constructions of a reified and regressive concept of 'African' masculinity (Morrell, Jewkes and Lindegger 2012). Thus, the constitutional guarantees of equality on the basis of sex, gender and sexual orientation exist in counterpoint to hegemonic cultures of heteropatriarchy. At the forefront are contestations about 'an authentic African identity' which emerged as part of postcolonial recuperation rooted in South Africa's racist past. Whereas African leaders decry homosexuality as a 'colonial import', lgbti activists assert that homophobia, introduced during colonialism, is 'unAfrican' (Msibi 2011; Van Zyl 2011). Foremost among those who condemn homosexuality are religious fundamentalists, who follow 'imported' colonial faiths. Within this context of entangled axes of power I examine the everyday working lives of lgbti participants in this study.

CITIZENSHIP AND BELONGING

Focusing on citizenship and belonging enables particular in/equalities to be exposed. This is achieved, in part, through eliciting both the affective and political dimensions of citizenship. I emphasise also the importance of 'active citizenship' for addressing historical inequalities in the workplace for lgbti rights in South Africa. Although democratic citizenship is generally understood to be based on ideals of equality, numerous theorists have demonstrated that citizenship is constructed normatively, reflecting social hegemonies. Feminists have shown its gendering (Lister 2003; Yuval-Davis 2011), queer theorists underscore its heteronormative dimension (Plummer 2003; Richardson 2005), whilst race and class theorists show how it is raced, ethnicised and classed (Dhaliwali 1995; Anthias 2001). Taken together, this research demonstrates how in/equality in citizenship is shaped by discourses of difference and power. Most acknowledge the intersectionality of inequalities (Yuval-Davis 2006)—the simultaneous and enmeshed discriminations impacting someone's social location.

Feminist theorists on citizenship argue that for democracy to work citizens should be politically active (Lister 2003)—that rights come with responsibilities. It includes participation not only in governance, but also in autonomous civil society movements and organisations (Yuval-Davis 1997; Lister 2003). Thus citizenship is more than the relationship between individual subject and state, requiring citizens' active participation such as the ongoing lgbti post-apartheid mobilisation despite South Africa's legislative gains in gender and sexual rights (Van Zyl 2005b). I use the 'thicker' concept of *belonging* to understand unevenness in entitlements to rights and responsibilities in citizenship and to acknowledge the affective dimensions of citizenship. Yuval-Davis (2011) suggests that *belonging* is about who we are and being part of a community; it is also about inclusion and recognition, feeling at home and feeling safe. In her analytical framework for deconstructing belonging, Yuval-Davis posits three interrelated but analytically distinct facets which mark out the boundaries of belonging: social locations; identities and attachments to communities; political values of inclusions/exclusions or identification with others. A *politics of belonging* becomes salient when the boundaries of belonging are contested through struggles and resistance, not only around the entitlements of belonging to a particular political community but also about the symbolic rights to define belonging—struggles about 'us' and 'them' (Yuval-Davis 2011). I use the different facets of *belonging* and the *politics of belonging* as a framework for analysing participants' belonging in the workplace.

Social Locations

Social locations are ascriptive positions for people in categories of, for example, race, class, gender, sex and so on; they carry 'weights in the grids of power relations operating in their society' (Yuval-Davis 2011: 13), positioning people simultaneously along multiple power axes (Yuval-Davis 2006). South African physical environments remain acutely shaped by apartheid geographies of class and race; therefore the majority of black lesbians, gay men and transgendered people are more likely to be poor, unemployed and living in a township. In addition, many sex-/gender-, class- and race-privileged lgbti South Africans have kept whiteness alive as the face of 'the' South African gay community (Oswin 2007; Craven 2011). For example, race and class differences in the 2012 Jo'burg Gay Pride led to its dissolution in 2013. Lgbti citizenship is often framed as 'sexual citizenship' (Weeks 1998) or 'intimate citizenship' (Plummer 2003)—'sexual, reproductive and other related rights concerning people's bodies and intimate relationships' (Yuval-Davis 2011: 60). But extending lgbti belonging to the workplace demands a focus on economic rights, or 'sexual and economic justice' (Binnie 2007: 1).

Gendering in the workplace is expressed in complex ways: the type of work being done; the proportion of women to men; the positions held by women and men; and participants' identities and relationships with coworkers (Booysen and Nkomo 2010). Many work cultures and spaces are masculinised—shaped by men's bodies, lives, experiences and skills (Du Toit 2012); this typically devalues femininity. However, not all men benefit from masculine cultures in specific workplaces because privilege stems from numerous identifications (Coston and Kimmel 2012; Rumens and Broomfield 2012).

Identities and Emotional Attachments

'Identities are narratives, stories people tell themselves and others about who they are (and who they are not)' (Yuval-Davis 2011: 14). Identities are not fixed but in a constant process of 'being and becoming'. They are shaped through dialectical relationships between self and other, where a desire for belonging signifies emotional attachments. The essentialisation of sexual dimorphism and the consequent ubiquity of compulsory heterosexuality 'forces' sex/gender/sexuality identities on lgbti, so that they experience a dissonance between 'socially desirable' gender and sexual identities and what they perceive as their 'authentic self'.

A significant indicator of belonging for lgbti identities is linked to 'passing' or 'coming out'—strands of a process by which a person hides or reveals his or her 'true' self. Being out is more than the outcome of a developmental process; it also involves strategic management of one's identities across different contexts and situations (Johnson 2008; Orne 2011)—how people assess their social environment before deciding whether it feels safe to disclose hidden identities such as sexual orientation. In coercively heteronormative environments, presenting as sex/gender/sexuality nonconforming spells danger for one's belonging as it is often accompanied by rejection, ostracism or even violence. Butch lesbians and transgender men who challenge hegemonic masculinities are often more vulnerable to homoprejudice (Human Rights Watch 2011), whilst simultaneously intersecting with other identities such as being African. Therefore threats to belonging may be handled through strategic identity management—deciding how, where and to whom to disclose one's same-sex identity. Workplaces operate on constructions of a normative 'us', where equality for 'others' is 'inclusion' on delimited terms. Sexual orientation is deeply linked to gender ideals set for 'real' men and 'real' women, therefore lgbti may be 'disqualified' as the subjects imagined in equality policies and legislation—'justifiable' targets of homoprejudice.

Ethical and Political Values

Ethical and political values underpin the way in which identities and social locations are judged by communities who purport to share the same values (Yuval-Davis 2011). Different communities determine where the boundaries are drawn, although these may be inconsistent across different discourses. Whereas the constitution explicitly asserts the equality of lgbti citizens, a dominant discourse has emerged labelling same-sex African identities as 'unAfrican' (Epprecht 2004, 2008; Van Zyl 2011). Contestations abound about the limits of African identities: religious discourses range from calling homosexuality 'an abomination' to arguing for tolerance and inclusiveness. In contexts where the Afro-communal concept of Ubuntu[2] is upheld, lgbti struggles for belonging therefore challenge discourses which seek to erase African lgbti subjectivities by confirming their African humanity.[3]

Studying white professional lesbians and gays at work, Hattingh (2005: 228) found that 'through employees' closetedness, organisations are allowed their comforting fantasy that gays and lesbians do not exist'. Van Zyl, Steyn and Orr (2003) found that lesbian and gay staff at a university did not feel safe to come out at work, and in a case study on Stellenbosch Municipality, Opperman (2009) found that sexual orientation was not included in the public service's diversity management programme. Trans people spoke about discrimination they faced at work, either for being perceived as lesbian or gay, or when they came out as transgender (Morgan, Marais and Wellbeloved 2009). Although legal channels exist for challenging discrimination, homoprejudice is often hard to prove. In a context of high unemployment in South Africa, people avoid risking their livelihoods through costly and time-consuming legal routes. Lgbti struggles for belonging are necessarily waged in a context where the discourse of equal rights is balanced against racist, sexist and homophobic cultural discourses.

Politics of Belonging—Employment Equity and Discrimination in the Workplace

The boundaries of belonging are defined by hegemonic groups until they are contested by marginalised groups through struggles for belonging (Yuval-Davis 2011). Although the constitutional provision of lgbti rights provides a powerful foundation for belonging in South Africa, most lgbti citizens are still struggling for belonging in their communities (Mkhize et al. 2010). Active citizenship effected through mobilisation addresses both the formal and affective dimensions of lgbti rights, ranging from social and cultural organisations to providing services and doing advocacy and lobbying. Much workplace discrimination falls under the purview of labour legislation, but NGOs such as the Equality Project and Gender DynamiX[4] will support lgbti people on all workplace issues.

Workplaces provide important spaces to examine belonging because employees spend approximately a third of their waking lives there. The formal boundaries of belonging are defined primarily by the constitution, comprehensive labour legislation and statutory institutions protecting employees against all forms of discrimination. The EEA focuses on redressing race, gender and disability inequalities, with employers having to comply with equity measures by submitting yearly reports of progress on employment equity plans. Employment equity has provided opportunities for people to transcend their class locations, demonstrated by the formation of a black élite closely linked to the ruling party (Southall 2004). Lgbti are not deemed to have been 'previously disadvantaged' on the basis of their sexuality, but because people have layered identities black lgbti are considered previously disadvantaged on grounds of race and/or gender.

Numerous labour-related legislative changes ensure economic equality for lgbti people: many focus on partnership equality such as medical aid, pension benefits and conditions of service. PEPUDA protects all employees from unfair discrimination. *Allpass v Mooiplaas Equestrian Centre* (2011) involved the dismissal of a gay man with HIV, while *Strydom v Nederduitse Gereformeerde Gemeente Moreleta Park* (2008) concerned a dismissal due to the complainant's sexual orientation. Both cases found in favour of the appellants for unfair discrimination. Since the Alteration of Sex Description Act (No. 49 of 2003), transgender persons may change their sex on all national registries like birth certifications and identity documentation. *Atkins v Datacentrix* (2009) and *Ehlers v Bohler Uddeholm Africa* (2010) both won cases for unfair dismissal after revealing their intentions to transition to women. Therefore, lgbti citizens who experienced labour discrimination have had their rights upheld by the justice system.

A number of studies on South Africa focus on violence against lgbti in everyday life (Nel and Judge 2008; Klein 2009; Mkhize et al. 2010), but this author found none that addresses violence, bullying or harassment against lgbti people in the workplace. Although harassment and discrimination are formally prohibited by law and equity policies, 'everyday' discrimination is pervasive. The next section will address lgbti recognition and belonging in the workplace.

WORKING THE MARGINS: WHAT LGBTI PARTICIPANTS SAY

I spoke to a diverse range of sex/gender/sexuality nonconforming people living in South Africa about their working lives. A snowball sample was generated through contacts in the lgbti sector in Cape Town. Key interviews in Xhosa, Afrikaans and English were captured on a digital voice recorder and were transcribed, coded and analysed using Nvivo10. Participants chose their name to be used in this chapter: fifteen chose their own names, an abbreviation or a diminutive; seven chose pseudonyms. They gave written informed consent for the interviews after being told that the research would be published in an academic book. They checked the transcripts and assented to how their stories were used in this chapter.

Out of twenty-two participants interviewed, thirteen lived in Cape Town, three came from Johannesburg, Bloemfontein and Durban, and six lived in rural towns. Participants' sex/gender/sexuality self-identifications were as follows: twelve lesbians, eight gay men, one man who admits to having sex with men (msm) but sees himself as heterosexual, and one male to female (mtf) trans woman. Their ages ranged from nineteen to sixty years, with the average being thirty-seven. They worked across different sectors: state—military, police, health, transport and education; private—health, commerce, construction and information technology; nonprofit; and university. Nine had achieved matric (grade xii), five had done post-matric training, four had graduated from university and four had completed postgraduate qualifications. There were eleven African, six Coloured and five white participants. Eleven were Xhosa-speaking, seven Afrikaans and four English, although thirteen interviews were conducted in English.

I asked them how they balance their rights and sense of safety and belonging in the workplace. I contextualise their experiences by firstly describing the gendered aspects of their workplaces and how they negotiate their places within them.

Gendered Workspaces—Social Locations

While gender, race and class are three key tropes for theoretical analyses of social locations, they need to be analysed contextually to understand how they are 'enmeshed and constructed by each other and . . . relate to political and subjective constructions of identities' (Yuval-Davis 2006: 205). Many workplaces or spaces in them are considered 'masculine' or 'feminine' (Wright 2008; Reid 2013). 'Masculine' workplaces could be 'macho' such as 'blue-collar' jobs or 'technical' such as information technology (IT). Similarly, caring work such as cleaning, nursing or teaching is frequently 'feminised'. Asanda, an out black lesbian, aged twenty-two, works in IT in the commercial sector: 'The more technical teams like networking tend to be more male—I'm in that team—other teams . . . would be more women than men . . . and HR always women'. Jongie is a thirty-eight-year-old gay black netball coach at a primary school, with more female than male staff, 'so you don't have that fight problem'. He told the women that he is gay but says, 'The guys also [know], but . . . won't actually say it'. Zanokhanyo, a gay black man, aged nineteen, works as a librarian at a high school where he was a pupil. Female colleagues know he is gay, but, he says: 'I find that the male teachers are the main concern, and the male students. Most of the time I don't even chat to the male teachers'.

The military is generally considered masculine, but the gynaecology department in a military hospital complicates gendering. Elizabeth, an out white lesbian of forty-nine, is head of a department of mostly women: 'In my profession there are many people who are gay and comfortable with it . . . so when I started working it was no problem since the senior people training me were also gay'. The police service is similarly gendered towards masculinity, where Vuyo, a young black lesbian of thirty-one is openly gay. She argues that there is no discrimination at work 'because when you're wearing that uniform, it doesn't show whether you're straight . . . because we're all men and women wearing the same clothes'.

Construction workers and heavy duty vehicle drivers are masculinised in 'macho' ways. Faried, a forty-seven-year-old Muslim builder has sex with men and identifies as 'straight'. Fifty-year old Christien is a mtf woman train driver who, when she told her HR department about transitioning, was sent for psychological evaluation and, although not suspended, was booked off driving trains for three months—illegal according to the EEA. Butch lesbian Lungi (thirty-six) drives trucks and is out to the other drivers. She is usually treated as 'one of the boys' but gets teased about how lesbians have sex, which she puts down to 'curiosity'. Babalwa, aged twenty-six, is a machine operator working shifts in a spice factory, where she is out to her coworkers: 'If there are people who don't like who I am, the work rules do not allow them to show that'.

Aphiwe (twenty-seven) works in a more feminised space, being a cleaner in a hospital where there are more females than males, and says, 'I've had no troubles', although they all know she is a lesbian and she lives and works in an area rife with hate crimes against lesbians. On the other side of privilege is Simone, a white thirty-eight-year-old general manager in the finance sector who is not out to her colleagues: 'My work colleagues don't even know I have a partner'. Anderson, a nineteen-year-old black gay man working in an NGO for HIV health research in an all-male team is also closeted: 'I've always hidden my sexuality . . . from my family . . . my community, even though it is sometimes killing me inside . . . I've got to hide it, to protect my being'.

'Who I Am?'—Identities and Emotional Attachments

Four people were not out in the workplace, with two actively passing as heterosexual. Three were out only to select people, often women. Three gave religious reasons for being closeted, either because of their own religious identity or for fear of being judged by others. Fifteen did not hide their sexuality in the workplace. This suggests complex relationships among participants, their workplaces and their coworkers, which depends more on participants' own sense of identity than structural factors. The four people who actively hid their sexuality from their colleagues were afraid of loss. When asked what he feared about coming out, Anderson said:

> Mostly it's loss. I might lose my job. I might lose my mom, she would kick me out at home . . . Maybe I'm an embarrassment to the community or the family . . . I don't want to lose what I have because of who I am.

Sharon, a forty-five-year-old coloured lesbian from a rural town, passes as straight because, divorced from their father, she fears losing her children. Faried compartmentalises his sexual practices from his 'straight' identity, with no intention of desisting. These participants hide their sexuality at work and at home. Simone was brought up in a religious home:

> For ten years I went through the whole belief that I could change, and the church could change me . . . until I was thirty when . . . I thought, Actually this is not working. So I accepted myself, and that was possibly the best gift I gave myself.

Despite having included sexual orientation in antidiscrimination policies at her workplace, Simone fears losing her authority as a manager: 'I know there's a lot of religious people in my office . . . and I know there would be judgement . . . which would make it harder for me to hold my role and keep my respect'. At thirty-eight she is finally out to her family and has introduced them to her partner and is planning to get married.

Three participants, who were selectively out to others, felt only people who knew them socially were entitled to know about aspects of their 'private' lives. Referring to a perception that black men are the most homophobic, Sibusiso, a twenty-three-year old gay black man who does development work, says: 'The most challenging part is that I'm working with men . . . in the townships [who] have different views of msm so . . . I have to act straight with [them]. Some . . . are not interested to listen to a gay man'. He explains that 'some of them believe that we gay people are running away from initiation school. I did initiation school. I'm still gay'. In Xhosa culture, a male who has not gone for initiation, which includes circumcision, is not considered a man. Zanokhanyo says, 'I wanted to prove . . . that even gay people can do circumcision'.

The participants who were out at work did not necessarily advertise their sexuality but did not hide it either. George (fifty-six) is a white gay man teaching at a girls' high school: 'I've never gone around saying it, but when people have asked, I haven't hidden it. They've also known that I live with a guy'. Merlot, a sixty-year-old coloured lesbian, was working in a commercial bank when she came out in the seventies: 'When they asked me, "Do you have a boyfriend?" "No". "Are you married?" "No". "Children?" "No. But I do have a girlfriend" . . . So I was out, nobody could cross-question me . . . nobody could talk behind my back'. The most formal coming out was when Christien (mtf) announced her transition to her employers by doing a presentation, assisted by a transgender person and advocacy workers. She has changed all her identity documentation, is taking female hormones and hopes to be able to complete her transition surgically by advocating for change in public health policy: 'I just want my body and my being to be the same . . . you are unacceptable to yourself . . . you want to get rid of your body'.

Participants thus strategically manage their identities at work: most are out because they want to 'be themselves' and show a sense of entitlement to their constitutional rights. The participants in this study are more open about their sexuality at the workplace than those conducted by Hattingh (2005) and Van Zyl, Steyn and Orr (2003), although the majority mentioned homoprejudice at work.

Discrimination at Work—Ethical and Political Values

Five out participants claimed they had never suffered lgbti discrimination at the workplace while others ranged from 'some' to 'lots'. The gynaecology department at the military hospital was described as lgbti positive: 'Numerous doctors have their life partners . . . coming to social functions' (Elizabeth). The ones who weren't out at work were sometimes party to homophobic comments and felt forced to participate for fear of 'outing' themselves: 'I've gotta laugh because everyone is laughing, while it's eating me up inside . . . you hear these cruel jokes and if you're not laughing then they might get suspicious' (Anderson).

Thirteen participants mentioned some homoprejudice at work. Babalwa differentiates between curiosity and sexual harassment, saying straight men 'ask you . . . personal stuff, "What do you do when you are sleeping with your girlfriend?", and when they say, "You think you are a man?" . . . I don't feel good, but . . . I defend myself, I don't stand back. Although straight women sometimes . . . have the same questions . . . it is curiosity'. Merlot and Sibusiso both recognise the intersectionality of their social locations: Sibusiso acknowledges the 'hierarchy' of oppressions:

> The discrimination is always there . . . they think . . . I don't understand Afrikaans . . . they say bad things about you behind your back. There is a racial dimension and also straight people . . . Constitution that protects us gay people, but they do not act according to the Constitution . . . all they care about is race.

Merlot was treated differently from another woman while receiving cancer treatment:

> There was a straight woman . . . white . . . diagnosed with cancer, and they . . . nurtured her very well . . . [nothing] like that with me . . . I had

my sales target. I said 'I can't, I don't feel well' . . . didn't have hair on my head, and my tongue was black . . . So I wasn't going to be able to sell anything. They weren't interested. Called me in and kept hammering me: 'You're not doing your job'. Oh it was awful. Whether it was because I was gay, or black, or a woman.

While most of the participants described various forms of homoprejudice, they preferred to deal with it in their own way rather than go to court. Zanokhanya says he is angry with colleagues, but 'if they don't want me the way I am, they can go to hell'. Thoko believes 'the laws are there, but . . . I've realised that not all of them are actually working for most people'. The only participant who took the legal route was Christien (mtf), who had suffered the worst discrimination. She tried to involve her company with her transition from the outset:

My colleagues were very shocked . . . I am changing from a man to a woman . . . I am asking for your support. I want you to look at this with open minds. I don't want you to discriminate against me and push me aside. So it happened. People ostracised me. They didn't want to talk to me.

Furthermore, a petition had been submitted denying her the use of the women's toilets, although she had informed the company's HR department of all the accepted international protocols for dealing with transitioning of an employee. She was forced to take her case to the Council for Conciliation, Mediation and Arbitration (CCMA).

What Should be Done?—A Politics of Belonging

A politics of belonging is about lgbti peoples' struggles for inclusion into a group or community. Most of the participants felt that homoprejudice should be addressed in the community. Dylan, Thoko, Sibusiso and Asanda all wanted to see more lgbti individuals on television as it had helped them. Thoko said 'Just by reading and watching TV I started understanding myself, and I realised, This is what actually is going on'. Many participants mentioned the need for workplace awareness campaigns, such as Jongie: 'Because we are different people . . . we have different identities so we need to educate them, starting from schools to universities to communities . . . [so] they can understand what kind of people we are'. Recommendations to address homoprejudice at work included training and workshops resembling those that are conducted countrywide on HIV and AIDS:

Coming to the workplaces, there need to be workshops with the staff . . . at school . . . there will be a workshop for teachers and a workshop for students. Teachers will be told, "Gays have rights, lesbians have rights, you don't have to discriminate". (Zanokhanyo)

Although all of the participants were aware of their constitutional rights, some felt it did not afford them 'real' protection. Only three who were familiar with labour legislation said they might use it in future. However, most participants dealt with everyday homoprejudice on a day-to-day basis, not envisaging using the courts. Christien was the exception:

> The company has turned me into a fighter . . . I felt as though I was not treated as a human being with dignity . . . it will change. The more informed people become, the more it will change. Over time . . . people who didn't accept me, who said, 'I won't speak to you', are talking to me today.

She had been allowed to return to driving trains after her CEO had sent an email to all staff emphasising that no discrimination would be tolerated, and the employer was ordered by the CCMA to produce a workplace policy which addresses discrimination against lgbti.

CONCLUSION: WORKING THE MARGINS

In South Africa today, in sharp contrast to the apartheid era, the constitution and comprehensive labour legislation formally protects lgbti employees from discrimination and requires that all workplaces have employment equity policies. Yet lgbti participants face everyday homoprejudice which most choose not to challenge through legal processes. Yuval-Davis's (2011) analytical framework for belonging enabled a disaggregation of citizenship to show how the participants' sense of belonging is shaped through entwined facets of identity, social locations and political values. In each of these facets there are boundaries of sex/gender/sexuality inclusions or exclusions which need to be strategically negotiated by the participants as they 'work the margins'.

How workplaces are gendered is significant to belonging, with participants being more wary of straight men than women. Intersecting social locations and identities such as being black and gay serve to challenge normative constructions about African identity and manhood. Here religion is a powerful discourse in 'othering' sex/gender/sexuality nonconforming participants. For many their sense of entitlement to be who they are is bolstered by knowing they have rights. Yet these rights were not gifted but won in strategic manoeuvres during the apartheid struggle and during the process of democratisation—and subsequently through active citizenship from civil society, showing that the politics of belonging for lgbtis in South Africa is uneven and ongoing.

Facing everyday homoprejudice in the workplace, the participants managed their identities strategically, deciding whether to come out and to whom and how they engaged with colleagues to feel secure. Yet, out of twenty-two participants eighteen were out at work, demonstrating that most felt safe enough to 'be themselves'. Being out can protect people against homopreju-dice, as colleagues know lgbti employees are protected by equity legislation, whereas those who are closeted, while not the targets, could be privy to homophobic expressions from straight in-groups. This study has shown that the judicial framework with its political values of legal rights aiming to pro-tect lgbti citizens provides a solid foundation for sex/gender/sexuality non-conforming people to express their identities. Although most participants still experienced homoprejudice, they did not doubt that they belonged inside the boundaries of citizenship and that other citizens needed to change their attitudes. As Thoko poignantly says: 'Ja. We are here, and we are here to stay. We are part of the society . . . We are just living our lives'.

NOTES

1. I do not capitalise the acronyms lgbti, msm or mtf in order to avoid essential-ising these identities.
2. Ubuntu refers to someone's humanity, which derives from being in relation-ships with others, expressed as, for example, 'I am because we are'.
3. Confirming their African identities, activists in a march during November 2012 in Khayelitsha near Cape Town carried posters claiming *Ubuntu Bethu* (our humanity).
4. An organisation that supports and advocates for the rights of transgender people.

REFERENCES

Anthias, F. (2001) 'The Material and the Symbolic in Theorizing Social Stratifica-tion: Issues of Gender, Ethnicity and Class', *The British Journal of Sociology* 52 (3): 367–390.

Armstrong, P., Lekezwa, B. and Siebrits, K. (2008) *Poverty in South Africa: A Pro-file Based on Recent Household Surveys*. Stellenbosch: Stellenbosch University, Bureau for Economic Research. Accessed October 2012 at: www.ekon.sun.ac.za/wpapers/2008/wp042008/wp-04-2008.pdf.

Binnie, J. (2007) 'Toward a Vision of Sexual and Economic Justice', Colloquium on *Towards a Vision of Economic and Sexual Justice,* Barnard College, New York 29–30 November 2007.

Booysen, L.A.E. and Nkomo, S. M. (2010) 'Gender Role Stereotypes and Requisite Management Characteristics', *Gender in Management* 25 (4): 285–300.

Coston, B. M. and Kimmel, M. (2012) 'Seeing Privilege Where It Isn't: Marginal-ized Masculinities and the Intersectionality of Privilege', *Journal of Social Issues* 68 (1): 97–111.

Craven, E. (2011) 'Racial Identity and Racism in the Gay and Lesbian Commu-nity in Post-Apartheid South Africa'. MA research report presented in May 2001 in the *Faculty of Humanities, Political Studies*. Johannesburg: University of the Witwatersrand. Accessed April 2014 at: http://wiredspace.wits.ac.za/bitstream/handle/10539/11358/MA_Research_Report_Emily_Craven_Final_corrections%5B1%5D.pdf?sequence=2

Dhaliwali, A. K. (1995) 'Can the Subaltern Vote? Radical Democracy, Discourses of Representation and Rights, and Questions of Race'. In Trend, D. (Ed.) *Radical Democracy: Identity, Citizenship and the State*. 42–61. London: Routledge.

Du Toit, L. (2012) 'Sexuality and the Workplace'. In Bosch, A. (Ed.) *The SABPP Women's Report 2012*. 7–11. Johannesburg: University of Johannesburg.

Epprecht, M. (2004) *Hungochani: The History of a Dissident Sexuality in Southern Africa*. Montréal: McGill-Queen's University Press.

Epprecht, M. (2008) *Heterosexual Africa? The History of an Idea from the Age of Exploration to the Age of AIDS*. Athens: Ohio University Press.

Hattingh, C. (2005) 'Struggles of Authenticity'. In Van Zyl, M. and Steyn, M. (Eds) *Performing Queer: Shaping Sexualities 1994–2004—Volume 1*. 195–233. Cape Town: Kwela.

Human Rigths Watch (2011) ' "We'll Show You You're a Woman" Violence and Discrimination against Black Lesbians and Transgender Men in South Africa'.

Johnson, S. M. (2008) 'My Revolving Closet Door', *Journal of Lesbian Studies* 12 (1): 59–67.

Klein, T. (2009) 'Intersex and Transgender Activism in South Africa', *Liminalis* 3: 15–41.

Lister, R. (2003) *Citizenship: Feminist Perspectives*. New York: Palgrave Macmillan.

Mkhize, N., Bennett, J., Reddy, V. and Moletsane, R. (2010) *The Country We Want to Live In: Hate Crimes and Homophobia in the Lives of Black Lesbian South Africans*. Cape Town: HSRC Press.

Mokgoro, J. Y. (2003) 'Constitutional Claims for Gender Equality in South Africa: A Judicial Response', *Albany Law Review* 67 (2): 565–573.

Morgan, R., Marais, C. and Wellbeloved, J. R. (2009) *Trans: Transgendered Life Stories from South Africa*. Johannesburg: Fanele, an imprint of Jacana Media.

Morrell, R., Jewkes, R. and Lindegger, G. (2012) 'Hegemonic Masculinity/Masculinities in South Africa', *Men and Masculinities* 15 (1): 11–30.

Msibi, T. (2011) 'The Lies We Have Been Told: On (Homo) Sexuality in Africa', *Africa Today* 58: 55–57. Accessed January 2013 at: http://go.galegroup.com/ps/i.do?id=GALE%7CA270362836&v=2.1&u=27uos&it=r&p=AONE&sw=w.

Nel, J. A. and Judge, M. (2008) 'Exploring Homophobic Victimisation in Gauteng, South Africa: Issues, Impacts and Responses', *Acta Criminologica* 21 (3): 19–36.

One in Nine Campaign (2012) 'LGBTI Activists Disrupt Jo'Burg Gay Parade 2012'. Accessed October 2012 at: www.youtube.com/watch?v=Hnxip-T_Hnw.

Opperman, T. (2009) *An Analysis of the Sexual Orientation Discrimination Framework in the Public Sector: The Case of Stellenbosch Municipality. Master of Arts (MA) in Public and Development Management*. Stellenbosch: Stellenbosch University.

Orne, J. (2011) ' "You Will Always Have to 'Out' Yourself": Reconsidering Coming Out Through Strategic Outness', *Sexualities* 14 (6): 681–703.

Oswin, N. (2007) 'Producing Homonormativity in Neoliberal South Africa: Recognition, Redistribution, and the Equality Project', *Signs* 32 (3): 649–669.

Plummer, K. (2003) *Intimate Citizenship: Private Decisions and Public Dialogues*. Seattle: University of Washington Press.

Reid, G. (2013) *How to be a Real Gay: Gay Identities in Small-Town South Africa*. Scottsville: University of KwaZulu-Natal Press.

Richardson, D. (2005) 'Claiming Citizenship? Sexuality, Citizenship and Lesbian/Feminist Theory', *Sexualities* 3 (2): 255–272.

Rumens, N. and Broomfield, J. (2012) 'Gay Men in the Police: Identity Disclosure and Management Issues', *Human Resource Management Journal* 22 (3): 283–298.

Schutte, G. (2012) 'Johannesburg's Gay Pride Parade: Not Much to be Proud of', *The South African Civil Society Information Service (SACSIA)*. Accessed October 2012 at: http://sacsis.org.za/site/article/1450#.UHM97VV62Lx.email.

Southall, R. (2004) 'The ANC and Black Capitalism in South Africa', *Review of African Political Economy* 31 (100): 313–328.

Van Zyl, M. (2005a) 'Cape Town Activists Remember Sexuality Struggles'. In Hoad, N., Martin, K. and Reid, G. (Eds) *Sex and Politics in South Africa*. 98–116. Cape Town: Double Storey, an imprint of Juta Academic.

Van Zyl, M. (2005b) 'Escaping Heteronormative Bondage: Sexuality in Citizenship'. In Gouws, A. (Ed.) *(Un)Thinking Citizenship. Feminist Debates in Contemporary South Africa*. 223–252. Cape Town: UCT Press.

Van Zyl, M. (2011) 'Are Same-Sex Marriages UnAfrican? Same-Sex Relationships and Belonging in Post-Apartheid South Africa', *Journal of Social Issues* 67 (2): 335–357.

Van Zyl, M., Steyn, M. and Orr, W. (2003) *'This Is Where I Want to Belong' Institutional Culture at Wits. Staff Perceptions and Experiences in 2002*. Johannesburg: University of Witwatersrand.

Weeks, J. (1998) 'The Sexual Citizen', *Theory, Culture & Society* 15 (3): 35–52.

Wright, T. (2008) 'Lesbian Firefighters', *Journal of Lesbian Studies* 12 (1): 103–114.

Yuval-Davis, N. (1997) 'Women, Citizenship and Difference', *Feminist Review* (57): 4–27.

Yuval-Davis, N. (2006) 'Intersectionality and Feminist Politics', *European Journal of Women's Studies* 13 (3): 193–209.

Yuval-Davis, N. (2011) *The Politics of Belonging: Intersectional Contestations*. London: SAGE.

Cases

Allpass v Mooikloof Estates (Pty) Ltd t/a Mooikloof Equestrian Centre (JS178/09) [2011] ZALCJHB

Atkins v Datacentrix (Pty) Ltd (JS02/07) [2009] ZALC 164; [2010] 4 BLLR 351 (LC); (2010) 31 ILJ 1130 (LC) (2 December 2009)

Ehlers v Bohler Uddeholm Africa (Pty) Ltd (JS296/09) [2010] ZALC 117; (2010) 31 ILJ 2383 (LC) (13 August 2010)

Strydom v Nederduitse Gereformeerde Gemeente Moreleta Park (26926/05) [2008] ZAGPHC 269; (2009) 30 ILJ 868 (EqC) (27 August 2008)

10 From Cradle to Grave
The Lifecycle of Compulsory Heterosexuality in Turkey

Mustafa Bilgehan Öztürk
and Mustafa Özbilgin

INTRODUCTION

In this chapter we draw on concepts borrowed from queer theory in order to problematize the lifecycle of compulsory heterosexuality in institutional settings, as experienced by gay men in Turkey. With our lifecycle approach, we build on the tradition of scholars in the areas of gender equality (Dale, 1987) and race equality (Thomas, Herring and Horton, 1994) and seek to account for the institutionalisation of inequality from cradle to grave. The lifecycle approach is a way of understanding life and career paths, processes and outcomes of individuals through their successive encounters with significant institutional discourses and practices in their own environment. The lifecycle approach promises to reveal not only cumulative and linear but also spontaneous and emergent effects of institutional encounters over a life course. We do not use the lifecycle as a concept of path dependence.

Queer theory makes it possible to explore institutional encounters as unfolding, emergent and unstable, rather than fixed, essential and constant phenomena (Butler 1990, 1993). Similarly, Foucault's (1995) sensitivity to the disciplining power of institutions guides us implicitly in our exploration of gay men's life-course experiences in the context of Turkey. Reflecting on Foucault's account of the discursive terrain of identity (Foucault, 1988, 1990a, 1990b), we focus on compulsory heterosexuality across a number of dominant social and economic institutions such as the family, the education system, the military and the workplace in Turkey. Although this is an ambitious task, our analysis demonstrates the interconnected nature of these institutions in shaping and crafting the life and career experiences of gay men in Turkey. Without assessing these significant domains of institutional discourse and practice, we would not be able to draw a coherent understanding of the life and career outcomes of this group.

QUEER THEORY

Queer theory showcases the pervasive nature of gendered experience and the centrality of gender in the normative and discursive construction of institutions and social life (Edelman, 2004; Halberstam, 2005; Hawley, 2001; Sedgwick, 1990; Warner, 1993). A queer perspective also questions the corrosive effects of power in the normative construction of forms of knowledge that societies generate through institutions, such as, inter alia, management (Parker, 2001), law (Beger, 2000), education (Snyder and Broadway, 2004) and medicine (Chambers, 2006). As such, queer theory problematizes the very legitimacy of discourses which serve to uphold the dominance of heterosexuality above other orientations.

Butler (1990) suggests that the crux of the taken-for-granted assumptions and beliefs about gender hinges on the idea of performativity. In her vision, gender does not have a predetermined and essential nature. Instead, gender is framed as a collection of performative acts, accepted as authentic and natural to the self and others, through repetition and reproduction (Butler, 1993). Located in language as well as institutional discourses, presumptive heterosexuality (1990, pp. xxvii, xxx) and the heterosexual matrix form the logic of compulsory heterosexuality in the social domain. Within the discursive workings of institutions, compulsory heterosexuality renders certain acts and practices untenable and marginalises entire groups of people pursuing them. Institutional discourses have a hold on the social world through the mechanism of patriarchy (cf. Rich, 1976, p. 57). In this framework, the discursive power of institutions can both distribute and withdraw recognition to various groups, shaping cultural intelligibility for subjects embedded in local contexts.

Despite its analytical promise, queer theory has been criticised for the absence of race, ethnicity, nation and class dynamics in its seminal texts (Nussbaum, 1999). Tatli (2012) critiques the continuing mirroring of this inattention in critical management research which sometimes utilises queer perspectives in analysis. A number of scholars have been exploring this gap in queer theorisation, and focused on intersectionality of disadvantage (see Eng et al., 2005; Johnson and Henderson, 2005; Muñoz, 1999; Ozturk, 2011). We contribute to this tradition by exploring sexual orientation discrimination in the context of Turkey which still largely remains outside the geographic imagination of queer theorisation. As two Turkish-born scholars, we are in a sense Saidian reflectors in exile (Said, 2002), pursuing difficult acts of critique of one context, in the comfort of another. This fluidity and rootlessness help to secure a perspective of authorial subalternity (cf. Spivak, 1988) and uncovers interlocking institutional discourses through a critical reading of emblematic instances of sexual orientation discrimination in the Turkish context.

THE LIFECYCLE OF COMPULSORY HETEROSEXUALITY FROM AN INSTITUTIONAL PERSPECTIVE

We explore the lifecycle of compulsory heterosexuality through significant institutions—the family, the education system, the military and the workplace—which shape gay men's experiences throughout their life course. We have selected these institutions, as they provide gay men with interconnected experiences through which complex mechanisms of inequality and disadvantage are activated. For example, the family plays a pivotal role in the educational choices and chances of individuals. Educational attainment determines the length and level of compulsory period of conscription. The military service provides a number of network benefits in finding jobs and promotion prospects for men, who mobilise these as well as educational and familial ties for crafting and navigating their careers. The absence of an equality body and protective legislation for sexual orientation in Turkey (Ozturk, 2011) has significance across all our examples, intersecting with institutions such as the family, education, military and employment systems to shape the lived experiences of gay men. We focus on the heteronormativity of these institutional settings, illustrating how the cumulative as well as emergent patterns of discrimination across the lifecycle of gay men constrain our ability to pinpoint a simple set of factors that account for the overall disadvantage experienced across the life course.

METHOD

We discuss queer theory and the 'lifecycle' as key to our analytical toolkit. In order to operationalize and illustrate examples of our key concepts we use secondary sources including academic literature from both English and Turkish language sources, legal codes and policy documents as well as authoritative newspaper accounts and lesbian, gay, bisexual and trans (LGBT) activist sources rather than primary sources. We note that most of our examples relate to gay men's life-course experiences specifically, and thus we refrain from overgeneralising our explanations to the LGBT community.

FAMILY

As the single most important social institution in Turkey, family, because of its significance, is publicly pronounced, culturally embedded and historically acknowledged. In the complex imbrications of religiosity and secularism, modernity and tradition, nationalism and regionalism, progressive ideology and nostalgia, the Turkish family occupies an oft-perplexing ideational fault-line of uncertainty, change and inertia (Gole, 1997; Ozbilgin, 2012; Ozbilgin and Healy, 2004; Ozbilgin, Kusku and Erdogmus, 2005). Although there has been a steadily expanding rights discourse for gender equality, patriarchy in its most violent as well as mundane effects still persist in Turkey (Baba, 2011; Cosar and Yegenoglu, 2011). Consequently, despite the European Union accession process as well as financial and trade liberalisation, Turkey has not yet achieved full gender equality (Commission of the European Communities, 2010).

Although there is evidence of nascent progress towards gender equality in Turkey (Ozbilgin et al., 2012; Stivachtis and Georgakis, 2011), such shifts often remain partial or superficial in nature when we explore power relations within the family. For example, despite the repeal of laws allowing schools to seek virginity tests for students suspected of 'immorality', families continue to have the right to seek virginity tests for their daughters and assert this right as an invasive means of sexual behaviour regulation (Altinay, 2000; Kemal, 2010; Parla, 2001). The policing of women's sexuality as well as the punishment of 'unacceptable' sexual conduct, such as lesbian sex or sex with a person who is not approved of by a woman's family, directly reinforces patriarchal ties which in turn exerts a powerful impact on gay men's experience of homophobia. This has long caused homosexuality to go underground and become invisible, as men could not be openly gay in the ritualised moments of family gatherings and significant events such as births, weddings, religious festivals and funerals.

Furthermore, patriarchy's most extreme penalty (honour killing) is prevalent and serves as a foreboding background condition for women (Ahmetbeyzade, 2008; Kogacioglu, 2004). In parallel, the patriarchal family ideology preserves its homophobic core in the honour killing of gay men. A case in point is the 2008 murder of Ahmet Yildiz, who is the most well-known victim of honour killings involving homosexuality in Turkey (Savci, 2010). Ahmet was an openly gay university student who came from a sequestered, tribal background in the south eastern part of Turkey. After moving to Istanbul for his university studies, Ahmet came out to his friends and joined the fledgling organised LGBT liberation movement in Turkey, eventually claiming the voice to identify himself as a gay man to members of his family. What distinguishes Ahmet from countless unresolved gay murder cases in Turkey is the almost incontrovertible evidence that suggests it was his father who, with the approbation of the family elders, based on a family council judgment, one night travelled from Diyarbakir to Istanbul, lay in wait for his son and fatally shot him as punishment for sullying the family name. One pertinent question here is, what fundamental anxieties, contingencies and vulnerabilities did Ahmet's homosexuality invoke, such that the heteronormative family council (the traditional society's informal home-based court) would position him as a threat that must be countered, disallowing him the possibility of a 'liveable life' (Butler, 2004)? It is possible that 'the negation, through violence, of that body is a vain and violent effort to restore order, to renew the social world on the basis of intelligible gender, and to refuse the challenge to rethink that world as something other than natural or necessary' (ibid., p. 34). Within heterosexism, there exists a 'cultural fantasy' that links 'imagining of homosexuality' to something 'fatal', which gives simultaneous interest and indifference to stories of murdered gay men (Edelman, 2004, pp. 39–40). The acceptability of homosexuality would mean the death of the existing sexual relations, often patriarchal in nature. Not only does this notion reinforce the dominant culture's equation of homosexuality and death, but also it implies that the threat posed by homosexuality against patriarchy may be resolved through murder, in this case, of a son by his father.

Turkey's recent EU accession process and the opening of the economy to global trade and finance may have the potential to alter the dynamics of the heterosexist equilibrium in Turkish families. Such liberalisation has provided opportunities of public expression for gay men. Conversely, relative relaxation in social rigidities serves to divert focus away from entrenched forms of inequality and injustice experienced at the micro-individual level in the context of families, which remains largely unaffected by the so-called liberalisation at the macro-national level. Gay men's sexual experiences previously could only manifest themselves in underground settings at ostensibly heterosexual pornographic movie theatres and Turkish bathhouses (*hamams*), which served as countercultural sites catering to gay men's immediate needs. In the new liberalising context of Turkey, such experiences find new outlets for social acceptability and legitimacy through the establishment of LGBT cafes, clubs and eateries and grassroots social support and action organisations such as Lambda Istanbul and KAOSGL as well as the university student network LEGATO. However, social acceptability has come at the cost of desexualisation. During this time of liberalisation, establishments which facilitated sexual encounters for gay men have also been raided and closed, sometimes in the name of purported protection of the sanctity of families living near such establishments, often at the behest of not just politicians but neighbourhood families themselves. This backlash is consistent with research that shows a trend of 'increased violence that has accompanied the general increase of gay visibility' (Berlant and Freeman, 1993, p. 206) elsewhere, such as in parts of the US.

Hate speech against gay male identities has become more pronounced not only in the media but also in official declarations by the state religious authority as well as cabinet ministers, with the express aim of protecting the 'virtue' and 'health' of the Turkish family. For example, 'the state minister in charge of women and family affairs, Aliye Kavaf', acting under the direction of the religious conservative AKP government, declared 'homosexuality a disease' (US Department of State, 2011, p. 38). This followed the previous year's decision by the director of religious affairs to declare homosexuality 'a behaviour disorder . . . spreading in a crazy way within society' (ibid.). A lone example of an evenhanded discussion of homosexuality broadcast by Haberturk TV received a hefty fine issued by RTUK, the state agency responsible for regulating television broadcasters, for 'presenting homosexuality as normal', which in RTUK's judgment 'harmed the Turkish family structure' (US Department of State, 2011, p. 39). The paradoxical role of the Turkish state in the course of the so-called liberalisation was that it gave rights with one hand and took away freedoms with the other, often using the traditional family concept as the pretext to do so.

EDUCATION

The institution of education in Turkey is constituted to render sexual orientation issues invisible, presenting heterosexuality as the only 'healthy' and 'natural' sexual orientation. The primacy of family as the foundational pillar of Turkish society is reiterated throughout schooling and university education. The family is also defined narrowly as a nuclear family, based on a matrimonial relationship between a woman and a man, with their siblings and elderly grandparents. This formulation not only marginalises and excludes LGBT families but also fails to include single-parent families or larger family formations (Ozbilgin, et al., 2011). This narrow definition of family permeates all levels of education. Gay men's presence is not accepted among students, teaching staff or parents. Students can be expelled from schools, teachers' work can be terminated and parents can experience various forms of exclusion if they come out as gay. Therefore, a gay man's presence is strictly limited to the closet. The situation is not brighter in higher education. Even in the most liberal Turkish universities there are no officially recognised LGBT networks. Although LEGATO, an informally organised LGBT network of students enrolled in Turkish universities, serves as the nascent countervailing force against this absence, the education sector more generally does not tolerate openly gay men. Instead, gay men are often perceived as threats to the social mores, causing a range of reactions from internalised homophobia to self-censorship among gay men, with the overall sense that survival involves (self-)silencing (Human Rights Watch, 2008). Silence often acts as a mechanism of suppression (Ward and Winstanley, 2003), and in the case of the Turkish education system it leads to the erasure of gay men from educational spaces.

The institution of education does not only refer to the experience of students but also interfaces with employment, as teachers and academics are strictly regulated by the state. A case that is illustrative of the unacceptability of homosexuality in educational spaces relates to the ongoing struggle by a gay male high school teacher, Zafer Hoca, who has been struck off from the profession for homosexual immorality (Basaran, 2010). Nearly a decade ago, in a small town by Nigde (a Central Anatolian city in Turkey), Zafer Hoca had a discreet casual sexual encounter with another man. In the aftermath of the encounter, Zafer Hoca was blackmailed by his casual partner, and when he refused to pay the man informed his school about the encounter, which caused Zafer Hoca to eventually lose his job. Despite blackmail, the unnamed man was never prosecuted, but Zafer Hoca has undertaken a long-running court battle for professional reinstatement (which he has so far lost at each successive court of appeal in Turkey) and is now preparing to take his case to the European Court of Human Rights. According to Zafer Hoca, homophobic discrimination was possible due to the vagueness of the provisions regarding the required 'chasteness' of a teacher, based on a long-standing regulation on the promotion and discipline of primary and middle school teachers (Basaran, 2010). This law promulgates that any 'proven dishonourable behaviour that is inconsistent with the position of a teacher against a student or in a context outside school results in exclusion from the profession' (*Official Gazette of Republic of Turkey*, 1930). Here Butler is most poignant in noting that 'presumptions about normative gender and sexuality determine in advance what will qualify as the "human" and "the livable"' (1990, p. xxii). Having stepped outside the presumptive hetero-sexual figure of a teacher, Zafer Hoca is no longer recognised as a teacher at all, and is irrevocably dehumanised by the profession as an overly sexualised subject rather than a person who has lost his livelihood.

MILITARY

Lacking the financial resources to sustain fully professionalised armed forces, Turkey has a vigorously enforced compulsory military service requirement for all male citizens, and a large portion of the Turkish military personnel is maintained by an influx of annually drafted enlistees. In this system, the higher a man's educational attainment is the shorter his conscription period will be, with the usual time-range from eight months to sixteen months. There are also exceptional circumstances such as permanent residency abroad, which can reduce the service to the bare minimum of twenty-one days of basic training. Often regarding its principal role as the guardian of the republic and the provider of the ultimate rite of passage into full-fledged manhood, the military as an institution acts as a symbolic manufacturing site of an idealised Turkish male identity shaped by a particular construction of hegemonic masculinity (Ertan, 2008; Selek 2009), a subjectivity that is hardened, conformist, order-preserving, nationalist, secular and overtly heterosexual. Pressurising this institutional community of deeply unequal power positions even further is a longstanding conflict between the armed forces and the guerrilla-style Kurdish fighters over the disputed Kurdish region in the southeast Anatolian region of the country, where young and inexperienced mandatory enlistees face existential fears alongside grappling with the moral weight of participation in semi-hot war zone activities (Aktas, 2009). These structural conditions produce a contextual quagmire difficult to navigate for any young male draftee, let alone a gay man who would be a subject of constant abuse, a condition which makes prospective gay male enlistees often unwilling to accept mandatory military service as a realistic option, even for a limited period of time.

One way to avoid the draft is for a gay prospective recruit to come out to the enlistment office when he is invited to start compulsory national service.

Because gay male citizens are deemed psychologically unhealthy and therefore prohibited from serving in the military, such self-identification should theoretically render the prospective enlistee unviable for duty. However, the process of gaining exemption is arduous and often compromises basic human dignity. The exemption process is intentionally made to have a traumatising impact to deter and penalise any heterosexual male posing as a gay man to dodge the draft and punish any genuine gay man for his 'unacceptable' sexual orientation. There is casual disrespect in the way the military doctors conduct anal examinations on the candidates and ask extremely intimate details of the candidates' personal sexual history in the examination room. There is a sense of overt rudeness as the military administrators process the paperwork, whilst the exemption seeker goes from one office to another in an interminable series of stages. The panel of military doctors (and sometimes an audience of medical students) who subject the candidate to one final formally convened interrogation are part of the standard procedure. However, what deeply disciplines and dehumanises a gay man in this process is the demand made by the military for the submission of pictures taken during sexual intercourse where the candidate is shown in the 'passive' role. Even after going through all the requested exemption hurdles, the failure to submit such deeply intimate pictures can result in the denial of the exemption application. Alternatively, the candidate's failure to provide pictures can cause a secondary proceeding of in-patient observation to be actioned, often lasting for a week in a military psychiatric ward, where the exemption candidate can be kept in the same quarters with people suffering from serious mental conditions. Whilst the military often denies the practice of requesting pictorial proof of homosexuality, in a recent review the Commission of the European Communities (2010, p. 30) states that the practice is still ongoing, although not each gay man is asked to provide such pictures. More recently, gay men are also told to bring their families for questioning to the military hospital, effectively ensuring a face-off between the gay individual and his family and outing him in the process (Altay, 2012). The military as an institution is potentially a deeply homoerotic space, and in this light the extreme symbolic violence it perpetrates against gay men may indicate the tendency of compulsory heterosexuality to recognise its very own contingency as well as permeability to homosexuality, and thus its desire to push away such fantasies into nontenability (Butler, 1993). As Butler (2004, p. 35) asserts: 'This violence emerges from a profound desire to keep the order of binary gender natural or necessary, to make of it a structure, either natural or cultural, or both, that no human can oppose, and still remain human'.

Until recently, those who successfully navigated the fraught process of the exemption application and gained formal release from military service were given discharge papers indicating 'psychosexual disorder (homosexuality)' as the reason of the exemption from mandatory service. With a recent change in the regulations, the above terminology has been dropped and instead the military health code applies the term 'sexual identity and behaviour disorders' as the basis of military exemption decisions, reproducing discourse that medicalises homosexuality as a problem (*Official Gazette of Republic of Turkey*, 2013). Importantly, in Turkey, job adverts almost universally state that male candidates must have no military service obligation, and this is checked rigorously prior to the contract-signing stage through an inspection of military-issued documents that must be provided by prospective male employees. Once submitted, the exemption documents issued to gay men effectively diagnose the job candidate as mentally ill, which can realistically entail the rescinding of a job offer.

The Turkish military has a particular historicity that allows it to be seen as a critical site of meaning that produces a common thread of national solidarity, albeit oftentimes through repression in a political context marred by repeated bouts of interethnic as well as religious/secular conflict. Furthermore, military service is perceived as tantamount to awakening into full manhood, providing service personnel with an array of national identity rituals mediated through community belonging and male coming-of-age (Altinay, 2004), exclusion from which can be deeply alienating to people of alternative sexual orientations. Experiences/encounters from the service period are productive of narratives and stories that give form and stature to the subsequent stages of a man's life in Turkey (Sinclair-Webb, 2000). Because the military enjoys a unique point of cultural value/norm/belief production in the Turkish social psyche, this exclusion creates a thick barrier to the recognition struggle of gay men.

The foregoing analysis suggests that unlike in many countries where gay men prefer to serve in the military (Bell, et al., 2011), in the Turkish case the majority of the cases involve gay men attempting to gain exemption from military service. This is possibly because of the heightened level of homophobic values and practices permeating the institution. To be sure, despite the professed heteronormativity of the Turkish military, some gay men still view military employment as a career choice as privates or officers. However, the professional branch of the Turkish military actively engages in discriminatory employment practices against existing and potential personnel identified (or sometimes rumoured) to be gay. The mode of institutional homophobia manifests itself through codified practice which allows the internal institutional disciplinary mechanisms to reject alternative sexualities as unfit for duty and erase their representation by expelling gay men from the ranks. In a policy change recently proposed to the cabinet, intramilitary discipline will be maintained through a points-based system, where homosexuality, coded 'unnatural relations', will receive the highest point penalty, the same as murder or the sale of military secrets, with certain expulsion from the profession as the punishment (Ozlen, 2012). From the perspective of the Turkish military, subjectivities falling short of satisfying the compulsory heterosexuality standard is indicative of unacceptable immoral conduct as well as a psychologically unhealthy life choice (Dalvi,

2003–2004), and ostensibly this forms the basis of their discriminatory stance. At a deeper level, however, as a principal site of the manufacture of conventional manhood, the military-induced subjectivities cannot coexist with gay male subjectivities. Significantly, Cockburn (2010, p. 113) argues that the whole ethos and evolution of the republic since 1923 is such that 'the Turkish man has been visualised before all else as a soldier'. Until the historically rooted production of patriotic, hypermasculine and heterosexual maleness is examined, the inclusion of gay men into the military nexus is thus bound to be penalised by the majority.

WORK

In Turkey, there is no regulation or governmental equality body that affords legal security against sexual orientation discrimination at the workplace (Commission of the European Communities, 2009; Yenisey, 2005). In addition, the normative environment organising the complex interactions of gay men and the heteronormative majority is deeply unequal, strongly privileging the majority as morally upright, psychologically healthy and 'normal' at the expense of gay men commonly treated in a variety of settings as objects of disgrace and repulsion (Human Rights Watch, 2008). In a wide-ranging investigation of the Turkish employment landscape, Ozturk (2011) finds that many lesbian, gay and bisexual workers remain in the closet with a great sense of anxiety, and those who are more open about their identity are variously ridiculed, distrusted, passed over for promotion, routinely mentally or physically bullied and abused and sometimes summarily dismissed.

The recent case of Halil Ibrahim Dincdag, a gay football referee banned from the profession for being gay, is illustrative of the depth of homophobia within the Turkish work culture (Ertetik, 2010). After serving as an amateur league referee for several years with an outstanding record, Halil completed the necessary procedures to convert his credentials into a professional referee certificate. However, when he was requested to supply his military discharge papers, Halil had to submit documents which indicated that he had been deemed exempt from military service on the basis of homosexuality as a 'psychosexual disorder'. With internal codes requiring professional referees to present a clean bill of health in regards to bodily and mental functions, the Turkish Football Federation rejected Halil's application on the basis that he had an unacceptable permanent mental illness. Despite many appeals through legal channels, Halil has so far been unsuccessful in claiming the professional position which he would have otherwise been given. Once his homosexuality was leaked to the press, Halil also lost his part-time job as a football commentator on a radio station. In one way, Halil's continuing battle through the court system and the media can be deemed futile. Conversely, it is possible to view in his long-running fight a serious attempt to overturn heteronormativity, which is represented by his capacity 'to invoke rights for which there are no prior entitlements . . . in the vein of "Black South Africans" ' who during the last phase of the apartheid 'arrived at the polling booths' despite having 'no prior authorisation for their vote' (Butler, 2004, pp. 224–225). As compulsory heterosexuality is based on an imposed, albeit often convincing, discursive artifice, continual micro-attempts at overturning the heterosexual matrix can eventually generate greater liberation.

CONCLUSION

Despite a number of promising changes such as the annual Pride march in Istanbul, the increasing availability of LGBT networks and the emergence of gay social venues, a lifecycle of compulsory heterosexuality in Turkey does not appear to be susceptible to radical positive shifts in the near future. This was particularly apparent when recently the legislature considered a proposal to establish a commission to inquire into the various forms of discrimination faced by LGBT citizens, which was roundly defeated and which the members of the ruling party used as an opportunity to reemphasize their view of homosexuality as a sign of moral depravity as well as a medical condition (Hurriyet Daily News, 2013). However, the encroachments upon various civil liberties by the current government may have begun to motivate a popular backlash. In May 2013 what started as a protest against the redevelopment of a small park (Gezi Park) into a shopping mall in central Istanbul, Turkey, expanded rapidly to seek redress for an extensive platform of grievances and to combat the general authoritarian tendencies within the political process (Kuymulu, 2013). Interestingly, rainbow flags were among those protester flags prominently displayed during the resistance activities, as LGBT networks worked in concert with various other civil society organisations. It is possible that the recent events could generate a legitimation effect for LGBT organisations and the issues they raise. However, as we have illustrated in this chapter, the negative consequences of openly identifying as a gay man are undeniable, and the heteronormativity across key institutions such as the family, education, military and the workplace still remain entrenched and largely unchallenged.

In this chapter, we have also explored some striking examples of resistance, instanced in different forms by Ahmet, Zafer Hoca and Halil. The forceful nature of the negative responses to appeals of basic human rights made by these gay men suggests that there is need for more informed debate on sexual orientation issues as part of a common human right agenda in Turkey. Despite the gloomy picture, Turkey provides an interesting setting in which to study compulsory heterosexuality and the resilience of the human soul. Regardless of the entrenched nature of institutional mechanisms that seek to eliminate homosexuality in Turkey, the gay male community is becoming more active. An increasing number of gay men, both on their own and in collectives, such as the KAOS GL and LEGATO organisations, bring their concerns to public attention, foster debate in the media and assert their human rights through national and European courts in a difficult context where such rights are continually disregarded and undermined.

REFERENCES

Ahmetbeyzade, C. (2008) 'Gendering Necropolitics: The Juridical Political Sociality of Honour Killings in Turkey', *Journal of Human Rights* 7(3): 187–206.

Aktas, F. O. (2009) 'Being a Conscientious Objector in Turkey: Challenging Hegemonic Masculinity in a Militaristic Nation-State', Unpublished MA Thesis, Budapest: Central European University.

Altay, E. (14 March 2012) 'New Psychological Torture for Gays from GATA: Facing the Family', KAOS GL, www.kaosgl.com/page.php?id=10824.

Altınay, A. G. (2000) 'Talking and Writing our Sexuality: Feminist Activism on Virginity and Virginity Tests in Turkey', in P. Ilkkaracan (ed.), *Women and Sexuality in Muslim Societies*. Istanbul: Women for Women's Rights Organization, pp. 413–412.

Altınay, A. G. (2004) *The Myth of the Military-Nation: Militarism, Gender and Education in Turkey*. London: Palgrave Macmillan.

Baba, H. B. (2011) 'The Construction of the Heteropatriarchal Family and Dissident Sexualities in Turkey', *Fe Dergi: Feminist Elestiri* 3(1): 56–64.

Basaran, E. (5 December 2010) 'Gay Religion Teacher Wants his Class Back', *Radikal*, www.radikal.com.tr/Radikal.aspx?aType=RadikalYazar&ArticleID=1031426.

Bell, M., Ozbilgin, M., Beauregard, A. and Surgevil, O. (2011) 'Voice, Silence and Diversity in 21st Century Organizations: Strategies for Inclusion of Gay, Lesbian, Bisexual and Transgender Employees', *Human Resource Management* 50(1): 131–146.

Beger, N. J. (2000) 'Queer Readings of Europe: Gender Identity, Sexual Orientation and the (Im)potency of Rights Politics at the European Court of Justice', *Social and Legal Studies* 9(2): 249–270.

Berlant, L. and Freeman, E. (1993) 'Queer Nationality', in Warner, M. (ed.), *Fear of a Queer Planet: Queer Politics and Social Theory (Vol. 6)*. Minneapolis: University of Minnesota Press, pp. 193–229.

Butler, J. (1990) *Gender Trouble*. London: Routledge.

Butler, J. (1993) *Bodies that Matter: On the Discursive Limits of Sex*. London: Routledge.

Butler, J. (2004) *Undoing Gender*. London: Routledge

Chambers, T. (2006) 'Closet Cases: Queering Bioethics through Narrative', *Literature and Medicine* 25(2): 402–411.

Cockburn, C. (2010) 'Militarism and War', in Shepherd, L. J. (ed.), *Gender Matters in Global Politics: A Feminist Introduction to International Relations*. London: Routledge, pp. 105–115.

Commission of the European Communities. (2009) *Turkey 2009 Progress Report*. Brussels.

Commission of the European Communities. (2010) *Turkey 2010 Progress Report*. Brussels.

Cosar, S. and Yegenoglu, M. (2011) 'New Grounds for Patriarchy in Turkey? Gender Policy in the Age of AKP', *South European Society and Politics* 16(4): 555–573.

Dale, A. (1987) 'Occupational Inequality, Gender and Lifecycle', *Work, Employment and Society* 1(3): 326–351.

Edelman, L. (2004) *No Future: Queer Theory and the Death Drive*. Durham, NC: Duke University Press.

Eng, D. L., Halberstam, J., Villarejo, A. and Freeman, E. (2005) (eds) *What's Queer about Queer Studies Now? Social Text 84/85:* Durham, NC: Duke University Press.

Ertan, C. (2008) 'Hegemonic Masculinity and Homosexuality: Some Reflections on Turkey', *ETHOS: Dialogues in Philosophy and Social Sciences* 1(4): 1–11.

Ertetik, I. (2010) 'Coming Out as a Political Act in the LGBT Movement in Turkey', Unpublished MA Thesis. Ankara: Middle East Technical University.

Foucault, M. (1988) *The Care of the Self: The History of Sexuality, Volume 3*. London: Vintage Books.

Foucault, M. (1990a) *The History of Sexuality: An Introduction, Volume 1*. London: Vintage Books.

Foucault, M. (1990b) *The Use of Pleasure: The History of Sexuality, Volume 2*. London: Vintage Books.

Foucault, M. (1995) *Discipline and Punish: The Birth of the Prison*. London: Vintage Books.

Gole, N. (1997) *The Forbidden Modern: Civilization and Veiling*. Ann Arbor: University of Michigan Press.

Halberstam, J. (2005) *In a Queer Time and Place: Transgender Bodies, Subcultural Lives*. New York: NYU Press.

Hawley, J. C. (2001) (ed.) *Postcolonial, Queer: Theoretical Intersections*. New York: SUNY Press.

Human Rights Watch (2008) *We Need a Law for Liberation: Gender, Sexuality and Human Rights in a Changing Turkey*. New York: Human Rights Watch Organization.

Hurriyet Daily News (30 June 2013) 'Main Oppostion Urges Protection of LGBT's, the Ruling Party Calls them Immoral', www.hurriyetdailynews.com/main-opposition-urges-protection-of-lgbts-ruling-party-calls-them-immoral.aspx?pageID=238&nID=47860&NewsCatID=339.

Johnson, E. P. and Henderson, M. G. (2005) (eds) *Black Queer Studies: A Critical Anthology*. Durham, NC: Duke University Press.

Kemal, Y. (2010) 'Social Changes and their Impact on Women in Turkey and Its Membership to the EU', *Journal of Women's Entrepreneurship and Education* 3/4(2): 80–93.

Kogacioglu, D. (2004) 'The Tradition Effect: Framing Honour Crimes in Turkey', *Differences: A Journal of Feminist Cultural Studies* 15(2): 119–151.

Kuymulu, M. B. (2013) 'Reclaiming the Right to the City: Reflections on the Urban Uprisings in Turkey', *City: Analysis of Urban Trends, Culture, Theory, Policy, Action* 17(3): 274–278.

Muñoz, J. E. (1999) *Disidentifications: Queers of Colour and the Performance of Politics*. Minneapolis: University of Minnesota Press.

Nussbaum, M (22 February 1999) 'The Professor of Parody', *The New Republic* 220(8): 37–45.

Official Gazette of Republic of Turkey (29 June 1930) 'Law on the Promotion and Discipline of Primary and Middle School Teachers'. Issue: 1532.

Official Gazette of Republic of Turkey (5 February 2013) 'Amendment to the Turkish Armed Forces Health Code'. Issue: 28550, Ankara.

Ozbilgin, M. (2012) 'Leadership in Turkey: Toward an Evidence-Based and Contextual Approach', in Metcalfe, B. D. and Mimouni, F. (eds), *Leadership Development in the Middle East*. Cheltenham, UK: Edward Elgar, pp. 275–296.

Ozbilgin, M., Beauregard, A., Tatli, A. and Bell, M. P. (2011) 'Work-Life Diversity and Intersectionality: A Critical Review and Research Agenda', *International Journal of Management Reviews* 13(2): 177–198.

Ozbilgin, M. and Healy, G. (2004) 'The Gendered Nature of Career Development of University Professors: The Case of Turkey', *Journal of Vocational Behaviour* 64(2): 358–371.

Ozbilgin, M., Kusku, F. and Erdogmus, N. (2005) 'Explaining Influences on Career "Choice": The Case of MBA Students in Comparative Perspective', *International Journal of Human Resource Management* 16(11): 2000–2028.

Ozbilgin, M., Syed, J., Ali, F. and Torunoglu, D. (2012) 'International Transfer of Policies and Practices of Gender Equality in Employment to and among Muslim Majority Countries', *Gender, Work and Organization* 19(4): 345–369.

Ozlen, T. (29 November 2012) 'Turkish Armed Forces is Institutionalising Discrimination', KAOS GL, www.kaosgl.com/page.php?id=12818.

Ozturk, M. (2011) 'Sexual Orientation Discrimination: Exploring the Experiences of Lesbian, Gay and Bisexual Employees in Turkey', *Human Relations* 64(8): 1099–1118.

Parker, M. (2001) 'Fucking Management: Queer, Theory and Reflexivity'. *Ephemera* 1(1): 36–53.

Parla, A. (2001) 'The "Honour" of the State: Virginity Examinations in Turkey', *Feminist Studies* (27): 65–88.

Rich, A. (1976) *Of Woman Born: Motherhood as Experience and Institution*. New York: WW Norton.

Said, E. (2002) *Reflections on Exile: An Other Literary and Cultural Essays*. Cambridge, MA: Harvard University Press.

Savci, E. (13 August 2010) 'Ahmet is my Family: Family, State and Sexuality in Contemporary Turkey'. Paper presented at the annual meeting of the American Sociological Association Annual Meeting, Hilton Atlanta and Atlanta Marriott Marquis, Atlanta, GA. http://www.allacademic.com/meta/p412598_index.html.

Selek, P. (2009). *Sürüne Sürüne Erkek Olmak*. Istanbul: İletişim Yayınları.

Sinclair-Webb, E. (2000) 'Our Bulent is Now a Commando: Military Service and Manhood in Turkey', in Ghoussoub, G. and Sinclair-Wevv, E. (eds), *Imagined Masculinities: Male Identity and Culture in the Modern Middle East*. London: Saqi Books, pp. 65–92.

Snyder, V. and Broadway, F. (2004) 'Queering High School Biology Textbooks', *Journal of Research in Science Teaching* 41(6): 617–636.

Spivak, G. C. (1988) 'Can the Subaltern Speak?' in Cary Nelson, C. and Grossberg, L. (eds), *Marxism and the Interpretation of Culture*. Urbana-Champaign: University of Illinois Press, pp. 271–313.

Stivachtis, Y. and Georgakis, S. (2011) 'Changing Gender Attitudes in Candidate Countries: The Impact of EU Conditionality—The Case of Turkey', *Journal of European Integration* 33(1): 75–91.

Tatli, A. (2012) 'On the Power and Poverty of Critical (Self)Reflection in Critical Management Studies: A Comment on Ford, Harding and Learmonth', *British Journal of Management* 23(1): 22–30.

Thomas, M., Herring, C. and Horton, H. (1994) 'Discrimination over the Life Course: A Synthetic Cohort Analysis of Earnings Differences between Black and White Males, 1940–1990', *Social Problems* 41(4): 608–628.

US Department of State, Bureau of Democracy, Human Rights and Labour (8 April 2011) '2010 Human Rights Report: Turkey', Washington, D.C.

Ward, J. and Winstanley, D. (2003) 'The Absent Presence: Negative Space within Discourse and the Construction of Minority Sexual Identity in the Workplace', *Human Relations* 56(10): 1255–1280.

Warner, M. (1993) *Fear of a Queer Planet: Queer Politics and Social Theory (Vol. 6)*. Minneapolis: University of Minnesota Press.

Yenisey, K. D. (2005) 'Harmonisation of Turkish Law with EU's Regulations in Respect of Equal Treatment', *Managerial Law* 47(6): 235–256.

11 Sexual Spaces and Gendered Dynamics
The Experiences of Male Cabin Crew

Ruth Simpson

INTRODUCTION

In this chapter I draw on literature on organizational space as well as some findings from my own research on men working in nontraditional occupations to explore how space is implicated in meanings relating to sexuality and gender. In particular, looking at the case of male cabin crew, I explore the performative nature of space and how male crew mobilise and utilise the spaces of their working lives. While a growing body of research has explored sexuality in the workplace (e.g., Burrell, 1984; Hearn and Parkin, 1995; Collinson and Collinson, 1996; Kerfoot and Knights, 1998; Brewis and Linstead, 2000), helping to overcome a 'sex-blind' approach to organizational life (Burrell, 1984; Hearn and Parkin, 1995), there has been limited work that has drawn simultaneously on issues of sexuality and space (Pullen and Thanem, 2010). As exceptions, some work has explored the significance of space and place within the 'sexploitation industry' (Thanem, 2010) such as 'red light' districts (Hubbard and Sanders, 2003; Skeggs, Moran and Tyler, 2005) as well as the diverse and complicated ways in which sex roles and gender roles interact in different contexts (Brewis and Linstead, 2000; Hearn and Parkin, 2001). However, there has been less work focussing on how (gendered, sexualised) meanings attached to space emerge and how these meanings may alter with the embodied performances of those working, moving and interacting within it. Informed by poststructural accounts, this chapter adds to emergent work on the performativity of space—that is, how space is made and remade through reiterative and transformative acts, perceptions, memories and meanings (Dodge and Kitchin, 2000; Crouch, 2003)—as well as, with reference to sexuality and gender, the creativity and complexities inherent within space-identity relationships.

It does this through a study of male cabin crew, part of a wider project conducted in the UK in 2002 through 2004 looking at the experiences of men in nontraditional occupations (Simpson, 2004, 2005, 2009). Seventeen interviews were conducted with male crew who were employed in five different airlines, two of which were short-haul, low-cost airlines with the remaining three being long-haul global carriers. All were based in the UK and were of British nationality. The experiences of male crew are potentially interesting given that the work is based upon a specific form of 'femininity' that draws on practices of deferential service as well as on notions of sexual 'availability' (Hochschild, 1983; Tyler and Abbott, 1998; Williams, 2002; Simpson, 2009). As Mills (1995) points out, the occupation has accordingly moved from what was previously a masculine domain, supported by airlines' earlier associations with militarism, to a largely feminine one, where the space of an aircraft can be seen as the site for the mobilization by airlines of a subordinated heterosexual femininity (Hochschild, 1983; Williams, 2003). This is often achieved through the presentation and performance of deferential female bodies (Tyler and Abbott, 1998; Tyler and Taylor, 1998), which are positioned erotically against the traditional masculinity of the flight deck (Mills, 1995). This can be seen as exemplar in the recent retro Virgin Atlantic advertisement where glamorous red-suited female crew ('still red hot!') are seen walking provocatively through an airport with a male pilot dressed in militaristic uniform that embodies (albeit with a post-feminist 'tongue-in-cheek') heterosexual masculine power, authority and control.

The feminized context of cabin crew therefore raises issues about the experiences of men when they enter a space that is saturated with gendered and sexualized meanings. As my research suggests, male crew members become associated with femininity and with a denigrated (homo)sexuality—irrespective of their actual sexual orientation (about half of the interviewees were gay; an approximate figure because not all crew offered this information). On the one hand, they may be valued for the special contribution they make to practices and perceptions of safety and security on the craft, at a time when dramatic incidents (notably the events and aftermath of 9/11) have put both under threat. On the other hand, however, they are also positioned as deviant Other in a context of a 'regulatory frame' of heterosexuality (Butler, 1993), where a subordinate female heterosexuality is presented as the norm. Men therefore need to manage an 'abject' identity within and through a space that is infused with gendered and sexual meaning.

In exploring these issues, this chapter first considers different orientations to space and organizations, highlighting and prioritising a view of space as 'lived experience' (Taylor and Spicer, 2007). It then reviews some of the work that has explored sexuality and space drawing specifically on literature that foregrounds the generative dimensions of space that goes beyond notions of space as mere context or 'container' of action. These dynamics are then applied to our understandings of the spatial and temporal features of the onboard service encounter within an aircraft. Here the chapter draws on my work with cabin crew to argue that we can appreciate how space and sexuality intersect: first through an understanding of the heteronormative gaze as spatialised in that it gains purchase partly from the spatial context in which it is exercised, and second through adopting a lens that sees certain spaces as 'heterotopic'—that is, as disorderly, unstable spaces of Otherness containing different layers of meanings. Taken together this highlights the performativity of space, discussed in the concluding section; namely, how it is brought into being through embodied performances that recite dominant discourses, for example, of sexuality and gender.

ORIENTATIONS TO ORGANIZATIONAL SPACE

As Taylor and Spicer (2007) argue in their review, literature on organizational space can be classed into three categories: studies of space as distance; studies of space as materialisations of power; and studies of space as experience. The first conceives of space as physical geometry or 'patterns of distance' that focuses on spatial outcomes such as workplace layout and how it may encourage certain behaviours and interactions. This orientation would therefore concern itself with the physical geometry of an aircraft—the physical separation and security of the flight deck and the safety implications of seating positions and how these spatial arrangements may influence the nature of the service encounter.

The second sees space as manifestations of organizational power, control and resistance—resonant with Goffman's (1959) analysis of 'front' and 'back' regions, where displays of conformity and resistance respectively can take place. In the context of airlines, because senior management is absent from the site of the service provision (i.e., the aircraft), there are strong managerial and prescriptive elements, supported by training in the way in which service in the 'front region' is to be carried out (Williams, 2003), as well as potential for noncompliance or for resistance in the 'back region' of the galley to such 'off-site' control. Crew, for example, often 'let off steam' in the privacy of the galley where, curtained off from the rest of the craft, they refer disparagingly to passengers and tell off-colour jokes.

Taking the dynamics of power and control further, the third orientation incorporates inhabitants' experiences and understandings and how these may influence space and the meanings attached. This focuses on how spaces are 'produced and manifest in the experiences of those who inhabit them' (Scott and Spicer, 2007: 333). Thus, passengers' experience of the space of an aircraft will be different from that of the crew. Space is therefore seen as a 'lived experience' and infused with different meanings. This takes us away from seeing space just as physical location to conceptualise it as activated and given meaning through the embodied performances and identity work of those within it (Lefebvre, 1991; Massey, 2004).

IDENTITY IN PLACE, SPACE AND TIME

This latter orientation places a focus on how identity is negotiated and managed in and through space. This highlights from a poststructuralist perspective the social and organizational contingency of subjectivity where identity is seen to be positional, temporal and relational. As Giddens (1979) argues, there is a 'time-space choreography' to people's existence that goes beyond (but can also in fact include) these dimensions as mere context or environmental 'backdrops' (Thrift, 1999; Keenoy and Oswick, 2003) to experience. Instead, these time-space relations can form the basis of power, opposition and control.

As Halford and Leonard (2006: 11) argue, place, space and time in organizations combine with more generic resources, such as those afforded by gender and occupation, to offer multiple and competing resources for the construction of working identities. These resources are invested with particular meanings that 'interplay with the discursive and material conditions' in which individuals are situated. Spaces can thus be seen to be 'performative' (Gregson and Rose, 2000) in that they are articulations of power produced inter-relationally through the performances and subject positions of men and women. In other words, spaces are 'animated by the embodied performances of the women and men who move through them' (Halford and Leonard, 2006: 77).

SEXUALITY AND SPACE

Challenging our understanding of sexuality as a biological 'given', some work (e.g., Ward, 2008) has highlighted how sexuality is discursively constructed and a product of power and knowledge. Thus, for Butler (1993) the binaries of gender and of sexuality are 'policed' through the regulatory frame of heterosexuality and the normative conceptions of what it means to be male, female and heterosexual. Men and women who do not conform to the 'norm' are negatively sanctioned and so controlled. There is thus a hierarchical system of sexual values, with homosexuality devalued. In this respect, from Butler, both sexuality and gender are performative— that is, the product of discourse. In other words, they are produced through repeated performances (citational practices) which signify or inscribe what that discourse (of gender, of sexuality) has named. Sexual identity is therefore not stable and intact 'once and for all' but has to be performed again and again according to these dominant meanings.

These different meanings are implicated in much of the work on sexuality and space—conforming to Taylor and Spicer's (2007) third orientation discussed above; that is, one which conceptualizes space as 'lived experience' and infused with different meanings. Recent interest has focused on public, private, virtual, formal and informal spaces—how the sexualizing of space is organized as well as how it affects organization. One strand has looked at the different spatial contexts such as 'red light' districts and the sex industry. Tyler (2010), for example, in her fascinating study of sales service work in the sex industry has investigated the gendered meanings attached to space—how gender is both done and undone—through an exploration of Soho, London, with its global association with commercial sex and a seedy night time economy. Penttinen (2010) has investigated the space of a sex bar in Finland, highlighting how 'shadow sexscapes' operate within landscapes of globalization as Eastern European women enact in Irigaray's (1985) terms the 'specular woman'—performing the position of feminine (and ethnic) Other in order to give men the possibility of asserting their masculinity by 'gazing at themselves in her' (Penttinen, 2010: 36).

Other work has explored how sexuality is formed through spatial practices and spatial 'Othering' that allows contestations of dominant forms of heterosexuality and the generation of new forms of sexual identity. With a focus on the artist Derek Jarman and his garden, and highlighting how gardens can be 'controversial' spaces associated with 'life and death, with order and disorder' as well as with different sexual identities, Steyaert (2010: 46) explores heterotopia as forms of disorganizing space and how 'queering' allows the opening of space to ever new practices of self-formation. Similarly, challenging a perceived trend to treat space primarily as 'reflection of and receptacle for socio-sexual relations' rather than as a 'generative facet' of these relations', Green et al. (2010: 8) explore the spatial dynamics of the bathhouse to show its structural features serve not just as a 'passive repository' for sexual exploration but 'generates, builds on and intensifies' the erotic experience (Green et al., 2010:14). Such work foregrounds the generative dimensions of space in relation to sexual practice, identity and desire that go beyond notions of space as 'containers' of activities and relationships.

SPACE, SEXUALITY AND THE AIRCRAFT

These spatial dynamics are implicated in the meanings attached to an aircraft as well as the practices that take place within it. In other words, the aircraft has specific spatial and temporal characteristics that frame and are framed by the relationships and embodied activities contained. These characteristics include close physical and temporal proximity of production and consumption where cultural expectations of consumers can shape the social interaction (Guerrier and Adib, 2004) and make specific demands on the public presentation of the (employee) self. Within the context of cabin crew, expectations of passengers, mobilized through discourses of consumer sovereignty and through promotional advertising that continue to draw on creations of available heterosexual femininity discussed above, can combine with the body proximity inherent in that service work to create a sexualized atmosphere within an encounter that can last for several hours (Tyler and Abbott, 1998).

Further, the aircraft can be seen to comprise a 'liminal' or 'in-between' space that is replete with ambiguity and uncertainty (Turner, 1977; Garsten,

1999) and where rules of engagement can be woolly, blurred or do not apply. Occupiers of such space are, as in an aircraft quite literally, 'passing through'. In this transitional space, passengers find themselves 'temporarily undefined'—separated from an existing social order 30,000 feet below; this may lead to a sense of personal freedom as, unbound by structural procedures (Garsten, 1999), individuals foster deviation and transcend constraints. Passengers may therefore engage in behaviours and practices in the air that they would consider less acceptable on the ground below—such as heavy drinking or inappropriate sexual activity.

Spaces can therefore be seen to be 'sexed' and gendered, shaping and framing attitudes and behaviours. The aptly named cockpit (or flight deck) and the aircraft cabin, for example, can be seen as masculine and feminine spaces respectively. As Mills (1996) has illustrated, the highly technologised space of the cockpit is underscored with meanings around rationality, danger and expertise that have core connections with discourses of heterosexual masculinity. Militaristic uniforms worn by the (mostly male) occupants are symbolic resources that further enhance the masculinity of this space. By contrast, the cabin, or main body of the aircraft, can be defined as a feminine space. It in this arena that consumption, service and the trivia of entertainment occur—culturally associated with heterosexual femininity.

It is in the context of these domestic activities and aesthetic bodily displays, saturated with gendered and sexualized meanings, that male crew accordingly manage their identity. Men often struggled against the subjectivities (based on subservience, deference and sexual Otherhood) imposed. Resistance was partly displayed through the high level of antagonism that was routinely displayed towards the privileged masculine space of the flight deck and its occupants—the latter perceived as arrogant, bullying and homophobic. Putting pilots in their place ('winding them up') was a preoccupation of many crew (as one male crew commented: 'I'm only a steward and you're flight deck . . . it's a male thing I suppose'). Gay crew engaged in potentially embarrassing banter ('you're a big boy aren't you!') and, through gestures, speech and body movements, 'camped it up' in a flamboyant parody of sexual alterity. All male crew resisted a servile role—practices that escalated and were given greater license when pilots moved out of the flight deck and into the space of the cabin:

> We had one (pilot) where he came out of the flight deck, and he said, 'There's nowhere to hang my jacket'. I said, 'Well try the wardrobe. It's in the bloody flight deck'. And he said, 'Yes, but there's no hangers. Could you go and get me one?' I was like, 'F*** off'. I said, 'Who do you think you're talking to?'

Meanings attached to space (e.g., around gender, sexuality) can accordingly underpin an inferiorization of subjectivity where the processes of and responses to Othering are heavily influenced by the specific temporal and spatial characteristics contained. The confined space of the interaction, the inability to leave the site of the service and the duration of the service encounter may well exacerbate the effects of any 'assault on self' (Williams, 2003) from dominant (e.g., heteronormative) discursive regimes. Generic discourses of gender, sexuality and occupation are accordingly negotiated through daily activities and interactions that are not only spatial in their context—that is, occur *within* space—but can be experienced (activated, constructed, resisted) *through* space.

VISIBLE SPACE AND THE GENDERED, HETERONORMATIVE GAZE

In the highly visible space of the cabin, crew are subject to a disciplining and normalizing 'gaze'—from passengers as well as from an absent management where the latter is still highly prescriptive, through training, in terms of aesthetic appearance and how the service encounter should be carried out. This appraisal is both disciplining and normalising in that it helps to structure and govern thought and action into preexisting norms, categories and behaviours.

The practices and relations embodied in the gaze have strong gendered and heteronormative associations. In terms of the former, a gendered vision is often bestowed on women by the 'gazer' (Perriton, 1999), capturing the power asymmetry that exists between the viewer and the viewed that is founded on phallocentric voyeurism and patriarchal objectification. In the context of airlines, Tyler and Abbott (1998) have referred to how female flight attendants are subject to instrumentally imposed aesthetic codes and how they must manage themselves as 'ornamental objects' within the working space of the craft. Through the gaze of airlines in particular, and patriarchally determined aesthetic codes of femininity more generally, women are expected to manage and maintain their bodies to reach an aesthetic ideal.

Rather than experiencing the panoptic gaze as oppressive or overly prescriptive, male crew often gained pleasure and pride from aesthetic bodily displays—enjoying and relishing the visibility their work afforded in the terminal and the aisle. The heteronormative gaze, however, was more oppressive—a gaze that can be seen to gain purchase from the meanings attached to the space in which subjects are viewed. The heteronormative gaze is a concept that reveals the expectations, demands and constraints produced when heterosexuality is taken as the norm. Here, individuals are expected to follow strict male/female behaviours that help to maintain a heterosexual sense of place. These hierarchically organized categories qualify homosexuality as a harmful and undesirable disposition—discourses that can be seen to dominate social institutions such as the family, education and the state. In the context of an occupational ideology that has positioned the 'sexy stewardess' as the normative model of service in the air (Tiemayer,

2007), male crew irrespective of actual sexual orientation are assessed as sexual Other and often, as my study confirms, subject to homophobic ridicule. In this respect, in a 'reversal of gaze' (Butler, 1990) and through 'movements of exhibition' (Irigaray, 1991) as they performed their role within the space of the aircraft, attention was drawn to men's Otherness. Within this 'gay space', men's bodies were objectified and a source of aversion: 'They (passengers) look at you in disgust, look at you like you're filth'.

Men are accordingly marked as Other within and through the highly visible and confined working space of the craft. This space is saturated with gendered and sexual meanings which, in turn, are inscribed, negatively, onto the bodies of men. While the corporate gaze can be a source of gratification—through which men manufacture and celebrate a 'clean' and professionally turned out appearance—the more generalised heteronormative gaze can be a source of oppressive homophobia. Through this gaze the individual is 'known'—a knowledge that is incomplete as it both highlights and conceals, supporting partial truths and obscuring what remains outside of its view. As the above suggests, the heteronormative gaze also gains significance from the space (its meanings, its embodied practices) in which it is exercised. The gaze therefore can 'adhere' more strongly to individuals (e.g., through perceptions of disgust) in spaces that threaten its regulatory frame such as those which carry nonheterosexual meanings. Individuals help give space meanings while at the same time they are marked, in the eyes of others, through the patriarchal and heteronormative gaze, by its dominant discursive regimes.

THE AIRCRAFT AND AISLE AS HETEROTOPIC SPACE

In his conceptualization of heterotopic—that is, 'other' spaces—Foucault (1986) captured the disorderly nature of (disorganizing) space where several layers of meaning may juxtapose in noncompatible ways. Jarman's garden, as Steyaert (2010: 50) points out in his analysis and as discussed above, is an example of heterotopic space because, given the unusual form of its cultivation (reassembled wasteland plants) as well as its location on a less than fertile 'sandy in-between space' near a nuclear power station, 'it reverses and upsets the concept of a garden itself'. It is a space where no one would expect a garden to be. Heterotopic space is accordingly nonhegemonic as a space of Otherness that contains sometimes hidden layers of meanings. The aircraft can be seen to be one such space in the juxtapositioning of speed and confinement; of being somewhere and nowhere; of domesticity and threat. We hurtle in a metal tube at 600 miles per hour and at 30,000 feet in subzero outside temperatures, sometimes crossing time zones as we progress. We are in space without place: we are nowhere whilst very much present—located and often pinioned in our seat. Yet despite this extraordinary movement, we sit still as we wait for time to pass and to 'arrive'. We are engaged in a potentially life threatening and dangerous activity—flying is not without personal threat—yet we are encouraged to 'enjoy' the comforts and securities of home: we eat, sleep, drink, watch films, read. We career, immobile, through space.

This juxtapositioning of meanings is also evident within the working space of the aisle where gender (masculinity, femininity) and sexuality (heterosexuality, homosexuality) cross cut and undermine each other in complex ways. Much of the work of cabin crew takes place in this space—either as a single 'walkway' running down the centre of the plane or as, on larger craft, a double corridor separated by a bank of seats. Here crew must manage the safety of the craft and undertake the service delivery and care of passengers. As we have seen, the cabin and the aisle can be seen to be 'feminine' space through the association with deferential service, domesticity and an eroticized and available female heterosexuality. However, these meanings can shift towards deviancy and Otherness with the presence of men. Male crew entering this space create meanings associated with a denigrated homosexuality (male pilots, on the other hand, who may occasionally transverse this space, confer a respected authority and status). Space is accordingly given meaning by the social definitions afforded to bodies of individuals who occupy its domains. At the same time, space itself confers meanings—ascribing the bodies of men with femininity and homosexuality. Space is therefore both gendered by the bodies and embodied activities within it and gendering (Halford and Leonard, 2006); by the same token it is both sexualised according to the social definition of bodies contained and 'sexualising' as it confers such meanings (erotic female sexuality; deviant homosexuality) onto others. This is further manifestation of the central notion, referred to previously, that activities and interactions are not only spatial in their context—that is, occur *within* space—but are also constructed (or resisted) *by* and *through* space.

As a form of heterotopic space, these meanings can juxtapose and intersect. During safety procedures, walking purposefully up and down the aisle (checking seat belts, closing overhead lockers, cross-checking security of doors and emergency exits) is integral to the work of cabin crew. Crew colonise this space—confident, visible and active as they perform their safety and security roles. While passengers are able to move within the aisle, their access is restricted and there are times when, perhaps unwillingly, they are confined to their seats. As Halford and Leonard (2006b) argue, movement such as walking is a particularly important spatial practice which, through comportment, eye contact, posture, tells 'rich stories' of relationships and power. In this context, the confinement of passengers (passive, feminine) is juxtaposed against the 'masculine' purpose and freedom of movement of crew, reflecting and containing gendered meanings attached to safety and security and drawing, potentially, on heterosexuality to ascribe authority and order.

In terms of the latter, as Ward (2008) found in his study of gay police officers, authority and order are not normally associated with homosexuality or ascribed onto the bodies of gay men. Gay men are seen as 'unreliable' in a context where officers need to practise a form of hegemonic masculinity to be authentic in the role and in order to be taken seriously. Gay men are 'good for a laugh' but lack conviction in the formal demands (creating order, discipline, authority) of the job. In the context of the aircraft, in a similar manner, practices and procedures relating to safety and security can be seen to be informed and influenced by discourses of heterosexual masculinity that help confer value, order and importance. In this way, during safety procedures, space can become normalised—as a 'masculinized' and heterosexual domain.

This more masculine, authoritative and heterosexual space, initiated partly by relations of movement and by the value afforded to safety (and heightened by recent terrorist threats), predominates during safety procedures and overlays more feminine meanings, outlined above. However, authority conveyed by movement alone is not fully secure and in this context can be undermined by associations with chore driven domesticity. Therefore, while movement and walking is often associated with a (masculine) purpose and authority, movement in response to the demands of others ('running around after passengers') can be seen to be part of deferential and hence devalued 'feminine' service. Here, the arrival of the trolley can cause a change in meanings attached to the aisle—as consumer sovereignty and deferential service ('milk in your tea sir?') undermine an earlier authority and as pleasure and gratification (i.e., giving satisfaction as part of quality service) normatively associated with femininity and homosexuality overlay an earlier, masculine and heterosexual seriousness of intent. This shift in meanings is partly captured in the quote below:

> Sometimes they (passengers) sit there by the (emergency) exit and just throw their bags and clothes, and they need to be clear, so you have to go and tell them and . . . you are the father who tells the child what to do. But then you go there with the trolley, and they go, 'Right, I'll have coffee and can you give them Pringles to my children over there'. And at that time you serve them.

In this juxtapositioning of responsibilities and of relations of power, the trolley as feminine artefact supports a feminization and (homo)sexualisation of the aisle, undermining more authoritative meanings and impressing on the identity of male crew (many crew members referred to the uncomfortable 'trolley dolly' image of their role). In one of my favourite quotes, a male crew member resisted a subordinated self through ironic recognition of the occupation's dominant meanings of deference and sexual availability ('you can't afford me')—playfully contrasting an acceptance of a subordinated identity with a more authoritative role:

> So you're a trolley dolly because they see you up and down the aisles with the coffee or tea, and I used to laugh and make a joke. I'd say, 'You

can't afford me, so you might as well have the tea or coffee or whatever, but when you collapse in the aisle with a heart attack, this trolley dolly has got to know what to do'.

The same space of the aisle therefore carries different gendered and sex-ualised meanings according to the embodied activities and movements of those within it and influenced by the symbolism that physical artefacts con-tain. These meanings can be tension-ridden and contestable and have mate-rial (e.g., dismissive behaviour from passengers) and discursive (e.g., feelings of inferiority) implications. Space thus emerges as complex and unstable—its meanings shifting with the activities and practices contained—both influ-encing and influenced by (gendered, sexual) identity processes.

As Foucault (1986) suggests, heterotopias are capable of juxtaposing sev-eral incompatible spaces within a single real place. Further, heterotopias function in relation to all spaces that exist outside of them. They mark a culturally definable space that is unlike any other space and that reflects larger cultural patterns or social orders. The aircraft can thus be seen as a heterotopic space. First, it is a site for the juxtapositioning of speed and con-finement, of being somewhere and nowhere and of domesticity and threat. Second, we can see how normative and 'other' disorderly spaces may inter-sect in noncompatible ways as meanings shift with the embodied activities that are contained. Spaces both 'mark' bodies and are brought into being by the embodied performances of men and women within them (Halford and Leonard, 2006). Finally, we have seen how the aircraft, while disconnected from the ground and at 30,000 feet, represents a microcosm of broader discourses that are partly historically determined through past practices and ideologies, that influence meanings and practices and that help make up a gendered and heteronormative gaze.

CONCLUSION

This chapter has explored some of the ways in which sexuality and space are intertwined—how spatial dynamics reflect and confer meanings and how these meanings may alter with the embodied performances of those work-ing, moving, interacting within it. In so doing, I have highlighted the insta-bility and socially constructed nature of space that takes us beyond notions of space as mere context or 'container' of experience. We have seen how the cabin of an aircraft is sexualized and sexualizing, gendered and gendering. It confers meanings relating to an available and subordinate female heterosex-uality on women and a denigrated sexual Otherhood on men—underpinned and reproduced through a patriarchal and spatially aware heteronormative gaze. At the same time these meanings are heavily influenced by broader discourses and by the social definitions attached to the bodies (moving, walking, working) it contains—supporting different and often incompatible layers of meanings within a heterotopic domain.

These meanings and processes can be seen to be implicated in space's performativity. As we have seen, Butler's (1993) seminal work conceptualized performativity as the repeated practices of everyday life that create an identity effect through the reiteration of norms. In that spaces can be understood as being brought into being through specific, embodied performances and as, from above, these performances constitute articulations of power and of particular subject positions, spaces too can be seen as performative (Gregson and Rose, 2000; Thrift and Dewsbury, 2000; Halford and Leonard, 2006b). Space is thus made and remade through reiterative and transformative acts, perceptions, memories and meanings (Dodge and Kitchin, 2000; Crouch, 2003). Inherently unstable, incomplete and in production (Massey, 2005; Unwin, 2000), space exists in hierarchal relations with other spaces (Gregson and Rose, 2000; Massey, 2005)—a hierarchy and relationality that can be both supported and challenged by particular performances. Activities and interactions are not only spatial in their context—that is, they occur *within* space but are also constructed (or resisted) *by* and *through* space.

The performative nature of space is evident in its relational and hierarchical nature (Massey, 2005). In this respect, activities and subjectivities of crew, moving rapidly in 'space without place' at 30,000 feet, can be seen to articulate broader power relations below. These relate, for example, to discourses of sexuality and gender which are manifest in the practices and power relations of the onboard service encounter as well as in embodied performances and a patriarchal and heteronormative 'gaze'. Equally, we have seen how the 'feminized' and, with the presence of men, homosexualised space of the cabin is positioned hierarchically (and for male crew often problematically) against the heterosexual, 'masculine' space of the flight deck. Spaces are thus separate yet, as Gregson and Rose (2000) point out, also 'threatened, contaminated, stained, enriched' by other spaces.

Performances do not take place in already existing locations—rather space is produced through embodied performances, as both articulations and exposures of power (Gregson and Rose, 2000; Crouch, 2003; Massey, 2005). Space can accordingly be seen as a process of doing or becoming (Unwin, 2000) through the citational activities of individuals within it. Another aspect of performativity therefore concerns the bodily dimensions as well as the tensions and instability of space. In this respect, we have seen how a 'masculine', heterosexual and authoritative space created through discourses and activities of safety and security can be easily disrupted and subverted by feminine and homosexualised activities of service and care—creating tensions for some men as they manage such contestations of meaning. Equally, the presence of male bodies can convert the cabin and aisle as sites of female heterosexuality, encouraged by past and current promotional practices suggestive of female service and availability (Tyler and Abbott,

1998; Tyler and Taylor, 1998; Williams, 2003), into a space saturated with and marked by homosexual meanings.

With sometimes painful discursive implications for crew, the aisle is thus precariously suspended, between masculinity and femininity, between heterosexuality and homosexuality, between authoritative and deferential space and the cabin as a whole marked by past history and by the body performances of men. Rather than being a 'given passive geometry' (Dodge and Kitchin, 2005), space is 'ontogenetic' in that it is continually brought into existence by the reiterative practices of individuals within them (Lefebvre, 1991; Massey, 1994; Mackenzie, 2003). This recursive view of space implies that it both shapes and is shaped by identity processes—mobilising and mobilized by social action and, along the lines of Gregson and Rose (2000), shifting with (historically contingent) citational activities and practices it contains.

In conclusion, through the case of male cabin crew, this chapter has highlighted how space and sexuality intersect through a spatially aware heteronormative gaze as well as through the dynamics inherent in understandings of heterotopic space. Drawing on notions of space as lived experience, we have seen how space and sexuality can intersect and how, in a performative sense, space is brought into being through embodied performances that recite dominant discourses of sexuality and gender.

REFERENCES

Butler, J. (1990) *Gender Trouble: Feminism and the Subversion of Identity*. London: Routledge.

Butler, J. (1993) *Bodies that Matter: On the Discursive Limits of Sex*. London: Routledge.

Brewis, J. and Linstead, S. (2000) *Sex, Work and Sex Work: Eroticizing Organization*. London: Routledge.

Burrell, G. (1984) 'Sex and Organizational Analysis'. *Organization Studies*, 5(2): 97–118.

Collinson, M. and Collinson, D. (1996) 'It's Only Dick': The Sexual Harassment of Women Managers in Insurance Sales'. *Work Employment and Society*, 10(1): 29–56.

Crouch, D. (2003). 'Spacing, Performing and Becoming: Tangles in the Mundane'. *Environment and Planning*, 35(11): 1945–1960.

Dodge, M. and Kitchin, R. (2005) 'Code and the transduction of space'. *Annals of the Association of American Geographers*, 95(1): 162–178.

Fineman, S. and Sturdy, A. (2001) 'Struggles for the Control of Affect', in A. Sturdy, I. Grugulis and H. Willmott (eds) *Customer Service*. Basingstoke: Macmillan, 135–156.

Foucault, M. (1986) 'Of Other Spaces'. *Diacritics*, 16: 22–27.

Garsten, C. (1999) 'Betwixt and Between: Temporary Employees as Liminal Subjects in Flexible Organizations'. *Organization Studies*, 20(4): 601–617.

Gherardi, S. and Poggio, B. (2001) 'Creating and Recreating Gender in Organizations'. *Journal of World Business*, 36(3): 245–259.

Giddens, A. (1979) *Central Problems in Social Theory: Action Structure and Contradiction in Social Analysis*. London: Palgrave Macmillan.

Goffman, E. (1980) *The Presentation of Self in Everyday Life*, 8th edition. London: Penguin.

Green, A., Follert, M., Osterlund, K. and Paquin, J. (2010) 'Space, Place and Sexual Sociality: Towards an Atmospheric Analysis'. *Gender Work and Organization*, 17(1): 8–27.

Gregson, N. and Rose, G. (2000) 'Taking Butler Elsewhere: Performativities, Spatialities and Subjectivities'. *Environment and Planning D: Society and Space*, 18: 433–452.

Grosz, E. (1994) *Volatile Bodies: Towards a Corporeal Feminism*. London: Allen and Unwin.

Guerrier, Y. and Adib, A. (2004) 'Gendered Identities in the Work of Overseas Tour Reps'. *Gender Work and Organization*, 13(3): 334–350.

Gutek, B., Cherry, B., Bhappu, A., Scheneider, S. and Woolf, L. (2000) 'Features of Service Relationships and Encounters'. *Work and Occupations*, 27(3): 319–352

Halford, S. and Leonard, P. (2006a) *Negotiating Gendered Identities at Work: Place, Space and Time*. Palgrave MacMillan.

Halford, S. and Leonard, P. (2006b) 'Place, Space and Time: The Fragmentation of Workplace Subjectivities'. *Organization Studies*, 27(5): 657–676.

Hearn, J. and Parkin, W. (1995) *Sex at Work: The Power and Paradox of Organizational Sexuality*. New York: St Martin's Press.

Hochschild, A. (1983) *The Managed Heart: Commercialisation of Feeling*. Berkeley: University of California Press.

Hubbard, P. and Sanders, T. (2003) 'Making Space for Sex Work: Female Street Prostitution and the Production of Urban Space'. *International Journal of Urban and Regional Research*, 27(1): 75–89.

Irigaray, L. (1991) *Philosophy of the Feminine*. London: Routledge

Keenoy, T. and Oswick, C. (2003) 'Organizing Textscapes'. *Organization Studies*, 25(1): 135–142.

Kerfoot, D. and Knights, D. (1998) 'Managing Masculinity in Contemporary Organizational Life: A Man(agerial) Project'. *Organization*, 5(1), 7–26.

Korczynski, M. (2003) 'Communities of Coping: Collective Emotional Labour in Service Work'. *Organization*, 10(1): 55–79.

Lefebvre, H. (1991) *The Production of Space*. Trans. D. Nicholson-Smith. Oxford: Blackwell.

Lewis, P. (2007) 'Emotion Work and Emotion Space in a Special Care Baby Unit', in P. Lewis and R. Simpson (eds) *Gendering Emotions in Organizations*, 75–88. Basingstoke: Palgrave Macmillan.

Mackenzie, A. (2002) *Transductions: Bodies and Machines at Speed*. London: Continuum Press.

Massey, D. (1994) *Space, Place and Gender*. London: Methuan.

Massey, D. (2005) *for Space*. London: Sage.

Mills, A. (1995) 'Cockpits, Hangars, Boys and Galleys: Corporate Masculinities and the Development of British Airways'. *Gender Work and Organization*, 5(3): 172–188.

Penttinen, E. (2010) 'Imagined and Embodied Spaces in the Global Sex Industry'. *Gender Work and Organization*, 17(1): 28–44.

Pullen, A. (2006) *Managing Identity*. London: Palgrave.

Pullen, A. and Thanem, T. (2010) 'Editorial: Sexual Spaces'. *Gender Work and Organization*, 17(1): 1–6.

Rose, G. (1999) 'Performing Space', in D. Massey, J. Allen and P. Sarre (eds) *Human Geography Today*, 65–72 Cambridge: Polity Press.

Simpson, R. (2004) 'Masculinity at Work: the Experiences of Men in Female Dominated Occupations'. *Work, Employment and Society*, 18(2): 349–368.

Simpson, R. (2005) 'Men in Nontraditional Occupations: Career Entry, Career Orientation and Experience of Role Strain'. *Gender Work and Organization*, 12(4): 363–380.

Simpson, R. (2009) *Men in Caring Occupations: Doing Gender Differently*. Basingstoke: Palgrave Macmillan.

Skeggs, B., Moran, L. and Tyler, M. (2005) 'Queer as Folk: Producing the Real of Urban Space'. *Urban Studies*, 41(9): 1839–1856.

Steyaert, C. (2010) 'Queering Space: Heterotopic Life in Derek Jarman's Garden'. *Gender Work and Organization*, 17(1): 45–68.

Taylor, S. and Spicer, A. (2007) 'Time for Space: A Narrative Review of Research on Organizational Space'. *International Journal of Management Reviews*, 9(4): 325–346.

Taylor, S. and Tyler, M. (2000) 'Emotional Labour and Sexual Difference in the Airline Industry'. *Work Employment and Society*, 14(1): 77–95.

Thanem, T. (2010) 'Free at Last? Assembling Producing and Organizing Sexual Spaces in Swedish Sex Education'. *Gender Work and Organization*, 17(1): 92–111.

Thomas, R., Mills, A. and Mills, J. (2004). 'Introduction: Resisting Gender, Gendering Resistance', in R. Thomas, A. Mills and J. Mills (eds) *Identity Politics at Work: Resisting Gender, Gendering Resistance*, 1–19. London: Routledge.

Thrift, N. and Dewsbury, J. (2000) 'Dead Geographies—and How to Make Them Live'. *Environment and Planning D: Society and Space*, 18(4): 411–432.

Tiemeyer, P. (2007) 'Male Stewardesses: Male Flight Attendants as a Queer Miscarriage of Justice, Genders'. www.genders.org/g45/g45_tiemeyer.html.

Tyler, M. (2010) 'Glamour Girls, Macho Men and Everything in Between: Un/Doing Gender and Dirty Work in Soho's Sex Shops', in R. Simpson, N. Slutskaya, P. Lewis and H. Hopfl (eds) *Dirty Work: Concepts and Identities*, 65–90. Basingstoke: Palgrave Macmillan.

Tyler, M. and Abbott, P. (1998) 'Chocs Away: Weight Watching in the Contemporary Airline Industry'. *Sociology*, 32(3): 433–450.

Turner, V. (1977) *The Ritual Process*. Ithaca, NY: Cornell University Press.

Unwin, T. (2000). 'A Waste of Space? Towards a Critical Understanding of the Social Production of Space . . .'. *The Institute of British Geographers*, 25(11): 11–29.

Ward, J. (2008) *Sexualities Work and Organization*. London: Routledge.

Weedon, C. (1993). *Feminist Practice and Poststructuralist Theory*, 2nd edition. Oxford: Blackwell.

Williams, C. (2003) 'Sky Service: The Demands of Emotional Labour in the Airline Industry'. *Gender Work and Organization*, 10(5): 513–550.

12 Is Your Workplace 'Gay-Friendly'? Current Issues and Controversies

Nick Rumens

INTRODUCTION

The import of the question used to title this chapter is suggested by significant cultural, social and political shifts and transformations that have taken place in recent decades regarding homosexualities and sexual diversity (Seidman, 2002; Weeks, 2007), prising open opportunities for lesbian, gay, bisexual and trans (LGBT) people to identify and live a plurality of sexualities and genders. If we live in what some have defined as an era of 'postmodern sexualities' (Simon, 1996), described in terms of sexual and erotic experimentation wherein sexuality and gender are characterised as constructed, multiple, fragmented, precarious and performative, it is apposite to examine whether constructions of workplaces as 'gay-friendly' actually represent a progressive step forward for LGBT employees. Put differently and somewhat simply, in what sense can gay-friendly workplaces be positively distinguished from gay-unfriendly work settings? Can we understand gay-friendly workplaces as contexts where there is a breakdown in heteronormativity? By heteronormativity I mean the power relations, knowledge and institutions that sustain normative constructions of heterosexuality as 'natural' and privileged. Positioned as a cornerstone of the sex-gender system, one that insists on the duality of man/woman and masculine/feminine, and one in which particular heterosexual identities, norms, intimacies and relationships to mention but a few are established as a normative standard. In that respect, might gay-friendly places of work condition an array of available subject positions for LGBT to live sexual diversity at work?

In beginning to address such questions, it is notable that as a previously unknown term, *gay-friendly* is increasingly common in everyday parlance. Well-thumbed travel guides such as *The Lonely Planet* refer to gay-friendly tourist destinations while liberal journalism aimed at LGBT people in the UK (e.g., *The Pink Paper*) and the US (e.g., *The Advocate*) regularly features articles on gay-friendly colleges, churches, hotels, countries, living areas and work environments. A cursory glance on the internet provides information on gay-friendly restaurants, lawyers and funeral directors. Elsewhere, LGB charities such as Stonewall in the UK publish annual surveys on 'gay-friendly employers'. Notably, the term has started to attract attention within academic circles. References to gay-friendly workplaces and organisational cultures can be found in the sexuality in organisation literature (Ragins and Cornwell, 2001; Tejeda, 2006; Fleming, 2007), but seldom is this term explained and interrogated. This strikes me as odd because the concept of a gay-friendly organisation seems to be underpinned by an implicit assumption of an ethics of tolerance and liberalism within the work environment, although what this means in terms of LGBT employees' ground level experiences is not always clear. In contrast, some scholars have tried to characterise gay-friendly workplaces (Correia and Kleiner, 2001) while others, drawing on critical theories, have interrogated this supposedly new organisational form—the 'gay-friendly organisation' (Giuffre, Dellinger and Williams, 2008; Williams, Giuffre and Dellinger, 2009; Williams and Giuffre, 2011)—broadly described by Williams, Giuffre and Dellinger (2009: 29) as 'work settings [that] attempt to eradicate homophobia and heterosexism'. Other researchers have analysed what LGBT employees think makes their employers LGBT-friendly (Colgan et al., 2007, 2009; Colgan and McKearney, 2011). From this slowly emerging literature, gay-friendly workplaces are said not to just tolerate LGBT employees but 'accept and welcome them into the workplace' (Williams, Giuffre and Dellinger 2009: 29). Crucially, however, it is contended that gay-friendly work settings continue to be characterised by inequalities along the lines of sexuality and gender, suggesting that even when framed as gay or LGBT-friendly, workplaces are complicit in keeping LGBT people entangled in the strictures of heteronormativity (Rumens and Kerfoot, 2009).

The basic premise of this chapter is that particular invocations of workplaces as gay-friendly, typically those that are appetising to employers, constitutes a notable and problematic turn of emphasis in how LGBT sexualities are being folded into organisational heteronormativity, one that signifies a narrowing of possible subject positions and ways of life available to LGBT people at work. Although it is currently possible to identify gay-friendly places of work in ways that were impossible or improbable decades earlier, I aim to think through the concept of the gay-friendly workplace from a different angle using a queer theory perspective. I do so because this involves an analysis of the situations that provoke the discourse of the gay-friendly workplace and the consequences to which it gives rise. It also demands attention is paid to the situations in which it is deployed, particularly those organisational contexts from which such a discourse derives its legitimation. Furthermore, a queer analysis is concerned with how the subjects of a gay-friendly workplaces are positioned discursively, giving rise to pertinent questions about who is included and recognised as 'normal' within such settings and who is marginalised and excluded. Taking this further, queer theory directs attention to the diverse realities in how genders and sexualities are performed and lived at work rather than how others such as employers, policy-makers or even researchers think they are experienced or *should* be understood. Pursuing these issues over the course of this chapter, I begin by examining why gay-friendly organisations matter to employers and those people who inhabit them, which is to consider concomitantly the contextual conditions of their possibility.

CONTEXTUALISING WORKPLACES AS 'GAY-FRIENDLY'

Understanding why gay-friendly places of work matter to employers who seek to claim such a label and those who work within them involves acknowledging the larger changes in the landscape of sexual politics and transformations in sexual and intimate life. There can be no question here of offering a detailed inventory of these changes (see Weeks, 2007), but it is worth mentioning some of these in broad terms. As noted by Weeks (2007), public attitudes towards gay and lesbian people appear to be noticeably liberal in the UK and some parts of the world. It has been generally observed that many LGBT people are currently more visible in the public eye. For example, Seidman (2002) examines the how some gay men and lesbians are constructed as 'normal' in mainstream film and TV programmes, insofar as they are constructed as figures who aspire to meet the heterosexual ideals of a living heteronormative life. Academics have also speculated about the demise of the 'closet' (Seidman, Meeks and Traschen, 1999) and the 'death of the homosexual' (Bech, 1999), signifying perhaps a new era in living sexual diversity that is less connected to shame, secrecy and negativity. In this vein, new normative and politically recognised schemes of relating intimately are indicative of the gains some LGBT people have made in terms of living 'normal' lives. The introduction of the Civil Partnership Act (2004) in the UK has been applauded but also slated as a pivotal moment in normalising gay and lesbian people within a legal and political framework of human rights (Stychin, 2006; Harding, 2008).

Whichever position one chooses to adopt within these debates, civil partnerships and same-sex marriages (where they are legally recognised) can be understood as cultural signs of gay-friendliness that convey something very important at a national level. As Puar (2011: 138) avers, to be 'gay-friendly is to be modern, cosmopolitan, developed, first-world, global north and, most significantly, democratic'. Indeed, claiming to be gay-friendly as a nation implies a commendable track record on LGBT rights. But the cracks are already beginning to show in some of these seemingly bold and progressive claims, and they deserve closer scrutiny. For example, Israel has courted controversy over its self-promotion as a gay-friendly nation: a champion of LGBT rights and equalities and a former host of World Pride in 2006. Critics have seen in Israel's positioning as gay-friendly something sinister: nefarious political motives to perpetuate propaganda on Palestine to maintain a schism between the two nations, with Palestine constructed as parochial and backward-thinking on LGBT issues (Puar, 2011). In that regard,

Israel has drawn sharp criticism about 'pinkwashing' over its own litany of misdemeanours regarding LGBT equalities and human rights.

Despite a sense of deep unease that surrounds some claims to be gay-friendly, an increasing number of employers are positioning themselves along these lines and for good reasons. In the UK, one of the most significant influencing factors has been the introduction and enforcement of protective legislation; namely, the Employment Equality (Sexual Orientation) Regulations (2003) and the Equality Act (2010). The Sexual Orientation Regulations (2003) have been hailed as a triumph in banning discrimination on the grounds of sexual orientation, while the Equality Act (2010) has introduced a single 'public duty', which demands all public bodies promote equality across the board. Similar transformations in the legislative and policy frameworks regarding discrimination on the grounds of sexual orientation are observable in other countries (Waaldijk and Bonini-Baraldi, 2006; Cavico, Muffler and Mujtaba, 2012), although such formal provisions and their effects on LGBT employees are by no means uniform and universal. While UK employers are required to meet their legal obligations here, an increasing number it seems are actively looking to avoid being labelled as, to put it simply, 'gay-unfriendly'. Studies on LGBT-unfriendly workplaces have over the last three decades or so exposed these organisational settings as homophobic and heterosexist, in which heterosexuality is often reproduced as a master and 'natural' category of sexuality against which homosexuality is cast as inferior and Other (Woods and Lucas, 1992; Humphrey, 1999; Bowring and Brewis, 2009; Ozturk, 2011).

As Colgan et al. (2007) rightly suggest, based on analysis of sixteen UK 'good practice' organisations, the legal protection provided by the (Sexual Orientation) Regulations (2003) is not a panacea for LGBT workplace discrimination, but it has exerted a positive influence as *another* driver for equality action. Previously, social justice and business case arguments for addressing sexual orientation at work served as the stimulus for employers to develop formal 'gay-friendly' signals such as policies that include sexual orientation, LGBT networks and support groups. Typically organisations in the public sector have been in the vanguard here, heralded as beacons of 'good practice' (Colgan et al., 2007). However, the 'modernization agenda' implemented by a former Labour government in the 1990s (Colgan and Wright, 2011) and lacerating cuts in public sector spending conditioned by a culture of 'austerity' have not just stifled 'good practice' in this area but, as Colgan and Wright (2011) suggest, also reversed it. On a more positive note, Colgan and McKearney (2012) submit that the initial impetus for developing a more inclusive work environment for LGBT employees can crystallise out of the activism of LGBT employees and their allies. They cite LGBT trade unions and more recently company network groups as contemporary examples of LGBT activism that seem to offer employee voice mechanisms in the UK. Notably, some of the LGBT company networks studied by Colgan and McKearney (2012) appeared to draw heavily on a business case argument for sexual diversity in the workplace. The business case discourse incentivises organisations to harness human differences on the basis that doing so will deliver, among other things, enhanced financial performance and efficiency. Still, LGBT workplace activism comes in many forms, not all of them driven by a business case for creating gay-friendly workplaces, such as those conditioned by workplace friendships (Rumens, 2011, 2012). Despite the varied conditions of possibility for gay-friendly workplaces, it is of note that they are typically understood and framed in a way that must be of benefit to employers as well as LGBT employees.

But how do people know which employers are gay-friendly? One major publication in that regard is the Workforce Equality Index, produced by the gay and lesbian rights organisation Stonewall. Published in 2005, the index is celebrated as the annual guide to Britain's most gay-friendly employers (Stonewall, 2013) and forms the centrepiece of the Diversity Champions accreditation scheme for employers, established in 2001. Submissions to the index are assessed against twenty-five questions across eight areas of good practice: (1) employee policy; (2) employee engagement; (3) staff training and development; (4) monitoring; (5) supplier policy; (6) LGB community engagement; (7) the 'pink plateau'; and (8) additional evidence and staff feedback. Such criteria operate as a mechanism for sifting and ranking the best UK companies for LGB people to work for. In addition to this criteria, Stonewall have published a number of documents that promulgate a business case for 'good practice' around sexual orientation (e.g., *Peak Performance: Gay People and Productivity* [2008]; *How to Engage Gay People in Your Work* [2011]). Colgan and McKearney (2012) acknowledge this also, noting how Stonewall recommends that LGBT company networks formulate a case that should benefit both employers and LGBT employees. Certainly the publication of an annual survey on Britain's gay-friendly employers does a commendable job of showcasing 'good practice' in the field of sexual orientation equality, but with it comes a number of unanswered questions that relate to how the term *gay-friendly* is being understood, measured and deployed as well as what it means to those it is intended to 'speak' to. Here then I have concerns. What structures my apprehension specifically is that *gay-friendly* is a polysemous term with multiple meanings, definitions and uses; yet it seems to achieve prominence and exert influence in a 'business-friendly' version that is palatable for employers. As such, I wish to articulate a number of issues and concerns about business-friendly constructions of gay-friendly organisations through a queer theory lens. Before doing so it is useful to elaborate on queer theory.

QUEER THEORY

Queer theory has become well-established within the social sciences since its emergence from the humanities departments of US universities during the late 1980s and now commands a substantial body of scholarship (Warner, 1993; Seidman, 1996; Edelman, 2004; Richardson Mclaughlin and Casey, 2012; Taylor and Addison, 2013). Growing out of poststructuralism, feminism and gay and lesbian studies, queer theory is a diverse body of conceptual resources and theorists favoured by those scholars for whom the heteronormative aspects of everyday life are troubling, in how they condition and govern the possibilities for individuals to build meaningful identities and selves. In this sense, it is crucial to acknowledge that queer theory is neither anti heterosexuality nor best understood as something intrinsically against what is 'heterosexual'. Rather, queer theory functions as a set of conceptual resources for challenging what is constructed as 'normal' and normative in different contexts and at any moment in time (Warner, 1993, 1999; Halperin, 1995). As such, the potential analytical focus of queer theory is potentially far wider than sexuality and gender (Halley and Parker, 2011). Although queer theory is a notoriously vague concept to define—this has sparked heated debate about its meaning, role and life expectancy (Halley and Parker, 2011)—it has stimulated and nourished ongoing critiques that seek to problematize and destabilize the normative status ascribed to heterosexuality.

While queer theories mean different things to different people in different contexts, Stein and Plummer (1994: 181–182) identify four 'hallmarks' of queer theory: (1) a conceptualisation of sexuality wherein sexual power runs through everyday life, 'expressed discursively and enforced through boundaries and binary divides'; (2) a concern with problematizing sexual and gender categories, and identities; (3) 'a rejection of civil rights strategies in favour of a politics of carnival, transgression, and parody', which may engender deconstruction, decentring and anti-assimilationist politics; and (4) a 'willingness to interrogate areas which normally would not be seen as the terrain of sexuality', such as conducting 'queer' readings of 'ostensibly heterosexual or nonsexual texts'. Indeed, the last few decades or so have been witness to a large boom in the number of 'queering' endeavours relating to consumer culture, literature, education, television and film, human relationships and religion to mention but a few. Queering may be understood as an activity that interrogates and deconstructs social and cultural norms, one that also searches for queer phenomena in places where we least expect to find it, which is to say that queering is a deconstructive and political practice (Warner, 1993). The process of queering and the other hallmarks associated with queer theories informs the theoretical scene against which this chapter examines gay-friendly workplaces.

EXAMINING WORKPLACES AS GAY-FRIENDLY THROUGH A QUEER THEORY LENS

Although queer theorists and queer theories are hegemonic in some academic contexts, notably those in the arts and humanities, they have started to venture into the field of organisation studies, finding sympathetic audiences at its critical fringes. This is evidenced by a rash of queer theory–inspired interrogations of management and organisation (Parker, 2001, 2002; Tyler and Cohen, 2008), leadership (Harding et al., 2011), workplace friendships (Rumens, 2012) and specific occupational fields such as construction and public administration (Lee, Learmonth and Harding, 2008; Rumens, 2013). As exemplified by this slowly growing body of research, queer theory is effective at challenging what we take for granted in organisation and chipping away at the binaries that structure organisational life. As another instance of this, I examine gay-friendly workplace using a queer lens.

On the Term *Gay-Friendly*

Given that queer theory contests the apparent stability of sexual and gender identity categories, one striking feature and problem about the concept of gay-friendly relates to the analytic architecture and intent of the term itself. The deployment of *gay* in *gay-friendly* as a blanket term to refer to LGBT people fails to convey the complexity of social diversity within and between sexual minorities. As such, the term itself is flawed at a conceptual level because it reproduces essentialist assumptions about what individuals, groups or communities are being invoked by the use of the word *gay*. Cronin and King (2010: 876) make a similar criticism of the term *gay* when it has been used as shorthand for describing diverse LGBT cultures and communities. As illustrated in this edited collection and elsewhere, it is commonplace among scholars to use a variety of identity-based acronyms (e.g., LGB, LGBT, LGBTQ, LGBTQI) in order to counter the tendency to refer to sexual minorities as single interest groups. Such acronyms are not without problems (Cronin and King, 2010), but arguably, they fare better in thwarting the essentialism implied in the term *gay-friendly*, which suggests homogeneity and uniformity in LGBT sexualities where there is often very little. Indeed, against a theoretical backcloth that acknowledges the fluidity, instability and multiplicity of sexual and gendered identities, the conceptual deficiencies of the term are thrown into sharp relief. Yet in literature on gay-friendly employers produced by Stonewall (2008, 2011) and in scholarly research, even that which seeks to critique the impact of gay-friendly workplaces on employees (Giuffre, Dellinger and Williams, 2008; Williams, Giuffre and Dellinger, 2009), a sharpened critical awareness about the theoretical inadequacy of the term itself is often found wanting. What concerns me here is not only that gay-friendly can be deployed unthinkingly and characteristically out of synch with recent research that has sought to examine the diversity *within* sexual and gendered identity categories (Rumens, 2012) but also how these categories intersect with other formations of difference such as class (Wright, 2011). My point then is that gay-friendly is an awkward term that wrings out the complexities of lived diversities in LGBT people's lives.

This has serious implications for advancing knowledge on how gay-friendly work environments may be understood and experienced differently between LGBT employees. For instance, one of the lesbian study participants in Giuffre, Dellinger and Williams's (2008) US study of gay friendly workplaces reported being treated like 'one of the boys' in conversations that objectified women sexually. In this example the female employee was subject to a form gender inversion based on a faulty stereotype of lesbians as naturally more masculine than heterosexual women, which presented problems in the company of male colleagues who assumed this employee shared sexist attitudes towards women because lesbians also date women. In this specific account of working as a lesbian in a gay-friendly workplace, experiences of work are mediated by other formations of difference such as gender. Yet referring to workplaces as gay-friendly can obscure these specific experiences shaped by gender, especially when they reveal such organisational contexts as sexist and discriminatory against women. Similarly, what might be a welcoming and friendly work context for some gay men might not be experienced in the same way by women who identify as lesbian or, indeed, as bisexual or trans (the latter two are rarely accounted for in studies on gay-friendly workplaces). In the same way, how might we understand organisations in which lesbian women are more accepted than gay men: as gay-friendly, lesbian-friendly or something else? It is not that I unswervingly advocate substituting one term with another or an acronym, but it is imperative to acknowledge the discursive closure levied by gay-friendly as a concept for understanding and normalising LGBT experiences in organisation. Through a queer theory lens, these variations are amenable to study. Examining how they are used in practice in organisations would help us to analyse less about whether workplaces can properly be described as gay-friendly and more about how organisational life is coloured as a result of being labelled gay-friendly. Still, assessing the gay-friendliness of various workplaces is an important endeavour pursued by some organisations, which brings forth a different set of concerns.

Measuring Gay-Friendly Workplaces

Stonewall has approached the issue of identifying and assessing how workplaces can be considered gay-friendly from a specific direction by designing criteria for evaluating manifestations of gay-friendliness in the workplace (cited above). These criteria cover all manner of issues that relate to organisational culture, policies, workplace relations and 'pink glass ceilings'. From this angle, Stonewall's Diversity Champions programme tends to position the organisation rather than the individual as the locus of change for advancing equality agendas on sexual orientation and employment. In one sense this is encouraging, but this is tempered by the fact that this accreditation scheme is voluntary, involving willing participants who actively seek to become 'diversity champions'. In this way, the attractiveness of such schemes is the capital they provide to employers in terms of achieving 'gay-friendly' status and the potential positive benefits this incurs (e.g., publicity, becoming an employer of choice for LGBT people). In contrast, organisations indifferent towards or reluctant to engage in sexual orientation equality work, arguably those most likely to gain from such forms of assessment, simply don't factor in.

Considering the above, a fundamental and more pressing question springs forth: can gay-friendly workplaces be identified and measured as such? Through a queer theory lens a deep-rooted assumption of Stonewall's Equality Index is unearthed: that gay-friendly employers can be recognized and ranked in gradations of gay-friendliness, the disciplinary effect of which is evident in how employers can be categorised as gay-friendly or not. This raises some knotty issues about measurement that need unravelling. As scholarly research reveals (Colgan et al., 2007; Giuffre, Dellinger and Williams, 2008; Williams, Giuffre and Dellinger, 2009), assessments about whether workplaces may be understood and experienced as gay-friendly can be regarded as context specific, subject to variation between individuals and open to alteration over time. Clearly then one troubling effect of producing indexes or lists is their capacity to transform the inchoate and complex disorderliness of organisational life into something static and tangible. In other words, the gay-friendly workplace can be constructed as something that is readily identifiable and thus culpable to managerial designs. In short, it is a legitimate target for management.

Articulating this further, it is useful to rely on the poststructuralist ancestry of queer theory by which it is possible to analyse how Stonewall draws on a business case discourse mobilised by those corporations which have mastered the art of measuring sexual diversity as a marketable signifier (Raeburn, 2004; Ward, 2008). On pragmatic grounds it is an effective discursive strategy. It affords the measurer a degree of prestige and authority, particularly in exercising power to label some employers as gay-friendly at a time when sexual diversity apparently matters to many employers (Colgan et al., 2007, 2009). Notably, the numbers of employers seeking accreditation through Stonewall's Equality Index continues to rise annually (Stonewall, 2013). What is more, engaging in a business case discourse occasions opportunities for LGBT organisations to connect with companies using a language they understand and find palatable. Other scholars have pointed to cases where queer and LGBT rights–based organisations on both sides of the Atlantic understand that, by emphasising sexuality as a diversity issue of commercial importance, they can potentially widen the range of their supporters, increase publicity and gain traction within the corporate realm (Ward, 2008). Be that as it may, engaging with a normative business case discourse on diversity can be hazardous, not the least of these hazards being the risk of co-optation. Indeed, some trade unions and more radical LGBT groups have criticised the business case discourse and Stonewall's increasing 'hegemony' in the sexual orientation equality area, but their power to influence the agenda along different directions of travel has been diminishing in the context of neoliberalism and austerity (Colgan and McKearney, 2012: 361, 372). From a queer theory perspective, dominant discourses are an important focal point of analysis given that they can neutralise (perhaps not completely) oppositional force levied by those discourses which are marginal (Seidman, 1996). Of specific concern then is how business-friendly assessments and constructions of workplaces and employers as gay-friendly can reproduce the very heteronormativities that damp down the disruptive and destabilising effects of particular LGBT identities and selves in the workplace. This represents an empirical knowledge gap, although theoretical accounts on the heteronormative components to business case discourses on diversity are emerging (Bendl, Fleischmann and Walenta, 2008). For empirical insights into how LGBT people understand their workplaces as gay-friendly, there is a small and important body of emergent scholarship from which I draw in the next section (Giuffre, Dellinger and Williams, 2008; Rumens and Kerfoot, 2009; Williams, Giuffre and Dellinger, 2009; Colgan and McKearney, 2011).

The Normalising Effects of Gay-Friendly Workplaces

Williams, Giuffre and Dellinger's (2009) US study is one of very few to use queer and feminist theories to serve up a tart corrective to the blithe assumption that gay-friendly workplaces represent a progressive step forward for the LGB employees who work within them. On the one hand, gay-friendly workplaces were largely defined by study participants as contexts in which they could openly disclose and participate as LGB in organisational life. On the other hand, interview accounts revealed the constraints inflicted by prevailing heteronormative expectations with gay-friendly workplaces about how LGB people should dress and behave. For some participants this meant being careful never to make gay jokes or 'camp it up' in a way that might provoke accusations from colleagues about 'flaunting' sexuality at work. As Williams, Giuffre and Dellinger (2009) argue, even in workplaces that study participants defined as gay-friendly, heteronormative power relations continue to exert a harmful influence, reproducing normative standards about what is a normal and what is an abnormal manifestation of homosexuality. Normative versions of homosexuality in gay-friendly workplaces were evident in available subject positions characterised by, among other things, the expression of conservative politics, being in a monogamous, long-term relationship and dressing 'professionally'. Williams, Giuffre and Dellinger (2009) shed light on how gay and lesbian identities are vulnerable to processes of heteronormalisation in the workplace, which squelches possibilities for living sexual diversity against the grain of heteronormativity. Viewed in this way, some employees actively sought to discard any potentially offensive qualities about being LGB in order to demonstrate that LGB people are *just like heterosexuals.* Mindful of this I share the concern voiced by Williams, Giuffre and Dellinger (2009) that maintaining 'normal' gay and lesbian identities grounded in a politics of heteronormativity can result in a state of 'invisibility' or a 'gay-friendly closet', as they put it, insomuch as becoming 'normal' means emphasising similarities and playing down differences with normative constructions of heterosexuality. Under these circumstances, there appears to be little room for constructing alternative sexualities such as queer sexualities, especially if queer sexualities are understood as harbouring potential for rupturing the discursive arrangements that sustain a heterosexual/homosexual binary which normalises sexual difference. Crucially, it is important not to take for granted the idea that a gay-friendly workplace is conducive to LGBT employees being able to live their lives against the grain of heteronormativity.

Pursuing this issue in another direction exposes another glaring omission in the study of gay-friendly workplaces: the analysis of heterosexualities. The attentiveness paid by queer theory to the study of sexualities has by and large given primacy to gay and lesbian sexualities. While there is good reason to invest in the ontological examination of gay and lesbian sexualities, conceptualising queer theories as a shifting zone of inquiry about what is 'normal' and 'normative' allows us to extend its analytical reach to include heterosexualities. So far, some of the most prominent research on gay-friendly workplaces has excluded heterosexuals from study samples (e.g., Giuffre, Dellinger and Williams, 2008; Williams, Giuffre and Dellinger, 2009), leaving unanswered questions about when and how heterosexuals might resist, disrupt or act complicity with heteronormative discourses that construct workplaces as gay-friendly. Similarly, we might ask what gay-friendly organisations mean to heterosexuals. Conceivably there is a lot at stake for heterosexuals in the construction of organisations as gay-friendly, whether as defenders of heteronormativity or as 'straight allies' who, acting on principles of social justice and alongside LGBT persons, wish to eradicate inequalities (Raeburn, 2004; Brooks and Edwards, 2009). Here we examine more closely how heterosexualities and privilege intertwine, especially with other formations of difference such as ethnicity, race, class, able-bodiness and age. After all, workplaces described as gay-friendly may also be understood as racist, sexist and ageist (Williams, Giuffre and Dellinger, 2009). More to the point of this chapter is the observation that we ought not to rule out the possibilities that some heterosexuals may wish to contest organisational heteronormativity, as nascent research on 'straight allies' testifies (Brooks and Edwards, 2009). Crucial to rendering this issue vulnerable to investigation is avoiding the essentialist trap of conflating heterosexuality with heteronormativity. Eliding the two threatens to silt up any discursive channels for critical reflection among heterosexuals on heterosexualities, especially as heteronormativities can have an inimical effect on heterosexuals in the workplace. It is entirely reasonable to imagine that heterosexuals might engage in critiques of heteronormativity, interrogating their investments in workplaces labelled gay-friendly in order to become powerful affiliates in queering organisational sexualities.

CONCLUDING REMARKS

Deriving conceptual insights from queer theories, I have across the pages of this chapter examined the inclination among commentators and organisations towards describing some workplaces and employers as gay-friendly. I have argued that gay-friendly is a polysemous term with multiple uses and meanings. Yet in some of its most conspicuous articulations it frequently finds expression in a business-friendly version that dovetails with the corporate bottom line. Notably also, the demands of some LGB charity organisations like Stonewall are being framed in a similar way that indicates compatibility with the bottom line rather than threatening the status quo. This suggests that some incarnations of gay-friendly workplaces are strategically aligned with notions of corporate success in terms of profit, efficiency and prosperity, although some trade unions, such as the Trade Union Congress (TUC) in the UK, have tried to counterpose this direction of travel. It is not my intention to discredit the work of organisations like Stonewall for these reasons; rather, it is my intention to inspire a mode of critique that sensitises us to how specific ways of framing workplaces as gay-friendly creates a seductive and seemingly reliable shorthand of value or worth. Nor can we assume that gay-friendly employers are synonymous with gay-friendly workplaces. It is quite possible that gay-friendly work contexts may emerge and disappear (un)predictably despite and in spite of employers who are reluctant to acknowledge LGBT sexualities.

As such, I sound a cautionary note against reading workplaces framed as gay-friendly as a 'natural' and logical next step in the development and materialisation of LGBT equalities at work. Unquestionably this chapter offers my own preliminary speculations in that regard. Still, I remain troubled by how certain constructions of workplaces as gay-friendly can operate symbolically and as a regulatory regime, doing little to undermine the heteronormativities entrenched in everyday work life and the organisational inequalities they reproduce. At best, the use of gay-friendly to label workplaces as such might signal some significant material gains for LGBT employees (e.g., domestic partner policies, company network groups, protection from discrimination, opportunities to disclose as LGBT), but I have been at pains to point out what may be obscured: alternative conceptualisations of gay-friendly workplaces from the perspectives of those who identify as LGBT, queer, heterosexual or something else.

Mindful of the above, where do we go from here? In bringing this chapter to a close, I offer the following avenues of future research for those interested in studying gay-friendly workplaces. Empirical and conceptual research is warranted on how normative discourses of gay-friendly workplaces are predicated on a politics of heteronormativity that (re)produces the dominance of normative heterosexuality. One question might be, are organisational expressions of gay-friendliness the latest turn of emphasis in the process by which gay and lesbian people are folded into normative heterosexual culture? Extending this line of inquiry, researchers might ask what place is there within gay-friendly workplaces for bisexual and trans employees? How can the perspectives of these individuals help to rupture the heterosexual/homosexual binary division upon which some constructions of gay-friendly are indebted? Furthermore, we need to address how workplaces can at one and the same time be understood as gay-friendly and sexist, racist and ageist to mention just a few discriminatory behaviours. Queer theory analyses can help here by accounting for the mobility of such things as sex, gender, race and ethnicity without evoking fixed points of intersection between and among these axes of difference. As with some scholars (Ward, 2008; Williams and Giuffre, 2011), we might turn our attention to 'queer organisations'. This might include organisational forms that emerge and are sustained when queer activism and politics has served as an organising principle. The study of 'queer organisations' might provide insights into what (if anything) is 'queer' about these organisations and whether they are different from gay-friendly organisations. Again, why and how might some organisations seek to construct themselves as 'queer', and what happens when organisational life is coloured by queer activism? Finally, we might envision queer futures in organisation that could provide the conditions for subjects to (re)construct and live different identity categories, realities and possibilities at work. It is reasonable to speculate that some organisations can occasion opportunities for subjects to engage in such queering activities at work, whereby queer is seen as an organising element of organisational life. One line of research is that we might search for queer instances that enable queer identified subjects to renew connections with a politics of shame, nonproductivity and failure (see Edelman, 2004; Halberstam, 2011). Concerning these avenues of inquiry, this chapter has pointed to a horizon of possibilities in that respect, arguing that queer theories can offer vital modes of critique that allow us to challenge the hetero/normative logics that sustain some constructions of workplaces as gay-friendly.

REFERENCES

Bech, H. (1999) 'After the Closet', *Sexualities*, 2(3): 343–349.

Bendl, R., Fleischmann, A. and Walenta, C. (2008) 'Diversity Management Discourse Meets Queer Theory', *Gender in Management: An International Journal*, 23(6): 382–394.

Bowring, M. and Brewis, J. (2009) 'Truth and Consequences: Managing Lesbian and Gay Identity in the Canadian Workplace', *Equal Opportunities International*, 28(5): 361–377.

Brooks, A. K. and Edwards, K. (2009) 'Allies in the Workplace: Including LGBT in HRD', *Advances in Developing Human Resources*, 11(1): 136–149.

Cavico, F. J., Muffler, S. C. and Mujtaba, B. G. (2012) 'Sexual Orientation and Gender Identity Discrimination in the American Workplace: Legal and Ethical Considerations', *International Journal of Humanities and Social Science*, 2(1): 1–20.

Colgan, F., Creegan, C., McKearney, A. and Wright, T. (2007) 'Equality and Diversity Policies and Practices at Work: Lesbian, Gay, and Bisexual Workers', *Equal Opportunities International*, 26(6): 590–609.

Colgan, F. and McKearney, A. (2011) 'Creating Inclusive Organisations: What Do Lesbian, Gay and Bisexual Employees in the Private Sector Think Makes a Difference?' in Wright, T. and Conley, H. (eds) *Handbook of Discrimination*, Gower: Aldershot, 97–110.

Colgan, F. and McKearney, A. (2012) 'Visibility and Voice in Organisations: Lesbian, Gay, Bisexual and Transgendered Employee Networks', *Equality, Diversity and Inclusion: An International Journal*, 31(4): 359–378.

Colgan, F. and Wright, T. (2011) 'Lesbian, Gay and Bisexual Equality in a Modernizing Public Sector 1997–2010: Opportunities and Threats', *Gender, Work & Organization*, 18(5): 548–570.

Colgan, F., Wright, T., Creegan, C., and McKearney, A. (2009) 'Equality and Diversity in the Public Services: Moving Forward on Lesbian, Gay and Bisexual Equality?' *Human Resource Management Journal*, 19(3): 280–301.

Correia, N. and Kleiner, B. H. (2001) 'New Developments Concerning Sexual Orientation Discrimination and Harassment', *International Journal of Sociology and Social Policy*, 21(8/9/10): 92–100.

Cronin, A. and King, A. (2010) 'Power, Inequality and Identification: Exploring Diversity and Intersectionality amongst Older LGB Adults', *Sociology*, 44(5): 876–892.

Edelman, L. (2004) *No Future: Queer Theory and the Death Drive*. Durham, NC: Duke University Press.

Fleming, P. (2007) 'Sexuality, Power and Resistance in the Workplace', *Organization Studies*, 28(2): 239–256.

Giuffre, P., Dellinger, K. and Williams, C. L. (2008) 'No Retribution for Being Gay?: Inequality in Gay-Friendly Workplaces', *Sociological Spectrum*, 28(3): 254–277.

Halberstam, J. (2011) *The Queer Art of Failure*. Durham, NC: Duke University Press.

Halley, J. and Parker, A. (2011) (eds) *After Sex? On Writing Since Queer Theory*. Durham, NC: Duke University Press.

Halperin, D. (1995) *Saint Foucault: Towards a Gay Hagiography*. New York: Oxford University Press.

Harding, N., Lee, H., Ford, J. and Learmonth, M. (2011) 'Leadership and Charisma: A Desire that Cannot Speak Its Name?' *Human Relations*, 64(7): 927–949.

Harding, R. (2008) 'Recognizing (and Resisting) Regulation: Attitudes to the Introduction of Civil Partnership', *Sexualities*, 11(6): 740–760.

Humphrey, J. C. (1999) 'Organizing Sexualities, Organized Inequalities: Lesbians and Gay Men in Public Service Occupations', *Gender, Work & Organization*, 6(3): 134–151.

Lee, H., Learmonth, M. and Harding, N. (2008) 'Queer(y)ing Public Administration', *Public Administration*, 86(1): 149–167.

Ozturk, M. B. (2011) 'Sexual Orientation Discrimination: Exploring the Experiences of Lesbian, Gay and Bisexual Employees in Turkey', *Human Relations*, 64(8): 1099–1118.

Parker, M. (2001) 'Fucking Management: Queer, Theory and Reflexivity', *ephemera*, 1(1): 36–53.

Parker, M. (2002) 'Queering Management and Organization', *Gender, Work & Organization*, 9(2): 146–166.

Puar, J. (2011) 'Citation and Censorship: The Politics of Talking About the Sexual Politics of Israel', *Feminist Legal Studies*, 19(2): 133–142.

Raeburn, N. (2004) *Changing Corporate America from Inside Out: Lesbian and Gay Workplace Rights.* Minneapolis: University of Minnesota Press.

Ragins, B. R. and Cornwell, J. M. (2001) 'Pink Triangles: Antecedents and Consequences of Perceived Workplace Discrimination against Gay and Lesbian Employees', *Journal of Applied Psychology*, 86(6): 1244–1261.

Richardson, D., Mclaughlin, J. and Casey, M. E. (2012) (eds.) *Intersections between Feminist and Queer Theory.* Basingstoke: Palgrave Macmillan.

Rumens, N. (2012) 'Queering Cross-Sex Friendships: An Analysis of Gay and Bisexual Men's Workplace Friendships with Heterosexual Women', *Human Relations*, 65(8): 955–978.

Rumens, N. (2013) 'Queering Men and Masculinities in Construction: Towards a research Agenda', *Construction Management and Economics*, 31(8): 802–815.

Rumens, N. and Broomfield, J. (2012) 'Gay Men in the Police: Identity Disclosure and Management Issues', *Human Resource Management Journal*, 22(3): 283–298.

Rumens, N. and Kerfoot, D. (2009) 'Gay Men at Work: (Re)constructing the Self as Professional', *Human Relations*, 62(5): 763–786.

Seidman, S. (1996) (ed.) *Queer Theory/Sociology.* Oxford: Blackwell.

Seidman, S. (2002) *Beyond the Closet: The Transformation of Gay and Lesbian Life.* New York: Routledge.

Seidman, S., Meeks, C. and Traschen, F. (1999) 'Beyond the Closet? The Changing Social Meaning of Homosexuality in the United States', *Sexualities*, 2(1): 9–34.

Simon, W. (1996) *Postmodern Sexualities.* London: Routledge.

Stein, A. and Plummer, K. (1994) ' "I Can't Even Think Straight": "Queer" Theory and the Missing Sexual Revolution in Sociology', *Sociological Theory*, 12(2): 178–187.

Stonewall (2008) *Peak Performance: Gay People and Productivity.* London: Stonewall.

Stonewall (2011) *How to Engage Gay People in Your Work.* London: Stonewall.

Stonewall (2013) *Workplace Equality Index 2013.* London: Stonewall.

Stychin, C. (2006) 'Las Vegas is Not Where We Are: Queer Readings of the Civil Partnership Act', *Political Geography*, 25(8): 899–920.

Taylor, Y. and Addison, M. (2013) (eds) *Queer Presences and Absences.* Basingstoke: Palgrave Macmillan.

Tejeda, M. J. (2006) 'Nondiscrimination Policies and Sexual Identity Disclosure: Do They Make a Difference in Employee Outcomes?' *Employee Responsibilities and Rights Journal*, 18: 45–59.

Tyler, M. and Cohen, L. (2008) 'Management in/as Comic Relief: Queer Theory and Gender Performativity in the Office', *Gender, Work & Organization*, 15(2): 113–132.

Waaldijk, C. and Bonini-Baraldi, M. (2006) *Sexual Orientation Discrimination in the European Union.* Hague: T.M.C. Asser Press.

Ward, J. (2008) *Respectably Queer: Diversity Culture in LGBT Activist Organizations.* Nashville: Vanderbilt University Press.

Warner, M. (1993) *Fear of a Queer Planet: Queer Politics and Social Theory.* Minneapolis: University of Minnesota.

Warner, M. (1999) *The Trouble with Normal: Sex, Politics, and the Ethics of Queer Life.* New York: The Free Press.

Weeks, J. (2007) *The World We Have Won.* London: Routledge.

Williams, C. and Giuffre, P. (2011) 'From Organizational Sexuality to Queer Organizations: Research on Homosexuality and the Workplace', *Sociology Compass*, 5(7): 551–563.

Williams, C. L., Giuffre, P. A. and Dellinger, K. (2009) 'The Gay-Friendly Closet', *Sexuality Research and Social Policy*, 6(1): 29–45.

Wood, P. B. and Bartkowski, J. P. (2004) 'Attribution Style and Public Policy Attitudes Toward Gay Rights', *Social Science Quarterly*, 85(1): 58–74.

Woods, J. D. and Lucas, J. H. (1993) *The Corporate Closet: The Professional Lives of Gay Men in America*. New York: The Free Press.

Wright, T. (2011) 'A "Lesbian Advantage"? Analysing the Intersections of Gender, Sexuality and Class in Male Dominated Work', *Equality, Diversity and Inclusion: An International Journal*, 30(8): 686–701.

13 Moving from 'Invisibility' into National Statistics? Lesbians and the Socioeconomic Sphere

Roswitha Hofmann, Karin Schönpflug and Christine Klapeer[1]

INTRODUCTION: SEXUALITY AS A CATEGORY IN SOCIOECONOMIC STATISTICS

A growing international body of research on LGBs'[2] living and working conditions (e.g., Colgan et al. 2007; Guasp and Balfour 2008; Plug and Berkhout 2008; Brand 2009; Losert 2009; Hofmann and Cserer 2010) and general policy discussions (e.g., Equality and Human Rights Commission 2009) as well as insights from within LGBTIQ[3] movements and theories indicate that sexuality has a tremendous impact on the socioeconomic status, labour market standing and social cohesion of lesbian women, gay men and bisexual people (Takács 2006). These theoretical and political discussions therefore highlight the need to consider sexuality less as a 'private matter' of 'erotic desire' or an individual 'sexual orientation' but rather as an analytical category, thus giving light to the stratificatory effects of sexuality and its deeply historical, political and social character (Foucault 1983; Evans 1993; Rubin 1993 [1984]). Michel Foucault (1983) refers to sexuality as a 'dispositif', a bundle of rules, discourses, practices and institutions that organize and regulate power structures in societies. Gayle Rubin strongly argued against libidinal or biological explanations of sexuality by demonstrating how and in which ways ('Western') societies are framed by a complex system of sexual stratification through social hierarchies on the basis of 'normal/ised' and 'deviant' sexual identities and behaviours (Rubin 1993 [1984]). Queer theorist David Evans indicated the socioeconomic effects of this modern system of sexual stratification by pointing to the 'material' consequences of living a lesbian/gay/queer life (Evans 1993).

Acknowledging sexuality as a stratificatory category and (hetero)sexuality therefore as a social institution, thus positioning LGBs in a particular way within heteronormative social and economic structures, provokes an interest in the 'sexual politics' of a society and the related social and political institutions and sociocultural norms (Butler 1990; Rich 1994). As a consequence of these vibrant theoretical and political discussions on the discriminatory and marginalizing effects of sexual stratification, not only international LGBTIQ organizations but also national and European public

bodies as well as academic scholars and researchers are increasingly pointing to the importance of data collection as a potent method to *quantify* the
stratificatory impact of sexuality on the socioeconomic status of LGBs, thus
allowing research to 'measure progress on tackling discrimination and tackling inequality' (Aspinall 2009; FRA 2009; Mitchell et al. 2009).

However, drawing on poststructuralist, governmentalist and queer theories, particularly Judith Butler's concept of heteronormativity (Butler 1990)
and Michel Foucault's concept of governmentality (2005), in which Foucault
describes a framework of power strategies that discipline and normalise
individuals and collectives in modern societies and states, this chapter seeks
to highlight some of the ambivalent and contradictory implications of quantitative research and data collection on LGBs. It will be argued that generating and working with socioeconomic statistics on lesbian women (and
LGBs in general) presumes and (re)produces certain problematic generalisations and (normalizing) categorisations with regard to sexuality and gender.
The lesbian 'data subject' established in socioeconomic statistics is thus 'not
always and already there awaiting identification' but is rather produced by
particular statistical practices along normative frameworks (Browne 2008;
Ruppert 2008; Browne 2010; Ruppert 2011, p. 224; Sokhi-Bulley 2011).
Hence, we would like to illustrate that processes of statistical data generation are not merely 'neutral' procedures of 'revealing' or making lesbians
'visible' but can be interpreted as a specific tool, as 'technologies of governmentality', thereby creating and assembling abstract categories and shaping
(sexual) subjects into 'forms that are calculable and able to be regulated'
(Sokhi-Bulley 2011, p. 141).

Besides these important epistemological discussions on the difficulties in the construction and production of (normalised) sexual identities
through statistical procedures, a critical approach on the socioeconomic
status of lesbians must also take into account the debates addressing the
general methodological and ethical challenges that occur in the process of
data collection on discriminated against and/or stigmatized groups. These
include, for example, questions of data misuse or methodological problems
in 'accessing' those populations (Brown and Knopp 2006; Ruppert 2011;
Sokhi-Bulley 2011; Phellas 2012). Hence, this chapter also demonstrates
that 'statistical visibility' is therefore not always connected to 'liberation' or
'progress' but is also ambivalent in its effect and intention.

RESEARCHING THE SOCIOECONOMIC STATUS
OF LESBIAN WOMEN

When attempting to 'measure' lesbian women and research their socioeconomic status, certain methodological and epistemological considerations
need to be addressed: first, lesbians do not exist in a similar way 'before'
they become statistically 'visible' because they have to be 'quantified' and

made 'countable' within a complex process of (self-)identification and statistical objectification (Ruppert 2008). People have to (or have to be able to) identify themselves in relation to prescribed categories or frameworks in order to be counted as 'lesbians' (for instance, gender/sex, cohabitation/marital status, sexual orientation). Therefore, this chapter also demonstrates that questions 'of what and how' something/someone is counted not only have to be considered with regard to methods and instruments of data collection but also with regard to certain political and ethical presumptions which (may) determine the entire methodological framework of data collection (Browne 2010, p. 233). Researching the socioeconomic status of lesbian women in particular entails sensitivity in matters of (heteronormative) power structures and sociocultural norms/language about sexualities, genders and family/relationship.

This leads to a second methodological problem in researching the socioeconomic status of lesbian women: lesbians are often subsumed under the group of LGBs, thereby assuming a 'similar experience' or comparable 'social standing'. Particularly so-called 'community research approaches' often focus on 'gays', 'homosexuals' or 'LGBs' and lack a differentiation of the embedded subgroups and their specific social standing (e.g., omitting lesbians). Whereas lesbians and gays share some experiences, they face very different socioeconomic realities as well as different forms and genealogies of discrimination and stereotyping (Klapeer 2013). Additionally, differences may not only arise from parenting and related social perceptions but also from the different economic situations associated with gender such as gender pay gaps, vertical and horizontal segregation on the labour markets and gendered discrimination in the workplace (Schönpflug 2012). Because, for example, lesbian women often work in professional areas such as education, social work and care work, where 'sexual orientation/sexuality' is especially understood as taboo, they often feel at risk and choose to remain closeted (see Colgan and Wright 2011). Lesbians are also affected by general gender-related bias (omitting a differentiation between men and women) and a bias based on gender related conceptions of sexuality (omitting homosexualities) in data-gathering methods. Much data may also ignore the interlinkage of categories of discrimination and special 'qualities' of intersectional discriminations (omitting intersectionalities).

Despite these problems, international research and official data gathering on the socioeconomic status of lesbian women and LGBs is slowly emerging. Existing qualitative as well as quantitative studies and rare examples of official data collection are landmarks mostly for the United States and UK context.[4] For European countries, besides certain qualitative case studies, no appropriate and comparable research and/or *official* statistical data exists for answering questions on the socioeconomic status of lesbians and LGBs. Therefore this chapter aims to critically examine the methodological problems and theoretical difficulties of data generation procedures which may be involved in collecting such data. It also aims to identify the availability and quality of data on the socioeconomic status of lesbian women from a queer-feminist and governmentalist perspective in order to highlight the tensions between the necessity of data and the 'normalising' implications of data gathering procedures on lesbian women and LGBs. To do this, we will draw on experiences from two research projects: first, we will discuss the results of an explorative study on Austrian lesbians and their working conditions (Hofmann and Cserer 2010); second, we will present some core findings from a study on the economic status of LGBs at the European level, which particularly highlights the discriminatory implications of current statistical practices (Schönpflug et al. 2013).

LESBIANS AT WORK (LAW)—AN EXPLORATIVE STUDY IN AUSTRIA

When the LaW project, the first survey of lesbians in Austria, was initiated in 2009,[5] legal protection against discrimination on grounds of sexual orientation in Austria existed only within working environments and a legal recognition of same-sex partnerships was still being negotiated.[6] The study's objective was to investigate the data situation of lesbian women in Austria on an official level and on a research level and to gather quantitative and qualitative data on the working and living conditions of lesbians in Austria. Investigating the data situation of lesbians was a difficult endeavour. Although the United Nations Economic Commission for Europe (UNECE) standards state that 'countries may wish to collect and disseminate data on same-sex partnerships' (UNECE 2006, p. 502), the nonbinding character of this standard became apparent for us when the Austrian national statistics institute was unable to provide data on lesbians and same-sex households from national household surveys in 2009. Before LGB partnerships could be registered, same-sex couples were 'cleared' from the gathered data pool or the sex of one household member was changed to be consistent with a heterosexual coupling situation. This meant that no statistical data was available on same-sex households in Austria prior to 2010. In order to achieve the second objective of the study—namely, gathering data on the working and life condition of lesbians in Austria—it was important to tackle some methodological issues connected to the above-mentioned challenges.

Sampling Issues

A first point at the methodological level is that the social invisibility and heteronormative exclusion of lesbian women results in limitations of standard sampling and estimation techniques in research projects. As a consequence, nonprobability methods of data collection are often used, such as convenience sampling (respondent-driven sampling) in communities (Salganik and Heckathorn 2004). Neither probability sampling nor nonprobability sampling methods can avoid all sampling biases such as differential response rates among different subgroups (Meyer and Wilson 2009). For example, in nonprobability samples, multiple inclusion and exclusion patterns of individuals cannot be controlled in a statistical sense; therefore, some individuals have a greater likelihood of being targeted than others. In the case of the LaW online survey, for example, we reached proportionally more lesbians with higher education qualifications. In addition, the stigmatisation of LGBs within empirical research often results in few self-identified LGBs taking part in surveys, thus making an extensive analysis, as well as any generalisations, difficult (Herek et al. 2010, p. 178). As a consequence, the results of LaW inevitably shows a nonrepresentative and therefore only exploratory picture of the socioeconomic situation of the participants. Still, these results were useful in highlighting for the first time the socioeconomic diversity of lesbians in Austria and so providing initial answers to specific questions and for research projects on lesbians in general.

Strong Needs for Anonymity

Whereas doing empirical research on highly stigmatized groups such as lesbian women, who are usually absent from research involving well-known populations (Aspinall 2009), strong needs for anonymity have to be taken into account. Lesbians and gays have much to lose from disclosing their sexual orientation/sexuality (Meyer and Wilson 2009). Therefore, a web-based online survey was used to guarantee anonymity for the participants and—considering the small research budget—to reach as many individuals as possible at low costs. The survey link was available for five weeks. During this period of time, 1,460 clicks on the link were reported. Nine hundred and sixty-two persons started the survey and 636 completed the whole survey. However, web-based surveys come with a range of biases, including different degrees of Internet usages and Internet affinity of certain groups as well as all the problems of a nonreactive research instrument (see Meyer and Colten 1999). In addition to these concerns, doing research on stigmatised groups such as lesbian women implicates further methodological challenges.

Labels and Wordings

'Sexualities' and 'sexual orientations' are highly fluid individual, collective and political phenomena and therefore multifaceted constructs (Herek et al. 2010, p. 177). Thus, on the one hand, sexualities and sexual orientations may change during a lifetime and therefore influence one's self-identification as, for example, 'lesbian', 'gay man' or 'bisexual woman' in surveys and other data collections. On the other hand, labels such as lesbian, gay, bisexual, heterosexual have a strong impact on the formulation and operationalisation of research questions, empirical research and statistical data collection. Especially from a queer perspective, the wording of identity categories in questionnaires for LGBs has to be elaborated thoroughly because it has to be taken into consideration that people prefer/reject different kinds of labelling such as 'lesbian', 'queer', 'women' and so on. As a consequence, in the case of LaW, we asked participants to self-identify their gender identity and sexual orientation in order to offer adequate space for different self-identifications (Hofmann and Cserer 2010, p. 52f).

In summary, on the methodological level, LaW provides an example of how to deal with normalising categorizations and labelling, social invisibility and the need for anonymity of lesbians due to the heteronormative structure of society.

CORE RESULTS OF LAW: THE DIVERSE LESBIAN

Despite some of the above-mentioned methodological problems and biases, the survey showed a first and diverse glimpse of Austrian lesbians. Ninety-five per cent of the 810 participants identified themselves as 'women' and 2 per cent as 'trans*persons', and 3 per cent chose another identity such as 'queer' or 'femme'. Eighty-five per cent identified themselves as 'lesbians' and 14 per cent, as 'bisexuals'. Thirty-eight per cent lived alone, 36 per cent lived together with their partner and 6 per cent lived with their partner and children. Ten per cent of the participants reported care duties regarding children or other persons. Compared to the total female population in Austria, the survey respondents had an above-average representation of people with higher education qualifications.[7] As a consequence, 37 per cent of the employed participants earned monthly (after tax) between 1.500€ and 2.000€ and 26 per cent, more than 2.000€.[8] These results highlight the socioeconomic diversity of lesbians in Austria on an exploratory level.

This diversity and the experiences with the official statistical body in Austria stimulated our interest in the quality of existing official statistical data on lesbians and LGBs and the related data gathering procedures in Europe. While working on LaW, we learned first-hand that national practices within EU countries remain linked to (a) national legislation on LGBs (e.g., partnership laws, nondiscrimination laws); (b) the decision of politicians and the national statistics institutions on whether and how to count LGBs; and (c) the technical protocols set to include or exclude counted data. This made us interested in comparing international practices concerning the processes of data collection and data availability on LGBs. We presumed that the lack and quality of statistical data on lesbians and LGBs were related to embedded governmentalist strategies of normalisation, for which the above-mentioned same-sex couple data clearing procedure in Austria was taken as an example.

THE EUROPEAN LGB DATA PROJECT

As a consequence, we sought funding from the Austrian National Bank for the LGB Data Project. The project was concerned with the data availability, data quality and data-gathering procedures on the socioeconomic situation of LGBs in the official statistical bodies of twenty-seven EU countries plus Iceland, Norway and Switzerland.

An Interdisciplinary Strategy

The LGB Data Project included an interdisciplinary literature review, a survey of practices of thirty national European statistics institutes, inputs from international community experts and researchers and a content analysis of the websites of national statistical institutes. The project includes first on an empirical level (a) an examination of the availability and quality of existing national data sets on the socioeconomic status of LGBs and (b) a critical analysis of the data generating processes with regard to sexuality/ LGBs/same-sex couples and households and the (discriminatory) implications of data collection methods. Second, its epistemological and theoretical aims were to (a) create transdisciplinary interlinkages between queer and de/constructivist approaches on sexuality(/ies) and quantitative economic, sociological and statistical discussions on 'measuring' LGB populations and (b) to also highlight methodological and epistemological challenges in determining the socioeconomic status of LGBs. Third, the political aims, informed by our queer-feminist and governmentalist perspective, were to foster and initiate further debates on the ambivalent relationship between the needs and benefits of data on LGBs and the danger of normalising sexual behaviour/activities/identities within data-collecting processes, and the misuse of LGB data in general.

Data Sources

At the EU level, data on 'Living Conditions and Social Protection' comes from the following sources: (a) two household surveys: the Household Budget Surveys (HBSs) and the EU-SILC (EUROSTAT 2004, EU Statistics on Income and Living Conditions); (B) national labour force surveys, (i.e., micro-census), which feed into (c) specifically conducted health, social life or education surveys or other general public surveys; and (d) community based respondent-driven surveys, such as the Lesbians at Work study (described above).

Data Trouble

Regarding European data sets, the following four fields of methodological difficulties for specifically identifying lesbian women and their socioeconomic status can be summarized as follows:

1. Living in coupling required: generally, in household surveys, respondents indicate their relationship to every household member. Thus,

cohabiting same-sex couples can be identified, no matter whether they are married, in a legal partnership or without any legal declaration of their relationship. Household data and also data on the interrelated individuals in each of those households can now be identified. This is an instance where lesbian women, their education level, their migration background, their work situation, their number of dependents, their health status and their living situations could theoretically be depicted. Problematic for the purposes of identifying lesbians in the population is that lesbian women (and also gay men) who do not live with their partner cannot be identified because household surveys generally do not include questions regarding sexuality.[9] Other minority groups—for example, people with migration backgrounds—are identified by questions concerning the nationality of their parents, their mother tongue and their time of residence in their new home country.

2. Legal status required: the next methodological problem when trying to extract lesbian women from household surveys concerns the inclusiveness of those surveys; we have identified a few options to deal with lesbians (and gays) in surveys:

   i. Counting registered partnership together with married couples: Austria has included registered partnerships in the EU-SILC and treats registered same-sex couples the same as married couples.

   ii. However, unlike in the SILC, in the Austrian micro-census (the Labour Force Survey) of 2012, the list of possible couples does not include the registered partnership, and lesbian and gay couples are not included.

   iii. Some European countries do not comply with Eurostat recommendations and do provide separate data for married heterosexual couples and registered LGB couples, whereas other countries refrain from doing so because this may lead to confidentiality problems, especially if data is made available on a micro-regional level.

   iv. A large group of countries—namely, those without legal partnership institutions for LGBs—do not count LGB couples at all. The National Statistical Institute of the Slovak Republic (February 2012) replied to our questionnaire:

We would like to inform you that the Statistical Office of the Slovak Republic does not survey data on Lesbians, Gays and Bisexuals. There is not in plan [sic] to collect mentioned data in the near future.

In other countries, sexuality is perceived as a 'private matter' or 'individual lifestyle/behaviour' instead of a sociopolitical category. The corresponding employee at the statistical institute of Luxemburg (date) stated:

Sexual orientation . . . is considered (like religion) as part of the private sphere which should be protected.

These two answers are in line with the observations from the literature review—namely, that statistical data collection and data analysis are influenced by discriminatory stereotypes of LGBs and that it is a common practice for same-sex couples living together to be treated as housemates whereas opposite-sex respondents living in the same house are treated as cohabitants (Purdam et al. 2008).

3. Plausibility checks and data correction: the third problem in identifying LGBs in the population arises from plausibility checks and data correction. Statistics Latvia (January 2012) explains in its questionnaire:

Data entry software normally doesn't allow to enter the same sex spouse or cohabiting partner. If such situation appears . . . at the stage of data cleaning at CSB such status is corrected according to de facto situation. [sic]

In comparison, the answer from the National Statistics Office of Iceland (date) seemed more promising, although it reveals some interesting biases:

We also ask a question of who is whose parent if not obvious from the list of household members. In case the parents are of the same sex . . . we code the older as the father and the younger as the mother. Eurostat always send a data check warning when for instance the 'father' is a woman.

4) Need for disclosure: the fourth and last methodological concern is related to the likelihood of the surveyed couples disclosing their sexuality/relationships in household surveys (see methodological discussion in the previous chapter). So far, we are only aware of two campaigns, one in 2010 by the US Census Bureau, which encourages same-sex couples to participate in the decennial count by advertising in LGBT publications and hosting town hall meetings. More recently, the Netherlands also started similar 'come out' campaigns. Concerns for disclosure need to be related to embedding surveys in a broader sociopolitical context (Black et al. 2000); the survey modes; racial/ethnic and culture considerations (Badgett and Goldberg 2009); issues of gender nonconformity (Weichselbaumer 2003, 2004); and the general wording of questions (Badgett and Goldberg 2009).

The Socioeconomic Status of Lesbians in European Countries

After passing these four hurdles, it seems surprising that any data on LGBs may become available from household surveys. Whereas the British Integrated Household Survey found that 1.5 per cent of adults in the United Kingdom identified themselves as gay, lesbian or bisexual in 2010/2011, there were indeed very few observations of same-sex couples in nearly all countries in the EU-SILC 2009. Only the Netherlands, France and Germany reach observation numbers of more than 20 per cent. Looking at the weighted numbers, we see that the share of people living in same-sex partnerships (registered/married or not) is low, being highest with 0.6 per cent in France, 0.5 per cent in the Netherlands and 0.4 per cent in Germany. Further, there are nine countries (Belgium, Bulgaria Cyprus, Estonia, Italy, Lithuania, Latvia, Romania and Slovakia) with no observations at all. With numbers of these magnitudes, it is impossible to generate valid accounts of the living situations of lesbian women (or LGBs) in any EU country (aside from the Netherlands), as the sample size is simply too small to differentiate any further and to deduct meaningful results for entire national populations.

From a queer-feminist and governmentalist perspective, we have to conclude that the 'lesbian and LGB data subject' is constructed and normalised in official data-gathering procedures in different ways. Lesbians are not appropriately counted by European household surveys due to four major factors: only cohabitating couples are counted, some surveys do not include lesbian (or gay) couples, lesbian women may not want to reveal their sexuality or partnerships and collected data may be cleared in plausibility checks. Furthermore, we conclude that the practices of questioning sexuality are highly inconsistent, even in data that is supposedly comparable across the EU. The household surveys analysed in the LGB Data Project have yielded even less information on the socioeconomic situation of lesbian women in European countries than the panel of the few women surveyed in the Austrian community sample of Law.

We also find that data generation and data collection is influenced by different forms of institutionalized heteronormativity, homophobic stereotypes and discrimination. First, we find that (heteronormative) family and household definitions anticipate data collection on sexual orientation/LGBs and same-sex households/couples. There is an invisibility of lesbian women and gay men in a large number of household survey questionnaires, and also as a topic or keyword on the websites of thirteen of the thirty reviewed national statistics institutes. (Comically, Statistics Belgium's search engine encouraged us to use a substitute when our search for the term *lesbian* yielded zero results: 'Did you mean belgian [sic]?'[10]) Second, but less entertaining, is the hyper-visibility of lesbians (and especially gays) when mentioned in connection with disease (HIV/AIDS) and criminal issues, on ten out of thirty websites.

CONCLUDING REMARKS

While we were evaluating the availability of data concerning the social and economic status of lesbian women in Austria and Europe, we became increasingly concerned with current political, methodological and epistemological debates on 'surveying sexual orientation'. In particular, we learned how data generation procedures are highly dependent on political/legal frameworks and power structures such as different forms of institutionalised and structural discrimination as well as homophobic stereotypes, family norms and partnership definitions. The heteronormative organisation of our societies—because it manifests itself in the lack of (social) acknowledgement and the ongoing social and cultural discrimination of lesbian women—has to be considered as an important issue related to data collection procedures and socioeconomic research about lesbian women. Public bodies and scholars engaging in such research have to therefore deal with the general problem of LGB people still experiencing discrimination; this leads to (justified) mistrust and suspicion by LGB people regarding how the data will be used and the belief that no improvements result from surveys (Equality and Human Rights Commission 2009, p. 1).

Therefore, we want to emphasize the need for contextualization and sensitivity when researching the socioeconomic status of lesbian women (or LGBs in general). Hence, data sets on LGBs have to be analysed in the context of multiple sociotechnical arrangements and epistemological, ontological and political presumptions as well as historical developments that have made the 'identification' of LGBs as a 'new' population possible and/or desired. On the methodological level, the social invisibility and heteronormative exclusion of lesbian women exposes the limitations of standard sampling and estimation techniques in research projects and in statistical procedures of EU member states and the EU as a whole. Especially given the importance of statistical data as a powerful policy tool (Colgan et al. 2007; Equality and Human Rights Commission 2009), improvement in the homophobic and potentially stigmatizing wording, labelling and definitions (Brackertz 2007) is essential. In addition, knowledge on possible sampling biases which may be misleading for further research and well as policymakers and practitioners (Meyer and Wilson 2009) is an important challenge for data gathering on LGBs. Furthermore, critical analyses on the socioeconomic status of lesbian women (and LGBs in general) must, thus, not only deal with 'technical' questions of data availability but also with the entire process of *how* and *why* lesbians are/can be identified or (are able to/may want to) identify themselves in the data-collection procedures.

Consequently, data collection efforts and procedures have to be perceived as political acts of (re)creating population groups along normative frameworks and 'official' categories therefore making a certain (sub)set politically visible and 'governable' (Browne 2010; Sokhi-Bulley 2011). This points to the fact that statistical categories and frameworks entail a 'normalising' and 'disciplining' effect because 'counting' presumes identification with entangled categories—for example, with categories that already have and imply a certain sociocultural meaning and norm. The two research projects therefore demonstrate that statistics can indeed be interpreted as a tool of governmentality and therefore 'subjectifying technology' because (only) certain groups/identities/relationships come into (a 'countable') existence by producing certain knowledge to make subjects 'governable' (Browne 2008; Ruppert 2008). Statistical procedures therefore always entail the danger of reestablishing, reessentialising and homogenising sexual/gender categories along heteronormative principles (or established sexual norms), thereby rendering the fluidity and complexity of sexual and gender identifications invisible.

These tensions between fostering the data collection on sexual orientation/LGBs/same-sex couples in order to be able to *quantify* discrimination and the dangers and risks of 'normalization' have to thus be considered. However, we still believe that 'counting' LGBs/same-sex couples/households and related research on the socioeconomic status on lesbian women can under certain circumstances queer(y) social and statistical presumptions about the 'normal' and thus challenge heteronormative assumptions (Black et al. 2000; Herek et al. 2010). Statistical methods have to be considered, like any other scientific method, as performative, which also means that 'dominant' versions and procedures of 'counting' can be changed in order to create and produce other 'realities'.

NOTES

1. In cooperation with Sandra Müllbacher and Hafdís Erla Hafsteinsdóttir.
2. The term *LGB* in this text refers to lesbian, gay and bisexual as forms of self-definition and self-articulation as well as social modes of existence. The problematic implications of these categories are acknowledged from a constructivist point of view and are therefore opposed to essentialist and ahistorical understandings of sexuality and sexual identity. Underlying cultural conceptions of sexual and gender identity, not just the terms used to describe these identities, are subject to change over time and place, and the relationships among sexual orientation, gender and gender conformity are understood to be complex. The category LGB (rather than LGBT) has been chosen for this project since we agree that 'it is inappropriate to list "trans" as a category under sexual orientation as it is an entirely different concept and such people may be heterosexual, gay, lesbian or bisexual' (Aspinall 2009, p. 34). Nevertheless, a gender performance deviant from the expected feminine or masculine mainstream may have different outcomes—for instance, in labour market hiring.
3. LGBTIQ refers to lesbian, gay, bisexual, transgender, intersexual and queer.
4. Examples for research topics are as follows: discrimination in the workplace (e.g., Badgett 2001, 2007; Frank 2006; Badgett and Frank 2007; Colgan et al. 2007; Antecol, Jong and Steinberger 2008; Pringle 2008; Colgan and Mc-Kearney 2011; Drydaskis 2011); intersectionalities with gender, 'race,' class, citizenship and ability (e.g., Robinson 2002; Albelda, Badgett and Schneebaum 2009); civil status (e.g., Albelda, Ash and Badgett 2005; Badgett, Gates and Maisel 2008); education (Rothblum et al. 2007); deviant gender performance (e.g., Weichselbaumer 2003, 2004; Badgett and Sears 2012).
5. The project (2009–2010) was conducted by the WU Vienna—Gender and Diversity Management Group and ordered and funded by the Association of Queer Business Women.

6. Since 2010, a law on legal same-sex partnership has existed in Austria, and the Austrian Statistic Institute provides corresponding data: www.statistik. at/web_en/statistics/population/registered_partnerships/index.html.
7. Forty-two per cent of those surveyed had a degree from a university, compared to the Austrian female average of 6.5 per cent.
8. In 2009 the average monthly income of employed women in Austria was 1,167€.
9. One exception is the Integrated Household Survey of the UK, where a sexual identity question is asked (Office for National Statistics 2011).
10. Source: Statistics Belgium, http://statbel.fgov.be.

REFERENCES

Albelda, R., Ash, M. and Badgett, L. (2005) 'Now that We Do: Same-Sex Couples and Marriage in Massachusetts', *Massachusetts Benchmarks*, 7(2), pp. 16–24.
Albelda, R., Badgett, L. and Schneebaum, A. (2009) *Poverty in the Lesbian, Gay, And Bisexual Community*. Williams Institute, UCLA, March. Available from: www. law.ucla.edu/WilliamsInstitute/pdf/LGBPovertyReport.pdf (accessed 7 July 2010).
Antecol, H., Jong, A. and Steinberger, M. (2008) 'The Sexual Orientation Wage Gap: The Role of Occupational Sorting and Human Capital', *Industrial and Labour Relations Review*, 61(4), pp. 518–543.
Aspinall, P. (2009) *Estimating the Size and Composition of the Lesbian, Gay, and Bisexual Population in Britain*. Equality and Human Rights Commission, Research Report 37. Available from: www.equalityhumanrights.com/uploaded_files/research/research__37__estimatinglgbpop.pdf (accessed 14 July 2010).
Badgett, L. (2001) *Money, Myths, and Change: The Economic Lives of Lesbians and Gay Men*, Chicago: University of Chicago Press.
Badgett, L. (2007) 'Discrimination Based on Sexual Orientation: A Review of the Literature in Economics and Beyond'. In Badgett, L. and Frank, J. (eds) *Sexual Orientation Discrimination: An International Perspective*, pp. 19–43. London: Routledge.
Badgett, L. and Frank, J. (eds) (2007) *Sexual Orientation Discrimination: An International Perspective*. London: Routledge.
Badgett, L., Gates, G. and Maisel, N. (2008) 'Registered Domestic Partnerships among Gay Men and Lesbians: The Role of Economic Factors'. *Review of Economics of the Household*, 6, pp. 327–346. Available from: http://williamsinstitute.law. ucla.edu/wp-content/uploads/Badgett-Gates-Maisel-Registered-DP-Economic-Factors-Mar-2007.pdf (accessed 8 November 2012).
Badgett, L. and Goldberg, N. (eds) (2009) *Best Practices for Asking Questions about Sexual Orientation on Surveys*. Williams Institute, UCLA, November. Available from: www.law.ucla.edu/WilliamsInstitute/pdf/SMART_WI_FINAL. pdf (accessed 7 July 2010).
Badgett, L. and Sears, B. (2012) *Beyond the Stereotypes: Poverty in the LGBT Community*. Available from: http://momentum.tides.org/beyond-the-stereotypes-poverty-in-the-lgbt-community (accessed 8 November 2012).
Black, D., Gates, G., Sanders, S. and Taylor, L. (2000) 'Demographics of the Gay and Lesbian Population in the United States: Evidence from Available Systematic Data Sources', *Demography*, 37(2), pp. 139–154.
Brackertz, N. (2007) 'Who Is Hard to Reach and Why?' ISR Working Paper, Swinburne Institute for Social Research.
Brand, P. A. (ed.) (2009) *Lesbians and Work: The Advantages and Disadvantages of "Comfortable Shoes"*. London: Rutledge.

Brown, M. and Knopp, L. (2006) 'Places or Polygons? Governmentality, Scale, and the Census, The Gay and Lesbian Atlas', *Population, Space and Place* 12, pp. 223–242.

Browne, K. (2008) 'Selling My Queer Soul or Queerying Qualitative Research', *Sociological Research Online*, 13(1). Available from: www.socresonline.org.uk/13/1/11.html (accessed 2 January 2012).

Browne, K. (2010) 'Queer Quantification or queer(Y)Ing Quantification. Creating Lesbian, Gay, Bisexual or Heterosexual Citizens through Governmental Social Research'. In Browne, K. and Nash, C. S. (eds) *Queer Methods and Methodologies. Intersecting Queer Theories and Social Science Research*. Abingdon: Ashgate, pp. 231–249.

Butler, J. (1990) *Gender Trouble. Feminism and the Subversion of Identity*. London: Routledge.

Colgan, F., Creegan, C., McKearney, A. and Wright, T. (2007) 'Equality and Diversity Policies and Practices at Work', *Equal Opportunities International*, 26(6), pp. 590–609.

Colgan, F. and McKearney, A. (2011) 'Spirals of Silence? Tackling the 'Invisibility' of the Sexual Orientation Strand and Sexuality in Academic Research and in Organisation

Colgan, F. and Wright, T. (2011) 'Lesbian, Gay and Bisexual Equality in a Modernising Public Sector: Opportunities and Threats', *Gender, Work and Organisation*, 18(5), pp. 548–570.

Drydakis, N. (2011) 'Women's Sexual Orientation and Labour Market Outcomes in Greece', *Feminist Economics*, 17(1), pp. 89–117

Equality and Diversity Policy and Practice', *Equality, Diversity and Inclusion*, 30(8), pp. 624–632.

Equality and Human Rights Commission (2009) *Beyond Tolerance. Making Sexual Orientation a Public Matter*. Policy Report. Available from: www.equalityhumanrights.com/uploaded_files/research/beyond_tolerance.pdf (accessed 14 July 2010).

EUROSTAT (2004) *Description of Target Variables: Cross-sectional and Longitudinal. EU-SILC 065/04: Version of 2004. Social and regional statistics and geographical information system. Unit E-2: Living conditions*. Available from: www.statistik.at/web_de/suchergebnisse/index.html (accessed 31 October 2012).

Evans, D.T. (1993) *Sexual Citizenship. The Material Construction of Sexualities*. London: Routledge.

Foucault, M. (1983) *Der Wille zum Wissen. Sexualität und Wahrheit Bd.1*. Frankfurt am Main: Suhrkamp.

Foucault, M. (2005) *Analytik der Macht*. Frankfurt am Main: Suhrkamp.

Foucault, M. (2007) *Security, Territory, Population*. Basingstoke: Palgrave Macmillan.

FRA—European Union Agency for Fundamental Rights (2009) *Homophobia and Discrimination on Grounds of Sexual Orientation and Gender Identity in the EU Member States*. Available from: http://fra.europa.eu/fraWebsite/attachments/FRA_hdgso_report_Part%202_en.pdf (accessed 13 July 2009).

Frank, J. (2006) 'Gay Glass Ceilings', *Economica*, 73(291), pp. 485–508.

Guasp, A. and Balfour, J. (2008) *Peak Performance. Gay People and Productivity*. London: Stonewall.

Herek, G.M., Norton, A.T., Allen, T.J., Sims, C. L. and Charles, L. (2010) 'Demographic, Psychological, and Social Characteristics of Self-Identified Lesbian, Gay, and Bisexual Adults in a US Probability Sample', *Sexuality Research and Social Policy*, 7, pp. 176–200.

Hofmann, R. and Cserer, A. (2010) 'Lesben am Werk. Explorationsstudie zur Erwerbstätigkeit lesbischer Frauen in Österreich'. Project Report—Working

Papers, No. 3, Abteilungfür Gender und Diversitätsmanagement, WU Vienna. Available from: http://epub.wu.ac.at/2791/1/WorkingPaper3.pdf (accessed 2 February 2012).

Klapeer, C. M. (2013) *Perverse Bürgerinnen. Staatsbürgerschaft und lesbische Existenz.* Bielefeld: transcript.

Losert, A. (2009) 'Je lockerer man damit umgeht, desto weniger Probleme hat man. Handlungsspielräume nicht-heterosexueller Beschäftigter am Arbeitsplatz'. In AG Queer Studies (ed.) *Verqueere Verhältnisse*, pp. 185–200. Hamburg: Männerschwarm Verlag.

Meyer, I. H. and Colten, M. E. (1999) 'Sampling Gay Men: Random Digit Dialing versus Sources in the Gay Community', *Journal of Homosexuality*, 37(4), 99–110.

Meyer, I. H. and Wilson, P. A. (2009) 'Sampling Lesbian, Gay, and Bisexual Populations', *Journal of Counseling Psychology*, 56(1), pp. 23–31.

Miles, N. (2008) *The Double-Glazed Glass Ceiling. Lesbians in the Workplace.* London: Stonewall

Mitchell, M., Creegan, C., Howarth, C. and Kotecha, M. (2009) *Sexual Orientation Research Review 2008.* Manchester: Equality and Human Rights Commission.

Office for National Statistics (2011) Statistical Bulletin. Experimental Statistics. Integrated Household Survey April 2010 to March 2011: Experimental Statistics. Available from: http://www.ons.gov.uk/ons/dcp171778_227150.pdf (accessed 31 October 2012).

Phellas, C. N. (ed.) (2012) *Researching Non-Heterosexual Sexualities.* Farnham: Ashgate.

Plug, E. and Berkhout, P. (2008) *Sexual Orientation, Disclosure and Earnings*, Institute for the Study of Labor (IZA), *IZA DP*, No. 3290.

Pringle, J. K. (2008) 'Gender in Management: Theorizing Gender as Heterogender', *British Journal of Management*, 19, Issue Supplement s1, pp. 110–119.

Purdam, K., Wilson, A. R., Afkhami, R. and Olsen, W. (2008) 'Surveying Sexual Orientation. Asking Difficult Questions and Providing Useful Answers', *Culture, Health & Sexuality*, 10(2), pp. 127–141.

Rich, A. (1994) *Compulsory heterosexuality and Lesbian Existence.* New York: Norton Paperback.

Robinson J. K. (2002) 'Race, Gender, and Familial Status: Discrimination in One US Mortgage Lending Market', *Feminist Economics*, 8(2), pp. 63–85.

Rothblum, E., Balsam, K., Solomon, S. and Factor, R. (2007) 'Lesbian, Gay Male, Bisexual, and Heterosexual Siblings: Discrepancies in Income and Education in Three US Samples'. In Badgett, L. and Frank, J. (eds) *Sexual Orientation Discrimination: An International Perspective*, pp. 62–75. London: Routledge.

Rubin, G. (1993 [1984]) 'Thinking Sex: Notes for a Radical Theory of the Politics of Sexuality'. In Abelove, H., Barale, M. A. and Halperin, D. M. (eds) *The Lesbian and Gay Studies Reader*. London: Routledge, pp. 3–44.

Ruppert, E. (2008) 'I Is; Therefore I Am. The Census as Practice of Double Identification', *Sociological Research Online*, 13(4). Available from: www.socresonline.org.uk/13/4/6.html (accessed 2 February 2012).

Ruppert, E. (2011) 'Population Objects. Interpassive Subjects', *Sociology*, 45(2), pp. 218–233.

Salganik, M. J. and Heckathorn, D. D. (2004) 'Sampling and Estimation in Hidden Populations Using Respondent-Driven Sampling', *Sociological Methodology*, 34(1), pp. 193–240.

Schönpflug, K. (2012) 'Gendered Work in a "Good Society"—a Paradox to Care About'. In Marangos, J. (ed.) *Alternative Perspectives of a Good Society*, pp. 33–56. New York: Palgrave.

Schönpflug, K., Hofmann, R., Klapeer, C. M., Müllbacher, S. and Schwarzbauer, W. (2013) *European LGB Data Project. A Compilation of Statistical Data on Sexual*

Orientation and an Application to Research on the Economic Status of LGBs. Research Report, Institute for Advanced Studies Vienna.

Sokhi-Bulley, B. (2011) 'Governing (through) Rights: Statistics as Technologies of Governmentality', *Social & Legal Studies*, 20(2), pp. 139–155.

Takács, J. (2006) *Limited Access to Active Citizenship: Social Exclusion Patterns Affecting Young LGBT People in Europe.* Available from: http://youth-partnership-eu.coe.int/youth-partnership/documents/EKCYP/Youth_Policy/docs/Citizenship/Limited_access_to_active_.pdf (accessed 3 May 2010).

UNECE—United Nations Economic Commission for Europe (2006) *Recommendations for the 2010 Censuses of Population and Housing.* Geneva: United Nations. Available from: www.unece.org/stats/publications/CES_2010_Census_Recommendations_English.pdf (accessed 7 July 2010).

Weichselbaumer, D. (2003) 'Sexual Orientation Discrimination in Hiring', *Labour Economics*, 10(6), pp. 629–642.

Weichselbaumer, D. (2004) 'Is It Sex or Personality? The Impact of Sex-Stereotypes on Discrimination in Applicant Selection', *Eastern Economic Journal*, 30(2), pp. 159–186.

14 Sexual Politics and Queer Activism in the Australian Trade Union Movement

Suzanne Franzway[1]

INTRODUCTION

Sexual orientation ideally should not cause problems for workers, their colleagues or their employers, let alone become of interest to trade unions. However, as the contemporary trade union movement has become aware, advocating for appropriate wages and decent conditions is not enough. Trade unions are not only confronted by the effects of neoliberalism with the renewed attacks by economic capital on the social contract between citizens and the state, on industrial conditions and on organised labour. Unions also recognise that their diverse union members and potential members bring much more than their skills, knowledge and labour power to the workplace.

Employers have fine-tuned interests in this diversity and display consistent preferences for specific collections of workers' attributes for specific jobs. Thus young women are preferred as workers in dress shops whereas middle-aged men seem preferable in senior management or boardrooms (Wajcman 1998; EOWA 2008). Such preferences are generally hidden behind assumptions that underlie normative ideas about workers' identities. Equally important is the assumption that whatever the nature of the workplace, decision-making power is appropriately held by men so that even feminised workplaces are likely to see the few men occupying the high-level positions (Vinnicombe 2008). Likewise, in Western societies, there continue to be widely held assumptions that women in the paid workforce also have family care responsibilities, whereas men's responsibilities focus on their families' economic well-being (Hochschild 1997; Smart 2007; Baker 2010).

Underlying these assumptions are societies' bedrock views that workers' sexual orientation is heterosexual, and these workers have normative family roles. The diversity of sexual orientations among workers as well as employers, clients and customers are heavily overshadowed by such assumptions. Yet, as this book demonstrates, workers have a wide range of sexual orientations which may be variable over the life course and over their working lives. The diversity and fluidity of workers' gender identities impact on workplace issues in two main ways: assumptions about invisibility can produce inappropriate and at times oppressive policies and practices and, second, such diversity can be the target of hostility and discrimination. Both fall within the remit of trade unions to address inequalities and injustices in the workplace.

However, considerable energy and activism are required to persuade trade union movements that workplace issues cannot be defined only in terms of their relevance to able-bodied white men. Those workers who do not fit this category therefore need considerable diligence and innovative strategies to gain recognition of their rights; as well, they need union resources to gain traction in workplaces and industrial agreements (Cobble 2004; Moghadam, Franzway and Fonow 2011; Ledwith and Hansen 2013). Elsewhere I have argued that such activism gains from, and at times depends, on alliances with groups and organisations outside the trade union movement (Franzway and Fonow 2009). Such alliances may be built by union activists with those in social movements and grass roots organizations that share political interests. For example, feminist union activists work with other feminists campaigning for improved domestic violence policies (Murray and Powell 2008). This chapter will consider examples of queer activism in the Australian trade union movement and examine the sexual politics involved in bringing such issues onto the industrial, social and political agenda.

QUEER ACTIVISM

First, I note that the terminology used here has itself arisen from the political activism that challenges normative and oppressive assumptions about sexual orientation that appear to be global. Terms have shifted from *homosexuality*, which was coined in 1869 by Karoly Maria Benkert but not widely used in English until the end of the century (Jagose 1996: 72). *Gay* was knowingly political in the 1960s and posed against the pathologised meaning that homosexual had accrued. References to 'gay and lesbian' groups have shifted to include bisexuality in GLB and then to LGBTI, noting that each stage has entailed a great deal of debate. The term *LGBTI* will be used in this chapter as the currently understood abbreviation to refer to people who identify as lesbian, gay, bisexual, transgender or intersex (Connell 2012), noting that an Australian Human Rights Commission report (2011) found intersex people are frequently omitted from discussions on workplace discrimination.

The term *queer* also has a history of shifting meanings depending on diverse theoretical and political purposes. In early sixteenth-century English it inferred odd, strange, suspicious, faint or ill, changing to include male homosexual by the late nineteenth century. As poststructuralist theories problematized understandings of identity, queer was adopted for its 'parodic invocation of historical cause and effect' (Jagose 1996: 76) and its implications of ambivalence, activism and theory. Whereas the term *LGBTI* is almost technical in its correct listing of diverse sexual orientations, *queer* continues to be flavoured by some of its earlier meanings. *Queer* includes a playfulness that is nevertheless seriously political in intent. *Queer* can be difficult and confrontational as it represents a challenge to the heteronormative dominance of union organisations and cultures (Warner 1993). This may explain why there is little evidence of its use in Australian trade union movement policies and campaigns. I use it deliberately here to highlight the riskiness entailed in union activism for LGBTI workers. I also seek to imply the creative strategies that are possible for queer activism in trade unions.

SEXUAL POLITICS

It is important to recognise that sexual orientation is a matter of gender, broadly defined, and the effects and meanings of gender in society are political. In order to bring the political back into our understanding of gender I adopt the term *sexual politics*, drawing on Kate Millet's definition in which the political is central to the forms and meanings of gender (Millet 1969). Thus normative heterosexual gender relations are achieved through political contestations over power to frame meanings of gender. Sexual politics points to gender relationships that are continually contested and thus are always changeable, even while appearing to be merely natural and ahistorical.

In gender theorising, Kate Millet's version of sexual politics has largely been replaced by a more direct emphasis on the sexual and sexualities, identifying a politics of sexual identities and difference (Seidman 1997; Collins 2004). American philosopher Judith Butler (2009) contrasts the politics of sexualities with the politics of gender relations, moving sexual politics to the centre of contemporary political life in a complex argument that links freedom and temporal progress. For the purposes of this chapter, sexual politics puts a useful stress on an ever-present relation of power that produces resistance and dominance, social contracts and diverse pleasures. If sexual politics are understood to incorporate both the sexual and the political, it provides a lens for understanding the dominance of heteronormativity and the often hostile or repressive responses to queer activism.

For the dominance of masculine heterosexuality to be sustained in much contemporary society, including in the labour movement, it must be continually restated, reaffirmed and reclaimed (Ledwith and Hansen 2013). In addition, sexual politics are engaged by deeply ambivalent meanings of difference, including those of sexual orientation, race, class, age, diversity and so on. It is this ongoing contestation that produces multiple discursive meanings of gender and power including complexities and diversities of power among nonheteronormative identities. In aiming for progressive and liberatory politics, sexual politics shifts the focus from an arithmetical 'gender inclusivity' in which LGBTI people disappear to one in which the dynamic and changing circumstances of gender relations contest and shape political opportunities and social identities that open up spaces for political action.

DIVERSITY

Sexual orientation and gender identities are important aspects of diversity within the workplace and broader population (Bell et al. 2011), but LGBTI workers are no more homogenous than any other group. As Githens (2009: 29) has argued, 'LGBT politics are sometimes problematic due to the presentation of LGBT issues as unified and shared among all people who identify as L, G, B, or T'. It is important, then to recognize the multiplicity of shifting gender identities and sexualities (Franzway 2002). The recently published report by the Australian Human Rights Commission (2011: 2) makes a clear difference between the terms 'sex and/or gender identity' and sexual orientation, a distinction which is carried into Australian law and offers significantly more protection against discrimination on the basis of sexual orientation than against discrimination on the basis of 'sex and/or gender identity'. State and territory laws currently protect LGB people from discrimination on the basis of sexual orientation, but only some state and territory laws provide protection to TI people from discrimination on the basis of gender identity (Australian Human Rights Commission 2011).[2]

In addition, state and territory rulings on sexual and gender discrimination can be overturned at the federal level, where current federal law protects against discrimination on the basis of sex but not against discrimination on the basis of sexual orientation and sex and/or gender identity (Australian Human Rights Commission 2010). These protections are further limited by the Australian industrial relations framework grounded in the Fair Work Act 2009, which prohibits discrimination on the basis of sexual orientation but not on the basis of gender identity.

Sexual orientation may not be inscribed on the body in the same way that other markers of diversity such as gender, 'race' and ethnicity are (Badgett 1996; Ryan-Flood 2004; Bell et al. 2011). As such, several studies have found that many LGB workers remain closeted or only come out to some colleagues in the workplace as a means of utilizing this invisibility to avoid discrimination and/or other negative outcomes in the workplace (Ryan-Flood 2004; Pitts et al. 2006; Colgan et al. 2007; Colgan and McKearney 2012). For example, the latest *Private Lives* study reports that 38.8 per cent occasionally or usually hide their sexuality or gender identity at work (Leonard et al. 2012). Being forced to remain closeted for fear of termination of employment is one way through which LGB workers can be silenced (Bell et al. 2011). In remaining closeted, LGB workers are unable to be completely themselves at work, an experience which Singh (in Hollibaugh and Singh 1999: 78) refers to as living 'the lie of normalcy'.

Sexual orientation may be 'invisible' in the workplace, whereas gender identity is frequently difficult to hide. As a result, transgender and intersex people face unique challenges in the workplace including being denied employment opportunities and not being recognized as their preferred gender (Australian Human Rights Commission 2011). The experiences of LGBTI workers may share many similarities, but there are also specific differences between LGB and TI workers which must be taken into account. In addition, even within these categories, there is great diversity in workplace experiences. For example, Bell et al. (2011: 133) suggest that 'employment probabilities for gay men and lesbians lie below those of married heterosexual men, but above those of heterosexual women'. Sexual orientation also has a significant impact on earning capacity, but in quantitative research and data, its typical invisibility within the categories of married or nonmarried workers leads to distortions of the analyses of causes of pay differentials and therefore the framing of political campaigns to achieve pay equity (Blandford 2003).

WORKPLACE CONCERNS

LGBTI people can experience workplaces as difficult and distressing. In Australia, research into their workplace experiences is limited and reduces the possibilities for appropriate development of policies and campaigns within the trade union movement. Three relatively large studies have been conducted in recent years. The *Private Lives* study explored aspects of health and wellbeing through online surveys, which were completed by 5,476 people (Pitts et al. 2006), and it was repeated in 2011, with 3,835 surveyed nationally (Leonard et al. 2012). The third study, by the Australian Human Right Commission (2011), was designed to explore the rights of LGBTI people, including their rights in the workplace, and it incorporated rountable consultations and written submissions from over 150 individuals and organizations.

Workplace problems for LGBTI workers range from the blatant, such as refusal of employment and violence, to the subtle practices of discrimination and invisibility. For those who are 'out', the treatment they receive can lead to depression, stress-related illness, substance abuse and even suicide (Flood and Hamilton 2005). Irwin's study found that 59 per cent of the people surveyed had experienced harassment or prejudicial treatment in the workplace as well as sexual and physical assault; actions included verbal abuse, destruction of property, ridicule, unfair work rosters, unreasonable work expectations and career restrictions (Irwin 1999). Bell et al. (2011: 133) have argued that 'living with the fear of being terminated, and lack of partner benefits are just a few of the concerns unique to GLBT employees'. Data collected by trade unions find that breaches of the labour rights of LGBTI workers are common (Education International 2007).

LGBTI workers experience both formal and informal discrimination aris-
ing from the dominance of heteronormative sexual politics and these present significant workplace challenges for them (Bell et al. 2011). Irwin's study
of LGT workers found that over 50 per cent of workers who participated in
the study had suffered from some form of discrimination (Irwin 1999: 28).
Formal discrimination takes place at an organizational level and includes
being denied employment, being dismissed from employment, being denied
promotions and raises and being excluded from family leave and insurance.
The first *Private Lives* study found that 10.3 per cent of participants had
been refused employment or promotion as a result of their sexuality (Pitt
et al. 2006). In addition, many of the participants in the AHRC consultations described 'being denied employment or promotion opportunities or
being dismissed or disciplined because of their sexual orientation' (Australian Human Rights Commission 2011: 9).

Informal discrimination happens on a more everyday level among
employees of an organization and includes harassment, lack of acceptance
of sexual orientation or gender identity by coworkers and supervisors, the
silencing of personal life and loss of credibility. It is difficult to measure,
monitor and evaluate this everyday informal discrimination, and outside
of the qualitative reports of LGBTI workers that report their experiences
(for example, Ryan-Flood 2004), little research has been done. At the
same time, action by both LGBTI community organisations and by the
trade union movement has been mixed. Whereas social and political activism in the past four decades has seen 'greater acceptance and visibility
for LGBT people in most developed economies' (Colgan and McKearney
2012: 359), LGBTI people still face significant workplace challenges and
issues.

TRADE UNIONS AND SEXUAL POLITICS

Trade unions have historically been dominated by masculine heterosexuality and so are challenged by questions of representation and organisation of
LGBTI workers (Ledwith and Colgan 2002). Yet, these workers experience
high rates of discrimination and prejudice whereas studies in other countries make similar findings, as we see in other chapters in this book. Trade
unions across the US, Canada, the UK and Australia have been described
as dominated by the sexual politics of the leadership of white heterosexual
men (Franzway 2001, 2002; Colgan and Ledwith 2002; Hunt and Haiven
2006; Wright et al. 2006; Franzway and Fonow 2011). As Bell et al. (2011:
138) have argued, this 'unrepresentative nature of union leadership restricts
the ability of unions to promote equality, diversity, and inclusion in employment effectively'. Questions have been asked about whether this dominant heterosexual masculinity in the union movement impacts on unions'
responses to the needs and demands of sexual minorities (Hunt and Haiven

2006), among other minority groups. Hollibaugh (in Hollibaugh and Singh 1999: 81) put it this way:

> The union movement . . . needs to recognize that identities are not rigid or always obviously defined, to have a complex understanding of diversity. If you want to bring all the players to the table, then you have to understand who the players are, what their issues are, and how their own issues color the way they see issues of commonality.

Similarly, Colgan and Ledwith (2002: 154) argued over ten years ago that the challenge for unions is 'to recognise that union membership is increasingly diverse, and diversely politicised, and that new structures and new cultures need to be developed to deliver union democracy and equality'. There has been a paucity of research since then on whether trade unions have been able to respond to this challenge. Research on LGBTI membership of trade unions and the experiences of LGBTI people within trade union movements remains scarce globally. It continues to be the case that issues of sexuality, 'particularly the hegemonic or homophobic dimensions of sexuality', are given little attention in any trade union movement (Franzway and Fonow 2011: 29).

Yet, in countries like Australia, where limited legislation exists to protect individual employees from discrimination on the basis of sexual orientation and/or gender identity, trade union membership can provide vital support and legal protection for LGBTI workers (Irwin 1999; Bell et al. 2011; Pride at Work 2012). Colgan et al. (2007) suggest that a number of factors help workers in deciding whether to come out in the workplace. These include the presence of an organisational LGBT group and getting involved in a trade union LGBT support network (p. 597). Trade unions and queer community organisations have important and useful roles in providing workplace environments that encourage and allow workers to challenge heteronormative sexual politics rather than having to hide behind invisibility or remain closeted. However, the responses of trade unions to LGBTI needs, as well as the access of LGBTI workers to trade unions, have a chequered history as the examples discussed below show. Where LGBT issues do surface, a great deal of uncertainty and timidity remains about how to frame them most effectively.

Some unions such as UNISON in the UK (Colgan 1999; Colgan et al. 2007; Ryan-Flood 2004) and the Australian Services Union (ASU), with its Gay and Lesbian Australian Services Union Members (GLAM) subgroup (Franzway & Fonow 2011), have been noted for their inclusive responses to diversity, in particular gender and sexual orientation diversity. GLAM, discussed below, was set up to articulate LGBT issues to the broad labour movement as well as within the ASU. In addition, Australian trade unions recently adopted the Social Inclusion policy at the 2012 Australian Council of Trade Unions (ACTU) congress. This policy is committed to building 'policies aimed at assisting workers to participate in the paid workforce' and focuses on particular minority groups including LGBT workers (Australian Council of Trade Unions 2012). As the ACTU is the overarching Australian body representing forty-six affiliated trade unions, it is hoped that the Social Inclusion policy or similar policies will be adopted by individual unions to the benefit of LGBTI workers.

In what follows I take examples from the Australian trade union movement to discuss the sexual politics involved in bringing such issues onto the industrial, social and political agenda. I draw on union documents and interviews I conducted with nine trade union officials in 2012 in South Australia. I selected interviewees, referred to with pseudonyms, who had leadership roles in their unions and who had responsibility for policy and campaign development. Two of the nine had gender equality in their portfolios.

QUEER ACTIVISM AND SEPARATE ORGANISING

Queer activism on workplace issues must contend with the reluctance of many LGBTI workers to become active in their unions. Many LGBTI workers still seem sceptical of the assistance unions might provide (Ryan-Flood 2004). Irwin's study found that, whereas 41 per cent of the participants were union members, very few took concerns about industrial issues or discrimination to their unions (Irwin 1999). LGBTI members who are activists generally have adopted similar strategies to those adopted by other minority groups in trade union movements. In particular, 'self-organizing' has become a common strategy, designed 'to build political spaces within unions from which they can make claims for representation and participation' (Franzway and Fonow 2009: n.p.). Colgan and Ledwith found that it is a strategy that helps 'to build sense of identity, political consciousness, confidence and solidarity and to develop and practice activist skills' (Colgan and Ledwith 2002b: 178). Self- or separate organising, as it is also known, appealed to LGBTI activists as a way to counter discriminatory sexual politics within and beyond the union leadership.

Self-organizing in unions began in the 1970s with the growth of public and service sector unions and a resurgent feminism extending to a renewed union feminism (Briskin and McDermot 1993; Cobble 2004). As Hunt and Haiven (2006: 674) observe, 'When a gay and lesbian rights movement emerged in the 1970s, the blatantly discriminatory practices of most organizations made the workplace an obvious target for change'. Feminists took up nontraditional concerns such as harassment and violence and argued that traditional union culture was part of the problem (Briskin and McDermott 1993; Colgan and Ledwith 2002a). Through self-organising within trade union movements, it has been possible for workers 'to gain self-confidence and build political strength inside their unions' (Hunt 2002: 261), and this has been one of the key initiatives which has increased visibility and support for LGBTI workers and their issues (Colgan et al. 2007). Such a strategy tends to be strongest in those unions where other minority groups have created spaces for their concerns and may include conferences, caucuses, committees, forums, workshops, special educational programs and websites (Briskin1993; Franzway 2001; Hunt and Boris 2007).

According to Curtin (1999: 33), separate spaces enable the development of discursive frameworks through which to constitute minority interest claims. The establishment of such spaces involves political activism in the face of inertia, resistance or even hostility from majority union members and leadership. Whereas such organising has limited success in overturning the hegemony of male leadership (Ledwith 2006), the strategies provide necessary opportunities to engage resources and to challenge dominant discourses about issues and agendas. Curtin (1999) has proposed that minority groups can establish their claims through building contingent solidarities with more dominant groups, although the challenge remains as to how to sustain these alliances over time. Such spaces may be clearly defined and defendable by activists, but their boundaries are not necessarily permanent or fixed.

The first such group in Australia, the Gay and Lesbian Trade Unionists Group (GayTUG), was formed in 1978. This was followed by the Sisters of Perpetual Indulgence, a group of Australian LGBT community activists who aligned with LGB workers by organizing to participate in the 1981 Australian May Day parade, the annual celebration of workers' rights. The group's colourful intervention, in spectacular queer style, was salutary for union activists, although some union leaders were opposed to it (Towart 2002). It led to the formal participation by several trade unions in the Sydney Gay and Lesbian Mardi Gras march, an annual event that attracts enormous crowds. Such activity required political activism within the unions in the face of a good deal of resistance, but this proved to be as valuable as the public event itself (Fortescue 2000). In these examples, a successful challenge to the unions' heteronormative sexual politics benefitted from broad alliances with other social movements.

'A POOFTER UNION'

One of the most effective examples of self-organising in Australia has been set up within the ASU, a broad-based union which covers social and community service workers and local government workers, as well as clerical, transport and energy workers and has over 60 per cent women membership, rising to more than 80 per cent in the community sector. GLAM (Gay and Lesbian Australian Services Union Members) was set up to overcome problems of invisibility very effectively through an unapologetic queer style, drawing on rainbow symbolism, dramatic gestures and the motto, 'Job security never goes out of style'.

Reflecting on its impact, one of my union informants recounted the experience of the local ASU secretary when GLAM was first established:

> He would go to the Trades Hall and they'd say, 'You're from that poofter union.' And John's no sort of dainty bloke. (Peter, union informant)

Such comments are not straightforward criticisms of support for diverse sexual orientation and gender identities. They also stem from the strongly held view that traditional issues of wages and conditions ought to be the central concerns of unions, without the distractions of explicit sexual politics. Elsewhere I have drawn attention to the ways that sexual politics in unions can cause obstacles to union representation of LGBTI workers' issues (Franzway and Fonow 2011). These can include the political perspectives of individual union leaderships as well as prevailing views across the wider union movement.

> So yes, there is discrimination. The unions approach it kind of organically . . . So for us, GLAM at that time was a very proactive thing, a brave thing to do. (Diane, union informant)

GLAM also exemplifies the impermanence of separate organising as well as the demanding issue of building and sustaining contingent solidarities. At present GLAM is in relative abeyance, so that its national website has not been updated for nearly two years, and few state or national activities have been evident over this period. However, I suggest that lack of permanence is not a necessary sign of failure. Assessment needs to question the effectiveness of its impact. Has this form of activism made a continued difference, or has the problem sunk back to its earlier status? According to my union informants, expressions of homophobia by union leaderships are no longer acceptable, and LGBTI workplace issues are now recognised as proper concerns for trade unions. In addition, GLAM is available to be rebooted for new campaigns for LGBTI workers and members. Such action is no longer seen as 'a brave move' on the part of the leadership but rather as a direct part of their obligation to respond to concerns raised by members.

'THAT'S SO GAY—MAKING SAFE SPACES'

Explicit hostility and discrimination may have subsided in the Australian trade union movement, but issues for LGBTI workers continue to be difficult to raise (Irwin 2002). The experience of members of the Australian Education Union (AEU) is revealing on this point. According to my union informants, teachers' workplace experiences range from covert barriers to career progress, the silencing of personal life stories to instances of 'nasty discrimination'. Australian teachers work in an environment clouded by three decades of moral panics about child sexual abuse, paedophilia and child pornography (Robinson 2008). These abuses have caused enormous damage to the lives of those who have been subject to them, but the consequences of fears about children's safety have spread very far. Primary and early childhood education finds it is even more difficult to recruit young men than it was when teaching was seen as women's work. LGBTI teachers are very wary about revealing their sexual orientation for fear it will cause alarm in the school community of parents, other teachers, students and educational employers (Miriam, union informant).

The everyday life experiences of LGBTI people are largely silenced, although two aspects of the current environment allow union activists to shine some light onto their LGBTI interests as well as onto matters of workplace concern. These are the widely accepted principle of 'the best interests of the child', particularly in education, which has led to strategies based on a dual focus on students and staff. And the contemporary public debates around marriage equity provide opportunities to speak about LGBTI issues more generally.

The AEU is a white collar union with over 70 per cent women membership and a long history of advocacy of progressive issues. In the 1970s, it established one of the first full-time women's officer positions in the country supported by a women's committee, a form of self-organising which has taken up LGB matters at union policy levels. The women's committee has worked to make safe spaces for cautious members. For example, a workshop titled, 'That's so Gay' brought activists from an interstate branch to discuss concerns about how to respond to student needs, training options and discrimination. Participants were encouraged to articulate their own workplace issues in the hope that confidence would be gained about breaking out of the invisibility of sexual orientation and gender identity. Building alliances with community and student activists are integral to the dual-focus strategy.

Most recently, the women's committee has worked to give the AEU a presence at the annual GLBTI festival, Feast, an initiative that arose in part from campaigns with secondary school student activists. The impact was described by one of my informants:

> A group of teachers and student activists came together to have a presence at Feast, especially the picnic. People bring their children to it, so we had a stall and lots of people said, 'It's really good the union is here'. But when I asked if they were union members they said yes but wouldn't say where they worked; they'd just wonder off, so that's about safety. They just don't feel safe. (Miriam, union informant)

A critical aspect to the union's strategy is the move to establish a 'formal voice' with embedded structures at the leadership level so that actions and campaigns are not dependent on the activism of specific individuals. The federal body of the union adopted a specific policy in relation to GLBTI[3] people at its 2006 annual conference as a result of the activities of members in several state branches. It was framed to promote and support 'the general welfare, personal, civil industrial and curriculum rights of GLBTI people as members' (Australian Education Union 2006).

Notably it adopted a dual focus on students as well as on staff. Thus the policy aimed to eliminate discrimination in employment through attention to ensuring inclusive workplace rights, including family matters and appropriate training as well as resources for specific committees and a national support network, but equally it paid attention to student needs including curriculum development as nonheterosexist and gender neutral and support mechanisms such as groups and aware counsellors. Winning endorsement of a policy is a critical stage in union politics, but implementation is equally crucial and depends on the efforts of committed and persistent activists.

CONCLUSION

Queer activism in the Australian trade union movement has a colourful if intermittent history of self-organising, building alliances and changing policy. It is a history which depends on the persistent efforts of relatively small groups of activists. It is not possible to argue that heteronormative sexual politics has been transformed, but it is clear that the rights and workplace issues of LGBTI workers can no longer be ignored. Although the visibility of these issues fades at times, in both trade unions and queer community organisations, essential gains have been made, as illustrated by the not-for-profit organization Pride in Diversity, which encourages 'good practice' among Australian employers who wish to become more inclusive (Pride in Diversity 2012). Success is contingent on constructions of alliances and campaigns.

However, this strategy depends in turn on the strength and focus of social movements and grass roots organisations. A number of my union informants commented that the campaigns for equal marriage both at local and international levels had given greater visibility to LGBTI people but had drained political energy away from the sexual politics of employment and the workplace. This situation is similar to that which most political activists around issues outside the mainstream face regularly. Queer activists in trade unions therefore also need patience during difficult political times as well as the capacity to recognise and take opportunities for action (Maddison and Scalmer 2006). Thus activism which aims at substantial change such as policy development and legislative reform provides firm ground for renewed campaigns and for challenging discriminatory cultures and practices. Given the prevailing heteronormative sexual politics of the trade union movement as well as of wider society, queer activism in trade unions will continue to be critical, in spite of its uneven history, to ensuring the workplace rights of LGBTI workers.

NOTES

1. With thanks for the skilful assistance by Melanie Baak.
2. No state or territory laws use the term *Intersex*; however, most refer to people of 'indeterminate sex' (Australian Human Rights Commission 2011).
3. GLBTI was the form used in this document. It was subsequently changed in the 2012 proposal.

REFERENCES

Australian Council of Trade Unions (2012) *ACTU Congress 2012: Social Inclusion Policy*, viewed 9 August 2012, www.actu.org.au/Images/Dynamic/attachments/7659/Social%20Inclusion%20Policy%20-FINAL.pdf.

Australian Education Union (2006) *Policy on Gay, Lesbian, Bisexual, Transgender and Intersex People*, Adelaide.

Australian Human Rights Commission (2010) *Protection from Discrimination on the Basis of Sexual Orientation and Sex and/or Gender Identity: Discussion Paper*, viewed 20 July 2012, www.humanrights.gov.au/pdf/human_rights/lgbti/lgbticonsult/SOGIdiscussion_paper.pdf.

Australian Human Rights Commission (2011) *Addressing Sexual Orientation and Sex and/or Gender Identity Discrimination: Consultation Report*, Sydney.

Badgett, M.V.L. (1996) 'Choices and Chances: Is Coming Out at Work a Rational Choice?' in Beemyn, B. and Eliason, M. (eds), *Queer Studies: A Lesbian, Gay, Bisexual, and Transgender Anthology*, New York: New York University Press.

Baker, M. (2010) *Choices and Constraints in Family Life*, 2nd ed., Oxford: Oxford University Press.

Bell, M. P. Özbilgin, M. F. Beauregard, T. A. and Sürgevil, O. (2011) 'Voice, Silence, and Diversity in 21st Century Organizations: Strategies for Inclusion of Gay, Lesbian, Bisexual, and Transgender Employees', *Human Resource Management*, 50(1): 131–146.

Blandford, J. (2003) 'The Nexus of Sexual Orientation and Gender in the Determination of Earnings', *Industrial and Labor Relations Review*, 56(4): 622–642.

Briskin, L. (1993) 'Union Women and Separate Organizing', in Briskin, L. and McDermott, P. (eds), *Women Challenging Unions: Feminism, Democracy and Militancy*, Toronto: Toronto University Press.

Briskin, L. and McDermott, P. (eds), *Women Challenging Unions: Feminism, Democracy and Militancy*, Toronto: University Press, Toronto.

Butler, J. (2009) *Frames of War. When is Life Grievable?* London: Verso.

Cobble, D. S. (2004) *The Other Women's Movement: Workplace Justice and Social Rights in Modern America*, Princeton, NJ: Princeton University Press.

Cobble, D. S. and Bielski, M. M. (2002) 'On the Edge of Equality?: Working Women and the US Labour Movement', in Colgan, F. and Ledwith, S. (eds), *Gender, Diversity and Trade Unions: International Perspectives*, London: Routledge.

Colgan, F. (1999) 'Recognising the Lesbian and Gay Constituency in UK Trade Unions: Moving Forward in UNISON?', *Industrial Relations Journal*, 30(5): 444–463.

Colgan, F., Creegan, C., McKearney, A. and Wright, T. (2007) 'Equality and Diversity Policies and Practices at Work: Lesbian, Gay and Bisexual Workers', *Equality, Diversity and Inclusion: An International Journal*, 26(6): 590–609.

Colgan, F. and Ledwith, S. (2002a) 'Gender, Diversity and Mobilisation in UK Trade Unions', in Colgan, F. and Ledwith, S. (eds), *Gender, Diversity and Trade Unions: International Perspectives*, Routledge, London.

Colgan, F. and Ledwith, S. (2002b) 'Gender and Diversity: Reshaping Union Democracy,' *Employee Relations*, 24(2): 167–189.

Colgan, F. and McKearney, A. (2012) 'Visibility and Voice in Organisations: Lesbian, Gay, Bisexual and Transgendered Employee Networks', *Equality, Diversity and Inclusion: An International Journal*, 31(4): 359–378.

Collins, P. H. (2004) *Black Sexual Politics: African Americans, Gender and the New Racism*, New York: Routledge.

Connell, R. (2012) 'Transsexual Women and Feminist Thought: Toward New Understanding and New Politics', *Signs*, 37(4): 857–881.

Education International (2007) *The Rights of Lesbian and Gay Teachers and Education Personnel. Triennial Report 2004–2007*, viewed 17 August 2012, www.ei-ie.org/en/.

Equal Opportunity for Women in the Workplace Agency (2008) *Australian Census of Women in Leadership*, Australian Government, Canberra, viewed 13 September, 2012. www.eowa.gov.au/Australian_Women_In_Leadership_Census/2008_Australian_Women_In_Leadership_Census/Media_Kit/EOWA_Census_2008_Publication.pdf.

Fair Work Act, (2009) Attorney-General's Department, Canberra.

Flood, M. and Hamilton, C. (2005) 'Mapping Homophobia in Australia', Australia Institute, viewed 10 August 2012, http://unilife.curtin.edu.au/sexualdiversity/documents/MappingHomophobiainAustralia.pdf.

Fortescue, R. (2000) 'Mardi Gras: The Biggest Labour Festival of the Year', *Hecate*, 26(2): 62–65.

Franzway, S. (2001) *Sexual Politics and Greedy Institutions: Union Women, Commitments and Conflicts in Public and in Private*, Annandale: Pluto Press Australia.

Franzway, S. (2002) 'Sexual Politics in (Australian) Labour Movements', in Colgan, F. and Ledwith, S. (eds), *Gender, Diversity and Trade Unions: International Perspectives*, London: Routledge.

Franzway, S. and Fonow, M. M. (2009) 'Queer Activism, Feminism and the Transnational Labor Movement', *The Scholar and Feminist Online*, 7(3), viewed 17 August 2012, http://sfonline.barnard.edu/sexecon/print_ff.htm.

Franzway, S. and Fonow, M. M. (2011) *Making Feminist Politics: Transnational Alliances between Women and Labor*, Urbana: University of Illinois Press.

Githens, R. P. (2009) 'Capitalism, Identity Politics, and Queerness Converge: LGBT Employee Resource Groups', *New Horizons in Adult Education & Human Resource Development*, 23(3): 18–31.

Hochschild, A. R. (1997). *The Time Bind: When Work Becomes Home and Home Becomes Work*, New York: Metropolitan Books.

Hollibaugh, A. and Singh, N. P. (1999) 'Sexuality, Labor, and the New Trade Unionism', *Social Text*, 17(4): 73–88.

Hunt, G. (2002) 'Organised Labour, Sexual Diversity and Union Activism in Canada', in Colgan, F. and Ledwith, S. (eds), *Gender, Diversity and Trade Unions: International Perspectives*, London: Routledge.

Hunt, G. and Haiven, J. (2006) 'Building Democracy for Women and Sexual Minorities: Union Embrace of Diversity', *Industrial Relations*, 61(4): 666–683.

Irwin, J. (1999) *The Pink Ceiling Is Too Low': Workplace Experiences af Lesbians, Gay Men and Transgender People*, Sydney: University of Sydney.

Irwin, J. (2002) 'Discrimination against Gay Men, Lesbians, and Transgender People Working in Education', *Journal of Gay & Lesbian Social Services*, 14 (2): 65–77.

Jagose, A. (1996) *Queer Theory*, Melbourne: Melbourne University Press.

Kirsch, M. H. (2000) *Queer Theory and Social Change*, London: Routledge.

Ledwith, S. (2006) 'Feminist Praxis in a Trade Union Gender Project', *Industrial Relations Journal*, 37 (4): 379–399.

Ledwith, S. and Colgan, F. (2002) 'Tackling Gender, Diversity and trade Union Democracy: A Worldwide Project', in Colgan, F. and Ledwith, S. (eds), *Gender, Diversity and Trade Unions: International Perspectives*, London: Routledge.

Leonard, W., Pitts, M., Mitchell, A., Lyons, A., Smith, A., Patel, S., Couch, M. and Barrett, A. (2012) *Private Lives 2: The Second National Survey of the Health and Wellbeing of Gay, Lesbian, Bisexual and Transgender (GLBT) Australians*, Melbourne: La Trobe University.

Maddison, S. and Scalmer, S. (2006) *Activist Wisdom: Practical Knowledge to Creative Tension In Social Movements*, Sydney: UNSW Press.

Millet, K. (1969) *Sexual Politics*, New York: Avon Books.

Moghadam, V., Franzway, S. and Fonow, M. M. (eds) (2011) *Making Globalization Work for Women: Women Workers' Social Rights and Trade Union Leadership*, New York: SUNY Press.

Murray, S. and Powell, A. (2008) *Working It Out: Domestic Violence Issues and the Workplace*, Melbourne: Australian Domestic and Family Violence Clearinghouse.

Pitts, M., Smith, A., Mitchell, A. and Patel, S. (2006) *Private Lives: A Report on the Health and Wellbeing of GLBTI Australians*, Melbourne: La Trobe University.

Pride at Work (2012) *Pride @ Work: Lesbian, Gay, Bisexual, and Transgender Labor and aur Allies*, viewed 9 August 2012, www.prideatwork.org/.

Pride in Diversity (2012) *Welcome to Pride in Diversity*, viewed 16 August 2012, www.prideindiversity.com.au/.

Robinson, K. (2008) 'In the Name of "Childhood Innocence": A Discursive Exploration of the Moral Panic Associated with Childhood and Sexuality', *Cultural Studies Review* 14(2): 113–129.

Ryan-Flood, R. (2004) 'Beyond Recognition and Redistribution: A Case Study of Lesbian and Gay Workers in a Local Labour Market in Britain', *New Working Paper Series*, viewed 3 July 2012, www2.lse.ac.uk/genderInstitute/pdf/Roisin.pdf.

Smart, C. (2007) *Personal Life: New Directions in Sociological Thinking*, Cambridge: Polity Press.

Vinnicombe, S. (2008) *Women on Corporate Boards of Directors*, Edward Elgar, Cheltenham.

Wajcman, J. (1998) *Managing Like a Man: Women And Men in Corporate Management*, Cambridge: Polity Press.

Warner, M. (1993) *Fear of a Queer Planet*, Minneapolis: University of Minnesota Press.

Wright, T., Colgan, F., Creegany, C. and McKearney, A. (2006) 'Lesbian, Gay and Bisexual Workers: Equality, Diversity and Inclusion in the Workplace', *Equality, Diversity and Inclusion: An International Journal*, 25(6): 465–470.

15 Going Global

International Labour and Sexual Orientation Discrimination

Gerald Hunt

INTRODUCTION

Over the past three decades, labour movements in a number of countries have taken up equity issues related to sexual orientation discrimination. There are now established lesbian, gay, bisexual and trans (LGBT) labour alliances in countries including Canada, the United States, Britain, Germany, Australia and the Netherlands (Bielski Boris 2010; Colgan and Ledwith 2002; Hunt 1999; Hunt and Eaton 2007; Krupat and McCreery 2001). These alliances have played an important role in advancing LGBT rights inside and outside of the workplace. Unions have helped secure non-discrimination policies, supported grievances based on sexual orientation discrimination, fought for collective agreement language to equalise benefit coverage for workers in same-sex relationships, mounted educational programs to raise awareness, and undertaken broader political, legal and social advocacy. The engagement of labour unions with sexual orientation issues has been uneven—more pronounced in developed, industrialized countries and in public sector unions—but advances toward a more inclusive agenda have been impressive (Colgan and Ledwith 2002). In Canada, for example, large public sector unions, the auto workers and the communications workers played a significant role in securing workplace rights and shifting the legal and constitutional scene through extensive lobbying and advocacy efforts (Hunt and Eaton 2007).

The advances that have been secured for LGBT workers in some parts of the world (often achieved with the assistance and support of organized labour) stand in stark contrast to the inequalities that are still 'normal' in many other parts of the world. Blatant discrimination against LGBT people, not least of which occurs in the workplace, is the reality in many countries. Homosexual acts are illegal, often with severe punishments, throughout much of Africa, Asia, the Caribbean, the Middle East and Russia. In Iran, Saudi Arabia, Yemen, Sudan, Mauritania, Northern Nigeria and Southern Somalia, homosexual acts can be punishable by death (ILGA 2013). As a result, many LGBT activists, including some working within the labour movement, have focused more of their attention and concern on the international scene.

In many of the countries with the weakest record on LGBT rights, national- or regional-based labour movements are often underdeveloped, weak and co-opted by governments (Schillinger 2005). Consequently, it would be very surprising if national labour movements in these countries had sexual orientation discrimination on their radar in any significant way. However, there is reason to believe that cross-nation labour movements might be more responsive to issues raised by sexual minorities and engaged in activities to address the discrimination they confront. First, given a grow-ing league of national labour movements are engaged with sexual diversity issues, it is reasonable to assume that some of these ideas have trickled up to the international level. Indeed, it is possible to imagine that national move-ments now exert pressure on their international counterparts to acknowl-edge sexual orientation discrimination and fight for its elimination. Second, the increased visibility of gays and lesbians around the world has resulted in a proliferation of national, and increasingly transnational, activist move-ments responding to the discrimination they face. Some of this activism is focused on workplace issues, implicating unions. Third, the expansion of forums for equity-seeking activists, including those groups focusing on sex-ual orientation and labour, has provided increased opportunities for inter-national collaboration. The growth of vehicles for such linkage comes in part as a defensive response to the neoliberal pressures of economic glo-balization as well as from overlapping agendas and areas of concern. Such linkages benefit from enhanced political attention to human rights concerns at the international level. Fourth, the renewal of international labour soli-darity in response to globalization has been accompanied by a resurgence and revitalization of the formal institutions that support it. Increasingly, these institutions declare a commitment to a broad equity agenda, which should include increased attention to sexual minorities.

THE TAKE-UP OF SEXUAL DIVERSITY IN
INTERNATIONAL LABOUR ORGANIZATIONS

Over the past century, various cross-border labour associations have emerged. Some have evolved and prospered whereas others have faded from the scene. During the last couple of decades, however, economic globaliza-tion has accelerated the growth, relevance and importance of multination labour institutions. Today, the largest and most influential international labour institutions are the International Trade Union Confederation, the International Labour Organisation and the European Trade Union Con-federation, as well as nine sector-based global unions (see Table 15.1). These 'globals' do not reflect the spontaneity of other forms of international labour cooperation, so visible in protests mobilized at major international gatherings of bankers and world leaders, but they are the strongest institu-tional embodiments of labour solidarity and cooperation. The globals are limited to developing policy directives, delivering educational programs,

Table 15.1   Global Union Confederations (2013)

Global Union	Worker/Sector
1. BWI: Building and Woodworkers International	Building trades
2. EI: Education International	Education workers
3. IAEA: International Arts and Entertainment Alliance	Artists and Actors
4. IFJ: International Federation of Journalists	Journalists
5. IndustriALL (merger in late 2012 of International Metalworkers' Federation [IMF], International Federation of Chemical, Energy, Mine and General Workers' Unions [ICEM] and International Textiles Garment and Leather Workers' Federation [ITGLWF])	Mining, Energy, Manufacturing (including Auto)
6. ITF: International Transport Workers' Federation	Transportation
7. IUF: International Union of Food, Agricultural, Hotel, Restaurant, Catering, Tobacco and Allied Workers' Associations	Food, Agriculture
8. PSI: Public Services International	Public sector workers
9. UNI: Union Network International	Office workers; media workers

hosting conferences, lobbying governments and attempting to sway their national membership to adopt common goals and initiatives. Nevertheless, because these globals have adopted policies and acted in a way that reflects the long-term potential for agreement across national and regional borders, this makes them important and relevant players in the international political economy (Cotton and Gumbrell-McCormick 2012; Fairbrother and Hammer 2005; Papadakis 2011; Pries and Seeliger 2013; Waterman 2005). Consequently, they are important institutions for monitoring equity initiatives and, specifically, sexual orientation discrimination.

This chapter considers how widely and thoroughly there has in fact been recognition of sexual orientation discrimination among cross-national unions and international labour organisations. The methodology used for assessing international labour's engagement with sexual orientation issues was to collect information from a number of key international labour organizations. The research was conducted from 2011 to 2013. Information was obtained through ten interviews with officials in the organizations and detailed analysis of organizational web sites, as well as content analysis of policy documents and publications produced by the organizations. Organizations included in this study were two large cross-nation labour confederations (International Trade Union Confederation and the European Trade Union Confederation), the International Labour Organization and nine global unions (see Table 15.1). Three of these global unions (Public Services International, Education International, Union Network International) were found to be particularly active on the sexual orientation file and are profiled in depth. In addition, a content analysis of eighty-nine International Federation Agreements (IFAs) signed between a multinational and one or more global unions was undertaken to determine whether sexual orientation was included in nondiscrimination language.

The International Trade Union Confederation (ITUC) was founded in November 2006 when former affiliates of the International Confederation of Free Trade Unions (ICFTU) merged with the World Confederation of Labour (WCL) and several other small trade union groups that had no global affiliation. The ITUC represents 175 million workers in 153 countries and territories and has 308 national affiliates. The ICFTU was the largest organisation in the ITUC merger, and it had taken on a number of initiatives on sexual orientation before the merger, being among the first international labour organizations to include lesbians and gays in its formal nondiscrimination language (a step it took in 2000). The ITUC incorporated this nondiscrimination provision in its founding constitution but has not taken many steps to tackle inequities based on sexual orientation beyond formal endorsement and co-operating with other globals. For example, at its second World Congress, in 2010, the ITUC endorsed a resolution promoting and defending fundamental workers' rights that specifically mentioned sexual orientation as a grounds of discrimination and called on its membership to affirm this resolution but did not map a strategic initiative in this area (ITUC 2010a). The ITUC has prioritized action on HIV/AIDS and does reference sexual orientation discrimination as an issue that needs to be addressed to curb the spread of the disease (ITUC 2010b). The ITUC does not appear to have directly confronted issues related to gender identity.

The International Labour Organisation (ILO) was formed in 1919 and became the first specialized agency of the United Nations in 1946. It is a tripartite organisation with 185 member states that brings together representatives from governments, employers and workers. Its primary role is to develop international labour standards that are endorsed by its members and enforced by the ILO. It currently has 186 conventions that cover topics ranging from child labour to safety in mines. Convention 111 (Discrimination in Employment and Occupation) came into force in 1960 and specifies that 'any distinction, exclusion or preference made on the basis of race, colour, sex, religion, political opinion, national extraction or social origin, which has the effect of nullifying or impairing equality of opportunity or treatment in employment or occupation is unacceptable' (ILO 2013). Even though Convention 111 does not directly address sexual orientation, sexuality has been a topic of discussion within the organization. In a 2003 report, called 'Time for Equity at Work', the ILO included sexual orientation as a 'new' source of discrimination. The issue was deemed to need further study and referred to an expert committee (ILO 2003). A follow-up report was issued in 2007, and it outlined what the committee found. This report listed in more detail the manifestations of sexual orientation discrimination and provided a summary of countries that had banned such discrimination in the workplace (ILO 2007). This report also acknowledges that this type of discrimination affected not only individual workers in terms of such things as hiring and firing but workers in same-sex relationships because same-sex partners were often denied workplace benefit packages available to opposite-sex partners. In the report there were thirty references to sexual orientation: one measure that the topic was on the ILO's radar screen more than it had been in the past. A third equity report was issued in 2011, and whereas this report once again highlighted and updated the issue of sexual orientation discrimination, it did not make any specific recommendations for change (ILO 2011). None of the reports went so far as to suggest that Convention 111 be updated to include sexual orientation as a designated category in need of protection. One sign of movement, however, was the publication in 2009 of a factsheet on eliminating discrimination in the workplace. This factsheet, which was made available to all members, specifically covered sexual orientation by formally acknowledging sexual orientation as a significant source of bias in the workplace and encouraging members to confront discrimination (ILO 2009). The ILO does have nondiscrimination provisions for its own employees and offers workplace benefits to same-sex couples. ILO materials do not deal with issues related to gender identity.

The European Trade Union Confederation (ETUC) consists of eighty-five members from a total of thirty-six countries in Western, Central and Eastern Europe, as well as ten European Trade Union Federations. As such, it is a large crossnation union confederation, second in membership only to the ITUC. The ETUC formally included sexual orientation in its nondiscrimination policies in 2000 and added gender identity in 2008. In 2013, the ETUC indicated prominently on the homepage of its website (ETUC.org) that it was at the 'forefront in defending human rights, trade union rights and equality for all workers'. This commitment includes equal treatment, respect and dignity for lesbians, gay men, bisexuals and transgendered workers. Recognizing that this commitment involves more than policy directives, the ETUC has mounted ambitious plans for tackling sexual orientation discrimination. In 2008, it organized the first Europe-wide trade union conference on LGBT rights and subsequently published a report with the lengthy title 'Extending Equity—Trade Unions in Action! Organising and Promoting Equal Rights, Respect and Dignity for LGBT Worker's (ETUC 2008). The report was made available in twenty-two European languages. It included an exchange of best practices amongst members and outlined ways for unions to promote equal rights, including collective bargaining strategies. It also encouraged its member unions to take more account of the T in LGBT and offered ideas for establishing linkages with NGOs in order to facilitate equality in the workplace and in wider society. Recently, the ETUC lead an initiative that partnered with the ITUC, and the International Lesbian and Gay Association, to strategize about combating homophobia, transphobia and bullying in schools, the workplace and society (ETUC 2012).

Public Services International (PSI) is made up of national unions with workers in public services in 150 countries. It was the first global union to tackle sexual orientation discrimination in the workplace. It approved a comprehensive policy statement in 1993, pushed in part by delegations from Canada (especially the Canadian Labour Congress and the Canadian Union of Public Employees), Britain (in particular UNISON), the Netherlands (especially ABVAKABO) and the United States (notably the municipal workers' union, AFSME). In 2005, a survey of equal opportunities conducted by PSI once every ten years included sexual orientation in its examination of structures, policies, programs and best practices for the first time. Much of PSI's campaign on sexual orientation discrimination has been in collaboration with Education International (EI) (discussed in the next section).

EI is the international labour confederation representing teachers' unions from around the world. It took up the sexual orientation file shortly after PSI; not surprisingly because teachers are an occupational group with a long history of being fired for being openly gay or lesbian. In 1998, EI developed a wide-ranging policy statement on sexual orientation. This resolution indicated that a sexual orientation bias was a violation of human rights and indicated its strong support for teachers to be open at work. The resolution called on its member unions to increase educational efforts and lobby their national government for reforms. Since that time, EI has undertaken a wide variety of educational activities. It has assisted several of its national unions in defending openly lesbian and gay teachers from harassment and dismissal, in some cases doing so in national contexts in which no legal protections were available. In 2001, it began publishing triennial reports on gay and lesbian educators, surveying their experiences across countries and chronicling cases of abuse. EI has issued formal letters to governments and other international organisations protesting rights violations, in cooperation with the relevant national affiliates. A spokesperson at EI indicated that there has been some pushback from conservative members but that the organisation has stayed the course. Recent campaigns have focused on Latin American and parts of Europe where LGBT rights are particularly fragile.

EI and PSI have worked closely to make sexual orientation discrimination a priority. Together they represent over 50 million workers, covering 950 different nationally based unions. In 1999, PSI and EI jointly published *Working for Lesbian and Gay Members*, mapping out a comprehensive strategy for trade union action. This report was updated in 2007 (PSI-EI 2007). Five years later, an International LGBT Forum was created with representation from national unions from both federations. The forum was created to generate awareness of sexual diversity issues among EI and PSI members, document cases of discrimination, organize training sessions and press for the inclusion of sexual diversity rights in international conventions and policies. It was also destined to serve as a vehicle for the development of an international network that could learn from the experiences of activists operating in very different local and national contexts. The first official meeting of the forum, which was in July 2004 in Porto Alegre, Brazil, produced a substantial declaration that called for more affirmative action at ILO, UNESCO, UN AIDS, governments and NGOs as well as their own sponsoring confederations (EI and PSI). It expressed concern about the workplace discrimination that still went largely unrecognized in international and national policies. It called for equality in the law, in access to public services, in relationship recognition, in the provision of support for young workers and in respect to the specific needs of transgendered people (PSI-EI 2007). In the follow-up to the Porto Alegre meetings, PSI and EI agreed to hold a joint LGBT forum at least once every three years as a precongress gathering. Meetings were subsequently held in Vienna in 2007 and in Cape Town in 2011. The 2011 forum held discussions about how to implement better complaint procedures when a LGBT teacher experiences discrimination. These meetings also include representatives from the ITUC.

Union Network International (UNI) is the result of amalgamations of various global unions. It is the most diverse global union covering workers in sectors such as cleaning, media, arts, gaming, sports and tourism. A spokesperson indicated that over the past decade, UNI has made equity initiatives a priority in almost all of it campaigns. It established an Equal Opportunity Department in 2008 with a mandate that included working with its member unions to improve collective bargaining language on equality clauses. Leaders at UNI indicate that sexual orientation discrimination had been an equity category that has been hard to convince some of its membership to prioritize, and one that has had pushback. As a result, UNI has emphasized educational programs as a first step in convincing member unions that sexual orientation discrimination is a serious problem worth pursuing. They have held training forums in four key locations (Africa, Asia, Europe and Latin American) on decent work with dignity, and these programs include information on sexual orientation. In 2010, UNI carried out a research project with nine large multinationals to determine the importance these corporations were giving to equality policies. This report indicated that all but three had nondiscrimination policies in place that included sexual orientation (UNI 2010). The information from this report is now being used in educational initiatives and to provide illustrations of language that can be used when bargaining for similar provisions in other settings.

The other six global unions (see Table 15.1) have been less active in the area of sexual orientation discrimination. However, most of them have negotiated framework agreements with international corporations that provide specific protections for sexual minorities. The next section of this chapter outlines the developments that have been taking place in this regard.

THE TAKE-UP OF SEXUAL DIVERSITY IN
INTERNATIONAL FRAMEWORK AGREEMENTS[1]

International framework agreements (IFAs) are contracts signed among a multinational corporation and one or more global union. These agreements cover the worldwide workforce of the multinational and often implicate the worldwide supply chain and subcontractor network of the firm. Commentators such as Papadakis (2011) argue convincingly that they represent the most important new tool for global relations to emerge in the two decades. In a study of thirty-eight IFAs, Hammer (2005) found there were two general types: those emphasizing rights and those emphasizing bargaining. He characterized rights agreements as those concentrating on fundamental rights for workers, often formalizing earlier codes of conduct. Bargaining agreements, in contrast, are those that deal with a somewhat broader range of issues beyond core labour rights, typically call for regular meetings and include a renewal date when terms can be renegotiated. Riisgaard (2005) concluded these agreements do help advance worker's rights, and Sobczak (2007) found the agreements had the potential to contribute to the social regulation of international companies and global supply chains. In a another study of sixty-two IFAs, Muller, Platzer and Rub (2008) indicated that although the agreements held little possibility of solving economic inequality produced by the globalization of production, they did have the potential to be a new tool for strengthening employee rights, especially in developing and emerging economies where such rights are often least developed.

As a minimum, IFAs reference all or most of the Core Labour Standards of the International Labour Organisation, as set out below:

- Convention 87—Freedom of association
- Convention 98—Right to collective bargaining
- Convention 111—Nondiscrimination in employment
- Convention 100—Equal remuneration for men and women
- Convention 105—Prevention of forced labour
- Convention 138—Minimum wage provision
- Convention 182—Child labour is not used

Some IFAs expand on these standards and may cover a broader range of ILO conventions and related worker concerns, including health and safety measures and environmental compliance. The first IFA was signed in 1988 between Danone, a food processing company, and the IUF. A few additional agreements were signed during the 1990s, but there has been a significant surge since 2000. In early 2013, there were ninety-nine IFUs covering over seven million workers (excluding supplier and subcontractors), many with well-known international companies such as IKEA, H&M and BMW.

In order to assess the degree to which IFAs include sexual orientation in their nondiscrimination language, a content analysis of IFAs was undertaken.

IFAs were obtained from the electronic data bank of the Council of Global Unions (Global Unions 2013). Ten of the ninety-nine agreements were unavailable for preview; as a result, eighty-nine IFAs were subject to detailed content analysis. Each agreement was assessed to determine whether sexual orientation (sexuality, sexual preference and lesbian/gay were deemed equivalent) was specifically mentioned. In addition, each agreement that did contain reference to sexual orientation was further assessed to determine if there were statements related to such things as best practices or education initiatives related to homophobia. Furthermore, the IFAs with this provision were analysed to determine the global union(s) involved, number of workers covered, year signed, national home base of the transnational corporation and dominant sector of the company.

Twenty-nine of the eighty-nine agreements—about one-third—were found to contain language specific to sexual orientation, sexuality or sexual preference. An overview of the results is summarized in Table 15.2. Further analysis revealed that the agreements fell under the jurisdiction of eight global unions (Table 15.3), involved multinationals from ten countries (Table 15.4), included most sectors (Table 15.5) and covered nearly 4.5 million workers. All of the agreements that specified sexual orientation were signed since 2001, with the frequency increasing each year (Figure 15.1). The first IFA agreements to include this language were at IKEA (2001), Volkswagen (2002) and Daimler-Chrysler (2002). Three new IFAs were signed in 2012 that included formal protections for sexual minorities, including one between Ford and the International Metal Federation (IMF), which has since merged with several other globals to become part of IndustriALL, making it the first American multinational to have an IFA. Three agreements (GDF, Brunel, Umicore) also contain statements indicating the need for education about sexual orientation discrimination.

As shown in Table 15.3, eight global unions have signed at least one IFA containing a provision for sexual orientation. The IMF has the most with sixteen, followed by the ICEM with five, UNI with four and PSI with two; all the others have one. The corporate home bases for these companies are all within Western Europe, except for one based in South Africa and the new one in the United States. As can be seen in Table 15.4, Germany leads the way as the home base for eleven transnational companies who have IFAs with sexual orientation provisions. Multinationals in seventeen different sectors are included, with the strongest representation coming from the auto sector.

WHAT EXPLAINS THE CONFIGURATION OF IFA COVERAGE FOR LGBT WORKERS?

The inclusion of sexual orientation as a ground for nondiscrimination in IFAs is a recent phenomenon. The agreements are largely with multinational corporations headquartered in Europe, so they are mainly a European

Table 15.2 International Framework Agreements with Sexual Orientation Discrimination Provisions*

Multinational corporation	Global union(s)	Workers covered**	Year signed	Corporate home base	Sector
SIEMENS AG	IndustriALL	402,000	2012	GERMANY	ELECTRONICS
FORD	IMF	164,000	2012	UNITED STATES	AUTO
MAN SE	IMF	47,670	2012	GERMANY	ENGINEERING
BANCO DO BRAZIL	UNI	118,900	2011	BRAZIL	FINANCIAL SERVICES
SODEXO	IUF	391,148	2011	FRANCE	HOSPITALITY
PETROBRAS	ICEM	80,497	2011	BRAZIL	OIL AND GAS
PFEIDERER AG	BWI	5,370	2010	GERMANY	BUILDING
GDF SUEZ ***	BWI, ICEM, PSI	214,000	2010	FRANCE	ENERGY
WILKHAHN	BWI	600	2009	GERMANY	FURNITURE
VALLOUREC	IMF	18,000	2008	FRANCE	METAL
BRUNEL***	IMF	5,300	2007	NETHERLANDS	ENGINEERING
UMICORE ***	ICEM, IMF	14,000	2007	BELGIUM	METAL
NAMPAK	UNI	17,000	2006	SOUTH AFRICA	PACKAGING
SECURITAS	UNI	217,000	2006	SWEDEN	SECURITY
PEUGEOT	IMF	187,000	2006	FRANCE	AUTO
INDITEX	ITGLWF	100,140	2006	SPAIN	RETAIL
BMW	IMF	106,000	2005	GERMANY	AUTO
FRANCE TEL	UNI, ICEM, PSI	167,000	2005	FRANCE	ENERGY
EADS	IMF	110,000	2005	NETHERLANDS	AEROSPACE
ROCHLING	IMF	8,000	2005	GERMANY	AUTO/PLASTICS
ARCELOR	IMF	95,000	2005	LUXEMBOURG	STEEL
BOSCH	IMF	225,000	2004	GERMANY	AUTO/ELECTRONIC
PRYM	IMF	4,000	2004	GERMANY	METAL
RENAULT	IMF	130,000	2004	FRANCE	AUTO
SCA	ICEM	46,000	2004	SWEDEN	PAPER
GEA	IMF	14,000	2003	GERMANY	ENGINEERING
VOLKSWAGEN	IMF	325,000	2002	GERMANY	AUTO
DAIMLER-CHRY	IMF	372,000	2002	GERMANY	AUTO
IKEA	BWI	127,000	2001	SWEDEN	RETAIL/FURNITURE
TOTALS 29	34	3,711,625	–	–	32

* The results are based on 89 IFAs. Ten of the 99 IFAs were unavailable to the researcher. As a result, there could be additional coverage in IFAs not consulted
** Employee numbers are estimates obtained from websites of company and ITUF web site
*** Includes strategies for dealing with homophobia (see notes in text)

Table 15.3   Sexual Orientation Coverage in IFAs by Global Union*

Global union	Number of IFAs	Worker coverage
IMF	16	1,824,970
ICEM	5	521,497
PSI	2	381,000
UNI	4	519,900
BWI	4	346,970
IndustriALL**	1	402,000
IUF	1	391,148
ITGLWF	1	100,140
TOTAL IFAs	34*	4,487,625*

* Three of the IFAs have been signed by more than one Global Union. This has been accounted for in calculating the total IFAs and total worker coverage for each Global Union.
** New global union, the result of a merger among IMF, ICEM and other confederations in 2012

Table 15.4   Sexual Orientation Coverage in IFAs by Corporate Home Base

Corporate home base	Number of IFAs
Germany	11
France	6
Sweden	3
Luxembourg	1
Belgium	1
Brazil	2
Netherlands	2
South Africa	1
Spain	1
United States	1
Total	29

development. It is, therefore, not surprising to find that the IFAs inclusive of sexuality provisions are primarily at European multinationals. Similarly, German multinationals lead the way in IFAs in general, so it is not surprising to find they have the most IFAs containing sexual orientation. In addition, many German unions were among the first national unions in the world to push for collective agreement language providing nondiscrimination coverage for gays and lesbians and the inclusion of benefits for same-sex couples (Holzhacker 1999). We can imagine this campaign was carried forward when negotiating international agreements with German companies.

Table 15.5   Sexual Orientation Coverage by IFAs by Sector and Worker Coverage

Sector	Number of IFAs	Worker coverage
AUTO	8	1,284,000
METAL	3	36,000
ENGINEERING	3	69,970
ENERGY	2	381,000
RETAIL	2	227,140
FURNITURE	2	127,600
ELECTRONICS	2	627,000
PAPER	1	46,000
AEROSPACE	1	110,000
PACKAGING	1	17,000
PLASTICS	1	8,000
SECURITY	1	217,000
STEEL	1	95,000
FINANCIAL SERVICES	1	118,900
HOSPITALITY	1	391,148
BUILDING	1	5,370
OIL AND GAS	1	80,497
TOTALS	32*	3,841,625*

* Some companies are in more than one sector. This has been accounted for in calculating the total number of IFAs and workers covered.

In addition, the main German automobile multinationals all have IFAs that include sexual orientation, reflecting the fact that such provisions have been in their national collective agreements for years. As a result, including coverage in their international operations represents an extension of their existing contractual language.

Although the Metal Workers Confederation (IMF) does not stand out as a global union active on a broad set of sexual orientation equity issues in the way that EI or PSI does, it is the global with the most IFAs covering LGBT workers. Note again, IMF is now part of IndustriALL, but the agreements referred to here were signed when it was IMF. There are a couple of plausible explanations for this. The first is the important lead of the IMF in signing IFAs generally: it outpaces all other global unions in the number of signed IFAs, it held a conference in 2007 to assert the importance they were giving to these agreements, and it subsequently published detailed guidelines for negotiating them (IMF 2007). Although these guidelines do not specify sexual orientation, it is a category that has been in IMF constitutional language since 2005. The second explanation has to do with the fact that so much of IMF's national union membership is based in Germany's large auto

Figure 15.1   Sexual Orientation Coverage in IFAs by Year

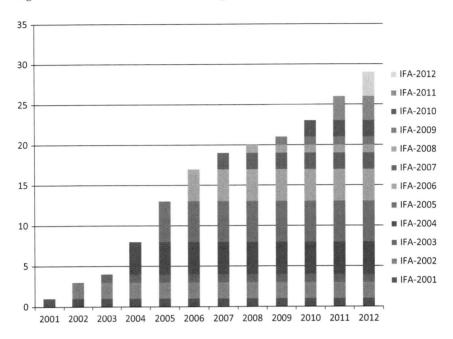

sector. It is therefore reasonable to assume that the combination of the IMF commitment to IFAs in general and the push by German national unions to recognize sexual orientation discrimination has been an important factor in recent developments.

Because IFAs are signed with large private sector multinationals, it follows that the public sector globals (PSI and EI) would not be involved with IFAs. Still, PSI is a cosigner on two IFAs with sexual orientation provisions (GDF and France Telecom), reflecting that multinational utility companies do operate in public sector environments. It is also the case that the International Federation of Journalists and the International Transportation Workers do not have IFAs, but they also tend not to have constituents working at multinational corporations and are less likely to have IFAs in general. The International Union of Food, Agriculture, Hotel, Restaurant, Catering, Tobacco, and Allied Workers' Association (IUF) only has one IFA with coverage for LGBT workers. This is because most of the IFAs signed by the federation were quite early, before sexual orientation was appearing in any such agreements. It is possible that sexual orientation coverage may get covered in subsequent revisions. UNI spokespeople indicate that they now prioritize the creation of IFAs as a strategy for enhancing cross-border worker rights. In combination with UNI's push on equity, this may mean that more of the IFAs cosigned with UNI will contain language specific to sexual orientation discrimination.

CONCLUSION

International labour is more responsive to sexual orientation discrimination than it has been in the past. The three largest, cross-sector international labour institutions (ITUC, ILO, ETUC) acknowledge the problem of sexual orientation discrimination in the workplace and the need to take some action to address it. The ETUC is the most responsive, having moved significantly beyond policy directives and rhetoric to expansive and inclusive education and support programs. Recently, the ILO has recognized sexual orientation in a number of its education and outreach efforts but has not amended Convention 111 to specify sexual orientation as a ground for non-discrimination. The ITUC supports the efforts being made by its national union membership and works co-operatively with global unions, especially EI and PSI, to advance the cause. The sector-based global unions also recognize that LGBT workers need protection, but only three (EI, PSI, UNI) have developed active campaigns designed to educate members, provide support and confront discrimination.

A new tool for cross-border labour regulation are the IFAs signed among multinational corporations and one or more global union. One-third of these agreements include discrimination language inclusive of sexual orientation, which covers over four million workers worldwide. Worker coverage may be even larger because the figure excludes the broader supply chain constituents that are often included in IFA language. Although many LGBT workers already have formal protection because they work in national settings where sexual orientation discrimination is prohibited, it is a significant and potentially transformative gain for workers in locations where there is no such provision. In some settings, these provisions may be the only formal protection for sexual minorities that exists. For example, GDF Suez, a large gas, water and electricity utility, signed an agreement with BWI, ICEM and PSI in 2010. This agreement has a clause ensuring equal opportunities and treatment of all employees, male or female—regardless of age, origin, nationality, religion, culture or political or sexual orientation. Further, the agreement indicates: 'Social exclusion and discrimination generate injustice, often rob people of their basic human dignity, and deprive society of the contributions of many. It may be overcome, including through education and training. Inside and outside the enterprise, diversity is positive and to be promoted' (GDF Suez 2013: 7). GDF Suez employs about 214,000 workers, and the agreement applies to subcontractors and suppliers, so the reach is large. Although it is based in France, its workers, subcontractors and suppliers are scattered across much of the world, including locations such as Latin America and Thailand, where sexual minorities do not have legal protections.

Interestingly, the developments taking place within the international wing of the labour movement appear to be following a similar path to those that took place at the national level over the past couple of decades. Global unions representing public sector workers and teachers have clearly taken the lead and progress is apparent in the global union most associated with the auto sector, the IMF. These developments add pressure on the ILO to revise Convention 111 and make it inclusive of sexual orientation. The addition of sexual orientation in this convention would have the immediate effect of making all IFAs inclusive of sexual orientation. Time will tell if this actually occurs. ILO officials suggested that sizeable blocks of their national members (much of Asia and Africa, for example) remain opposed to extending formal equality rights to LGBT workers, and an amendment would be unlikely to pass.

Further research is needed to determine the impact these protections in IFA contracts have on workers around the world. The fact that some IFAs now provide recourse for workers fired, excluded from promotion and advancement opportunities or denied benefits readily available to heterosexuals because they are a sexual minority is noteworthy. It provides a new doorway for initiating grievances and other legal actions at the level of the firm, potentially up the hierarchy to the human resources department and to union stewards at the multinational headquarters. Whether or not sexual minority claimants will act on this new type of protection remains to be seen. The degree to which multinationals and global unions will be prepared to support and investigate cases of discrimination based on sexuality, especially in cultural and political settings where homosexuality is outlawed or highly repressed, is also unclear. Colgan (2011: 719) makes the interesting observation that a corporate social responsibility framework (CSR) offers the best vision for getting multinationals to endorse sexual orientation issues because it helps to situate LGBT discrimination within a broader commitment for human rights. A CSR framework may be one way to give added momentum to IFAs.

It is now clear that increasing numbers of IFAs contain nondiscrimination language for LGBT workers. When this is combined with the initiatives taken by cross-national union confederations and global unions, we can conclude that there are significant developments taking place in the worldwide fight for equality and dignity in the LGBT labour force. In other words, there is movement afoot, and activists have a number of additional tools to tackle LGBT discrimination around the world.

NOTE

1. Portions of this section of the chapter were adapted from Hunt (2011) 'International Framework Agreements and Sexual Orientation Discrimination', *Journal of International Management Studies*, 11(1), pp. 99–109. Used with permission of the copyright holder (International Association of Business and Economics). All information was updated to 2013

REFERENCES

Bielski Boris, M. (2010) 'Identity at Work: U.S. Labor Union Efforts to Address Sexual Diversity through Policy and Practice', *Advances in Industrial and Labor Relations*, 7, pp. 185–205.

Colgan, F. (2011) 'Equality, Diversity and Corporate Social Responsibility: Sexual Orientation in the UK Private Sector', *Equality, Diversity and Inclusion*, 30(8), pp. 719–734.

Colgan, F. and Ledwith, S. (eds) (2002) *Gender, Diversity and Trade Unions: International Perspectives*. London: Routledge.

Cotton, E. and Gumbrell-McCormick, R. (2012) 'Global Unions as Imperfect Multilateral Organizations: An International Relations Perspective', *Economic and Industrial Democracy*, 33(4), pp. 707–728.

Croucher, R. and Cotton, E. (2009) *Global Unions, Global Business: Global Union Federations and International Business*. London: Middlesex University Press.

ETUC. (2008) *Extending Equity—Trade Unions in Action! Organising and Promoting Equal Rights, Respect and Dignity for LGTB Workers*. Brussels: ETUC.

ETUC. (2012) *ETUC, ETUCE and ILGA-Europe Commit to Work Jointly to Combat Homophobic Bullying in Schools, in Workplaces and in Society*. Brussels: ETUC (accessed online: www.etuc.org/a/9981).

Fairbrother, P. and Hammer, N. (2005) 'Global Unions: Past Efforts and Future Prospects', *Relations Industrielles/Industrial Relations*, 60(3), pp. 405–431.

Global Unions (2013) 'Framework Agreements' (accessed online: www.global-unions.org/framework-agreements.html).

Hammer, N. (2005) 'International Framework Agreements: Global Industrial Relations between Rights and Bargaining', *European Review of Labour and Research*, 11(4), pp. 511–530.

Holzhacker, R. (1999) 'Labor Unions and Sexual Diversity in Germany'. In Hunt, G., ed., *Laboring for Rights: Unions and Sexual Diversity across Nations*. Philadelphia: Temple University Press.

Hunt, G. (ed.) (1999) *Laboring for Rights: Unions and Sexual Diversity Across Nations*. Philadelphia: Temple University Press.

Hunt, G. (2011) 'International framework agreements and sexual orientation discrimination', *Journal of International Management Studies*, 11(1), pp. 99–109.

Hunt, G. and Eaton, J. (2007) 'We Are Family: Labour Responds to Gay, Lesbian, Bisexual, and Transgendered Workers'. In Hunt, G. and Rayside, D. eds, *Equity, Diversity and Canadian Labour*. Toronto: University of Toronto Press.

ILO (2003) *Time for Equality at Work*. Geneva: International Labour Organisation.

ILO (2007) *Equality at Work: Tackling the Challenges*. Geneva: International Labour Organisation.

ILO (2009) *Eliminating Discrimination in the Workplace (Factsheet No. 5)*. Geneva: International Labour Organisation.

ILO (2011) *Equality at Work: The Continuing Challenge*. Geneva: International Labour Organisation.

ILO (2013) 'C111 – Discrimination (Employment and Occupation) Convention, 1958 (No. 111)' (accessed online: www.ilo.org/dyn/normlex/en/f?p=1000: 12100:0::NO::P12100_ILO_CODE:C111).

IMF (2007) Recommendations of the International Framework Agreement Conference' (accessed online: www.imfmetal.org/IFA).

ITUC (2010a) 'Defending and Promoting Fundamental Human Rights', Vancouver: 2nd ITUC World Congress Resolutions (accessed online: www.ituc-csi.org/IMG/pdf/CONGRESS_Decisions_EN.pdf).

ITUC (2010b) 'Fighting HIV/AIDS', Vancouver: 2nd ITUC World Congress Resolutions (accessed online: www.ituc-csi.org/IMG/pdf/CONGRESS_Decisions_EN.pdf).

Krupat, K. and McCreery, P. (eds) (2001) *Out at Work: Building a Gay-Labor Alliance*. Minneapolis: University of Minnesota Press.

Müller, T., Platzer, H. and Rüb, S. (2008) 'International Framework Agreements: Opportunities and Limitations of a New Tool of Global Trade Union Policy', *Friedrich Ebert Stiftung (Briefing Papers No. 8)*. Bonn: Friedrich-Ebert-Stiftung Publishing.

Papadakis, K.(ed.) (2011) *Shaping Global Industrial Relations: The Impact of International Framework Agreements*. Basingstoke: Palgrave Macmillan.

Pries, L. and Seeliger, M. (2013) 'Work and Employment Relations in a Globalized World: The Emerging Texture of Cross-Border Labor Regulation', *Global Labour Journal*, 4(1), pp. 26–47.

PSI-EI (2007) *Trade Unionists Together for LGBT Rights*. Brussels: Education International.

Riisgaard, L. (2005) 'International Framework Agreements: A New Model for Securing Workers Rights?' *Industrial Relations*, 44(4), pp. 707–737.

Schillinger, H. (2005) 'Trade Unions in Africa: Weak but Feared', Geneva: Occasional Papers, Global Trade Union Program (access online: http://library.fes.de/pdf-files/iez/02822.pdf).

Sobczak, A. (2007) 'Legal Dimensions of International Framework Agreements in the Field of Corporate Social Responsibility', *Industrial Relations*, 62(3), pp. 466–489.

UNI (2010) *Policies on Equality at Work in Global Companies*. Nyon: UNI Global Union.

Contributors

Michèle Bowring is a faculty member in leadership studies in the department of business at the University of Guelph, Canada. Her primary research interests lie at the intersection of leadership, gender, sexuality and diversity in the workplace. Other recent areas of exploration include consumption and online communities, qualitative methods, media and culture. For relaxation, Michèle has been known to take photographs of flowers and other pretty things in the Canadian wild, make a not-too-bad stained glass panel or two and/or watch as many science fiction television shows and films as she can find.

Jo Brewis works at the University of Leicester School of Management (UK) where she is deputy head; she also looks after PhD students in the wider College of Social Science. She specializes in teaching research methodology and research skills. Her research interests sit at the intersection between the body, identity, sexuality, culture and processes of organizing. In her leisure time Jo is often to be found at indiepop gigs, watching her box sets of *The West Wing* or *Burn Notice* for the hundredth time or catching up with celebrity goings-on via *heat* magazine (all in the name of her intellectual endeavours, obviously).

John Broomfield gained his PhD from Warwick Business School's department of organisation and human resource management (UK). His PhD research analysed the work experiences of gay men in the police and the performing arts industry, exploring the lives of gay workers within traditionally perceived 'gay hostile' and 'gay-friendly' occupations. John has coauthored articles based on the findings of this research published in journals such as *Human Resource Management Journal* and *Organization*. Since completing his PhD, John has worked as a social researcher for the Civil Service in his hometown of Cardiff, Wales. He currently works as an analyst for local government policy.

Todd Brower is the judicial education director for the Williams Institute on Sexual Orientation Law and Public Policy at UCLA School of Law

(US). He is a professor of constitutional law at Western State College of Law in California. He has an LL.M from Yale Law School, a J.D. from Stanford Law School and an A.B. from Princeton University, and was a Fulbright scholar in France. Professor Brower served on the California Judicial Council—Access and Fairness Advisory Committee and is the author of various law review articles, research studies and publications on the treatment of lesbian, gay, bisexual and transgendered persons in the courts of the United Kingdom, California and New Jersey. He has worked with the courts of many US states and federal agencies on judicial education programs and with national and international judicial organisations.

Fiona Colgan is senior lecturer (teaching and research) and course leader for the MA in human resource and employment management in the faculty of business and law at London Metropolitan University (UK). She supervises research students and teaches in the areas of employee relations, equality and diversity and research methods. She has published on a range of topics in the equality, diversity and employment relations field. Recent publications include articles on sexual orientation and employment issues in *Equality, Diversity and Inclusion, Gender, Work & Organisation* and *Human Resource Management Journal*; she also wrote a forthcoming book chapter (2013) on 'Employment Equality and Diversity Management in a Russian Context' for *International Handbook on Diversity Management at Work* (Edward Elgar).

Catherine Connell is assistant professor of sociology at Boston University (US). Her research focuses on how gender and sexuality norms are reproduced and resisted in organizations and occupations. She is currently finishing a book about how gay and lesbian public school teachers negotiate tensions between the rhetoric of gay pride and professional ethics of discretion. Her most recent published work includes articles in *Gender & Society, Sexuality Research & Social Policy*, and *Women's Studies Quarterly*.

Suzanne Franzway is a professor of gender studies and sociology at the University of South Australia. Her research interests focus on sexual politics and labour movements; the politics of ignorance, social movements and the body; and epistemologies of workplace change and gendered violence and women's citizenship. She published *Making Feminist Politics: Transnational Alliances between Women and Labor* (2011, University of Illinois Press) with Mary Margaret Fonow, and *Challenging Knowledge, Sex and Power: Gender, Work and Engineering* (2013, Routledge) with Julie Mills, Judith Gill and Rhonda Sharp. Her influential books *Staking a Claim: Feminism, Bureaucracy and the State* (1989, Polity Press) with Dianne Court and R. W. Connell and *Sexual Politics and Greedy*

Institutions: Union Women, Commitments and Conflicts in Public and in Private (2001, Pluto Press) are both widely cited. She is active in feminist labour movements and the UNESCO Women's Studies and Gender Studies Research Network.

Roswitha Hofmann is a sociologist, scientific consultant and lecturer at the WU Vienna (Austria). Her main teaching and research focus is on gender diversity, sexual orientations, intersectionality and sustainable diversity management from a queer perspective. Roswitha has conducted field studies in Austria and internationally. She has published a large number of articles in peer reviewed journals as well as in applied media and edited books. She is a member of the Editorial Advisory Board of Diversitas.

Gerald Hunt is a professor in organizational behaviour and human resources management at Ryerson University in Toronto, Canada. He teaches in the area of organizational change, industrial relations and human resources at undergraduate and graduate levels. His research focuses on organized labour's response to equity issues related to sexual diversity, gender and race. Publications include *Equity, Diversity, and Canadian Labour* (2007, University of Toronto Press) and 'Gender and Specialty in Business Management Education' (2013) in the *Canadian Journal of Higher Education*.

Christine M. Klapeer holds a postdoctoral position at the department of development studies at the University of Vienna (Austria). She has published on institutionalized forms of heteronormativity, sexual/queer(ing) citizenship and the problematic relationship between citizenship and lesbian life. Her dissertation 'Perverse Bürgerinnen Staatsbürgerschaft und lesbische Existenz' will be published in May 2014. Her current research interests also include intersections of queer/postcolonial approaches with theories of post-/development particularly focusing on transnational sexual rights discourses/policies and LGBTIQ-inclusive development strategies.

Elizabeth McDermott is a senior lecturer in health research in the faculty of health and medicine at Lancaster University (UK). Her research interests focus on mental health inequalities and their relation to age, sexuality, gender and social class. Her forthcoming book, *Queer Youth and Self Harm: Psychosocial Perspectives* (Palgrave Macmillan), coauthored with Katrina Roen (University of Oslo), will be published in 2014. She has published in a wide range of journals including *Sexualities*, *Journal of Social Policy*, *Youth & Society* and *Social Science & Medicine*. Elizabeth is currently leading a two-year Department of Health, UK government–funded research grant investigating LGBT youth suicide, self-harm and help-seeking (2014–2015).

Mustafa Özbilgin is a professor of organisational behaviour and human resource management at Brunel University London (UK). He also holds chairs at Université Paris-Dauphine and Koç University in Istanbul. His research focuses on equality, diversity and inclusion at work. He is the editor in chief of the *British Journal of Management.*

Mustafa Bilgehan Öztürk is a senior lecturer in management at Middlesex University Business School (UK). His research primarily focuses on identifying strategies to combat discrimination, exclusion and marginalisation experienced at the workplace by sexual and gender minorities.

Nick Rumens is a professor of organization behaviour at Middlesex University London (UK). His main research interests include lesbian, gay, bisexual and trans (LGBT) sexualities in organisations and how queer theories might generate disruptions to heteronormativities within the field of organisation studies. His research has mobilised queer theories to examine the organisational lives of LGBT people, gay and bisexual men's workplace friendships and intimacies, and how we might 'queer' the business school and critical management research. He has published articles on these topics in journals including *Human Relations, Organization, Human Resource Management Journal, Construction Management and Economics, Gender Work & Organization* and *The Sociological Review*, and he has contributed to recent edited collections such as *Queer Absences and Presences* (Palgrave Macmillan, 2013) and *The Oxford Handbook of Gender and Organization* (Oxford University Press, 2014). Well-received books include *Queer Company: Friendship in the Work Lives of Gay Men* (Ashgate, 2011) and *An Introduction to Critical Management Research* (Sage, 2008).

Karin Schönpflug is an economist and works as a researcher at the Vienna Institute for Advanced Studies (Austria). She is also a lecturer at the University of Vienna, at the department of development studies. She is interested in discourses of economic theory and creating realities with data processing. She has published on feminist utopian literature and its embedded economic models, the distribution of work, and economic crisis in *Feminism, Economics, Utopia: Time Traveling through Paradigms* (2008, Routledge).

Ruth Simpson is a professor of management at Brunel Business School (UK). She has published widely in the area of gender, emotions and careers, with recent work focussing on the experiences of men in nontraditional roles and on men doing 'dirty work'. Authored and coauthored books include *Men in Caring Occupations: Doing Gender Differently* (2009, Palgrave Macmillan); *Gendering Emotions in Organizations* (2007, Palgrave Macmillan); *Emotions in Transmigration: Transformation,*

Movement and Identity (2012, Palgrave Macmillan) and *Dirty Work: Concepts and Identities* (2012, Palgrave Macmillan).

Paul Willis is a senior lecturer in social work at Swansea University (UK). Prior to working in academia, Paul qualified in social work at the University of Tasmania, Australia, and his practice experience included supporting LGBQ-identifying young people in counselling and community development roles in rural Tasmania. His research interests include sexuality and care in adult relationships, sexuality and ageing, social inclusion in organisations and the social identities and wellbeing of queer youth. He has recently completed a mixed methods study into the inclusion of older LGB residents in care organisations in Wales with colleagues at Swansea. Paul is currently cochair of the UK Sexuality in Social Work Interest Group.

Mikki van Zyl is an independent scholar and lifelong human rights activist based in South Africa. She has been a consultant to the NGO sector for twenty years, doing participatory action research and training around gender and sexualities. She also lectures in diversity studies and disability studies. Her current research focus is on lesbian hate crimes, social mobilisation against homophobia, same-sex marriage, sexual belonging and rights in citizenship and an African ethics of care in the context of HIV and AIDS. Recent publications include *Performing Queer* and *The Prize and the Price*, which she coedited with Melissa Steyn, and several published papers on same-sex marriage and belonging, activism against lesbian hate crimes, and developing a southern lens for an ethics of care, with Amanda Gouws.

Index